European Union and its Neighbours in a Globalized World

Volume 27

The series publishes monographs and edited volumes in the field of European and international law and policy. A special focus is put on the European neighbourhood policy, current problems in European and international law and policy as well as the role of the European Union as a global actor. The series supports the publishing and distribution of research results of cross-border research consortia. Besides renowned scientists the series is also open for publication projects of young academics. The series emphasizes the interplay of the European Union and its neighbouring countries as well as the important role of the European Union as a key player in the international context of law, economics and politics.

Francesco Decarolis • Barbara Marchetti
Luisa Torchia
Editors

The EU Digital Regulation and its Impact on Member States

Springer

Editors
Francesco Decarolis
Bocconi University
Milano, Italy

Barbara Marchetti
University of Trento
Trento, Italy

Luisa Torchia
Roma Tre University
Rome, Italy

ISSN 2524-8928 ISSN 2524-8936 (electronic)
European Union and its Neighbours in a Globalized World
ISBN 978-3-032-06489-9 ISBN 978-3-032-06490-5 (eBook)
https://doi.org/10.1007/978-3-032-06490-5

This Springer imprint is published by the registered company Springer Nature Switzerland AG
The registered company address is: Gewerbestrasse 11, 6330 Cham, Switzerland

Preface

In Europe, the digital landscape is undergoing significant transformations, driven by both technological advancements and regulatory changes. The primary challenges lie in managing the influence of dominant large platforms and regulating artificial intelligence to create a fairer, more accessible, and competitive European digital market while protecting fundamental rights from the risks posed by AI. In response, the European Union has initiated a regulatory revolution with major legislative acts such as the Artificial Intelligence Act (AI Act), the Digital Markets Act (DMA), and the Digital Services Act (DSA).

This book offers a unique contribution by bridging legal, economic, and institutional perspectives to provide a comprehensive, comparative analysis of how European digital regulations are taking shape in practice. Unlike existing studies that focus primarily on the design of the Digital Markets Act, Digital Services Act, and Artificial Intelligence Act, this volume shifts the emphasis to their implementation by Member States and to their institutional and organizational impacts on Member States. It reveals the many institutional transformations, enforcement challenges, and unintended consequences that emerge at the national level. By systematically examining five key Member States—Italy, Germany, Spain, France, and Estonia—the book uncovers the tensions between national regulatory autonomy and European harmonization, shedding light on the varied governance models adopted across jurisdictions. This comparative approach not only highlights best practices but also identifies potential regulatory blind spots, offering valuable insights for policymakers seeking to refine the EU's digital governance framework in an era of rapid technological change.

Given the significance and cross-disciplinary nature of the topic, the book consists of two sections. The first section addresses the Artificial Intelligence Act (EU Reg. 2024/1689) and its impact on the regulatory framework and administrative systems in the five Member States analyzed. More specifically, it examines the various uses that national administrations are making of AI, the legal frameworks developed by courts and legislators to address the challenges posed by this technology, and the new principles of administrative law designed to mitigate risks. The section also explores how these principles could align with the regulatory framework of the

AI Act and investigates the organizational and institutional changes necessary to respond effectively to this technological challenge.

The second section delves into the complex landscape of the newly introduced Digital Markets Act (DMA) and Digital Services Act (DSA), focusing on the various institutional arrangements adopted by Member States and their national competent administrations to support this new EU legal regime. By analyzing the implementation of these regulations in Estonia, France, Germany, Italy, and Spain, this section offers a detailed examination of how different national approaches shape the regulatory landscape and affect the effectiveness of enforcement mechanisms.

The book's project main aim is to present concrete, comparative insights from five key Member States. Accordingly, the essays in both sections of the book seek to contribute to a deeper understanding of how digital market governance is evolving across Europe. These case studies reveal important divergences in regulatory approaches, with some Member States taking proactive stances in enforcing new digital market rules, while others adopt a more cautious or fragmented approach. The analysis also touches on some of the unintended consequences of digital regulation.

A key aspect of the analyses presented in the studies concerns the institutional interplay between national and European regulators. For instance, the implementation of the DMA and DSA involves multiple governance levels, including national competition authorities, data protection agencies, and newly designated Digital Services Coordinators (DSCs). The book explores the challenges and trade-offs associated with coordinating these institutions, particularly in light of overlapping national and EU-level enforcement responsibilities.

Overall, the different essays provide policymakers, scholars, and industry stakeholders with a nuanced perspective on the opportunities and challenges of enforcing these regulations. Ultimately, they underscore the importance of adaptive and well-coordinated regulatory frameworks to ensure the society at large can benefit from advances in the tech sector.

Milano, Italy
Trento, Italy
Rome, Italy
June 2025

Francesco Decarolis
Barbara Marchetti
Luisa Torchia

Acknowledgments

We are grateful to our co-authors, with whom we have developed the ideas and research contributions that underpin this book. Our discussions and joint work over the years have been a constant source of insight and intellectual stimulation.

We also wish to thank the many colleagues and friends who generously offered comments, suggestions, and perspectives at various stages of this project. Their engagement has enriched the final result in countless ways.

A special thank you goes to Guido Roveri for his invaluable assistance throughout this research project. His dedication and support have been essential to bringing this work to completion.

We would like to conclude with a heartfelt thought for Professor Tanel Kerikmäe, who passed away in August 2025. His contribution to this book stands as a testament to his remarkable intellectual commitment to legal studies and to the evolving landscape of digital regulation in Europe. It is an honour to acknowledge his work and to preserve a trace of his vision within these pages.

Decarolis gratefully acknowledges support from the European Research Council (ERC-2020-COG, Grant Agreement ID: 101002867 CODIM – Competition in Digital Markets).

Contents

Editors and Contributors

About the Editors

Francesco Decarolis Full Professor, Department of Economics, Bocconi University—Milan.

In addition to his role at Bocconi University, he is a Temporary Professor of National School of Administration of the Italian Presidency of the Council of Ministries; a CEPR Research Affiliate; an associate editor of *The Review of Economic Studies* and of *Econometrica*.

He previously held various temporary positions at the University of Wisconsin Madison, University of Chicago, University of Pennsylvania, Boston University, Columbia University, Stanford University and the Einaudi Institute for Economics and Finance.

Over the last fifteen years, he has held various advisory roles for different public bodies, including the European Commission, the Italian Presidency of the Council of Ministers, the Italian Antitrust Authority, and the Milan Court of Justice.

He got a PhD in Economics from The University of Chicago in 2009.

His area of research is Industrial Organization, and he mostly works on topics in competition economics, antitrust, market design, public procurement, and the regulation of digital platforms.

Among his recent publications, the most representatives are: "Rules, Discretion, and Corruption in Procurement: Evidence from Italian Government Contracting" (with R. Fisman, P. Pinotti and S. Vannutelli) forthcoming at the Journal of Political Economy—Microeconomics; "Regulating online search in the EU: From the android case to the digital markets act and digital services act" (with M. Li) International Journal of Industrial Organization, Volume 90, September 2023; "Bid Coordination in Sponsored Search Auctions: Detection Methodology and Empirical Analysis" (with M. Goldmanis, A. Penta and K. Shakhgildyan), Journal of Industrial Economics, Volume 71, Issue 2 June 2023, Pages 570–592; "Gender and bureaucratic corruption: Evidence from two countries" (with R. Fisman, P. Pinotti, S. Vannutelli and Y. Wang) Journal of Law, Economics and Organization, Volume

39, Issue 2, July 2023, Pages 557–585; "Buyers' Role in Innovation Procurement," (with G. de Rassenfosse, L. Giuffrida, E. Iossa, V. Mollisi, E. Raiteri and G. Spagnolo), Journal of Economics & Management Strategy, 2021, 30, pp. 697–720; "From Mad Men to Maths Men: Concentration and Buyer Power in Online Advertising" (with G. Rovigatti), CEPR Discussion Paper 13897, 2019, American Economic Review, 2021, 111(10); "Bureaucratic Competence and Procurement Outcomes" (with L. Giuffrida, E. Iossa, V. Mollisi and G. Spagnolo), The Journal of Law, Economics, and Organization, Volume 36, Issue 3, November 2020, Pages 537–597; "Marketing Agencies and Collusive Bidding in Online Ad Auctions," (with M. Goldmanis and A. Penta), Management Science, 2020, 66(10), pp. 4359–4919; "Subsidy Design in Privately-Provided Social Insurance: Lessons from Medicare Part D" (with M. Polyakova and S. Ryan), Journal of Political Economy, May 2020, vol. 128, no. 5, pp. 1712–1752; "Open Enrollment Periods and Plan Choices" (with A. Guglielmo and C. Luscombe), Health Economics, July 2020, Volume29(7), pp. 733–747; "Comparing Procurement Auctions," International Economic Review, Vol. 59, No. 2, pp. 391–419, May 2018; "Insurers Response to Selection Risk: Evidence from Medicare Enrollment Reforms" (with A. Guglielmo), Journal of Health Economics, 56, 2017, pp. 383–396; "Detecting Bidders Groups in Collusive Auctions," (with T. Conley) American Economic Journal: Microeconomics, Vol. 8, No. 2 May 2016, pp. 1–38; "Renegotiation of Public Contracts: An Empirical Analysis" (with G. Palumbo) Economic Letters, Vol. 132, July 2015, pp. 77–81; "The Unintended Effects of the Medicare Part D Low Income Subsidy," Health Policy, Vol. 119, Issue 5, May 2015, pp. 597–603; "Local Public Procurement Regulations: The Case of Italy," (with C. Giorgiantonio) International Review of Law and Economics, Vol. 43, August 2015, pp 209–226; "Entry and Subcontracting in Public Procurement Auctions," (with N. Branzoli) Management Science, Vol. 61, Iss. 12, December 2015, pp. 2945–2962; "Medicare Part D: Are Insurers Gaming the Low Income Subsidy Design?" American Economic Review, April 2015, 105(4): 1547–80; "Awarding Price, Contract Performance and Bids Screening: Evidence from Procurement Auctions," American Economic Journal: Applied Economics, Vol. 6, Iss. 1, January 2014, pp. 108–132.

Further details are available here: https://faculty.unibocconi.eu/francescodecarolis/.

Barbara Marchetti (1967) is Professor of Administrative Law in the University of Trento, Italy.

She graduated summa cum laude at the Faculty of Law of the University of Trento and in the same university she discussed her Ph.D. thesis on *The Collateral Challenge of Administrative Decisions: A Comparative Analysis (France, Europe, England and Italy)*.

Her main research interests are AI and public administration, administrative justice, EU administrative law, and comparative administrative law.

Her publications include five books as author: *Manuale di diritto amministrativo*, Giappichelli, 2023 (with M. Dugato, G. Della Cananea, A. Police, M. Ramajoli); *Searching for the fundamentals of Administrative law*, Giappichelli, 2019; *Pubblica amministrazione e corti negli Stati Uniti. Il judicial review sulle administrative agencies,* Padova, Cedam, 2005*; L'esecuzione della sentenza amministrativa prima del giudicato,* Padova, Cedam, 2000; *L'eccezione di illegittimità del provvedimento amministrativo. Un'indagine comparata*, Quaderni del Dipartimento di Scienze giuridiche, Trento, 1996; and some books as editor: *Administrative Remedies in the European Union. The Emergence of a Quasi-Judicial Administration,* Torino, Giappichelli 2017; *L'amministrazione europea e le sue regole* (editor with Luca De Lucia), Bologna, Il Mulino, 2015; *Pubblico e privato nell'organizzazione e nell'azione amministrativa* (editor with Giandomenico Falcon) Padova, CEDAM, Wolters Kluwer Italia, 2013; *Pubblico e privato. Oltre i confini dell'amministrazione tradizionale* (editor) Padova, CEDAM, Wolters Kluwer Italia, 2013; *L'amministrazione europea: caratteri,* accountability *e sindacato giurisdizionale* (editor) Padova, Cedam, 2009 (editor).

Some of her articles deal with Comparative and European Administrative law: *La sentenza Loper Bright e il ripensamento dei rapporti tra legge, amministrazione e giudice, in Giornale di diritto amministrativo, 2025, 3, 399; La regolazione europea del mercato dell'intelligenza artificiale, in Rivista della Regolazione dei Mercati, 2024, 1, 3; Vincoli sovranazionali e discrezionalità amministrativa, in Riv. it. dir. pubbl. comun., 2022, 5–6, 721; Il sistema integrato di tutela,* in B. Marchetti and L. De Lucia (editors) *L'amministrazione europea e le sue regole*, Bologna, Il Mulino, 2015, 197–230; *I possibili ostacoli ad una disciplina unitaria della governance globale,* Riv. Trim. dir. Pubbl., 2014, n. 4, 917–925; *Efficienza amministrativa e protezione del cittadino nella riforma del judicial review inglese,* Giorn. Dir. Ammin. 2014, n. 1, 418–426; *Il giudice amministrativo tra tutela soggettiva e oggettiva: riflessioni di diritto comparato*, Dir. Proc. Amm. 2014, n. 1, 74–106; *Le garanzie procedurali e processuali delle imprese nella Rete europea della concorrenza,* in Rivista Della Regolazione Dei Mercati, 2014, n. 1, pp. 5–28; *Diritto privato e amministrazione pubblica: problemi e spunti di comparazione*, in G. Falcon, B. Marchetti (editors), *Pubblico e privato nell'organizzazione e nell'azione amministrativa. Problemi e prospettive*, Padova, CEDAM, Wolters Kluwer Italia, 2013; *Su Rule of Law e legalità globale*, in Quad. Cost., 2013, n. 4, 1035–1043; *Fondi strutturali e tutela giurisdizionale: variazione degli schemi regolatori e conseguenze sull'architettura giudiziaria dell'Ue*, in Riv. It. Dir. Pubbl. comun., 2012, n. 6, 1105–1128; *Il principio di motivazione* in M. Renna, F. Saitta (editors), *Studi sui principi del diritto amministrativo*, Milano, Giuffrè, 2012, 521–532; Much Ado About (Almost) Nothing: *il Rapporto della House of Lords sulla Corte di Giustizia UE*, in Giornale di diritto amministrativo, 2012, 206–212; *Comparing EU and Global Judicial Systems: some reflexions*, in G.B. Mattarella, E. Chiti (editors) *Global Administrative Law and EU Administrative Law. Relationships, legal Issues and Comparison*, Springer, 2011.

Recently she published some articles on AI and public authorities: among them *Artificial intelligence and public authorities: does the European AI Act protect public values?*, in Eur. Rev. publ. law, 2024, 36, 1, 67; *Divergenti? Le strategie di Unione europea e Stati Uniti in materia di Intelligenza artificiale* (con Edoardo Chiti), in Riv. della regolazione e dei mercati, 2020, 1, 28; *Prime osservazioni sulla proposta di regolamento dell'Unione europea in materia di intelligenza artificiale* (con C. Casonato), in Biolaw Journal, 2021, 3, 415–437; *Smart cities e amministrazioni centrali di fronte all'intelligenza artificiale: esperienze a confronto* (con E. Chiti e N. Rangone), in Biolaw Journal, 2022, 1, 24; *L'impiego di sistemi di intelligenza artificiale nelle pubbliche amministrazioni italiane: prove generali* (con E. Chiti e N. Rangone), in Biolaw Journal, 2022, 2, 489–507; *Amministrazione digitale*, in Enc. Diritto - Funzioni amministrative, Milano: Giuffrè Lefebvre, 2022, pp. 75–109.

Membership: *European Group of Public Law, Istituto per le ricerche sulle pubbliche amministrazioni*—Irpa; *Carreer and Recruitment Committee*, University of Trento; *Co-President ICON-s Italian Chapter; Network Jus Publicum; Italian Association of Administrative Law Profe-ssors*; Italian Institute of Administrative Sciences (I.I.S.A.); ReNEUAL (Research Network of European Administrative Law). She is member of the Scientific Board of Collana di Studi di Diritto pubblico (editors A. Sandulli - R. Bin), and she is member of the Steering Committee of some Legal Journals (*Rivista della regolazione dei Mercati, Diritto pubblico, Rivista italiana di diritto pubblico comunitario, Rivista di diritto sportivo,* Blog *Diario di diritto pubblico*) and member of the Advisory Group for legal publications for Il Mulino Publisher.

Luisa Torchia (1957) is Full Professor of Administrative Law in the University of Roma Tre, Italy.

She graduated summa cum laude at the Faculty of Law of the University of Roma Sapienza.

Her main research interests are AI and public administration, EU administrative law, comparative administrative law, public law, and economics.

Her publications include nine books as author: *Lo Stato digitale. Una introduzione*, Bologna, Il Mulino, 2023; *Diritto amministrativo. Una conversazione* (with S. Cassese), Bologna, Il Mulino, 2014; *Guida alla ricerca per giovani giuristi* (with S. Battini, L. Casini, S. Cassese, E. Chiti, B.G. Mattarella, G. Napolitano, A. Sandulli, G. Vesperini), Edizioni Irpa, 2012; *Il governo delle differenze. Il principio di equivalenza nell'ordinamento europeo*, Bologna, Il Mulino, 2006; *La responsabilità dirigenziale*, Padova, Cedam, 2000; *Il controllo pubblico della finanza privata*, Padova, Cedam, 1992; *Le amministrazioni nazionali*, Padova, Cedam, 1988; *Le funzioni del Governo locale* (with F. Merloni e V. Santantonio), Milano, Giuffré, 1988; *I raccordi tra Stato e regioni. Un'indagine per casi su organi e procedimenti* (with C. Desideri), Milano, Giuffré, 1986; and some books as editor: *La dinamica del diritto amministrativo. Dieci lezioni*, Bologna, Il Mulino, 2017; *L'Unione europea in crisi*, Milano, Giuffrè, 2017; *La tecnificazione* (editor with S. Civitarese Matteucci), in *A 150 anni dall'unificazione amministrativa. Studi*, ed. by L. Ferrara e D. Sorace, vol. IV, Firenze, Firenze University Press, 2016; *Attraversare i confini del diritto. Giornata di studio dedicata a Sabino Cassese*, Bologna, Il Mulino, 2016; *I nodi della pubblica amministrazione*, Napoli, ES, 2016; *Italian Public Law in XXI Century* (editor with S. Cassese), London, Esperia Publication Ltd, 2012; *Lezioni di diritto amministrativo progredito*, II ed., Bologna,

Il Mulino, 2012; *Metamorfosi del diritto delle società? Seminario per gli ottant'anni di Guido Rossi* (editor with F. Brescia and A. Zoppini), Napoli, ES, 2012; *Lezioni di diritto amministrativo progredito*, Bologna, Il Mulino, 2010; *Il sistema amministrativo italiano*, Bologna, Il Mulino, 2009; *La scienza del diritto amministrativo nella seconda metà del XX secolo* (editor with E. Chiti, R. Perez and A. Sandulli), Napoli, ES, 2008; *Sviluppo o declino. Il ruolo delle istituzioni per la competitività del Paese* (editor with F. Bassanini), Passigli, 2005; *Welfare e federalismo*, Bologna, Il Mulino, 2005; *Fondazioni bancarie tra autonomia privata e guida pubblica*, monographic issue of *Il Ponte*, 2003; *La riforma del governo. Commento ai decreti legislativi n. 300 e n. 303 del 1999 sulla riorganizzazione della Presidenza del Consiglio e dei ministeri* (editor with A. Pajno), Bologna, Il Mulino, 2000; *Lo Stato autonomista* (editor G. Falcon and in cooperation with M. Cammelli, F. Merloni, G. Pastori, L. Torchia), Bologna, Il Mulino, 1998; *Il procedimento amministrativo: profili comparati*, Padova, Cedam, 1993; *La sperimentazione amministrativa regionale* (editor with E. Buglione and C. Desideri), Bologna, Il Mulino, 1991; *Stato e Regioni. La funzione statale di indirizzo e coordinamento*, Roma, NIS, 1990; *Lavoro pubblico e lavoro privato. È ancora attuale la distinzione?* (editor with L. Gaeta), Napoli, ESI, 1989.

Some of her recent articles deal with: *Poteri pubblici e poteri privati nel mondo digitale*, in Il Mulino, n. 1, 2024; *La giustizia amministrativa digitale*, in M. Ramajoli, *Una giustizia amministrativa digitale?*, Bologna, Il Mulino, 2023; *Carlo Azeglio Ciampi* (con B. Settis), in S. Cassese, A. Melloni, A. Pajno, *I presidenti e la presidenza del Consiglio dei ministri nell'Italia repubblicana. Storia, politica, istituzioni*, tomo secondo, Editori Laterza, 2022; *I poteri di vigilanza, controllo e sanzionatori nella regolazione europea della trasformazione digitale*, in Rivista trimestrale di diritto pubblico, n. 4, 2022; *La giustizia amministrativa digitale*, in *Studi in onore di Maria Immordino*, Napoli, Editoriale Scientifica, 2022; *Riforma amministrativa*, in *Enciclopedia del diritto, Funzioni amministrative*, diretto da B.G. Mattarella e M. Ramajoli, Milano, Giuffrè, 2022; *Lo Stato digitale e il diritto amministrativo*, in *Liber amicorum* per Marco D'Alberti, Torino, Giappichelli, 2022; *Commento all'art. 119 - Riti abbreviati relativi a speciali controversie*, in *Commentario breve al codice del processo amministrativo*, Padova, Cedam, 2021; *La Relazione sull'attività della giustizia amministrativa nel 2020*, in *Giornale di diritto amministrativo*, 2021; *L'europeizzazione dei diritti delle pubbliche amministrazioni*, in *Ragionando di diritto delle pubbliche amministrazioni. In occasione dell'ottantesimo compleanno di Domenico Sorace*, a cura di Simone Torricelli, Esi, 2020; *Socio e società di fronte alla responsabilità per danno erariale dopo il testo unico sulle società pubbliche*, in "*Le società a partecipazione pubblica,*" Quaderni di diritto commerciale, Milano, Giuffrè, 2019; *Il giudice amministrativo e l'amministrazione: controllo, guida, interferenza*, in Rivista trimestrale di diritto pubblico, n. 1, 2019; *La responsabilità degli organi sociali nelle imprese a partecipazione pubblica*, in *Giornale di diritto amministrativo*, n. 2, 2018; *Le misure per la qualità e l'innovazione nel Codice dei contratti pubblici*, Quaderni di ricerca giuridica, Banca d'Italia, 2018; *La Costituzione dei diritti e la Costituzione delle prerogative* (con S. Cassese), in *Foro italiano*, febbraio 2018; *Teoria e prassi delle decisioni amministrative*, in *Diritto amministrativo*, n. 1, 2017; *La regolazione del mercato dei contratti pubblici*, in *Rivista della regolazione dei mercati*, 2016; *In crisi per sempre? L'Europa fra ideali e realtà*, in *Rivista trimestrale di diritto pubblico*, n. 3, 2016; *Funzione consultiva e funzione normativa: il Consiglio di Stato e le riforme*, in *Giornale di diritto amministrativo*, n. 3, 2016; *Moneta, banca e finanza fra unificazione europea e crisi economica*, in Rivista italiana di diritto pubblico comunitario, n. 6, 2016; La nuova direttiva europea in materia di appalti di lavori, servizi e forniture nei settori ordinari, in Diritto amministrativo, n. 2-3, 2015; La responsabilità della pubblica amministrazione, in Istituzioni di diritto amministrativo (con E. Morlino), a cura di Sabino Cassese, V ed., Milano, Giuffrè, 2015; Giustizia ed economia, in Giornale di diritto amministrativo, n. 4, 2014.

Memberships*: European Public Law Organization*; *General Council of Icon-S* (International Society of Public Law); *Italian Association of Administrative Law Professors*; *Istituto di ricerca sulla pubblica amministrazione*—Irpa; *Evaluation committee for the recruitment of lecturers* at the Bocconi University; *Advisory Board of the Development Programme,* Department of Law, University of Palermo. She is the director of the second-level master's degree "Lo Stato digitale" at the University of Roma Tre. She is member of the Scientific Board of *Teoria e prassi del diritto* and *Aedon* and she is member of the Steering Committee of *Rivista Trimestrale di Diritto Pubblico* and *Giornale di diritto amministrativo.*

Further details are available here: https://www.uniroma3.it/en/persone/RU1jVl1HRE9hOGhpQk5vaVpOMVcyVlRKankvQjMwWkpBVEt6anNwT0lRUT0=/.

Contributors

Lucie Cluzel-Métayer Nanterre University, Law Department, Nanterre, France

Susana de la Sierra University of Castilla-La Mancha, Toledo, Spain

Alexandre de Streel University of Namur, Namur, Belgium

Néstor Duch-Brown Joint Research Centre, European Commission, Brussels, Belgium

Cristina Fraenkel-Haeberle University of Speyer and German Research Institute for Public Administration (research area: civil service), Speyer, Germany

Jens-Uwe Franck University of Mannheim, Department of Law, and Mannheim Centre for Competition and Innovation (MaCCI), Mannheim, Germany

Kristi Joamets Tallinn University of Technology, Tallinn, Estonia

Tanel Kerikmäe Tallinn University of Technology, Tallinn, Estonia

Nina Lasbleiz Nanterre University, Law Department, Nanterre, France

Estela Fernández López University Carlos III, Madrid, Spain

Mariateresa Maggiolino Bocconi University, Department of Law, Milan, Italy

Frédéric Marty CNRS, GREDEG, Université Côte d'Azur, Nice, France

Viktoria Mazur Tallinn University of Technology, Department of Law, Tallinn, Estonia

Marianna Merler University of Trento, Trento, Italy

Ebru Metin Tallinn University of Technology, Tallinn, Estonia

Camilla Ramotti Luiss Guido Carli University, Rome, Italy

David Ramiro Troitiño Tallinn University of Technology, Department of Law, Tallinn, Estonia

Public Administrations and AI: National Law and AI Act

AI and Public Administration

Barbara Marchetti and Luisa Torchia

Contents

This contribution stems from a common reflection. Barbara Marchetti wrote the parr. 1, 1.1, 1.2, 1.3, 1.4, 1.5, 3, 3.1, 3.2, 3.3. Luisa Torchia wrote the parr. 2, 2.1, 2.2, 2.3, 2.4, 2.5.

B. Marchetti (✉)
University of Trento, Trento, Italy
e-mail: barbara.marchetti@unitn.it

L. Torchia
Roma Tre University, Rome, Italy
e-mail: luisa.torchia@uniroma3.it

F. Decarolis et al. (eds.), *The EU Digital Regulation and its Impact on Member States*, European Union and its Neighbours in a Globalized World 27,
https://doi.org/10.1007/978-3-032-06490-5_1

Abstract The chapter explores the relationship between artificial intelligence and public administrations. It is structured into three parts.

The first part examines the different types of artificial intelligence and the various ways in which public administration can employ it, in order to assess the risks and highlight the opportunities it presents.

The second part analyzes the framework of national and European regulations governing the use of AI in the exercise of public functions, with particular attention to the case law of national courts and the complex European regulatory framework, represented by Regulation 2024/1689 (AI Act).

The third part focuses on the main challenges facing algorithmic administration, including the adequate training of public officials, the procurement processes necessary to equip the administration with AI systems, and the role of cybersecurity, whose importance grows as public administration accelerates its digitalization process.

1 AI and Public Administration: The Importance of Distinguishing

Almost every study or piece of research concerning artificial intelligence (AI) underscores both its opportunities and risks. Enthusiastic and dystopian perspectives often emerge, depending on whether one perceives the beneficial or harmful potential of AI, the opportunities it creates, or the risks it poses to citizens' rights.[1] In a study focused on the use of AI by public authorities, a discussion of both the benefits and risks is therefore indispensable, as we are addressing applications that, on one hand, have the capacity to significantly enhance administrative services and functions, but on the other hand, due to the intrinsic characteristics of AI, could also endanger fundamental values of public administration, such as transparency, accountability, impartiality, comprehensibility, and the justiciability of administrative decisions.[2] However, in a work that seeks to analyze the issues arising from the use of AI in the public sphere, a general and abstract approach which treats AI as a monolithic technology would prove of limited value. It is, in the author's view, more appropriate and beneficial to adopt a methodology that distinguishes between different types of AI and their various applications in public administration. The

[1] See Crawford (2021), Suleyman (2024), Kissinger et al. (2021), Floridi (2020), Floridi (2022), Ferrarese (2022), Habermas (2023), Zuboff (2019), Casini (2022), Finocchiaro (2024).

[2] On the debate related to use of AI by public administrations, see Coglianese and Lehr (2017), Coglianese and Lehr (2019), Palmer Olsen et al. (2022), Pasquale (2022), Engstrom et al. (2020). The citation "Glaze et al. (2023)" has been changed to "Glaze et al. (2022)" to match the author name/date in the reference list. Please check if the change is fine in this occurrence and modify the subsequent occurrences, if necessary. Glaze et al. (2022), Rachovitsa and Johann (2022). For the Italian debate, see Avanzini (2019), Marchetti (2022), Torchia (2023).

potentialities and risks associated with symbolic AI (so-called expert systems or hard rules-based systems), machine learning (ML) AI, or generative AI (LLMs), as well as their respective uses in cognition, facilitation, support, or decision-making, are, in fact, distinct.

For instance, the use of a ML AI system, characterized by significant opacity in its decision-making logic and the possibility of bias, to determine the allocation of public housing or the granting of a subsidy, is inherently a very different (and riskier) operation from deploying an expert system to sort e-mails within an administration or to manage a chatbot. It thus appears necessary to avoid broad generalizations regarding the advantages and disadvantages of the use of such technology. Instead, the approach should focus on identifying, for each specific system, the distinct risks associated with its varied applications, in line with a risk-proportionate approach that, not coincidentally, also inspires European Regulation 2024/1689 on Artificial Intelligence (the AI Act, hereinafter referred to, as discussed in Sect. 2.3).

The first part of this paper will seek to elaborate on this methodological foundation by examining the range of possible applications of AI within the public sector and the various challenges they present. Following this, and while maintaining these premises in the background, the European and national regulatory frameworks governing the matter will be scrutinized, with particular emphasis on the general or sector-specific nature of the regulations, the risk-mitigation strategies embedded within them, and the administrative apparatus established for their enforcement. In the third part of the paper, the implications of the administrative digitization process will be explored, both in terms of the skills and capabilities required of civil servants and with specific reference to the methods and procedures of procuring or producing AI, analyzing the pros and cons of in-house production versus outsourcing.

In conclusion, a series of general observations will be offered.

1.1 What Is Meant by AI?

The definition of AI contained in Article 3 of the European Regulation immediately accounts for the plural nature of this technology: it encompasses systems with varying degrees of autonomy, with or without adaptive capacity, based on different methods and techniques, capable of performing highly diversified tasks.[3]

These structural differences have consequences on the explainability of the system, on the amount of input data required to train and validate the system, on the decision-making logic, and on the type of outputs generated by the machine. These, in turn, may come into greater or lesser tension with the rules and principles

[3] See Art. 3, EU reg. 2024/1689: «AI system means a machine-based system that is designed to operate with varying levels of autonomy and that may exhibit adaptiveness after deployment, and that, for explicit or implicit objectives, infers, from the input it receives, how to generate outputs such as predictions, content, recommendations, or decisions that can influence physical or virtual environments».

applicable to the public sphere and with the way administrative decisions must be constructed.

Without delving too deeply into the technical aspects, it is necessary at least to distinguish between systems based on hard rules algorithms[4] (so-called expert systems) and systems based on machine learning (ML) algorithms.[5]

The former are based on a causal logic, well summarized by the *if-then* formula: the model is built on a series of steps in which knowledge of a specific domain is codified, and the machine reaches a predefined conclusion when the established conditions are met. The advantage of these systems is that the path taken to reach the final output is re-constructible and intelligible, meaning it is explainable. Of course, its comprehensibility requires the translation of the technical rule into a legal rule—since the algorithm appears as a set of mathematical formulas and functions, hardly understandable to non-experts—but the fact that it arrives at the output based on steps connected by a causal relationship allows for an explanation of how the machine has processed the data and performed its work.

Therefore, their use can be considered compatible with the principles of transparency and explainability, without significantly altering the relationship between citizens' rights and public authority and the fundamental guarantees embedded therein. On the other hand, they can enhance predictability and legal certainty due to automation. Even if they do not pose major concerns, they are, at the same time, not particularly effective or high performing.[6]

Conversely, ML and deep learning (DL) algorithms are highly performant but, when used by public authorities, may entail significant risks concerning the rule of law due to their opacity (the so-called black box issue) and their potential for errors and discrimination.[7] Constantly learning and modifying their internal structure through experience, they lack transparency, accessibility, and traceability. Effective participatory mechanisms are precluded, and conditions for their reviewability appear to be lacking. Courts cannot establish causal links between input data (even if known) and produced outputs—which are fundamental for reasonableness and proportionality review—as there is only a statistical-probabilistic correlation between the two extremes of the algorithmic process.

This is why using ML for making final administrative decisions, such as benefits allocation or university admissions, raises the most critical concerns.

Since 2022, moreover, generative AI has entered the AI landscape, which, as is well known, is based on a textual prompt and can generate novel content through deep neural networks, structured in multiple layers, that create large language

---

[4] Algorithm is a set of instructions that is designed to accomplish a task. Algorithms usually take one or more inputs, run them systematically through a series of steps, and provide one or more outputs. Algorithms are typically associated with computing and are an essential element of computer programming.

[5] See Traverso (2022), Russell and Norvig (2010), Santosuosso and Sartor (2024).

[6] See Santosuosso and Sartor (2024).

[7] See Santosuosso and Sartor (2024).

models (LLMs). These foundation models are trained on broad datasets using large-scale self-supervision, then adapted to a wide range of downstream tasks.

The opportunities these models present for public authorities are vast, as are the risks they pose.[8] On one hand they may seamlessly complement human labor (helping public officials in many of their tasks like writing emails, preparing texts, translating, searching norms and references) but they could also amplify bias, undermine trust of information (because of the so-called hallucinations) and compromise data protection, revealing sensitive citizen data or internal governmental data.[9]

This is why generative AI presents substantially few risks if used, for instance, for managing chatbots in public services, while, on contrary, could be very risky if used in computationally-assisted processes to assign benefits[10] or, more generally, for decision-making:[11] being based on LLMs, for example, these programs would score claims based on the words that appear in them (and relationships between these words), identifying some set of claims as particularly meritorious claims, without understanding the meaning of any of these legal texts.[12]

1.2 *AI for Routine and Conversational Tasks*

As evidenced by national reports, there is a high number of AI applications that can make public administrations' work significantly more efficient and faster while presenting minimal or negligible risk. This does not mean, of course, that such applications have no impact on administration and its organization, or on the workforce employed therein, but the benefits they bring outweigh the potential disadvantages, as they are deployed in activities and operations of a predominantly preparatory and routine nature.

Consider applications used for sorting emails within an administration, or systems promoted by the European Commission to enhance the «document summarization capabilities» of its officials or to provide «services to leverage the vast data, information, and knowledge base that the administration has across various business areas».[13] Likewise, AI used to assist officials in translation functions, such as

[8] See Weerts (2025), Cantens (2024), Dreyling et al. (2024), Pasquale and Malgieri (2024).

[9] See Weerts (2025).

[10] See Pasquale and Malgieri (2024).

[11] See Pesch (2025).

[12] See Pasquale and Malgieri (2024): «In the administrative benefits landscape, score-based natural language processing (SBNLP) offers promising efficiencies while generative AI seems a tempting solution for providing requisite explanations. Nonetheless strict limits on their use will be necessary. The true essence of administrative due process-genuine transparency, fairness and accountability—must remain at the forefront of any integration of such technology into benefits management».

[13] See Weerts (2025).

the European eTranslation system, or the chatbot Albert, which supports French civil servants in their tasks.[14]

Alongside these systems, designed to assist officials in their daily activities, fall in the same category—high efficiency and low risk—the chatbots developed to respond to citizens' queries. For example, the chatbot developed in Italy by INPS (Istituto Nazionale della Previdenza Sociale) for its users, the SIGMA chatbot created for Portuguese citizens, or the Aristotle chatbot created for French students can be mentioned.

The advantages of using AI for such tasks (routine and conversational) are evident both in terms of administrative efficiency and speed and in terms of facilitating relations with citizens. Consider the possibility of addressing questions and queries to the administration 24/7 via chatbot.

However, some risks, albeit not high, are associated with the use of these applications. Three key aspects emerge: the first concerns the potential exclusion effect linked to the digital divide in the case of conversational AI. This issue is particularly relevant for institutional chatbots, considering that, for instance, in Italy, there remains a significant digital divide between the north and south of the country and between the younger and older populations.

The second risk relates to both deskilling and misinformation, which may result from the use of these models. On the one hand, there could be a gradual loss of linguistic and writing skills among public personnel; on the other, errors and omissions could arise in the absence of adequate oversight by officials.

The third and final aspect concerns the potential consequences in terms of staff reductions, as tasks previously performed necessarily by civil servants could gradually be carried out by machines. Consider, for example, personnel engaged in text translation within European institutions.

However, in light of the advantages generated and subject to the necessary human oversight of the machine—an essential requirement for the reliable use of AI—the applications referenced (which remain outside the exercise of discretionary functions) appear, in balancing pros and cons, to have minimal impact on rights, adequately mitigate risks—if an email sorting system misdirects an email, the office will reassign it to the appropriate unit[15]—and offer considerable advantages in terms of efficiency and speed of public administration operations.

Not surprisingly, the same European regulation excludes systems dedicated to these types of tasks from being considered high-risk, either because they perform activities that do not impact citizens' rights or because they do not substantially influence the exercise of powers. This can be inferred from both the analysis of Annex III of the Regulation and the reading of paragraph 3 of Article 6, dedicated to the hypotheses of declassification of systems (which would be theoretically high-risk).

---

[14] See Koller (2024), Ada Lovelace Institute (b) (2024).

[15] See Weerts (2025).

1.3 *AI Replacing the Human Official*

At the opposite extreme—in terms of criticality and problematic aspects for public values and the rule of law—compared to the internal or conversational use of AI, lies its decision-making use.[16] By decision-making use, it is meant that through AI the administration directly adopts decisions that have a significant impact on the sphere of the concerned individuals. Even in this case, however, the scenario changes depending on whether a rule-based expert system is used, in which the logical steps leading to the decision can be reconstructed, or a machine learning (ML) system is employed. In the first case, as mentioned, it is possible to explain to the concerned individual the instructions given to the machine, the data used, and the path followed by the system to reach the decision. In contrast, where the decision is adopted using systems characterized by inexplicability and operational opacity, such possibility does not exist, and the risks of errors, biases, and hallucinations potentially leading to actual rights violations are heightened.[17] In such instances, as demonstrated by national reports, there are strong tensions with the values and principles intrinsic to administrative action previously referenced: transparency, motivation, justiciability, and accountability.[18] This is even more relevant considering that many systems may be supplied by private providers, who are not bound to incorporate public values within the algorithm but rather to pursue choices that ensure profit maximization.[19]

For this reason, as of today, the use of ML AI for adjudication proceedings is highly limited within the European context, whereas it appears to be more widespread in the United States, particularly regarding welfare state benefits. This is the case, for example, with systems used by the Social Security Administration (SSA) to determine the urgent allocation of state benefits,[20] to establish eligibility for disability benefits,[21] or even to grant patents.[22] In Europe, the most well-known case was the SyRI algorithm, developed by the Dutch Government to identify citizens committing fraud against the welfare system. The algorithm was annulled by the Court due to its discriminatory nature, leading to a scandal that ultimately resulted in the fall of the government.[23]

---

[16] See Avanzini (2019), Marchetti (2022), Torchia (2023).

[17] See Ames et al. (2020).

[18] See Coglianese and Lai (2022), Coglianese (2020).

[19] See Langer (2024).

[20] See Pasquale and Malgieri (2024).

[21] See Glaze et al. (2022).

[22] See Engstrom et al. (2020), Coglianese and Ben-Dor (2021).

[23] See Rachovitsa and Johann (2022), Torchia (forthcoming).

1.4 AI Supporting the Human Official

When examining European experiences as analyzed in national reports, it emerges that many AI applications currently in use serve a supportive function to subsequent actions carried out by human officials. Technically, therefore, these can be described as decision-support systems. Unlike the previously examined categories, AI is neither confined to routine activities nor intended to replace human officials in making the final decision. Instead, it provides assistance to the authority in various ways to enable the optimal exercise of its powers.

There are numerous use cases. On one hand, there are applications that allow the administration to extract knowledge from large volumes of data to better guide its policies (data-driven policies): for instance, a system analyzing data on pedestrian and vehicle circulation in a given urban area to optimize traffic and public transport; or a system analyzing social media data to assess public sentiment on economic recovery, drawing conclusions for monetary policy decisions.

These systems offer unprecedented advantages to the administration by expanding its knowledge base, enabling it to prepare and develop policies in ways previously unthinkable. However, risks remain: on one side, such systems may provide incorrect or incomplete representations of reality if the dataset construction lacks accuracy and representativity; on the other, privacy violations may arise if the data used include personal or sensitive information that has not been properly anonymized or pseudonymized.

Additionally, some applications provide risk assessments to the administration to enhance control and oversight activities. Examples include systems used by financial authorities to identify potential tax evaders or those employed by the Bank of Italy to detect links between companies and organized crime through financial analysis, or to assess customer complaints to refine financial oversight strategies.

In all these cases, the AI system does not make final decisions but directs and influences subsequent human-led investigative and decision-making activities.

For all such ML-based systems, key concerns arise regarding the type of data used for training, considering both the European data protection regulation, which imposes a principle of data minimization (Article 5(1)(c) GDPR), and the European AI regulation, which establishes precise obligations for data management and control for both providers and deployers.

For instance, in France, Article 154 of the 2020 Finance Law (Loi n. 2019-1479 of 28 Décembre 2019) authorizes the tax administration, on an experimental basis, to automatically collect and process publicly available information from users' social media profiles, excluding content accessible only through password-protected areas. This data is used to detect undeclared activities. Although no automatic link exists between the automated control results and the final administrative decision, the algorithm's findings influence whether a tax investigation is initiated or dismissed.

A similar approach has been adopted in Italy, following the delegation law (Law no. 111 of 9 August 2023), which authorizes the tax authority to conduct web scraping to identify potential tax evaders.

Furthermore, predictive systems of this kind may result in discriminatory outcomes depending on the criteria used to select the scrutinized subjects. Depending on the methodology employed, there is a risk of disproportionately targeting specific categories of individuals, increasing the likelihood of violations being detected within those groups.[24]

Even more critical is the risk assessment system used in the judicial sector: the well-known case of the COMPAS algorithm, employed in the US to assess the recidivism risk of defendants, has demonstrated how biases in training data generate clear discriminatory effects against the black population.[25]

Thus, even for decision-support systems, a case-by-case approach is required to assess the system's role in decision-making, its influence on final decisions, its potential impact on fundamental rights and data protection, and its utility for its intended purpose:[26] These factors must guide administrative choices regarding system adoption and risk-mitigation measures, particularly those ensuring human oversight. Furthermore, mechanisms must be established to detect and report algorithmic discrimination, as has been done, for example, in Estonia.

1.5 Transparency and AI

The use of AI by public administrations must not result in making their actions opaque and inscrutable. This principle has multiple implications. First, as mentioned, it concerns the ability to understand and explain algorithm-based decisions.

Second, it involves access to the source code, which may be protected by intellectual property rights,[27] particularly when the system is supplied by private entities.

How can these opposing needs be reconciled? Can intellectual property rights override the public's right to access administrative acts? Or must proprietary rights yield when the system is used by a public authority[28]?

Article 1(2)(b) of Directive 2016/943 on the protection of undisclosed know-how and business information (trade secrets) states that such protection «does not affect the application of Union or national rules requiring trade secrets to be disclosed to the public or to administrative or judicial authorities for the performance of their duties».

---

[24] See Torchia (2023).

[25] See Liu et al. (2019), Angwin et al. (2016).

[26] See Palmiotto (2024).

[27] See Bloch-Wehba (2020).

[28] See Bloch-Wehba (2020).

Thus, intellectual property protection finds a potential limit in the necessity to safeguard public interest, though the balance point may vary significantly.

In Italy, this issue arose in a judicial case[29] concerning the Ministry of Education's use of an algorithm protected by intellectual property rights. The first-instance court denied access to the source code based on IP rights, but on appeal, the Council of State ruled that such rights must yield to the need for transparency in public administration. Recently also the Spanish Tribunal Supremo (1119/2025 Decision), in the BOSCO Case, reached the same conclusions in terms of right to access to an algorithm deciding on social bonus (Chapter V).

Less clear-cut, however, appears to be the solution adopted within the United States legal system,[30] where the courts seem to assess the required level of transparency with a certain degree of pragmatism, also considering the rights at stake. Here, the alternative is not simply between full access to the source code or its complete protection; rather, judges may require the disclosure of the most relevant elements of the algorithm without necessarily mandating the revelation of the source code. This has significant implications for the procurement process of such technology, as the public entity, during contract negotiations, must «take into account the need to have access to and be able to disclose sufficient information about the algorithm, the underlying data, and the validation results to satisfy transparency norms».[31]

A third implication concerns the general obligations of communication and transparency incumbent upon the administration when using artificial intelligence systems. More specifically, administrations are required to publish on their institutional websites the characteristics of the systems and models used, the data employed for training, the procedures or activities for which the systems are deployed, and the role they play within the decision-making process.

In Italy, such an obligation has only recently been introduced by Article 30 of Legislative Decree 36/2023, albeit with a provision that appears of little utility in ensuring an effective understanding of the uses of this technology in the public sphere and its implications for citizens' rights. Indeed, the rule merely requires public authorities to publish on their website, in the transparency section, a list of the applications used, without further specifications.

More interesting and effective, instead, is the communication model adopted, for example, in the United Kingdom. The *Algorithmic Transparency Recording Standards*[32] provide for two levels of information—one more elementary, aimed at non-experts, and a more technical one, designed to specifically explain the functioning of the system. Under these standards, the administration does not merely list the

[29] See in this volume Merler and Ramotti, *Italian public administration in the face of digital transformation*

[30] See Coglianese and Lampmann (2020).

[31] See Coglianese (2020).

[32] See https://www.gov.uk/government/publications/guidance-for-organisations-using-the-algorithmic-transparency-recording-standard/algorithmic-transparency-recording-standard-guidance-for-public-sector-bodies

applications in use but must also disclose their operating logic, the training, validation, and testing datasets of the system, and its intended purposes.

2 The Rules for the Use of AI

Artificial intelligence applications have been made available on the global market and, unlike most products and services, without any prior authorization process, in the absence of rules specifically addressing their use, and allowing, at least initially, free access to anyone wishing to use them.

There are two fundamental reasons why the process of production and commercialization of artificial intelligence applications differs from other production and commercialization processes. The first reason relates to the intrinsic and unavoidable difficulty of regulating innovation: regulation, by definition, is an activity that requires a defined object, but innovation—again by definition—introduces into the world and the market previously non-existent objects, which therefore cannot be regulated until they come into existence. The awareness of this difficulty underpins the approach of the European regulation on artificial intelligence, aimed at regulating not so much specific applications but rather the risks potentially associated with any application, thereby allowing a broad margin of flexibility in the (future) identification of even products that do not yet exist today.

The second reason, however, derives from the nature of the production process of artificial intelligence applications, which are introduced to the market also with a view to future refinements, for which "training" derived precisely from user interaction is essential. Unlike a drug or a machine, for which marketing without a prior authorization process ensuring safety and verifying potential side effects or malfunctions would be deemed unacceptable, artificial intelligence evolves by "learning" from its own use and would therefore require an equally evolutionary, flexible, and dynamic regulation—an objective difficult to achieve, especially considering the complexities of the regulatory process in all legal systems and particularly within the European legal framework.

With specific regard to the public sector, however, various legal systems have faced a preliminary issue before that of regulation itself: the very possibility of resorting to artificial intelligence for the exercise of public power or, at any rate, the conditions for its use. Even algorithmic administration, in fact, must comply with the principle of legality, affirmed in national legal systems as well as in European law. This principle, on the one hand, cannot be circumvented because of the use of technological tools, and on the other hand, may require a different articulation—compared to traditional administrative activity—for algorithmic administration.[33]

[33] See Santosuosso and Sartor (2024).

The solution to this issue has been identified through the search for an enabling norm, which may have a general scope or refer to specific cases, depending on the circumstances.

It is possible to resort to a general enabling norm if the use of artificial intelligence is considered a tool for exercising powers already attributed to public administration and not, instead, a new type of power, which, under the principle of legality, needs a specific legal basis. According to a widely held view,[34] such general authorization could be inferred from the GDPR provision enshrining the right (of any individual) «not to be subject to a decision based solely on automated processing, including profiling, which produces legal effects concerning him or her or similarly significantly affects him or her» (Article 22). Indeed, according to this thesis, the very recognition of this individual right would derive from the generalized acknowledgment of the possibility of making administrative decisions through automated processing, which is nonetheless allowed, albeit by way of exception, in certain specific cases (for instance, if automated processing is necessary for the conclusion of a contract, or is authorized by the EU or a Member State with accompanying safeguards, or if the data subject consents to a fully algorithmic administrative decision).

In various national legal systems, there are also norms that not only authorize but encourage the use of artificial intelligence for administrative functions. In Italy, both the law on administrative procedure,[35] the Digital Administration Code[36], and the Law 132/2025 contain provisions that not only permit the use of artificial intelligence in dealings with citizens but go so far as to establish a "digital citizenship" principle that should inspire the conduct of administrative procedures. In France, the *Code des relations entre le public et l'administration* was amended by the *Loi pour une République numérique of 2016,*[37] extending the guarantees provided for traditional administration to algorithmic administration. In Spain, a constitutional norm was introduced stating that «la ley limitará el uso de la informática para garantizar el honor y la intimidad personal y familiar de los ciudadanos y el pleno ejercicio de sus derechos» (art. 18.4) and the 2015 *Régimen jurídico del sector público*

---

[34] See Civitarese Matteucci (2021), Dalgado (2019).

[35] The provision stipulates that, in order to achieve greater efficiency in their activities, public administrations shall act by means of computerised and telematic tools, in their internal relations, between the different administrations and between these and private parties. Literally, «per conseguire maggiore efficienza nella loro attività, le amministrazioni pubbliche agiscono mediante strumenti informatici e telematici, nei rapporti interni, tra le diverse amministrazioni e tra queste e i privati» (art. 3-bis, L. no. 241/1990).

[36] The CAD requires public administrations to use information and communication technologies to pursue the objectives of efficiency, effectiveness, cost-effectiveness, impartiality, transparency, simplification and participation in compliance with the principle of equality and non-discrimination and to ensure the effective recognition of the rights of citizens and businesses (art. 12) and provides in general terms for public administrations to engage in the process of administrative digitalisation, using new technological solutions to rationalise and simplify not only management activities, documents and payment methods for citizens, but also administrative procedures.

[37] On the amendments to the Code see Bourcier and De Filippi (2019).

provided for the possibility of carrying out administrative activity exclusively through automated systems (Article 41).

A partially different choice was made in Germany, where fully automated administrative decisions are permitted only on condition that an explicit legal basis exists and that they concern binding, non-discretionary decisions, while the legislator remains free to identify specific procedures and measures for which automated processing is authorized.[38] Yet another approach was adopted in Denmark, where the so-called "administrative law by design" principle applies, requiring the direct regulation of technological tools used by the administration to ensure their compliance with general legal principles, thus directly influencing the development and programming processes of such tools to guarantee their adherence to the general principles governing all administrative activity.

The presence of enabling rules is, however, only a prerequisite for the use of artificial intelligence by public administrations and leaves numerous problems open as regards the conditions of legitimacy and the actual possibility of controlling automated administrative decisions. In the absence of rules on these profiles, at least until the adoption and entry into force of the AI Act (on which see below), some principles were defined by national courts in the first cases of challenges to automated administrative decisions.

2.1 The Judicial Way to Regulation: Courts and Technology

In the vast array of cases brought before national and international courts, issues relating to privacy regulation, intellectual property, competition, and liability for content control and moderation prevail. However, certain issues concerning algorithmic administration have also emerged, for which judges have applied general principles and identified particular limits and conditions.

In Italy, for example, the administrative court has established that when administrative power is exercised through the use of algorithms, it must comply with three general principles: a principle of enhanced transparency, which must ensure not only the knowability but also the comprehensibility of algorithmic decision-making process; a principle of non-exclusivity of automation, with the mandatory requirement of human intervention, according to the "human in the loop" principle; a principle of non-discrimination, whereby even the use of algorithmic tools is subject to the principles of equality and equal treatment.[39]

The principle of transparency has also been affirmed by the French Conseil Constitutionnel, which has established its precedence over rules concerning trade secrecy or intellectual property, in such a way that if transparency cannot be ensured due to the protection of intellectual property or trade secrecy, the administration

[38] See Fraenkel-Haeberle (2020).

[39] See Carloni (2020), Gallone (2023).

may not use algorithmic tools to make decisions. Similarly, the review of such decisions through administrative appeals or judicial proceedings cannot be entirely automated. In analogous terms, the German Constitutional Court intervened in its ruling of 16 February 2023 on predictive policing algorithms.

The intervention of the courts has thus provided a form of embryonic bottom-up regulation, which, however, naturally only concerns the conditions of legitimacy for the use of artificial intelligence, as it would be impossible to establish, in a judicial case, actual rules on the processes of production, commercialization, and implementation of new products and services.

This has forcefully revived the debate on the choice between self-regulation—the approach preferred in the United States—and external regulation, according to the European legal tradition. The discussion on the advantages and disadvantages of both options is lively and has recently focused on the European AI Act and new artificial intelligence applications based on Large Language Models (LLMs), which also have a global reach.

2.2 *The Difficulty of Regulating AI*

It has already been mentioned that regulating innovation is difficult precisely because it entails governing a phenomenon that is continuously evolving and assumes unprecedented characteristics. A clear example of this difficulty is evidenced by the European AI Act, which, at the beginning of the legislative process for its adoption, contained a definition of the object to be regulated that had to be subsequently modified due to the proliferation of general intelligence applications based on LLMs. Initially, the rules referred to «software developed using one or more of the techniques and approaches listed in Annex I, which can, for a specific set of objectives defined by humans, generate outputs such as content, predictions, recommendations, or decisions that affect the environments with which they interact». In the final text, however, they refer to «a machine-based system that is designed to operate with varying levels of autonomy and that may exhibit adaptiveness after deployment, and that, for explicit or implicit objectives, infers, from the input it receives, how to generate outputs such as predictions, content, recommendations, or decisions that can influence physical or virtual environments».

The difficulty in regulation is further exacerbated, in the case of artificial intelligence, by two additional factors: the need for the regulator to possess technical expertise that is almost entirely monopolized by *Big Techs*, and, conversely, the simultaneously widespread and global dissemination of this new technology within the social and political sphere, which therefore requires general rules—sometimes of a constitutional dimension—that in turn must necessarily impact social and political life, both individually and collectively.

These difficulties probably explain why, until now, both states and international organizations have preferred to adopt soft regulation measures, define general principles, encourage self-regulation, and promote the adoption of codes of conduct rather than implementing a true regulatory regime in this field. However, the situation has changed following the spread of the first artificial intelligence applications based on natural language, which, according to widespread and at least partially shared opinion—even paradoxically among the major producers of these applications—are innovations fraught with serious risks, up to and including concerns about the domination of machines over humans and the potential extinction of humanity.[40]

The inadequacy of self-regulation had, in any case, already been evident for some time, and the debate on the pros and cons of regulation has highlighted not only the risks to individual rights and democracy posed by the spread of new technologies, but also the implausibility of narratives attributing solely to the absence of regulation the ability to innovate and build global platforms (for which any national regulator is thus at an asymmetric disadvantage). The frequently cited Section 230 of the Communications Act, regarded as the foundational basis for the transformation of innovative start-ups into major platforms due to their liability exemption, would certainly not have been sufficient if those start-ups had not also benefited from the availability of venture capital and extensive public intervention characteristic of the American system.[41]

Conversely, the absence of regulation has evidently produced negative effects, not only in terms of the proliferation of fake news and hate speech, social and political polarization, data abuse, and violations of individual and collective rights,[42] but also in terms of the market itself. In the absence of effective antitrust rules, large platforms today hold oligopolistic or monopolistic positions, acquire all potential competitors, and have made it impossible or at least extremely difficult for the primary advantage of innovation—the disruption of established market positions and hierarchies in favor of new entrants—to take place. The current scale of *Big Techs* is now such that traditional tools used to limit private power and prevent abuses, such as competition law and the definition of liability regimes, have become at least partially ineffective.[43]

The issue of regulation has thus become even more complex, as it would not suffice merely to extend existing rules to *Big Techs*—for example, by eliminating the original liability exemption under Section 230—but requires the construction of new and more suitable regulatory regimes.

---

[40] Already in 2015, S. Hawking, Elon Musk, Steve Wozniak and other technology experts signed a public letter calling for stricter regulation on artificial intelligence research and warning of the risks involved in creating machines with higher intelligence than humans. More recently, several experts and industry leaders, including Sam Altman (CEO of Open AI) signed a statement in May 2023 stating that "mitigating the risk of extinction due to AI should be a global priority" and Geoffrey Hinton (often called the "godfather of AI"), left Google in 2023 and publicly expressed his concerns about the potential existential risk of AI.

[41] See Bradford (2024).

[42] See Zuboff (2019), Crawford (2021).

[43] See Olson (2024).

The European Union has embarked on this path, albeit with difficulties, by adopting a series of regulations—among the most recent being the Digital Markets Act (DMA), the Digital Services Act (DSA), and the AI Act—aimed at establishing uniform rules for the entire European internal market, yet possessing a sort of extraterritoriality, as they apply to all products and services marketed and provided within the European legal framework, regardless of the nationality of the producer or provider. Concerning the specific subject of this part of the volume, particular importance is given to the regulation on artificial intelligence, whose essential features are analyzed below.

2.3 The European Regulation 1689/2024 and the Space for National Legislators

The European regulation on artificial intelligence has three main objectives: to introduce a control system that allows for the verification of the compliance of artificial intelligence systems with the fundamental values and rights ensured within the Union; to define a regulatory framework that guarantees at least a certain degree of uniformity and legal certainty while at the same time not hindering investment and innovation in the sector; and to build an effective governance system for the security of artificial intelligence that overcomes the fragmentation of the single market that could result from uncoordinated national legislation. The regulation applies to any artificial intelligence system marketed or used within the single market, regardless of its origin or development outside the Union.

For the first time, the regulation introduces a ban on certain artificial intelligence practices, such as those that use subliminal techniques or social scoring systems,[44] while also establishing, again for the first time, harmonized rules for the placing on the market, commissioning, and use of artificial intelligence systems within the Union. Specific requirements are thus imposed for high-risk AI systems (many of which are classified as such due to their use in typically public sectors) and obligations for all operators of these systems, while a governance framework is defined to ensure market monitoring and supervision.[45]

[44] On 4 February 2025, the Commission Guidelines on prohibited artificial intelligence practices established by Regulation (EU) 2024/1689 (AI Act) were published.

[45] The AI Act was published in the Official Journal of the European Union on 12 July 2024 and came into force on 1 August 2024, but the actual implementation has different deadlines: from February 2025 the ban on AI systems with unacceptable risk will become effective; from May 2025 the codes of conduct will apply; from August 2025 the governance rules and obligations for general purpose AI will apply; from August 2026 the provisions for AI systems (including Annex III) will apply; from August 2027 the entire regulation for all risk categories (including Annex II) will apply.

Among the many relevant elements of this complex regulation, two are particularly noteworthy: the regulatory approach based on risk management[46] and the determination of rules and obligations for the entire chain of entities involved.

The regulation only sets out the minimum requirements for the admissibility of artificial intelligence systems within the European legal order and calibrates these requirements based on the type of risk associated with different types of tools, differentiating them according to risk intensity. The regulation identifies different types of risk: unacceptable risk, high risk, non-high risk, and minimal risk, for artificial intelligence systems. For low or minimal-risk systems, only information obligations or adherence to Codes of Conduct are required. High-risk regimes, on the other hand, are subject to a discipline that provides for specific requirements and obligations, including those related to risk management, system transparency, and human oversight.[47] Systems that entail unacceptable risks are, finally, subject to a prohibition regime unless expressly exempted.

This regulatory framework also includes provisions on general artificial intelligence models based on LLMs—both in standalone versions and in cases where they are integrated into a system and allow user interaction through an application—for which a specific procedure is established to identify potential systemic risks associated with them.[48]

Furthermore, the rules apply to all entities involved in any capacity in the production, marketing, or use of the relevant tools: not only to programmers, designers, manufacturers, and suppliers—regardless of whether they are established in the Union or a third country—but also to users of artificial intelligence systems located in the Union or even in a third country if the system's output is used in the Union. The subjective application criterion is also extended to both public and private entities, regardless of the different rules of action that usually apply to public action compared to private activity, although in some cases the public nature of the user has entailed the imposition of specific obligations, such as the requirement to conduct a fundamental rights impact assessment of the system before its deployment.

The regulation also provides for some exemptions, for example, for AI systems placed on the market, commissioned, or used exclusively for military defense or national security purposes, for AI systems specifically developed and commissioned solely for scientific research and development purposes, and for AI systems released under free and open-source licenses (if they are not high-risk).

Despite establishing uniform and broad-ranging rules, the regulation does not cover the entire subject matter, leaving room for Member States to intervene, both

---

[46] Risk is defined as «the combination of the probability of damage occurring and the severity of the damage».

[47] The main obligations with immediate application relate to prohibiting the design of AI systems with unacceptable risk that may cause serious harm, subjecting new high-risk AI products to conformity assessments before placing them on the market, registering high-risk AI systems in a European database that can be consulted by users, ensuring adequate human oversight of the high-risk AI systems used, and reporting any serious AI-related incidents to the competent authorities.

[48] On the AI Act, see Casonato and Marchetti (2021), Rangone (2025), Rangone and Megale (2025).

legislatively and in terms of implementation and monitoring. At the legislative level, each Member State is primarily responsible for regulating the authorization of applications that directly impact fundamental rights, such as remote biometric identification (RBI), although national law must still remain within the limits set by the regulation regarding the purposes for which such applications may be used. National laws must be notified to the Commission within 30 days of adoption and will be published by the Commission on a dedicated website Various legislative proposals on this matter are currently under approval in different Member States. In this regard, reference can be made to Italian Law 132/2025, *Disposizioni e deleghe al Governo in materia di intelligenza artificiale* (Chapter II), as well as to the approval by Spanish Government, on 11 March 2025, of the *Anteproyecto de Ley para el Buen Uso y la Gobernanza de la Inteligencia Artificial*) (Chapter V).

In terms of implementation and monitoring, the regulation provides for a mixed governance system based on cooperation between European institutions and national administrations. Each Member State must either establish a new or designate an existing national notification authority and a national market surveillance authority to ensure the regulation's application and enforcement, which is largely entrusted to national administrations, albeit within the framework of the general rules defined by the regulation. These authorities must exercise their powers independently, impartially, and without bias, but do not necessarily need to have the characteristics of a fully independent authority, as is the case in other sectors of the European internal market, such as competition protection or privacy protection. Therefore, they may be constituted or designated from among existing administrations that maintain a traditional link with the executive, if they respect a principle of enhanced impartiality in the performance of their activities. The same characteristics are replicated at the European level, as will be seen in the next section.

Some Member States have chosen to designate existing entities as market surveillance authorities—Italy, for example, has designated the Agenzia per l'Italia Digitale (AgID) and the Agenzia per la Cybersicurezza Nazionale (ACN)—while other Member States are proceeding with the establishment of new authorities: in Spain, on 22 August 2023, a royal decree was approved for the establishment of the Agencia Española de Supervisión de Inteligencia Artificial (AESIA), in collaboration between the Ministry of Finance and the Civil Service and the Ministry of Economic Affairs and Digital Transformation, dedicated to overseeing the operation of artificial intelligence systems. In France, post-market surveillance competencies for systems should be attributed to the Commission Nationale de l'informatique et des Libertés (CNIL).

2.4 *The New AI Administrations Between Expertise and Independence*

The European governance system in the field of artificial intelligence is based on the establishment of two new entities: the Office for Artificial Intelligence and the European Artificial Intelligence Board. Through the first Office, the Commission contributes to the implementation, monitoring, and supervision of AI systems, with powers of monitoring, information requests, and the ability to assess AI models. The regulation stipulates that member states «facilitate the tasks entrusted to the Office for AI». This is, therefore, a typical instrument of institutional cooperation between a central office and national administrations in the implementation and application of the same rules, with the new office remaining within the Commission's executive structures. The Board, on the other hand, is composed of representatives from the member states and the Commission and carries out functions related to the implementation of the regulation, cooperation between national supervisory authorities, advisory functions, and is also tasked with collecting and disseminating best practices among member states. It is, therefore, a forum where national experiences are shared, and new tools are developed to be disseminated across all national legal systems.

At the organizational level, the creation of a European database of high-risk artificial intelligence systems is also foreseen, managed by the Commission and configured as a registry of systems, with a requirement for prior registration of the system before it is placed on the market or put into service. All competent authorities have extensive powers to access all relevant data and information, including training, validation, and testing datasets used by the provider, as well as the AI system's source code, and they have sanctioning powers in case of violations of the regulation.

In addition to the administrative bodies, there are also forums for public consultation, with a dedicated Forum, and a consultation body for technical and scientific matters, with the group of experts. Governance is further complemented by some soft regulation tools, such as codes of conduct and the AI Pact. The codes of conduct can be voluntarily adopted by entities developing, providing, and using AI systems to establish ethical principles aimed at ensuring the respect of fundamental rights, as well as good practices to ensure comprehensibility and responsible use of artificial intelligence. The codes of conduct can be structured differently depending on the risk level of the various AI systems indicated by the regulation. The AI Pact is also a voluntary tool, promoting responsible, ethical, and secure use of artificial intelligence, aligned with European principles and regulations, and encouraging the adoption of good practices in the field through the development of guidelines and operational standards, involving public institutions, research bodies, businesses, and other interested parties. Both with the codes of conduct and the AI Pact, the participants voluntarily commit to complying with certain ethical and legal standards.

2.5 General and Sectoral Rules for Public Sector Applications

Within this complex regulatory framework, the use of artificial intelligence by public administrations, while generally permitted, is nonetheless subject to legitimacy conditions directly linked to the typical guarantees of public power exercise. The spread of AI is, therefore, necessarily uneven and depends not only on the availability of specific applications but also on the intensity of guarantees that must be provided in accordance with European law, as well as national constitutions and laws. It is no coincidence, for instance, that this diffusion is very limited in the field of justice,[49] as judicial activity and the conduct of trials require the full respect of at least the rights of defense, the right to be heard, equality between the parties, and often the possibility of more than one level of judgment, with the evident impossibility of using the same AI system in both the first and second instances, or having different systems for each level of judgment. The autonomy of the human judge and the ability to defend the parties involved in a trial remains, therefore, an activity that is still eminently, if not exclusively, human.

As for administrative activities more specifically, it has already been observed earlier that AI systems can be used without too many difficulties for routine or serial activities that require mere checks or verifications, based on objective data. Even with greater caution, as reflected in national reports, trials are underway in several countries, especially regarding the use of AI for public order functions, such as investigative activities or tax investigations, or for the granting of benefits and social services, provided that a proper balance is maintained with privacy protection and the final decision respects the principle of "human in the loop". Experiences in this field have not always had positive outcomes—as shown by the cases of the British postal service[50] and the Duch welfare system[51]—but other countries have used these experiences to improve their capacity to choose appropriate systems. In some countries, like Italy, there is also a push to use artificial intelligence for food safety inspections, the awarding and management of public contracts, and financial market supervision.[52]

---

[49] See Civinini (2024).

[50] In Great Britain between 1999 and 2015, hundreds of employees were wrongly accused of theft and fraud and even sentenced to prison terms, based on anomalies reported by a faulty computer system called Horizon, developed by Fujitsu to centralise the accounting of postal branches. In 2019, a judge recognised that the Horizon system was faulty and therefore the convictions were based on errors and should be overturned and the victims compensated.

[51] In the Netherlands, a scandal related to the discriminatory operation of algorithms used by tax authorities to identify potential fraud in child benefit payments led to the resignation of the government in 2021. Thousands of families were falsely accused of tax fraud between 2012 and 2019 on the basis of blatantly discriminatory criteria, such as "foreign-sounding names" and "dual nationality", which particularly affected families with Bulgarian nationality and low and middle income, who were forced to repay large sums of money and often ended up in poverty, losing their homes, jobs and in some cases even their minor children (more than a thousand minors were removed from their homes and placed in state custody).

[52] See Armiento (2024).

Despite the general framework provided by the European regulation on artificial intelligence, it is possible for each country to develop specific rules differentiated according to the type of administrative function to be exercised. The advantage of this tendency lies in the ability to use as a basis for regulating specific AI systems the rules already present in each legal system that define the role of public administration and the objectives it must pursue through the exercise of that activity. On this basis, it is then possible to adapt the sector-specific regulations to new technological tools, thus gradually building tailored legal frameworks.

3 An Administration Equipped for the Use of AI

Whatever the use to which the public administration puts AI, three conditions should always be met to ensure its reliable and secure use. The first concerns the training of public sector staff involved in the operation of AI; the second relates to the evaluations to be carried out to acquire the AI system intended for use; the third concerns the measures to be taken to ensure its cybersecurity. The importance of these three factors is evident. First of all, governing, making decisions, and delivering public services with AI requires specific skills to understand both its benefits and risks, and to ensure the human-machine interaction,[53] which is at the heart of a human-centered AI. These skills should not be confined to certain administrations but must be built and integrated into all administrations using AI to exercise their powers and functions.

Additionally, appropriate structuring of choices related to how to procure the AI system is necessary: the alternative between in-house provision and outsourcing has numerous pros and cons, so choosing between the two options involves weighing many factors, not only economic, and adopting the most appropriate choice for each specific case.

Finally, it is crucial that the administration can develop the necessary technical skills to ensure the robustness and cybersecurity of its systems and associated support infrastructures, including those related to data.

3.1 *The Guarantee of the Human Oversight and Officials Training*

The widespread use of algorithms requires an adequate level of AI literacy not only in civil society but also within the administration. The European regulation on AI itself establishes, in Article 4, that «[p]roviders and deployers of AI systems shall take measures to ensure, to their best extent, a sufficient level of AI literacy of their

[53] The so-called meta-autonomy discussed by Floridi and Cowls (2022)

staff and other persons dealing with the operation and use of AI systems on their behalf, taking into account their technical knowledge, experience, education and training and the context the AI systems are to be used in, and considering the persons or groups of persons on whom the AI systems are to be used».

Proper training and preparation of staff are, in fact, the condition for governing AI systems and assessing their implications in the context in which they operate. Moreover, if, as noted above, the human-centered nature of AI is guaranteed by human oversight, it is clear that the official interacting with AI or otherwise relying on its support must understand how the system works (e.g., whether based on causal logic or statistical-probabilistic reasoning), the data it was trained on, the purpose for which it was developed, and the potential risk components.

Article 14 of the European regulation, dedicated to human oversight, outlines the measures that must be taken, proportional to the risks of the system, to ensure such control. These include (a) properly understanding the relevant capacities and limitations of the high-risk AI system and being able to duly monitor its operation, including in view of detecting and addressing anomalies, dysfunctions, and unexpected performance; (b) remaining aware of the possible tendency to automatically rely or over-rely on the output produced by a high-risk AI system (automation bias), particularly for high-risk AI systems used to provide information or recommendations for decisions to be made by natural persons; (c) correctly interpreting the high-risk AI system's output, taking into account, for example, the interpretation tools and methods available; (d) deciding, in any particular situation, not to use the high-risk AI system or to otherwise disregard, override, or reverse the output of the high-risk AI system; (e) intervening in the operation of the high-risk AI system or interrupting the system through a "stop" button or a similar procedure that allows the system to come to a halt in a safe state. These measures, as is evident, require a critical understanding of AI issues in general and specific knowledge of the system in use.

Under the European regulation, these measures must be implemented by the deployer of high-risk systems (as mentioned above). However, given the responsibilities and principles governing administrative action, one might ask whether it is not reasonable to require human oversight for every AI application, including those that, based on the tasks they perform, may be classified as low-risk or minimal-risk.

In addition to being a prerequisite for ensuring effective human oversight, adequate training and preparation of public officials are also necessary for properly managing AI procurement procedures. As highlighted by the French Council of State in its report on *Inteligence artificielle et action publique: construire la confiance, servire la performance*,[54] even when the administration does not develop the system in-house, «l'externalisation requiert également des compétences internes afin de définir le cahier des charges, de sélectionner et de piloter les prestataires. S'agissant de la sélection, il est indispensable que l'administration comprenne ce qu'elle achète exactement».

[54] See Conseil d'Etat, etude (2022).

These skills are needed both to avoid information asymmetries that could place the public buyer at a disadvantage vis-à-vis the private contractor and to allow the contracting authority to adequately weigh the benefits and risks of the technological solution offered, including with respect to data management.

Naturally, the type of expertise required within the administration varies depending on whether the administration intends to develop its own AI systems or simply act as a deployer. In the former case, it must have personnel with IT and programming skills (computer scientists and data analysis experts); in the latter, however, the administration will primarily need to provide technical training to its staff to equip them with basic, cross-disciplinary IT skills.

3.2 *How to Procure AI: In-house vs. Outsourcing*

The decision whether to develop an AI system in-house or purchase one from the market is complex.[55] It should first be preceded by a planning activity to identify the administration's needs, the type of AI system capable of fulfilling that task, the risks and benefits expected, and the economic-financial and environmental costs.

Once this analysis is completed, the administration will have the necessary information to decide whether to develop the system in-house or turn to the market. In some cases, this may be an obligatory decision: for example, smaller administrations may lack the necessary technical expertise to design and develop an AI application, so purchasing from the market could become the only viable option.

For larger administrations, such as ministerial bodies or independent authorities, the choice between in-house production and outsourcing presents numerous variables. First, in-house production can take different forms: the system can be developed by internal technical staff, or its design and development can be entrusted to an in-house body controlled by the administration, or the application's development could result from an agreement with another public research institution, such as a university.

Whichever form is chosen, in-house production can certainly bring three main advantages. Firstly, the system can be designed to meet the specific needs of the administration and incorporate choices inspired by public values, thereby avoiding possible misalignments associated with AI development by private entities, driven primarily by profit-maximizing motives.[56]

Secondly, in-house production allows for the retention of data within the public sphere, avoiding their transfer to private parties. The administration will be able to maintain full control over the quality of training, validation, and testing data and take measures to prevent or minimize bias and errors.

---

[55] See Ada Lovelace Institute (a) (2024), Engstrom et al. (2020), Chiti et al. (2022), Chiti et al. (2022).

[56] See Casonato (2025), Hickok (2024).

Lastly, by developing the system in-house, the administration can intervene effectively in the event of malfunction, as there is no separation between provider and deployer, unlike in outsourcing scenarios.

However, in-house production also has its costs, both in economic-financial terms (for example, LLMs incur high training, development, and operational costs, including energy and environmental costs) and in terms of the competitiveness of the products. In particular, in-house development seems unlikely to offer truly innovative and high-performance systems, due to the administration's limited capacity to attract computer scientists and industry experts.

In many cases, therefore, outsourcing becomes either an obligatory or preferable choice. If this occurs, the contractor selection and contract award stage become crucial to ensuring the administration's accountability.[57] As noted by Coglianese and Lampmann,[58] «the contracts between government agencies and third-party vendors thus provide an important tool for ensuring both the responsible design of Ai tools and overall accountability of their use».

In this sense, a contracting approach to algorithmic accountability can help ensure, even in the absence of specific regulations, three objectives. First, the administration can require the provider to supply basic information about the algorithm and its operation. This is essential not only to avoid the administration losing control over how its decisions are formed by outsourcing certain segments but also to explain to citizens the logic behind these decisions.

The private provider could thus be contractually obliged to disclose all information necessary to ensure sufficient transparency as required by Article 13 of Regulation 2024/1689.

Secondly, adequate standards can be imposed during the bidding process: algorithms are not neutral, and such standards could ensure that the algorithm incorporates choices aligned with public rules, respects privacy regulations, manages public data appropriately when its transfer to a private entity is necessary, and ensures system accuracy and cybersecurity. The provider could be required to demonstrate compliance with a range of obligations set by the administration, even regardless of the system's classification as high-risk.

Lastly, the bidding process could also serve as the moment when the administration addresses potential intellectual property issues,[59] or prevent the supplier from using this as an obstacle to the administration's understanding—and thus the public's understanding—of the key components of the system and its training data.[60]

In the English case *R (Bridges) v. Chief Constable of South Wales*, for example, the administration was found responsible for violating the Public Sector Equality Duty (PSED) because, having been unable to access the datasets used by the

---

[57] See Hickok (2024).

[58] See Coglianese and Lampmann (2020), Coglianese (2024)

[59] See Muscolo (2022), Ghidini and Austoni (2022).

[60] See Coglianese and Lampmann (2020).

provider for facial recognition, it had essentially delegated the verification of fairness to the supplier.

The full understanding of the system by the administration is, moreover, required by the provisions contained in the European regulation regarding the obligations of deployers of high-risk systems.

First, Article 26 of the regulation establishes that the «deployer shall ensure that input data is relevant and sufficiently representative in view of the intended purpose of the high-risk AI system», which implies knowledge of the data sets used by the algorithm.

Furthermore, under Article 27, the administration is required to conduct an impact assessment on fundamental rights, which must include, among other elements, «the specific risks of harm likely to have an impact on the categories of natural persons or groups of persons identified pursuant to point (c) of this paragraph, taking into account the information given by the provider pursuant to Article 13».

This impact assessment is only required under the European regulation for high-risk systems; however, many systems, including the Estonian system, consider it crucial to conduct systematic algorithmic audits, as they help to identify bias in AI-driven decision-making processes (Mac[61]).

Lastly, full knowledge is required by Article 86 of the regulation when the administration must provide a specific explanation of the role played by AI in the formation of a harmful individual decision: according to this provision, «[a]ny affected person subject to a decision which is taken by the deployer on the basis of the output from a high-risk AI system [...] shall have the right to obtain from the deployer *clear and meaningful explanations* of the role of the AI system in the decision-making procedure and the *main elements* of the decision taken».

Together, these obligations place precise responsibilities on the administration regarding understanding the system and the risks it presents. Thus, the decision to purchase a system from the market must be accompanied by an awareness of the associated risk profiles and the search for appropriate guarantees to mitigate them.

3.3 Defense Against Attacks on ICT Systems: The Role of Cybersecurity

The management, storage, and transmission of public data, the digitization of a portion of state services and functions, the transition of many public contracts to digital platforms, and the development and use of AI systems in the context of e-government have made the issue of the security of digital infrastructures urgent. This is not only for internal security reasons but also to ensure the integrity of state information

[61] See Mac (2024).

systems against external threats, thereby safeguarding digital sovereignty and independence.[62]

Thus, after an initial phase in which cybersecurity was primarily a matter of intelligence, it has now acquired a broader dimension, requiring the adoption of both supranational and national frameworks and the establishment of an administrative apparatus capable of ensuring its implementation.

On the regulatory front, the European Union first introduced the European Cybersecurity Strategy at the end of 2020, followed by the enactment of the Network and Information Systems Directive 2016/1148 (NIS Directive), later amended by NIS2, which extended the NIS regulation to other sectors and introduced risk analysis.[63] The Cybersecurity Act (Reg. 2019/881), which specifically strengthens the role of the EU Agency for Cybersecurity (ENISA), and the Cyber Resilience Act (2024/2847), which amends previous legislative acts to establish common security standards for products containing digital components, such as software and hardware, to protect consumers and businesses.[64]

In 2023, the Commission also presented a new regulation proposal, called the Cyber Solidarity Act, aimed at enhancing the European common response to cyberattacks, including the introduction of a Comprehensive Cyber Emergency Mechanism.

Overall, the European regulatory framework aims, on one hand, to establish common security standards for digital networks and services, to protect consumers, but on the other hand, to create a strengthened European cooperation system. This system is based on the imposition of obligations on states and sector operators, who are required to adopt organizational and technical measures to protect their infrastructures. ENISA plays a central role in this new common system: on the one hand, the Agency provides support to states (also through the Computer Security Incident Response Team Network—CSIRTs Network), while on the other hand, it is tasked with developing a unified certification system for ICT services and networks (*EU-wide Certification Scheme Standards for Information and Communications Technology*[65]).

Building on the European regulatory framework, states have implemented national regulations and established or strengthened their respective sectorial institutions. The Italian state, for example, has defined the National Cybersecurity Perimeter (PSNC) through Decree Law 105/2019, outlining the public and private entities that, as providers of essential public services, are required to not only adopt the necessary measures to defend their infrastructures against cyber-attacks but also

---

[62] See Giupponi (2024), Ursi (2023).

[63] EU Directive 2022/2555, transposed in Italy by Legislative Decree 138/2024.

[64] See Raffiotta (2022), Sheperd (2022).

[65] See https://digital-strategy.ec.europa.eu/en/news/first-eu-wide-cybersecurity-certification-scheme-make-european-digital-space-safer

notify the Computer Security Incident Response Team (CSIRT) of any incidents or attacks affecting their networks or digital infrastructures.[66]

On the organizational front, the National Cybersecurity Agency (ACN) was established in 2021,[67] through Decree Law 82/2021. This agency serves as the single national contact point within the European cybersecurity system and is responsible for exercising the many competencies that were previously assigned to various authorities, including the Presidency of the Council of Ministers (which retains some powers), the AgID (Agency for Digital Italy), and the intelligence services.

The ACN is now responsible for coordinating the various entities involved in the cybersecurity function, certifying ICT products and systems, and developing preventive measures and effective responses to attacks and incidents affecting national digital infrastructures.

Similar agencies exist in all EU member states. In France, the *Agence Nationale de la Sécurité des Systèmes d'Information*, established in 2008 under the control of the government, operates as a node within the European network and exercises certification powers. Compared to the Italian Agency, it has more extensive regulatory powers.[68]

In Germany, the Federal Office for Information Security (*Bundesamt fur Sicherheit in der Informationstechnik—BSI*[69]) was established as early as 1991, but its powers have recently been expanded in line with the new European regulatory framework and the increasing need for protection related to e-government.

At the lowest level of the institutional architecture of cybersecurity are the individual administrations, which are required to adopt the necessary security measures to protect their technological infrastructures and ICT systems. In Italy, the Agid has established three levels of protection: a minimum level, a standard level, and a high level, depending on the complexity of the information system and the type of administration considered. The highest level of protection must be ensured for public authorities most exposed to risks, also due to the information they store or the services they manage.[70] A precise set of obligations was established by Law No. 90 of 17 July 2024, *Disposizioni in materia di rafforzamento della cybersicurezza nazionale e di reati informatici*, which further enhanced the security of public information systems (establishing specific notification obligations for all administrations identified by the law and creating internal structures responsible for compliance). The same law also introduced a revision of cybercrimes, with a provision for harsher penalties.

---

[66] See Giupponi (2024).

[67] See Parona (2021).

[68] See https://cyber.gouv.fr/publications/recommandations-de-securite-pour-un-systeme-dia-generative

[69] See https://www.bsi.bund.de/EN/Das-BSI/Auftrag/auftrag_node.html

[70] See https://www.agid.gov.it/it/sicurezza/misure-minime-sicurezza-ict

The system thus built is multi-level. The regulations governing it are both European and national, and their application is entrusted to the European Agency and the central administrations of the states.

The effectiveness of the overall system in ensuring the protection of digital infrastructures will depend on several factors: the ability of national agencies to coordinate the involved stakeholders in exercising the cybersecurity function, the functioning of alarm and notification systems, and the organisational capacity of individual administrations. However, a decisive factor will also be its ability to evolve technologically, as cyber-attacks, aided by AI, become increasingly sophisticated and thus more dangerous.[71]

4 Public Administrations Between Innovation and Risks

Public administrations are called upon to use AI to improve the delivery of services and the exercise of public functions, but they must also consider the risks that the use of technology may pose to fundamental values protected in the public sphere—primarily equality, transparency, accountability, and explainability of decisions—and therefore adopt all necessary remedies and measures to avoid or at least mitigate these risks.

First and foremost, the administration must carry out careful planning to identify its "technological needs", i.e. to understand which systems can improve the services to be delivered, with what characteristics in terms of models and operating logic, and to subsequently identify the means for their acquisition. The choice to apply AI must also be accompanied by a rigorous risk assessment, which may depend on both how the system is employed in decision-making processes and the type of system: symbolic AI (expert systems), for example, poses fewer risks to both the principle of equality and the challenge of explainability and comprehensibility than ML-based AI systems.

Careful consideration must also be given to the data used by the system: the administration must ensure that the data are of high quality and representative of the context in which the system will operate, and this verification must occur whether the system is provided by a private supplier (Article 26) or developed in-house (Article 10).

This planning is necessary both to ensure the compliance of public administrations with the obligations established by European regulation and, more generally, to respect the rule of law and the principles that govern public action.

The administration must also carry out thorough verification and monitoring of the results achieved and any problems that arise, and this activity must be documented transparently, including for dissemination within the public system, to build a culture and common awareness.

---

[71] See Camacho (2024).

To ensure these objectives, the administration must possess the necessary skills and expertise, which are currently largely lacking in most national administrations, where officials with a background in law or economics prevail. Therefore, continuous training systems and recruitment strategies must be developed to ensure the availability of personnel capable of managing strategic planning, the conscious use of technology, and providing citizens with clear communication about the use of AI.

Building a technologically prepared administration, capable of managing applications, using them to provide services and performance, acquiring them or developing them in-house, and planning the necessary technology represents probably the most complex challenge of the new algorithmic administration.

References

Ada Lovelace Institute (a) (2024) Buying AI. https://www.adalovelaceinstitute.org/report/buying-ai-procurement/

Ada Lovelace Institute (b) (2024) Evidence review, Foundation models in the public sector. https://www.adalovelaceinstitute.org/evidence-review/foundation-models-public-sector/

Ames D, Handan-Nader C, Ho DE, Marcus D (2020) Due process and mass adjudication: crisis and reform. Stan L Rev 72:1

Angwin J et al (2016) Machine bias. PROPUBLICA. https://www.propublica.org/article/machine-bias-risk-assessments-in-criminal-sentencing

Armiento MB (2024) Pubbliche amministrazioni e intelligenza artificiale. Strumenti, principi e garanzie. Editoriale Scientifica, Naples

Avanzini G (2019) Decisioni amministrative e algoritmi informatici. Predeterminazione analisi predittiva e nuove forme di intellegibilità. Editoriale scientifica, Naples

Bloch-Wehba H (2020) Access to algorithms. Fordham Law Rev 88(4):1265

Bourcier D, De Filippi P (2019) Les algorithmes sont ils devenus le langage ordinaire de l'administration? In: Koubi G, Cluzel-Métayer L, Tamzini W (eds) Lectures critiques du Code des relations public et administration. LGDJ, Paris, pp 193–220

Bradford A (2024) The false choice between digital innovation and regulation. Northwest Univ Law Rev 377

Camacho NG (2024) The role of AI in cybersecurity: addressing threats in the digital age. J Artif Intell Gen Sci 3(1):143–154. https://doi.org/10.60087/jaigs.v3i1.75

Cantens T (2024) How will the state think with ChatGPT? The challenges of generative artificial intelligence for public administration. AI & Society, pp 1–12

Carloni E (2020) I principi della legalità algoritmica. Le decisioni automatizzate di fronte al giudice amministrativo. Dir amm 2:271

Casini L (2022) Lo Stato (im)mortale. I pubblici poteri tra globalizzazione ed era digitale. Mondadori, Milan

Casonato C (2025) L'intelligenza artificiale fra pubblico e private: una sfida per il costituzionalismo. DPCE 1

Casonato C, Marchetti B (2021) Prime osservazioni sulla proposta di regolamento dell'Unione europea in materia di intelligenza artificiale. Biolaw J 3:415

Chiti E, Marchetti B, Rangone N (2022) L'impiego di sistemi di intelligenza artificiale nelle pubbliche amministrazioni italiane: prove generali. In: Pajno A, Donati F, Perrucci A (eds) Intelligenza artificiale e diritto: una rivoluzione? vol 2. Il Mulino, Bologna, p 43

Civinini MG (2024) Nuove tecnologie e giustizia. In: JuLIA handbook artificial intelligence, judicial decision-making and fundamental rights

Civitarese Matteucci S (2021) Public administration algorithm decision-making and the rule of law. Eur Public Law 27(1):129

Coglianese C (2020) A framework for governmental use of machine learning. https://www.acus.gov/sites/default/files/documents/Coglianese%20ACUS%20Final%20Report%20w%20Cover%20Page.pdf
Coglianese C (2024) Procurement and artificial intelligence. In: Paul R, Carmel F, Cobbe J (eds) Handbook on public policy and artificial intelligence. Elgar Publishing, p 235
Coglianese C, Ben-Dor LM (2021) AI in adjudication and administration. Brook L Rev 86:791
Coglianese C, Lai A (2022) Assessing automated administration. Public law and legal theory research paper series no 22-28
Coglianese C, Lampmann E (2020) Contracting for algorithmic accountability. Admin L Rev Accord 180
Coglianese C, Lehr D (2017) Regulating by Robot: administrative decision making in the machine-learning era. Geo IJ 105:1167
Coglianese C, Lehr D (2019) Transparency and algorithmic governance. Adm Law Rev 71:7
Conseil d'Etat (2022) Inteligence artificielle et action publique: construire la confiance, servire la performance. https://www.conseil-etat.fr/publications-colloques/etudes/intelligence-artificielle-et-action-publique-construire-la-confiance-servir-la-performance
Crawford K (2021) Atlas of AI. Power, politics, and the Planetary Costs of Artificial Intelligence. Yale University Press, New Haven
Dalgado IM (2019) Automazione, intelligenza artificiale e pubblica amministrazione: vecchie categorie concettuali per nuovi problemi? Istituzioni del federalismo 3:643
Dreyling RM, Koppel T, Tammet T, Pappel I (2024) Challenges of generative AI Chatbots in public services – an integrative review. ACM Manuscript Submission Template
Fernandez JV (2023) Artificial intelligence in government: risks and challenges of algorithmic governance in the administrative state. Ind J Global Leg Stud 65
Ferrarese MR (2022) Poteri nuovi. Privati, penetranti opachi. Il Mulino, Bologna
Finocchiaro G (2024) Intelligenza artificiale. Quali regole? Il Mulino, Bologna
Floridi L (2020) Pensare l'infosfera. La filosofia come design concettuale. Raffaelo Cortina editore, Milan
Floridi L (2022) Etica dell'intelligenza artificiale. Sviluppi, opportunità, sfide. Raffaello Cortina editore, Milan
Floridi L, Cowls J (2022) A unifies framework of five principles for AI in society. https://doi.org/10.1002/9781119815075.ch45
Fraenkel-Haeberle C (2020) Fully digitalized administrative procedures in the German legal system. Eur Rev Digital Admin Law 1-2:105
Engstrom DF, Ho DE, Sharkey CM, Cuéllar M-F (2020) Government by algorithm: artificial intelligence in federal administrative agencies
Gallone G (2023) Riserva di umanità e funzioni amministrative. Indagine sui limiti dell'automazione tra procedimento e processo. CEDAM, Padova
Ghidini G, Austoni I (2022) Intelligenza artificiale e proprietà intellettuale. Quadro generale. In: Pajno A, Donati F, Perrucci A (eds) Intelligenza artificiale e diritto: una rivoluzione? vol 3. Il Mulino, Bologna, p 43
Giupponi TF (2024) Il governo nazionale della cybersicurezza. Quad Cost 2:277
Glaze K, Ho DE, Ray GK, Tsang C (2022) Artificial intelligence for adjudication: the social security administration and AI governance. In: Bullock J (ed) The Oxford handbook of AI governance. Oxford University Press, Oxford
Habermas J (2023) Nuovo mutamento della sfera pubblica e politica deliberativa. Raffaello Cortina, Milan
Hickok M (2024) Public procurement of artificial intelligence: new risks and future proofing. AI & Soc 39:1213–1230
Kissinger H, Schmidt E, Huttenlocher D (2021) The age of AI. J Murray Publisher, London
Koller R (2024) Comment a été développée Albert, l'IA générative de l'Etat français. https://www.ict-journal.ch/news/2024-04-26/comment-a-ete-developpee-albert-lia-generative-de-letat-francais

Langer C (2024) Decision-making power and responsibility in an automated administration. https://doi.org/10.1007/s44163-024-00152-1
Liu H-W, Lin C-F, Chen Y-J (2019) Beyond State v. Loomis: artificial intelligence, government algorithmization and accountability. Int J Law Inf Technol 27:122
Mac TA (2024) Bias and discrimination in ML-based systems of administrative decision-making and support. Comput Law Secur Rev 55:106070
Marchetti B (2022) Amministrazione digitale. In: Mattarella BG, Ramajoli M (eds) Funzioni amministrative, Enc Dir I tematici III:75
Muscolo G (2022) Big data, algoritmi, intelligenza artificiale: perchè proteggerli con un brevetto? In: Pajno A, Donati F, Perrucci A (eds) Intelligenza artificiale e diritto: una rivoluzione? vol 3. Il Mulino, Bologna, p 209
Olson P (2024) Supremacy: AI, ChatGPT and the race that will change the world. Macmillan Business, London
Palmer Olsen H, Livingston Slosser J, Troels Hildebrandt T (2022) What's in the box? In: Micklitz H, Pollicino O, Reichman A et al (eds) Constitutional challenges in the algorithmic society. Cambridge University Press, Cambridge, p 219
Palmiotto F (2024) When is a decision automated? A taxonomy for a fundamental rights analysis. German Law J. https://papers.ssrn.com/sol3/papers.cfm?abstract_id=4578761
Parona L (2021) L'istituzione dell'Agenzia per la cybersicurezza nazionale. Giornale di diritto amministrativo 6:709
Pasquale F (2022) Inalienable due process in an Age of AI: limiting the contractual creep toward automated adjudication. In: Micklitz H, Pollicino O, Reichman A et al (eds) Constitutional challenges in the algorithmic society. Cambridge University Press, Cambridge, p 42
Pasquale F, Malgieri G (2024) Generative AI, explainability, and score-based natural language processing in benefits administration. J Cross-Discip Res Comput Law 2(2) https://papers.ssrn.com/sol3/papers.cfm?abstract_id=4826707
Pesch PJ (2025) Potentials and challeges of large language models (LLMs) in the context of administrative decision-making. Eur J Risk Regul:1–20
Rachovitsa A, Johann N (2022) The human rights implications of the use of AI in the digital welfare state: lessons learned from the Dutch SyRI case. Hum Rights Law Rev 22
Raffiotta EC (2022) Cybersecurity regulation in the European Union, and the issues of Constitutional Law. Rivista AIC 4:1
Rangone N (2025) Intelligenza artificiale, tutela dell'ambiente e regolazione europea. Biolaw J (1):529–548
Rangone N, Megale L (2025) Risks without rights? The EU AI act's approach to AI in law and rule-making. Eur J. Risk Regul: 1–16
Russell S, Norvig P (2010) Artificial intelligence. a modern approach, 3rd edn. Pearson Education Inc, New Jersey
Santosuosso A, Sartor G (2024) Decidere con l'IA. Intelligenze artificiali e naturali nel diritto. Il Mulino, Bologna
Sheperd AJK (2022) The EU security continuum. Blurring internal and external security. Routledge, London
Suleyman M (2024) The coming wave. AI, power, and our future. Penguin Books, London
Torchia L (2023) Lo Stato Digitale. Il Mulino, Bologna
Traverso P (2022) Breve introduzione tecnica all'intelligenza artificiale. DPCE online 1:155
Ursi R (ed) (2023) La sicurezza nel cyberspazio. Franco Angeli, Milan
Weerts S (2025) Generative AI in public administration in light of the regulatory awakening in the US and EU. Camb Forum AI Law Gov I:1–19
Zuboff S (2019) The age of surveillance capitalism. Public Affair, Hachette Book Group, New York

Barbara Marchetti is Full Professor of Administrative Law, Law Department, University of Trento. Her contributions are mostly on EU Administrative Law, AI and public authorities, Administrative Justice. Recently she wrote L'esecuzione della regolazione digitale dell'Unione europea e il ruolo della Commissione, RTDP, 2024, 4, 1097; Artificial Intelligence and public authorities: does the European AI Act protect public values?, ERPL, 2024, 36, 1 67.

Luisa Torchia is Full Professor of Administrative Law, Law Department, University of RomaTre. She has written extensively on regulation of financial markets, federalism, European law, law and economics, public procurement, regulation of digital technology. Her most recent works include Poteri pubblici e poteri privati nel mondo digitale, in Il Mulino, n. 1, 2024; Lo Stato digitale. Una introduzione, Bologna, Il Mulino, 2025.

Italian Public Administration in the Face of Digital Transformation

Marianna Merler and Camilla Ramotti

Contents

Marianna Merler wrote the paragraphs 1, 1.2, 3, 4, 5, 5.1, 5.2, 6, 6.1, 6.3; Camilla Ramotti wrote the paragraphs 1.1, 2, 2.1, 2.2, 2.3, 6.2.

M. Merler (✉) · C. Ramotti
University of Trento, Trento, Italy

Luiss Guido Carli University, Rome, Italy
e-mail: marianna.merler@unitn.it

F. Decarolis et al. (eds.), *The EU Digital Regulation and its Impact on Member States*, European Union and its Neighbours in a Globalized World 27,
https://doi.org/10.1007/978-3-032-06490-5_2

Abstract The chapter explores the implications of EU Regulation 2024/1689 ("AI Act") on the Italian public administration. It begins with a brief description of the digital transformation faced by public administrations, in which artificial intelligence ("AI") is included as part of this evolutionary process. It continues with administrative court rulings and the principles they affirmed in relation to algorithmic administration and analyses how the AI Act intervened with the aim of ensuring compliance with the rule of law. The chapter then looks at the impact of AI legislation, both supranational and national, on the organisational structure of public administration and focuses on the knowledge and skills to be provided to public employees in order to interact effectively with the digital world (in general) and AI (in particular). Finally, the chapter deals with a specific sector, that of public contracts, in which the use of AI finds specific legislative discipline, and analyses some cases of use of AI applications by Italian public administrations.

1 The Digital Transformation of Italian Public Administration

The public administration's use of artificial intelligence (hereinafter "AI") is part of the broader digital transformation process that started in the 1990s. The first wave of digitalisation in the public sector was mainly directed towards the use of information and communication technologies (hereinafter "ICTs") to achieve dematerialisation: public administrations started transforming paper documents into digital ones, storing them and transmitting them digitally. Meanwhile, the use of ICTs in the public sector has been accompanied by the adoption and implementation of specific legislation.[1] The 2000s represented a decisive turning point in the process of digitalisation of the Italian administration: in 2005 Article 3-*bis*, entitled «Use of telematics», was introduced in the Administrative Procedure Act (Law No 241/1990)[2] and in that same year the Digital Administration Code (Legislative Decree No 82/2005, hereinafter "CAD") was adopted.[3] While the former is a general provision that directs public administration's activities towards the use of telematics, the latter represents an organic regulation that brings together and organises rules relating to digitalisation. Several regulatory interventions and policy documents followed the adoption of the CAD (Carloni, 2015), giving rise to an ever-changing regulatory framework.

[1] See Legislative Decree No 29/1993, Legislative Decree No 39/1993, Law No 59/1997, d.P.R. No 513/1997, d.P.R. No 445/2000.

[2] See Law No 241/1990, Law No 15/2005, Cardarelli (2017), Costantino (2016), Legislative Decree No 82/2005 (CAD).

[3] See Carloni (2005), De Giovanni (2018), Marchetti (2022).

In spite of the difficulties in the application and implementation of the outlined legislation, as witnessed by the numerous amendments to the CAD,[4] since the 2000s Italian public administrations have started to make increasing use of ICTs in the organisation and performance of their activities. The public sector has therefore embarked on a path of computerisation and modernisation aimed at rationalising processes, simplifying the relationship with citizens and providing more effective and efficient public services.[5] The process of digitalisation was, however, much slower than expected.[6]

The 2020 amendment of Article 3-*bis* of Law No 241/1990 made the use of ICTs in the public sector the rule (*"public administrations act by means of computerised and telematic tools*"), emphasising the close link between the use of ICTs and the principle of good administration enshrined in Article 97 of the Italian Constitution and Article 41 of the Charter of Fundamental Rights of the European Union. The COVID-19 crisis has further accelerated Italy's digitalisation process and an even bigger boost was given by the National Recovery and Resilience Plan (PNRR), the national plan implementing the European Union's post-Covid recovery program (Recovery and Resilience Facility – RRF) supported by the Next Generation EU.[7] Among the resources, EUR 6,74 billion, namely 27% of the total, was specifically dedicated to the complete digitalization of the public administration. The financial support thus enabled Italian public administrations to invest in the purchase of ICT tools and to experiment with the use of increasingly complex digital technologies, giving a strong acceleration to the digitalisation process.[8]

The use of AI by public authorities is part of this evolving process, giving rise to a new wave of digitalisation which is *"laying the foundation for the transition from E-Government to Algorithmic Government"*.[9] AI is not just one thing, but it is an umbrella term which encompasses a family of very different technologies. Therefore, first and foremost it is crucial to distinguish between different approaches to AI, namely knowledge-based AI and machine learning, since the challenges they pose to principles that govern public powers are different.[10] Indeed, while knowledge-based AI does not alter the public power's structure, machine learning brings about a qualitative change in the exercise of administrative power, and therefore requires a rethinking of principles and rules that have traditionally governed it.[11] Indeed, machine learning exhibits certain characteristics, such as reliance on statistical correlations, improved performance after implementation, and increased complexity,

[4] See Carloni (2011), Tentoni (2011), Carotti (2017), Carotti (2018).

[5] See Bombardelli (2002), Merloni (2005), Duni (2008), Civitarese Matteucci and Torchia (2016), Sgueo (2016), Maddalena (2017), Cardarelli (2017), Pesce (2018), Martines (2018), Auby (2019).

[6] See Carloni (2019).

[7] See Torchia (2020, 2021).

[8] See Galetta (2022).

[9] See Marchetti (2024a).

[10] For a technical discussion of the difference between these approaches See Sartor (2022), Traverso (2022). See in this volume Marchetti, Torchia, *AI and Public Administration*

[11] See Avanzini (2019), Cavallo Perin and Galetta (2020), Marchetti (2022), Torchia (2023a, b).

which entail risks in terms of potential discrimination, lack of transparency, reduced accountability, as well as potential infringement of privacy and data protection. Moreover, it is crucial to distinguish between different uses of AI systems by public authorities, as concerns for public values and fundamental rights of individuals are different. The use of AI for decision-making purposes (e.g. AI for the allocation of public benefits to individuals), for instance, raises more concerns than the use of AI to identify relevant facts, for facilitation purposes or for other auxiliary tasks (e.g. the use of chatbots to facilitate citizens' access to digital public services). Despite the differences highlighted, Regulation EU/1689/2024 (hereinafter referred to as the "AI Act") applies indiscriminately in all these cases to public authorities, whether they are providers or deployers of AI systems. The fact that the AI Act applies without distinguishing between different approaches and different uses of AI systems raises some doubts about its effectiveness in ensuring adequate protection of individuals in the face of AI-powered public administration, at least when considered in isolation.

As in other countries, the leap from simple technologies to AI, especially the one based on advanced machine learning and deep learning , occurred in the absence of an adequate regulatory framework. In Italy, it was first the courts with an *ex post* regulation that found the rules and guarantees needed to protect citizens while waiting for supranational and national legislators to intervene. This naturally only pertains to the conditions of legitimacy for the use of AI by public authorities, as it would be neither feasible nor appropriate to delineate substantive rules governing the production, commercialisation and implementation of AI systems within the confines of judicial adjudication.

1.1 The Administrative Jurisprudence on the Legitimacy of the Algorithmic Public Administration

In Italy, administrative courts have played a prominent role in addressing issues concerning algorithmic decision-making in public administration, particularly in the education sector's public competitions.

In several rulings,[12] the courts emphasised that algorithms, though pre-programmed to consider various personal circumstances, must not replace human oversight but rather serve as tools subordinate to human judgment. Computerised proceedings must remain instrumental and auxiliary, supporting but not supplanting human decision-making. Over-reliance on algorithms would violate principles such as transparency, procedural participation, and the duty to provide reasoning for decisions.

The Council of State weighed in to stress the value of digitalisation and automation in administrative processes, especially for routine, high-volume tasks

[12] See T.A.R. Lazio, no. 9224–9230/2018, Galetta (2020a, b).

where data is certain and discretion is absent.[13] However, the ruling clarified that algorithms should be treated as pre-defined rules set by human actors, qualifying as computerised administrative acts. Their use must not undermine fundamental principles of administrative law. To this end, algorithms must be transparent, comprehensible, and open to full judicial review.

In a later decision,[14] the court recognised that automatic classification of applications, based on predetermined rules, could align with efficiency and economic goals. However, algorithmic tools should be regarded as organisational modules that cannot violate core administrative principles. This decision went a step further by considering the application of such technologies not only to legally bound decisions but also to discretionary ones. Nevertheless, algorithmic rules must still adhere to three key principles: (i) the principle of transparency (knowability, the process and rules must be knowable), (ii) the principle of non-exclusivity of algorithmic decision-making (algorithmic decision-making must not operate independently of human oversight), and (iii) the principle of non-discrimination in algorithms (algorithms must not introduce or perpetuate bias).

These rulings reflect varying levels of openness towards algorithms in administrative processes. However, a shared concern among Italian administrative courts is the adherence to core administrative principles. The cases highlight the inadequacy of traditional procedural law in addressing algorithmic decision-making and the need for new legal principles to ensure such practices remain compliant with law and within the bounds of administrative law.

1.2 From Case Law to a New Legislative Framework

After three years of negotiation the AI Act finally entered into force on August 1st, 2024.[15] It is well known that the AI Act adopts a risk-based approach,[16] identifying different levels of risk of AI systems, namely unacceptable risk, high risk, limited risk and minimal risk. Accordingly, it classifies AI systems into different categories: prohibited AI practices (unacceptable risk), permitted AI systems but subject to requirements set out in Chapter III, Section 2 (high-risk AI systems), AI systems permitted and subject to transparency obligations (limited risk) or codes of conduct for the voluntary application of specific requirements (limited and minimal risk). Therefore, depending on the specific risk level of the AI system, public administrations must comply with the relevant obligations under the AI Act.

In relation to prohibited practices identified in Article 5, for example, public authorities must avoid their use or assess whether the specific use of the AI system

---

[13] See Cons. Stato, no. 2270/2019, Canalini (2019), Laviola (2020).

[14] See Cons. Stato, no. 881/2020, Marchetti (2021).

[15] See Hacker (2024), Fernández-Llorca et al. (2024).

[16] See Novelli et al. (2024a, b), Marchetti (2024a, b, c).

falls within the exceptions provided for in the provision. Significant vagueness has been highlighted in relation to this part of the legislation, which makes the scope of application of the prohibitions uncertain and risks opening up a wide area of discretion on the part of providers, deployers and the public authorities themselves who are called upon to oversee the legislation.[17] In relation to high-risk AI systems, most of which are closely related to public tasks, services and functions (Annex III lists education, access to and enjoyment of essential public services and benefits, law enforcement, migration, asylum, and border control management, administration of justice and democratic processes) public authorities must take measures to ensure compliance with the requirements and obligations set out in Chapter III, Sections 2 and 3 of the AI Act. Requirements for high-risk AI systems concerns the adoption of a risk management system (article 9), an adequate data governance (article 10), technical documentation and record keeping (articles 11 and 12), sufficient transparency (article 13), human oversight (article 14) and an appropriate level of accuracy, robustness and cybersecurity (article 15). As it is well known, the placing on the market or use of a high-risk system cannot take place unless its compliance with the requirements, which is entrusted to the CE marking procedure, is first verified. In addition, the AI Act lays down other obligations that vary depending on whether the public administration is a provider and/or a deployer of the AI system (Chapter III, Section 3 of the AI Act). Among these, one of the most relevant aspects when the deployer is a public administration is the obligation to conduct a fundamental rights impact assessment (FRIA) (article 27). Therefore, in addition to the data protection impact assessment (DPIA) required by the GDPR in specific cases,[18] public administrations are required to evaluate, before the deployment, the impact of their use of a high-risk AI system on individuals' fundamental rights. Another relevant obligation is enshrined in Article 86, which requires clear and meaningful explanations from the deployer—especially if it is a public administration—about the role of the AI system in the decision-making process and the main elements of the decision taken. All these requirements and obligations are aimed at ensuring respect for the rule of law and related public values, *i.e.* transparency, equality and non-discrimination before the law, and preventing the abuse of power.[19]

The AI Act is a regulation, therefore according to Article 288 TFEU it has general application and is binding in its entirety and directly applicable in all Member States. Public administrations must therefore implement provisions laid down therein without having to wait for a transposing legislative act. Nevertheless, the AI Act leaves some margin of appreciation on specific aspects and requires Member States to make some essential choices regarding the rules for the adaptation of their domestic legislation. Moreover, the AI Act does not apply to areas that are not covered by EU law. Accordingly, the adoption of national legislation remains indispensable for safeguarding a high level of protection at the domestic level. This is

[17] See Marchetti (2024a, b, c).

[18] See Article 35 GDPR.

[19] See Marchetti (2024a, b, c).

essential both in areas that fall outside the material scope of the AI Act and thus require national regulatory intervention, and in those fields where the AI Act provides only a minimum harmonized framework for the admissibility of AI systems within the European legal order, leaving room for Member States to intervene (e.g. with respect to real-time remote biometric identification systems).

Even before the AI Act came into force, in April 2024 the Italian government proposed the Draft Law No 1146/2024 "Disposizioni e deleghe al Governo in materia di intelligenza artificiale" which stressed some specific national nuances.[20] Following a one-year parliamentary process, Law No. 132/2025 was published in the Official Journal of the Italian Republic. This legislation sets out the guiding principles for the research, experimentation, development, deployment, and application of AI systems and models within the Italian legal order. More specifically, it outlines the principles that should inform the use of AI within the Italian legal framework, including principles of transparency, proportionality, security, protection of personal data, confidentiality, accuracy, non-discrimination, gender equality and sustainability, respect for human autonomy and decision-making power, prevention of harm, knowability, and explainability. It also addresses areas closely linked to domestic legislation, such as the use of AI systems in healthcare and disability (articles 7-10), employment (articles 11-12), intellectual professions (article 13) and justice (article 15). It also covers property rights (article 25) and criminal sanctions (article 26).[21][22]. Among the most relevant provisions is article 14, concerning the use of AI systems in public administration. The provision requires public administrations to utilize AI systems with a view to improving the efficiency and effectiveness of their activities, reducing the time required to conclude procedures, and improving both the quality and the quantity of services provided to citizens and businesses. The provision mandates that public administrations must ensure that interested parties are able to comprehend the functioning of the AI systems employed and to trace their use. Accordingly, public authorities are expected to tailor the content and form of information and explanations to the particular recipient to whom they are addressed. In any case, the use of AI systems is confined to an instrumental and supporting role in administrative decision-making, without prejudice to human autonomy and decision-making power, thereby aligning with the human oversight obligation set forth in article 14 of the AI Act. Accordingly, the ultimate responsibility for decisions and procedures involving the use of AI systems continues to rest exclusively with civil servants. They therefore need proper training and preparation in order to govern AI systems and assess their implications within their operating context. Finally, the provision mandates that public administrations adopt technical, organisational and training measures designed to ensure the responsible use of AI systems and to develop transversal skills among its users. Law No 132/2025 also

[20] for a first discussion see Burelli (2024), Romano (2024). In August 2024, the Italian Data Protection Authority (DPA) gave its positive opinion on the proposed legislation, emphasising the necessary data protection conditions to be met. See Data Protection Authority (2024), Cappai (2024)

[21] See Article 22 Draft No 1146/2024.

[22] See Data Protection Authority (2024), Cappai (2024).

introduces delegations to the Government to adopt one or more legislative decrees establishing a comprehensive framework on the use of data, algorithms and mathematical methods for the training of AI systems, as well as in all cases referred to in Article 24 (e.g. delegation of authority for regulating the use of AI in police activities and in preliminary investigations). While the adoption of a national law represents a positive development, the measure does not, at this stage, appear to introduce any substantial additional safeguards for individuals. Much will ultimately depend on the manner in which the government exercises the delegated regulatory authority. [23].

Beyond the Law No. 132/2025, the first Italian legislative provision that specifically referred to AI is Article 30 of the Public Procurement Code (Legislative Decree No 36/2023). It represents the first national legal basis for the use of AI by public administrations and encapsulates, translating them into the specific context of tendering procedures, the principles that the administrative jurisprudence affirmed for the legitimacy of algorithmic administrative activities.[24] Nevertheless, since the provision sets out general principles, it can extend its scope of application, moving out of the specific context of public procurement, and acquire general applicability by applying those principles to other uses of AI by public administrations (Avanzini 2024a).

2 The Principles Governing the Use of AI in Public Sector

As previously noted, administrative proceedings are built upon essential principles like legality, participation, and transparency. However, the incorporation of algorithms into such processes raises serious concerns about preserving their foundational values. Alongside traditional norms, new principles—such as knowability, non-exclusivity, and non-discrimination—are emerging in response to these technological developments. The integration of algorithms in public administration adds layers of complexity to the interpretation and application of established legal principles, necessitating a nuanced understanding of their role in this evolving landscape.

[23] See C(2024) 7814.

[24] See Council of State, Sec. IV, 2270/2019, 8472–8473-8474/2019, 881/2020, Carloni (2020), Torchia (2023a, b).

2.1 Legality

A key legal question is whether algorithmic decision-making aligns with the principle of legality.[25] If algorithms are considered mere administrative tools, no specific statutory authorisation may be required. However, if they constitute a novel exercise of administrative power, each instance of use may necessitate express legislative authorisation.[26]

It is essential to examine the normative underpinnings of the former position. A pertinent provision is Article 3-*bis* of Law No. 241/1990, which promotes the generalised adoption of computerised and telematic tools by public administrations to enhance efficiency. Similarly, Article 12(1) of the Code of Digital Administration (CAD, Legislative Decree No. 82/2005) obliges public administrations to employ ICT tools in their activities to achieve objectives such as efficiency, effectiveness, cost-effectiveness, impartiality, transparency, simplification, and participation, all in line with the principles of equality and non-discrimination. Furthermore, Article 41(1) of the CAD explicitly requires public administrations to conduct administrative procedures using ICT.

In the Italian legal framework, public administrations are thus broadly empowered to adopt new technologies, with their use recognised as a right. This right imposes corresponding obligations on public authorities without necessitating case-specific authorization.[27]

At the supranational level, Article 22 of the General Data Protection Regulation (GDPR) grants individuals the right not to be subject to decisions based solely on automated processing. Since this regulation establishes a specific right for individuals to avoid fully automated decisions, it may be inferred that algorithmic administrative procedures, provided they are not fully automated, are lawful and legitimate.

As this analysis suggests, there is a prevailing view that algorithms serve as organisational tools, largely a matter of administrative discretion, which does not inherently require explicit legal empowerment.[28]

Compliance with the principle of legality, however, is not sufficient to deem a legal system as founded upon the Rule of Law. For this, additional guarantees are required, including legal certainty, non-discrimination, participation in public decision-making and transparency.[29]

As will be demonstrated, adherence to these principles in the context of algorithmic use varies significantly depending on the specific applications of such systems and the type of algorithm employed.

---

[25] See Satta (1969), Fois (1973), Bassi (2001), Cassese (2003).

[26] See Avanzini (2019), Civitarese Matteucci (2019), Delgado (2019), Carloni (2020), Marchetti (2022), Torchia (2023a, b).

[27] See Torchia (2023a, b).

[28] See Torchia (2023a, b).

[29] See Marchetti (2024a, b, c).

In this direction and as a preliminary note, it is important to consider the distinction between deterministic algorithms and machine learning algorithms.[30] Deterministic algorithms operate on a set logic that can be retraced, resembling legal reasoning through their «if/then» structure. In contrast, machine learning algorithms—especially those utilising neural networks—generate outputs based on complex patterns within training data. These processes often remain opaque, or «black boxes»,[31] rendering the decision-making process challenging, if not impossible, to trace.

As will be analysed below, and as has already been partially anticipated, the AI Act accounts for the distinction between different types of algorithms and establishes regulation developed on a risk-based approach. It is essential to evaluate whether this framework can ensure that algorithmic decision-making aligns with the principles of the Rule of Law.

There are, in particular, Articles 10 to 14 AI Act, which, as will be shown, seek to uphold several key principles applicable to high-risk systems.

Among these, Article 10, concerning data and its governance, warrants early attention. This article establishes that datasets used in training machine learning models must comply with strict data management requirements. These obligations include careful design decisions, data collection processes, and operations such as annotation, labeling, and cleaning. Moreover, datasets must be reviewed to assess potential biases and identify any weaknesses or limitations, sufficiently representative and free from inaccuracies and gaps.[32]

In the following paragraphs, some of the other Articles will also be analysed in an attempt to draw some common considerations.

2.2 *Participation and Non-exclusivity (HITL)*

The most effective way to introduce participation in algorithmic decision-making is to remember that «[t]he administrative procedure is the form of administrative functions, meaning that the course of a function is a procedure as it is ordered by the evidence of interests».[33] In essence, administrative procedures are structured as sequences of actions aimed at balancing and reconciling various interests, with private individuals playing a pivotal role in the decision-making process. Through participation, the State seeks to incorporate «as much society as possible»,[34] ensuring

[30] See Carullo (2021).

[31] See Pasquale (2015), Coglianese and Lehr (2017), Lo Sapio (2021a, b), Masucci (2022), Troisi (2022).

[32] See Marchetti (2024a, b, c).

[33] See Giannini (2000).

[34] See Nigro (1980).

that the management and protection of interests are entrusted to those directly affected.[35]

Participation by interested parties constitutes a critical phase in the procedural sequence.[36] A pressing question, therefore, is whether, and to what extent, meaningful participation can be accommodated within algorithmic decision-making processes.

In this sense, concerns emerge about the feasibility of effective participation. Two primary issues are: (i) determining if algorithmic processes allow room for dialogue with private parties, and (ii) assessing the role of the person in charge of the procedure,[37] whose involvement may be reduced or eliminated by automation.

Regarding the first concern, the notice of initiation of proceedings[38] serves a crucial role in rendering administrative actions cognisable, thereby enabling interested parties to exercise their participatory rights.[39] Some scholars have proposed that ICT and automated decision-making could enhance these rights. For example, technology might facilitate the identification of third parties involved in proceedings and reduce the time and costs associated with such processes.[40]

Once the notice has been received, interested parties must be afforded the opportunity to participate in the decision-making process. These guarantees, however, are articulated differently within algorithmic procedures: (i) the interested party must be assured full transparency regarding the criteria and models employed; (ii) the decision must be attributed to the authority vested with the relevant power, which must retain the ability to verify both the logic and the legitimacy of the outcomes (as will be discussed shortly, this is the so-called principle of the «human in the loop»). Consequently, algorithmic administration entails a reconfiguration of traditional participatory guarantees, as ensuring meaningful participation in an algorithmic decision-making process is, in essence, unfeasible.[41]

According to some scholars, the rules governing participation are of such significance that they acquire a legitimising value akin to that of the legislative provisions governing administrative procedure.[42] A potential method of legitimation could be the introduction of «notice and comment» mechanisms[43] for algorithmic decision-making, to be conducted at the conclusion of the proceeding and before the adoption of the final measure.[44] This solution, however, is deemed unworkable, as no

[35] See Benvenuti (1996).

[36] See Cassese (1971), Chiti (1977), Levi (1977), Villata (1992), Cassese (1993), Zito (1996), Virga (1998), Di Nitto (1999), Giglioni and Lariccia (2000), Caranta and Ferraris (2000), Cognetti (2000), Sandulli (2000).

[37] See Sandulli (1991), Canavesio (1992), Impinna (2015).

[38] See Article 7(1), Law No. 241/1990.

[39] See Terracciano (1994), Saitta (2000), Sandulli (2004), Civitarese Matteucci (2005).

[40] See Masucci (1993), Galetta (2020a, b), Torchia (2023a, b).

[41] See Marchetti (2022).

[42] See Cavallo Perin (2020).

[43] See Clarich (2005), Albisinni and Peci (2017).

[44] See Cavallo Perin (2020).

specific provisions to this effect currently exist. Moreover, the role of the person responsible for the procedure becomes problematic, as it is entirely subsumed by the fully automated decision-making process.[45]

To ensure the correct functioning of an algorithm and the desired outcomes, the input data and the programming of the software are of fundamental importance. These elements result from human decisions, specifically those made by the person in charge of the procedure and the software developer, respectively. This underscores the importance of the *human in the loop* (HITL) principle.[46] Enshrined in Article 22, GDPR and by Article 14, AI Act and reinforced by administrative courts,[47] this principle ensures human oversight in algorithmic decision-making, affirming the non-exclusivity of such processes.

It is necessary to distinguish between three different models of human-machine interaction, as reported in the 2019 *Ethics guidelines for trustworthy AI*:[48] the *human in the loop* (HITL), which implies the possibility of human intervention in every logical step taken by the system; the *human on the loop* (HOTL), which envisages human involvement only in the programming and monitoring phase of the software; the *human in command* (HIC), according to which human control over the activity of the software is to be carried out as a whole, deciding when and how to use the system.

Two main concerns in algorithmic accountability are human oversight and responsibility assignment. As already mentioned, while deterministic algorithms operate predictably and facilitate accountability, machine learning systems pose challenges due to their unpredictability and opacity in decision paths.

Some scholars argue that the initial selection of data is so crucial[49] that this phase constitutes the core of the decision-making process.[50] However, this assertion is partial, as it holds true only in cases where the administration selects the data for the software developed in-house. The situation becomes more complex when the development of the system is outsourced to private entities, a scenario in which the administration may not even be aware of the data being used.[51]

However, this does not absolve the administration from its duty to exercise control both during and after the process.[52] Such oversight should involve, first, ensuring that interested parties are able to participate in the proceedings and, second, enabling the administration to verify the results before adopting the final measure.

Courts have supported the requirement for human accountability in automated processes, focusing on whether decisions can be legally attributed to a human

[45] See Avanzini (2019).

[46] See, Oddenino (2020), Marchetti (2021), Mosqueira-Rey et al. (2023), Armiento (2024).

[47] See Cons. Stato, no. 8472/2019, Cons. Stato, no. 881/2020.

[48] See European Commission (2019), Previti (2022).

[49] See Orofino and Gallone (2020).

[50] See Avanzini (2019).

[51] See Marchetti (2022).

[52] See Paolantonio (2021).

official. The issue of imputability is, in fact, the second concern regarding the presence of human oversight in algorithmic decision-making processes. The fact that a decision made using algorithms is attributable to an official carries several legal implications. It affects whether the decision itself can be classified as an administrative act, and thus subject to judicial review; it impacts the official's responsibility for ensuring that the decision aligns with the public interest for which the administrative power is exercised; and it relates to the official's liability for any harm caused to third parties.[53]

Responsibility assignment is crucial, as attributing an algorithm's decision to an official has legal ramifications, such as enabling judicial review and ensuring decisions reflect the public interest. Deterministic algorithms generally allow for this accountability, while machine learning poses a challenge since it evolves independently. Nonetheless, accountability for algorithm-generated decisions ultimately resides with the administration.[54]

Human oversight is given significant emphasis in the AI Act, particularly in Article 14.[55] This provision is located within Section 2 of the regulation, which pertains specifically to high-risk AI systems, and is therefore applicable solely to these categories. This focus represents a limitation of the provision, yet it remains commendable for several reasons.

Firstly, Article 14 stipulates that human oversight must extend to the design and development phases of such systems (paragraph 1), with the aim of preventing or mitigating risks to health, safety, and fundamental rights (paragraph 2). This oversight must always be proportionate to the type of AI in question and its contextual application (paragraph 3).

Notably, paragraph 4 underscores the powers that must be granted to individuals responsible for oversight. These include: (i) possessing sufficient knowledge and understanding of the high-risk AI system to effectively monitor its operation; (ii) being aware of the natural human tendency to rely on AI system outputs; (iii) correctly interpreting the outputs and having the necessary tools to disregard or adjust them where appropriate; and (iv) the ability to safely interrupt the operation of AI systems when required.

2.3 *Transparency, Knowability and Comprehensibility*

The mechanisms provided by the legal system to safeguard individual rights and foster a «glass house» approach within public administration are, in themselves, insufficient to guarantee meaningful transparency within the State. For transparency to be effective, legislative measures must be both efficient and functional, while the

[53] See Marchetti (2021).

[54] See Delgado (2017).

[55] See Lo Sapio (2024).

concept of transparency itself must evolve—normatively and practically—in line with social, cultural, and conceptual shifts in administrative activity.

The technological transformation currently affecting public administration demands that transparency be adapted to align with the new tools used in administrative processes. Algorithmic opacity, in particular, poses significant challenges to transparency, as reconciling these intelligent systems with open governance proves complex. The primary issues arising from algorithmic decision-making in public administration are twofold: (i) the reliance on big data, characterised by its volume, variety, and velocity, which complicates the traceability and intelligibility of decisions; and (ii) the autonomous decision-making capabilities of algorithms—particularly those powered by machine learning—that render such processes unpredictable.[56] Consequently, transparency has once again become a critical issue concerning the use of algorithms in public decision-making.

This challenge directly impacts the rights of those affected by administrative decisions, extending beyond mere access to documents or records generated by an algorithmic process to include, where possible, access to the algorithm's source code. Moreover, individuals must be able to challenge and defend themselves against decisions derived from algorithmic processes.[57] Achieving this—where transparency in terms of access rights becomes relevant—requires a clear understanding of the rationale behind each decision, as in cases where human agents make determinations.

A distinction can therefore be drawn between two types of transparency: «fishbowl transparency» and «reasoned transparency».[58] The former, as its metaphor suggests, relates to the capacity of stakeholders to scrutinise the administration's actions and obtain pertinent information. This translates into the exercise of access rights over data, documents, and information held by public bodies. Conversely, reasoned transparency concerns the rationale underpinning administrative actions, providing insight into the logic behind decisions made. Though conceptually distinct, these two forms of transparency are interdependent, as the administration must first make information accessible to explain the logic and reasoning applied in any given decision. This allows the principle of comprehensibility of the algorithmic decision-making to be considered guaranteed.

In the realm of algorithmic governance, fundamental principles are at stake, particularly those ensuring the accessibility and comprehensibility of both the decision-making processes and the resulting administrative decisions. Coherent with this framework and with what has already been highlighted, the GDPR enshrines these principles. A combined reading of Article 13(2)(f) and Article 14(2)(g) of the GDPR reveals two key principles: (i) the principle of knowability, which requires the data controller to inform data subjects of any automated processing of their personal

[56] See Carloni (2022).

[57] See Colapietro (2023).

[58] See Coglianese and Lehr (2019).

data; and (ii) the principle of comprehensibility, which obliges controllers to explain the operational logic of algorithms and anticipated consequences to data subjects.[59]

Article 15 of the GDPR completes this framework of transparency, establishing the data subject's right to obtain confirmation from the data controller that their data is being processed and to access further information.

Unlike Articles 13 and 14, which address pre-processing stages, Article 15 provides for transparency throughout the ongoing data processing and beyond.[60] This comprehensive approach ensures transparency at all stages, encompassing both the knowability of data processing and the comprehensibility of its logic and outcomes.

These principles intersect with national legislation and the evolving jurisprudence of administrative courts, which have produced significant guidelines on algorithmic transparency. It is clear that the future of administration is digital; however, this does not imply that it will automatically become more transparent or democratic. Such outcomes are achievable only if regulated with the appropriate legal instruments.[61]

The relationship between algorithms and transparency is, at times, incendiary, highlighting the significant challenges in achieving transparency given the inherent opacity of algorithms.[62] This opacity can be *linguistic* (the technical programming language), *legal* (intellectual property protections), or *structural* (the complex, often inscrutable nature of machine learning algorithms).

Given the pervasive integration of artificial intelligence, including its opaque «black boxes», into the metaphorical glass house of public administration,[63] it becomes essential to define these black boxes and consider how the opacity they generate might be remedied. A «black box» denotes the highest degree of algorithmic opacity, particularly in machine learning and deep learning processes, where the transformation of inputs into outputs is obscured. This inscrutability is so profound that even developers may be unable to reconstruct the logic by which such systems achieve their outcomes.[64]

In accordance with the principles of the GDPR, the Italian administrative judiciary has undertaken significant steps to address these challenges. Algorithms rely on data inputs processed via source codes—the textual instructions in programming languages that govern computational operations. Understanding this source code, a prerequisite for achieving fishbowl transparency, is critical for comprehending algorithmically driven administrative actions and ensuring compliance with reasoned transparency.

---

[59] See Wachter et al. (2017), Malgieri and Comandè (2017).

[60] See Colapietro (2023).

[61] See Alti and Barbieri (2023).

[62] See Lo Sapio (2021a, b).

[63] See Otranto (2021).

[64] See Lo Sapio (2021a, b), Armiento (2024).

This issue has been addressed in Italy in the context of teachers' mobility,[65] where the administration initially denied access to the source code, classifying it as a non-administrative document.[66]

The administrative judge rejected this argument, holding for the first time that there are no legal obstacles to recognising the right of access to the source code of an algorithm utilised within an automated administrative process.

The judge reasoned that accepting the administration's position would legitimise the obfuscation of acts central to public administration's activities, such as the management of public competitions, thereby undermining transparency. This would also create a «double track», whereby transparency loses significance in IT-managed procedures compared to traditional ones. As such, the source code was deemed an accessible administrative document.

This judicial precedent marked a significant advance in promoting algorithmic transparency. However, it also highlighted a critical limitation: access to source codes, while necessary, is not sufficient to achieve comprehensive transparency. Genuine transparency demands not only access to the source code but also intelligibility of the underlying logic and data inputs, allowing for insights into the rationale behind decisions. This dual focus is essential for realising both fishbowl transparency (what the administration does) and reasoned transparency (how and why it does it).

Italian administrative jurisprudence has further refined the criteria for ensuring transparency in algorithmic decision-making.[67] The principles of knowability and comprehensibility of the algorithmic rule have been affirmed as a reinforced interpretation of the principle of transparency. This requires full knowability of a rule expressed in a non-legal language, extending across all phases of the procedure. This comprehensive approach allows verification that criteria, prerequisites, and outcomes comply with the law while ensuring the procedure's rules and modalities are clear. Comprehensibility must encompass the logical processes employed by the machine to make decisions, thereby realising both fishbowl and reasoned transparency. This would effectively dispel the opacity inherent to algorithmic decision-making.

At the European level, the AI Act[68] complements the GDPR by classifying AI practices into three risk levels, each corresponding to distinct protective establishing in Article 13 further sufficient operational transparency, enabling users to interpret outputs and use them appropriately. High-risk systems must also include instructions for use that are concise, complete, correct, clear, relevant, accessible, and understandable. In other words, Article 13 mandates that high-risk AI systems must be designed with transparency to ensure that users can understand and utilise them

---

[65] See T.A.R. Lazio, no. 7526/2020, Forgione (2018), Prosperetti (2019), Bravo (2020).

[66] See Previti (2022).

[67] See Cons. Stato, sez. VI, decision no. 2270, April 8, 2019, Cons. Stato, sez. VI, decision no. 8472, December 13, 2019, Cons. Stato, sez. VI, decision no. 881, February 4, 2020.

[68] See Finocchiaro (2022), Messina (2022), Resta (2022).

effectively. These systems must be accompanied by clear and comprehensive instructions, which should include: (i) information about the provider of the AI system; (ii) details regarding the system's capabilities and limitations; (iii) an outline of any potential risks associated with its use. Additionally, the instructions must clarify how to interpret the system's outputs, account for any pre-determined modifications to the system, and provide guidance on its maintenance. Where applicable, they should also address the procedures for collecting, storing, and interpreting data logs.

This reflects a shift from mere logic-based processing transparency (as required under GDPR Articles 13 and 14) to ensuring interpretability, providing protection through comprehensibility rather than mere knowability.

Public administrations must thus understand the language, operation, and logic of algorithms to enable those affected by decisions to do the same. Only then can the principle of comprehensibility, as defined in case law and supranational frameworks, be realised. Access to algorithmic components, while a necessary condition, is insufficient to meet the transparency demands of such systems. Practical application of transparency rights requires ensuring comprehensibility in addition to mere knowledge of algorithmic operations to mitigate the risk of «knowing without understanding».[69]

Finally, situated between the guarantees relating to stakeholder participation and those pertaining to the transparency of algorithmic decision-making processes is Article 86 of the AI Act, which addresses the right to an explanation of individual decision-making processes.

This article provides that any person affected by a decision rendered by the deployer on the basis of the output of a high-risk AI system shall have the right to obtain clear and meaningful explanations from the deployer. These explanations must concern the role of the AI system in the decision-making process and the principal elements of the decision taken. The output in question must produce legal effects or similarly significantly affect the individual in a manner they consider having an adverse impact on their health, safety, or fundamental rights (paragraph 1).

This provision shall not apply to the use of AI systems where exceptions or limitations to this obligation are provided for under Union law or national law adopted in conformity therewith, or where the right is otherwise not provided for under Union law (paragraphs 2–3).

However, as previously noted, compliance with the criteria set out in the AI Act—especially in Articles 10 to 14—should, in theory, enable public administrations employing algorithms to adhere to the principles safeguarding the Rule of Law.[70] The European regulatory framework is designed to steer administrative action towards a more structured and principled direction. Nonetheless, certain fundamental guarantees—such as participation, transparency, non-discrimination—remain exposed to significant risks of erosion.

---

[69] See Torchia (2023a, b).

[70] See Marchetti (2024a, b, c).

This vulnerability arises from the fact that, regardless of how specific and detailed the regulatory provisions may be, the nature of algorithms, particularly those employing machine learning techniques, introduces an intrinsic and unresolved conflict with these guarantees. The opacity of machine learning systems, their capacity for autonomous adaptation, and the difficulty in fully understanding or explaining their outcomes create substantial challenges to ensuring that these fundamental rights are preserved.

In light of these concerns, much will depend on the choice granted to national legislators under the AI Act and the approach they take to implement these provisions within their respective legal systems. It will be critical to examine how this discretion is exercised in practice and whether national laws and policies succeed in bridging the gap between the promises of the regulatory framework and the realities of algorithmic governance.

3 A Complex and Constantly Evolving Organisational Structure

The AI Act establishes a complex and rigid governance structure which involves both the supranational and the national level.[71] The former encompasses the AI Office, the European Commission, the European Artificial Intelligence Board, the Scientific Panel of Independent Experts and the Advisory forum. The national level, on the other hand, encompasses the Notifying Authorities, Notified Bodies, and Market Surveillance Authorities. More specifically, Article 28 requires Member States to designate or establish at least one notifying authority responsible for setting up and carrying out the necessary procedures for the assessment, designation, notification and monitoring of conformity assessment bodies (i.e. notified bodies). Furthermore, Article 70 requires each Member State to establish or designate as national competent authorities at least one notifying authority and at least one market surveillance authority to ensure the enforcement of the Regulation and to designate a market surveillance authority to act as the single point of contact for the purposes of the AI Act (Article 70).

National Authorities play a crucial role in enforcing the obligations set out in the AI Act, as the regulation places the responsibility for its implementation primarily on the Member States, with the notable exception of obligations relating to General-Purpose AI models, the enforcement of which lies with the European Commission [72].

The designation of competent national authorities further expands the already complex organisational structure in the digital sphere. As far as Italy is concerned, a multiplicity of public actors are involved in the digital transformation process (Bontempi 2020; Marchetti 2022). At the national-central level, the Prime Minister,

[71] See Novelli et al. (2024a, b).

[72] See Article 88 AI Act, Marchetti (2024a, b, c).

or the delegated Minister, directs, coordinates and promotes initiatives related to technological innovation and digitalisation.[73] The Interministerial Committee for Digital Transition (CITD) promotes, steers, coordinates and monitors government actions in implementing the country's digital transition. The Department for Digital Transformation (DTD) and the Agency for Digital Italy (AgID) are the structures that support the Prime Minister or the delegated Minister in carrying out his activities. The DTD promotes and coordinates the government's actions, defining a unified strategy for the country's digital transformation (d.P.C. June 19, 2019). To this end, implementing the Prime Minister's directives, the Department for Digital Transformation directs, coordinates and stimulates the definition and implementation of programmes, projects, and action plans on digital transformation. The latter is the technical agency of the Council Presidency.[74] AgID has regulatory and executive functions, including supervisory powers over the effective and correct implementation of the relevant regulatory framework, and sanctioning powers in order to ensure the realisation of the objectives of the Italian Digital Agenda (Article 14-bis CAD). Another fundamental body is the National Cybersecurity Agency (hereinafter "ACN"), established by Decree-Law No 82/2021 as part of the European Cybersecurity Strategy and tasked with safeguarding security and resilience in cyberspace.[75] ACN has multiple functions, namely certification, supervisory and sanctioning powers. It also coordinates authorities which have competences in the cybersecurity sector and to this end elaborates the National Cybersecurity Strategy, then adopted by the Prime Minister.[76] Finally, a crucial role is played by the Italian Data Protection Authority (DPA), whose powers are laid down by the General Data Protection Regulation (Regulation EU/679/2016) and the Data Protection Code (Legislative Decree No 196/2003). At the public administration level, the Chief Digital Officer (RTD) is the mandatory public administration managerial figure whose functions are to guide and coordinate the digital transformation of all Italian public administrations.[77]

Even from the brief description of their tasks, the complexity of the organisational structure in digital matters is evident, enlightening possible overlapping competencies and coordination problems.[78] These aspects eventually contribute to fragmentation, potentially limiting the effectiveness of ICT implementation across the public sector. Moreover, as anticipated the structure is further complicated by the enforcement of the AI Act.

With regard to the designation of National Authorities, the AI Act leaves a significant margin of discretion to Member States. However, in the choice, requirements in terms of expertise, independence, impartiality and absence of bias must be

[73] See Decree-Law No 22/2021 converted by Law No 55/2021.

[74] See Commissione Parlamentare (2017), Carloni (2012), Notarmuzi (2010), Merloni (2005).

[75] See Montessoro (2019), Parona (2021), Rossa (2023), Renzi (2024), Giupponi (2024).

[76] See ACN (2022).

[77] See Article 17 CAD, Circolare No 3 1 October 2018.

[78] See Carloni (2019), Bontempi (2020).

ensured.[79] Moreover, National Authorities shall have the adequate technical, financial and human resources and infrastructure to fulfil their tasks effectively.[80] Italy has chosen to integrate the new functions envisaged by the AI Act within existing institutions, designating AgID and ACN as the competent National Authorities and delineating their respective competences and functions, without prejudice to the designation of the Bank of Italy, CONSOB and IVASS as market supervisory authorities pursuant to, and in accordance with, Article 74(6) of Regulation (EU) 2024/1689 .[81] More specifically, article 20 of the Law No 132/2025 designates ACN as the market surveillance authority, endowed with monitoring, inspection and sanctioning powers over AI systems and AgID as the notifying authority, entrusted with promoting AI innovation and development, as well as with establishing procedures for the notification, evaluation, accreditation, and monitoring of entities responsible for verifying the conformity of AI systems. A coordination Committee, composed of the Directors General of AgID and ACN and the Head of the Department for Digital Transformation, is established at the Presidency of the Council of Ministers. Furthermore, the competences, tasks and powers of the Data Protection Authority (hereinafter "DPA") remain unaffected.

The choice of AgID and ACN as National Authorities can be criticised under three main grounds. First, since the AI Act expressly requires the designation of DPAs as competent authorities for the application of a number of its provisions,[82] one would have expected the Italian DPA to be one (or the) competent National Authority. Indeed, the European Data Protection Authority (EDPB) expressly stated that the choice of Member States to designate DPAs as competent authorities would meet the criteria of rationality and simplification.[83] Second, both AgID and ACN are government agencies, meaning that the Prime Minister or the delegated Minister has powers of direction and supervision over their activities, thus limiting their discretionary powers and eventually straining the independence requirement stressed by the AI Act.[84] However, Italy was not the only Member State to opt for a government agency as the national competent authority under the AI Act. Spain, for example, established the Spanish Artificial Intelligence Supervisory Agency (AESIA) as an autonomous agency of the Spanish Department of Digital Transformation. Third, the designation of two different bodies may lead to a fragmentation of governance and create coordination problems in carrying out their respective activities, which would be further worsened by coordination with the activity of the DPA, which continues to perform its functions. The need for a single, fully independent national authority dealing with both AI and data protection was therefore emphasised.[85] A

[79] See Article 70 par. 1 AI Act.

[80] See Article 70 par. 3 AI Act.

[81] See Article 18 Draft.

[82] See Article 74 par. 8 AI Act.

[83] See EDPB (2024).

[84] For an interesting discussion on the topic see Cappai (2025).

[85] See DPA (2024).

different perspective, however, might look favourably on the investiture of authorities other than the DPA as competent national authorities. In fact, the AI Act is a complex piece of legislation in which multiple interests, in addition to data protection, come into play. ACN, for instance, is the authority that is certainly best placed to ensure that adequate levels of cybersecurity are achieved, in line with the requirement of the AI Act that requires competent national authorities to take appropriate measures to ensure an adequate level of cybersecurity.[86] Nevertheless, the European Commission's detailed opinion[87] seems to criticise the choice of ACN and AgID as national authorities. Indeed, the European Commission recalls that national competent authorities[88] must possess the same level of independence as that provided by Directive (EU) 2016/680 for DPAs in law enforcement, migration management and border control, administration of justice and democratic processes.

The action of all public entities involved must follow precise paths to ensure an adequate usage of AI and an effective implementation of the AI Act in the public sector. The first document adopted by Italy on the specific topic of AI is the *White Book on Artificial Intelligence at the service of the citizen* drawn up by AgID in 2018. It is addressed to public administrations and contains recommendations and indications on how to make the most of the opportunities offered by AI, limiting its critical and problematic aspects in order to develop increasingly citizen-friendly public services.[89] However, the most relevant document when ICTs and public administration are concerned is the *Three-year Plan for IT in Public Administration*, drawn up by AgID as of 2017. The Plan is an essential tool for promoting the digital transformation of the Italian public administration through the declination of the digitalisation strategy into operational guidelines, specifying relevant objectives and targets. The *Three-Year Plan 2024–2026*, which is part of the broader framework defined by the strategic European programme Digital Decade 2030, focuses, among other aspects, on data and AI in public administration (Chap. 5). For the first time thus Italy included AI as a strategic line in the *Three-Year Plan*, envisioning multiple targets that must be achieved in the near future. Among other targets, AgID is called to elaborate guidelines on the methodological and organisational steps that public administrations must follow in order to adopt, procure, develop and implement AI solutions (Objective 5.4). In this regard, between 18 February and 20 March 2025, a public consultation was conducted on the *Guidelines for the Adoption of Artificial Intelligence in Public Administration*, adopted through AgID's Determination No. 17/2025 and still undergoing the formal adoption process.

Completing the strategic line envisioned in the *Three-Year Plan 2024–2026*, in July 2024 Italy presented the *Italian Strategy for Artificial Intelligence 2024–2026*, which updated the previous *Strategic Program for Artificial Intelligence* of 2021. The Strategy reflects the government's commitment to create an environment in

---

[86] See Article 70 par. 4. See in this volume Marchetti, Torchia, *AI and Public Administration*.

[87] See C(2024) 7814.

[88] See Articles 18 and 22 Draft.

[89] See Tresca (2018)

which the Italian vision of AI can be fully realised and defines strategic actions in line with the macro-objectives identified by the government, namely to support the creation and adoption of AI applications, to promote foundational and applied scientific research and to create favourable contextual conditions to enhance AI value generation. The 2024–2026 Strategy focuses on four macro-areas, namely research, public administration, enterprises and training, encouraging multiple actions, such as collaboration between public administrations and private actors, coordination of public administrations' activities, promotion of research and dissemination of knowledge in the field of AI, provision of measures and incentives aimed at the entrepreneurial and industrial development of AI. Law No 132/2025 deals with the AI National Strategy in Article 19, specifying the subjects called upon to prepare and update it (Department for Digital Transformation, in agreement with the National Authorities referred to in article 20), approve it (Interministerial Committee for Digital Transition), and coordinate and monitor its implementation (Interministerial Committee for Digital Transition, AgID and ACN).

Despite the fact that the Italian public administration has equipped itself with policy lines—such as the *Three-Year Plan 2024–2026* and the *Italian Strategy for Artificial Intelligence 2024–2026*—neither a data culture nor adequate infrastructures and skills for the effective adoption of AI technologies are yet sufficiently widespread. Indeed, despite progress in recent years, Italy currently ranks 25th in terms of AI readiness in the public sector.[90] Therefore, doubts persist about the ability of Italian public administrations to properly implement the obligations imposed by the AI Act.

4 Digital Skills of Civil Servants as a Prerequisite for the Digital Transformation

AI has already had a fundamental impact on the public sector, both in quantitative and qualitative terms, and this impact is destined to increase in the coming years. The entry of AI into the public landscape brings about a real transformation of public work, which requires a structural reform of the Italian public administration to embrace it. Moreover, the implementation of the provisions of the AI Act requires civil servants with adequate knowledge and skills on the specific topic of AI, currently lacking in the Italian public administration.

Over the last decade, the Italian public administration has had to face many challenges, mainly due to public spending cuts, that have led to a reduction in the number of public employees, hiring freezes and an increase in the average age of public personnel. This has led to an increasing mismatch between the skills available in the public sector and those required by the current digital or "algorithmic" administration. In the *Digital Decade Country Report 2024* it was pointed out that

[90] See Oxford Insights (2024).

despite Italy's recent improvements, challenges in digital skills persist and remain below EU levels. The situation is critical with regard to both the basic digital skills of the population and the digital skills of the active workforce.[91] This is far from reassuring. Digital competences are of utmost importance when ICTs are used in the public sector, especially in order to optimise the use of financial resources,[92] ensure the proper use of digital technologies, derive value from them, make appropriate, efficient and informed decisions in relation to the use and purchase of IT solutions.[93] On the contrary, lack of skills generates unreasonable choices (mis-uses) or even lack of choices (missed-uses).[94] The situation is even more critical in relation to specific skills in AI related topics. A recent study conducted by FormuPA[95] highlights that the exposure of Italian civil servants to AI is sufficiently high (more than 57% of civil servants is highly exposed to AI and 28% is moderately exposed to AI), with some figures more exposed than others, such as those in leadership and managerial positions. To derive value from the opportunities that digital technologies (in general) and AI (specifically) can offer, it is therefore crucial to empower the entire public workforce. First and foremost, it is crucial to enhance existing employees by making them acquire the appropriate digital skills and especially AI-related skills to navigate, interact and operate effectively in the digital environment.[96] Secondly, it may be necessary to require skills other than administrative competencies in future recruitment.

While the possession of digital competences is specifically requested by the CAD[97] with specific attention to the development of the technological, legal IT and managerial skills of managers,[98] the AI Act focuses on AI-related skills. Article 4 AI Act states the binding obligation on public administrations, whether they are providers or deployers of AI systems, to *"take measures to ensure, to their best extent, a sufficient level of AI literacy of their staff and other persons dealing with the operation and use of AI systems on their behalf"*. Indeed, specific competencies on AI are necessary to ensure the effective implementation of provisions of the AI Act. Human oversight set out in article 14, for example, requires natural persons (*i.e.* the public official) to whom the oversight is assigned to be able to properly understand the relevant capacities and limitations of the high-risk AI system and be able to duly monitor its operation, to correctly interpret its output, to decide not to use the AI system or to otherwise disregard, override or reverse the output and to intervene in the operation of the high-risk AI system or interrupt the system.[99] Despite the clarity

---

91 See European Commission (2024).

92 See Carloni (2019).

93 See Commissione Parlamentare (2017).

94 See Del Gatto (2021).

95 See FPA (2024).

96 See FPA (2024).

97 See Article 13.

98 See Article 13, par 1-bis, Article 17.

99 See Article 14 AI Act.

of these statements, the tasks required are far from easy to ensure. This is even more difficult due to the tendency of automatically relying or over-relying on the output produced by a high-risk AI system, as recognised in the AI Act.[100]

From a general perspective, in 2015 the *Digital growth strategy 2014–2020* was published, appointing AgID as the responsible entity that promotes, supports and coordinates the various projects implemented on the topic of e-skills. In 2018 AgID published a document titled *Digital Competences* which defined the new professional figures for the digital transformation of the public administration. A significant boost to the consideration of e-skills came from the PNRR, which devotes ample space in Mission 1 precisely to the competences of public personnel. In order to guarantee the upskilling and reskilling of civil servants, Italy has launched a variety of initiatives. The panorama is fragmented, with numerous projects developed, promoted and coordinated by a multitude of different entities. In 2020, based on the *Strategy Digital Italy 2026*, the *Digital Republic Initiative* was set up, representing the national strategic initiative coordinated by the Department for Digital Transformation and aimed at promoting digital skills at different levels of the Italian economy and society. In the last years, initiatives connected to the *Digital Republic Initiative* were numerous. In the same year, Italy launched the *National Coalition for Digital Skills*, which currently includes 5070 public administrations involved in advanced e-skills training activities. Furthermore, in 2020 the *National Strategy for Digital Skills,* strongly supported by the PNRR, was adopted, providing for measures dedicated to digital skills development and human capital training aimed at strengthening and developing the digital skills in the active workforce, particularly in the public sector. The Strategy is complemented by Operational Plans, aimed at linking multiple initiatives in order to achieve the objectives set out therein.

An active role in developing civil servants' digital competences has been played by AgID which organises training sessions and events aimed at public administrations, as well as ICT and innovation companies, academia and citizens. The Department of Public Service has played a fundamental role in steering the digital skills of administrative employees thanks to the *Initiative PA 110 e Lode* and the learning hub *Syllabus "Digital Skills for Public Administration"*, which helps to identify the training needs and offers personalised e-learning courses. Specific courses on the subject of AI are also offered. In March 2024 the registered public administrations on Syllabus were 7.174 and the civil servants whose training was programmed were 684.000. At the territorial level, thanks to an agreement between the National Association of Italian Municipalities (ANCI) and the Department for Digital Transformation, the *ANCI Academy* has been set up, specifically dedicated to the training of municipal officials and managers. For the local administration, the Department for Digital Transformation started the Initiative *Progetto FAST* and AgID organised webinars on public administration and innovation and training laboratories specifically directed to Chief Digital Officers. Other initiatives have been carried out by central administration, such as the Ministry of University and

[100] See Article 14, par. 4 lett. b.

Research, the Ministry of Culture and by the Ministry of Enterprise and Made in Italy, that aim to improve digital skills in order to support digital transformation in their specific sectors.

A great improvement, but still insufficient, especially considering that digital skills do not coincide with those related to AI, which represents a very specific, albeit crucial, family of advanced digital technologies. On the specific topic of AI, the *Three-Year Plan for Information Technology 2024–2026* emphasises that one of the guiding principles for the use of AI in public administration is to train civil servants, especially those in leadership positions, and to develop the skills needed to effectively manage and apply AI in public services. The Italian Strategy on AI also deals with the training of the public workforce (Strategic Action F.5). Moreover, among the delegations to the government on the subject of AI, Law No 132/2025 also mentions the *"provision of literacy and training courses on the use of artificial intelligence systems"* (Article 24(2)(e)). It also specifies that public administrations shall take technical, organisational and training measures to ensure a responsible use of AI and to develop the transversal skills of its users (Article 14).

However, although the provisions of Law No 132/2025 and the programmatic documents specifically stress the importance of improving AI-related knowledge and skills in the public sector, the practical efforts are unsatisfactory. Some specific initiatives on AI topics have been promoted by the National School of Administration (SNA), by FormezPA, an association under the supervisory powers of the Department of Public Service, and by other entities, such as the Observatory Digital Agenda. Universities also offer a multiplicity of master's degrees, modules or specialist courses on the topic of AI. However, there are currently no detailed training plans for civil servants—or at least for public managers—on AI-related issues. Other countries, on the other hand, are investing more on AI competencies in the public workforce. An example is the U.S. *AI Training Act* which requires the Office of Management and Budget (OMB) to establish an AI training program to ensure that the workforce of the federal administrations has the adequate knowledge and skills to effectively interact with AI. Similarly, the U.K. is launching courses on AI on Civil Service Learning to boost civil servants' skills and knowledge on the topic.

In conclusion, competences are crucial for Italy's digital-readiness, especially when AI comes into play. To this end, the public sector is pursuing multiple fragmented initiatives and activities to improve the digital skills of civil servants. However, most of them focus on digitalisation in general and they do not specifically deal with AI. Although it seems that the digital competences of public sector employees have acquired an increasing attention in the last few years, all these efforts, while having a qualitative impact, are insufficient to meet the overall demand for e-skills, particularly in the AI domain. Moreover, there is a current shortage of ICT experts (in general) and AI specialists (in particular) in the public sector. This shortage thus poses significant challenges to the effective implementation of AI projects in the Italian public administration. Much more should be done to train civil servants and develop their knowledge and skills on AI issues necessary to ensure effective human oversight as required by the AI Act and avoid automation bias. As recognised by the *Digital Decade Country Report 2024*, Italy demonstrates limited dynamics and in the last few years there has been no overall significant improvement.[101]

5 Artificial Intelligence and Public Procurement

The public procurement sector is the one that first saw the issue of AI addressed from a regulatory point of view. Article 30 Code of Public Procurement specifically deals with the use of automated procedures in the contract lifecycle, including the use of innovative technological solutions, such as AI. Addressing the topic of AI and public procurement necessarily requires a dual perspective. In fact, AI can be the subject of tenders or the tool used by the contracting authority in the course of tenders to make public action more efficient. Moreover, the relationship between national provisions and the AI Act is analysed. It is noteworthy that the public procurement sector will not be strongly affected by the provisions of the AI Act, considering that most of them are aimed at the high-risk systems included in Annex III where no reference is made to the contracting activity of the public administration.

5.1 AI as the Object of Tendering Procedures

By way of introduction, the public administration can decide whether to outsource the AI system (contracting out) or to develop it in-house (in-house providing). This section does not delve into the advantages and disadvantages of the two options and focuses exclusively on the first hypothesis.[102]

The general provisions related to the purchase of ICTs by public administrations are Articles 68 and 69 CAD, as completed by AgID's guidelines and technical rules. Although the provisions generally refer to "software", they have a broad scope and can thus also cover the purchase of AI systems.[103] In particular, Article 68 identifies the relevant principles (cost-effectiveness and efficiency, investment protection, re-use and technological neutrality) and rules that must guide the public administration in the purchase of software or parts of it. In making its choice, the public administration must carry out a comparative technical and economic assessment among different solutions available on the market (software developed for the public administration; reuse of software developed for the public administration; free or open-source software; proprietary software; combination of these options) and must consider technical and economic criteria (the overall cost of the software; the interoperability of the software with others available, the level of security and pri-

[101] See European Commission (2024).

[102] See Marchetti (2022). See in this volume Marchetti, Torchia, *AI and Public Administration.*

[103] See Marchetti (2022).

vacy protection guaranteed by the software). Article 69, on the other hand, encourages the re-use of software owned by public administrations.

The general provisions must be integrated with specific provisions of the Public Procurement Code and eventually those of the AI Act. A crucial aspect in the purchase of AI systems, highlighted by Article 30(2) of the Code, is that the public administration must guarantee the availability of the software's source code, the relevant documentation and any other element useful for understanding the logic of its operations. The request for source code availability is consistent with recent administrative jurisprudence, which has emphasised that the principle of transparency of public administration must prevail over intellectual property rights.[104] The Public Procurement Code thus emphasises the preference for open source solutions over proprietary software.[105] Similarly, Article 68 CAD allows public administrations to purchase proprietary software only in cases where free and open-source solutions are not available (Article 68 par 1-*ter*). Moreover, the national legislation is perfectly in line with supranational legislation. Indeed, recital 102 of the AI Act states that "*Software and data, including models, released under a free and open-source licence that allows them to be openly shared and where users can freely access, use, modify and redistribute them or modified versions thereof, can contribute to research and innovation in the market and can provide significant growth opportunities for the Union economy*". The preference for open source solutions is also closely linked to the principle of knowability and comprehensibility in Article 30(3) of the Public Procurement Code, the availability of the source code being precisely a means to fully realise the latter. In addition to the source code, the public administration must make available any other element that may be useful to fully understand the functionality of the software.[106]

Article 30(2) stipulates that contracting authorities shall introduce clauses in tender documents to ensure the necessary support and maintenance services to correct errors and unwanted effects (such as bias) resulting from automation. With this provision, the Public Procurement Code sought to remedy the disconnect that occurs in the procurement of software between those who develop it and those who use it, who often lack the skills and means to intervene and correct its functioning.

Furthermore, article 5(1)(d) of the Law No 132/2025 deals specifically with the purchase of AI systems from private companies, directing the public administration's choice towards AI systems that comply with the specific characteristics set out in the provision. In particular, article 5(1)(d) mandates that, in the selection of suppliers of AI systems and models, preference may be given to solutions that ensure the localisation and processing of strategic data within data centres located on national territory, whose disaster recovery and business continuity procedures

[104] See Council of State, Sec. IV, 8472–8473-8474/2019, TAR Lazio-Roma, Sec. III-bis 7370/2020. In any case, public administrations cannot shield themselves behind the alleged unknowability of the technological mechanisms they employ in the exercise of their functions. This principle was once again reaffirmed by the Council of State, Sec. VI, 4929/2025.

[105] See Del Gatto (2021).

[106] See Avanzini (2024a, b).

are implemented in data centres situated within national territory, as well as to models capable of guaranteeing high standards of security and transparency in the training and development of applications based on generative AI, in compliance with competition law and the principles of non-discrimination and proportionality. Moreover, AgID is to publish guidelines on the purchase of AI that are intended to guide public administrations in the choice of purchasing procedures and the definition of supply specifications, in order to ensure that needs of the public administration are met, adequate levels of service are provided and the regulatory framework is complied with.

These provisions emphasise a crucial aspect of public procurement, which has been regarded as a valuable policy instrument to achieve other objectives besides those strictly related to the purchase of works, goods or services. This can also be made possible by the technical specifications *ex* Article 79 and Annex 5 of Legislative Decree No 36/2023. Indeed, in relation to AI, tendering procedures can be used to purchase AI systems that have specific technical characteristics and guarantee transparency and explainability, data protection, cybersecurity and accuracy.[107]

5.2 *AI as a Tool for Tendering Procedures*

The second perspective to consider is the use of AI as a tool by the contracting authority. The new Public Procurement Code[108] opted for a complete regulatory framework on digitalisation.[109] It envisioned a national digital procurement ecosystem (e-procurement) with self-executing provisions aimed at automating the entire contract lifecycle, from the planning phase to the complete execution of the contract.[110] With the new Code, the use of ICT in tendering procedures has become the rule: digitization simplifies the procedures, makes planning, procurement, and contract management activities more effective and eventually prevent corruption, as it allows transparency, traceability and control of all activities.[111] However, the use of AI systems in tendering procedures cannot reduce the guarantees for economic operators, and in particular cannot conflict with the rule requiring that every single decision of the public administration, including in the field of tenders, must remain accessible, reasoned and justifiable.

To this end, Italy adopted Article 30 Code of Public Procurement which transposes, translating them into the specific context of public procurement, the principles rooted in European law and recently affirmed by the administrative jurisprudence to regulate algorithmic administrative decisions. In a recent ruling (No. 4857/2025),

[107] See Licata (2024).

[108] See Legislative Decree No 36/2023.

[109] See Articles from 19 to 30.

[110] See Buratti (2024), Avanzini (2024a, b), Palamoni (2024).

[111] See Commissione speciale del Consiglio di Stato (2023).

the Italian Council of State clarified that the principles stated in Article 30 of the Public Procurement Code apply only to "algorithmic administrative decisions" and not to decisions only supported by AI systems. While the former involves the algorithmic system making the decision itself, the latter involves the algorithmic system functioning solely as an auxiliary tool, with the decision-making power fully entrusted to humans. First of all, Article 30(3)(a) recalls the principle of knowability and comprehensibility. The provision encapsulates a right of every economic operator to know whether an automated decision-making process concerning him/her exists. Therefore, the contracting authority has a precise duty to inform the economic operator of an existing automated decision-making process. In addition to this information, when an automated decision-making process is in place, the economic operator has a right to receive meaningful information on its functioning, necessary to respect the principle of comprehensibility.[112] Some insights can be found in the provision itself. First, the principle of comprehensibility is closely linked to the availability of the source code. The latter, together with the relevant documentation, can enable the contracting authority, albeit with known limitations, to better understand the functioning of the software and to provide the necessary explanations. Second, comprehensibility is closely linked to the principle of non-exclusivity of the algorithmic decision and requires motivating human interaction with the output of the algorithm. The dataset used to train the algorithm can also be relevant for a better comprehension of the algorithmic decision.[113] Being conscious of the existence and of the functioning of an automated procedure is crucial for the full exercise of the right of defence by the economic operator concerned and for the review of legitimacy by the administrative judge. The national provision recalls the requirements of transparency and information in Article 13 AI Act for high-risk AI systems and the right to an explanation of the individual decision-making process in Article 86 AI Act, but the justification provided does not appear to be comparable to that required by Article 3 Law No 241/1990.

The principle of transparency is further strengthened by Article 30(5), which requires contracting authorities to publish the list of the technological solutions used to perform their activities in a specific section of their institutional website ("Transparent Administration", Article 9 of the Legislative Decree No 33/2013). Despite some limitations, this provision is of utmost importance, as it provides an overview of the uses of AI by contracting authorities, providing them with an incentive to use these tools correctly due to possible public scrutiny. Nevertheless, the usefulness of the provision will be diminished if it merely results in a list of the AI systems used by the public administration, without any further specification. Better transparency could be achieved by following the - albeit more general - examples of the Amsterdam and Helsinki *AI registers* or by following the British government's *Algorithmic Transparency Standards*.

---

[112] See Lo Sapio (2021a, b), Colapietro (2023).

[113] See Galetta (2023).

Article 30(3)(b) states the principle of non-exclusivity of the algorithmic decision. It requires that the public official appointed by the contracting authority and responsible for the specific procedure must have the competences and the power of reviewing the outcome of the AI system, controlling, validating or refuting the automated outcome. The provision specifically recalls the human oversight requirement for high-risk AI systems enshrined in Article 14 AI Act which goes into more detail on the subject. Both the provisions represent the legislative translation of the "human-in-the-loop" or "reserve of humanity" principle[114] and assume the use of the AI system to support the human being and not to replace him. Indeed, there is no doubt that the contracting authority should remain solely responsible for the final decision.[115] Nevertheless, the real concern is the risk of "automation bias", meaning that the public official, instead of justifying why he/she deviated from the algorithm's decision and taking responsibility for it, will more easily tend to adhere to the algorithm's outcomes, as recognised by Article 14 AI Act.[116] In order to ensure the effective implementation of this requirement, the contracting authority has to identify the entity responsible for human oversight and provide that it has the necessary knowledge and skills.

Article 30(3)(c) affirms the principle of algorithmic non-discrimination, which requires the contracting authority to implement appropriate technical and organisational measures to prevent discriminatory effects against and between economic operators. It is necessary that the technical and organisational measures put in place are adequate to rectify the factors leading to inaccuracies in the data, minimise the risk of errors, guarantee the security of personal data and prevent discriminatory effects.[117] Indeed, the risk of discriminatory effects arising from the use of AI systems is well known, especially when it comes to machine learning or deep learning algorithms. In the specific context of tendering procedures, for example, a discriminatory result could occur in relation to an AI system that, due to an error in the instructions provided, would lead to a national economic operator being favoured over a foreign one contrary to the basic principles that govern tendering procedures.

As anticipated, in addition to the principles expressly incorporated in Article 30, the AI Act may become relevant. Therefore, it is necessary to identify the specific level of risk to which the AI system falls and to apply the relevant requirements. The use of AI in tenders is not in itself a high-risk sector, as Annex III of the AI Act does not explicitly consider it. It is therefore necessary to check on a case-by-case basis whether the use of AI in the specific procedure falls within a sector that the legislator has considered to be high-risk, such as in relation to critical infrastructure.[118] In this case, all AI obligations for the deployer (and possibly provider if the AI system was implemented in-house) will apply.

---

[114] See Benanti (2022), Gallone (2023).

[115] See Avanzini (2024a, b).

[116] See Garapon and Lassègue (2021), Marchetti (2021).

[117] See Article 30(4) Code, Recital 71 GDPR.

[118] See Barberio (2023).

In conclusion, some considerations should be emphasised. First, the provision leaves wide margins of discretion to contracting authorities. In fact, the rule provides that contracting stations *"where possible"* should automate the procedure using innovative technologies and refers in general to AI without specifying the concept further. With regard to the first aspect, the rule does not specify the prerequisites in the presence of which to automate the procedure, apparently leaving contracting authorities complete discretion on whether and how to use an AI system, such as in hypotheses of constrained or discretionary activity, for decision-making purposes (e.g. awarding the contract) or for preparatory tasks (e.g. to identify corrupt practices in tenders, facilitate communication with economic operators). In relation to the second aspect, the provision leaves it up to the contracting authority to choose which type of AI system to use, including both knowledge-based AI systems and ML AI systems. As in all other contexts, the major concerns focus on machine learning, rather than on knowledge-based AI systems.[119] Although non-learning algorithms are mostly used in current tendering contexts, in the near future the availability of large amounts of data may allow the training of learning algorithms to be applied to the most complex tendering procedures.[120] A few experiences have already been described.[121] Furthermore, it should be noted that guarantees and principles of Article 30(3) have been affirmed by the administrative courts in relation to knowledge-based AI systems, where the translation of the technical rule into a legal one is simpler than in the case of machine learning. The doubt therefore remains as to whether the economic operator is actually protected when machine learning comes into play in procurement procedures for decision-making purposes.[122] Finally, public officials need to be sufficiently AI literate to ensure the effective implementation of these provisions thus requiring the acquisition of the necessary digital skills. Thirdly, there are some limitations in regulating by principle the use of AI in tender procedures, especially with regard to the effective protection of the economic operator in the face of automated procedures.[123]

6 Some Use Cases of Artificial Intelligence in the Italian Public Sector

In a comparison with other European countries, Italian public administrations seem to show less effort in developing, adopting and implementing AI solutions. However, the financial support of the PNRR has led more public administrations to undertake AI-based projects. In 2021, an interesting project was conducted to map, through

[119] See Avanzini (2019), Auby (2019).

[120] See Commissione speciale del Consiglio di Stato (2023).

[121] See Corrado (2023).

[122] See Marchetti (2024a, b, c).

[123] See Perfetti (2023), Avanzini 2024a, b

the use of surveys, the projects based on AI implemented or tested by different administrations, at central or territorial level. The result provided an interesting overview of the way in which Italian administrations are exploiting the opportunities offered by AI and addressing the challenges related to it.[124] As of 2021, use cases have increased: public administrations are currently using AI to support decision-makers, for cognitive (extracting knowledge from data), facilitation (chatbots) or recommendation purposes, and in some cases for decision-making (such as in public competitions). Different types of AI are being used, such as knowledge-based AI, machine learning (ML) and foundational models (such as LLMs). The target for 2025 set by the *Three-Year Plan 2024–2026* is to launch 150 innovative AI-based projects, while the target for 2026 is 400 projects. It is noteworthy that all these projects shall be developed and implemented in conformity with provisions set out in the AI Act and in the national legislation on AI. In the following section, different use cases are analysed.

6.1 National Institute for Social Prevention (INPS)

The National Institute for Social Prevention (INPS) is the Italian main social security institution which manages the settlement and payment of pensions and social security and welfare benefits. INPS provides multiple services to millions of citizens. With the *Strategic Digital Plan 2022–2026*, progress has been made towards digitalisation to improve simplification and efficiency. AI is playing a central role in this evolutionary process[125] as demonstrated by the numerous projects that INPS has initiated and concluded. One interesting example is the development of chatbots, such as the generalised *Masterbot* and specialised *Skillbot*, to simplify and personalise the interaction with the user, improving accessibility and usability of services. INPS is also using AI to manage customer service requests and for the automatic classification of e-mails.[126] Recently, AI has been used to improve the SAVIO data mining platform for medical check-ups[127] and currently INPS is experimenting AI for legal disputes.[128]

In order to gain value from the use of AI, minimising risks, and to comply with the provisions set out in the AI Act, INPS adopted a *Strategy on AI for INPS*.[129] The Strategy envisages the creation of a Data Competence Centre, which provides for

[124] See Chiti et al. (2021a, b, 2022a, b), Federico et al. (2021), Meneghetti (2022), Buono (2022), Rangone (2022). Similarly, AgID conducted a survey entitled "L'intelligenza Artificiale nella Pubblica Amministrazione", published in 2025, in order to identify AI projects within central public administrations and national public service providers.

[125] See Buono et al. (2022).

[126] See INPS (2024).

[127] See Boscarino et al. (2018), Boeri et al. (2021).

[128] See Buono et al. (2022).

[129] See INPS (2024).

the constant updating on the latest AI developments and the dissemination of AI knowledge. It also envisages the mapping of all completed and ongoing AI projects activated by INPS. To this end, INPS is developing an App (named *Censimento sistemi di Intelligenza artificiale per la compliance allo AI ACT*). Furthermore, the Strategy focuses on the identification of risks, compliance and monitoring aspects. Finally, the Strategy envisages a framework (INPS IA@SCALE) used for defining modalities for launching and developing AI-based projects and defining a standardised model that must be followed to develop AI-based solutions within the Institute. The framework focuses on data acquisition and preparation, model training and deployment following a precise roadmap. The Strategy stresses the importance of people and their competences, operational models and processes and governance.

INPS represents a virtuous example of responsible implementation of AI into the public administration's structure. This is mainly due to the fact that INPS has the human, material and financial resources, as well as the necessary knowledge and skills to develop AI systems in-house and to manage AI-based projects from the initial to the final phase. This makes it easier to apply the principles stressed by the administrative judge, the binding rules set out in the AI Act and the legislative provisions that will later be passed at national level.

6.2 *Italian Revenue Agency*

The Italian tax authorities, led by the *Agenzia delle Entrate* (Revenue Agency), face significant challenges in navigating the digital transformation.[130] Tasked with managing state tax revenues, the Agency prioritises fostering tax compliance through taxpayer assistance and measures to combat tax evasion and non-compliance.

To enhance compliance, the *Indici Sintetici di Affidabilità Fiscale* (ISA) were introduced in 2017.[131] These indicators, based on statistical-economic methods and multi-period tax data, assess the reliability of taxpayers' business or professional activities on a scale from 1 to 10. Reliable taxpayers, including individuals and businesses, benefit from reduced scrutiny and additional administrative advantages.[132] The algorithm underpinning the ISA "report card"[133] is developed by *Soluzioni per il sistema economico s.p.a.* (SOSE), a company majority-owned by the Ministry of Economy and Finance (88%) and the Bank of Italy (12%).

---

[130] See Bontempi (2022).

[131] See Art. 9 bis, d.l. no. 50, April 24, 2017, converted by l. no. 96, June 21, 2017, Macchia (2020), Mascolo (2021).

[132] See art. 9 bis, par. 1, decree-law no. 50/2017, Agenzia delle Entrate (2023a, b).

[133] See Bontempi (2022).

Despite its advantages, ISA raises concerns typical of black-box systems, particularly regarding accountability for inconsistencies in outcomes,[134] and the rigidity of its processes, which lack provisions for cross-examination or clear mechanisms for taxpayer interaction.[135] Consequently, difficulties arise in identifying the parties responsible for providing explanations on the algorithm's functioning and the rationale behind its conclusions.

Another notable AI initiative is *Verifica dei Rapporti finanziari* (VERA), designed to identify tax evasion risks.[136] The system integrates data from the *Anagrafe Tributaria* with information from the *Archivio dei Rapporti Finanziari.*

In June 2022, the Revenue Agency issued guidelines to ensure the system balances fairness with administrative efficiency.[137] Subsequently, in July 2022, the Italian Data Protection Authority (GPDP) reviewed the system's data protection impact assessment, focusing on risks of discrimination and breaches of transparency and fairness in automated decision-making (GPDP opinion of July 30, 2022, no. 276).

The GPDP underscored the principles of knowability, algorithmic non-discrimination, and the non-exclusivity of algorithmic decisions in administrative processes. While authorising the system's operations, the GPDP imposed specific conditions, including: stakeholders consultation during processing activities; publication of a summary of the data protection impact assessment (excluding sensitive annexes); periodic reporting on model performance, covering metrics, activities, issues identified, and corrective measures implemented.

In a subsequent document, the Revenue Agency outlined its methodologies for risk analysis, which ensures human oversight at all stages.[138] The risk analysis process involves several stages, and human intervention is guaranteed throughout (no fully automated decision-making processes are in place).

The document also distinguishes between two types of analysis employed by the algorithms: deterministic and stochastic analysis.

Deterministic relies on models and techniques that process data related to specific taxpayers or tax periods to identify known risks using predefined, non-probabilistic criteria.

Employing AI and inferential statistics, stochastic analysis identifies previously unknown risks and develops autonomous selection criteria, attributing probabilities to the occurrence of known risks.

A technical annex to the document elaborates on the logic underlying these algorithms.

---

[134] See Gabanelli and Marinelli (2019).

[135] See Macchia (2020).

[136] See Art. 1, pars. 681–686, l. no. 160, December 27, 2019, which was implemented by a decree of June 28, 2022, of the Mef.

[137] See Agenzia delle entrate, circular no. 21/E of June 20, 2022.

[138] See Agenzia delle Entrate (2023a, b).

Moreover, in 2023[139] pursuant to an amendment to the Taxpayer's Charter of Rights, the entitlement to cross-examine tax authorities was excluded in relation to acts involving automated, substantially automated, expedited settlements, and formal declaration review processes.

The technological tools deployed by the Revenue Agency highlight broader concerns about algorithmic opacity. Adherence to the principles of knowability, non-exclusivity, and algorithmic non-discrimination remains crucial. Ensuring transparency within such systems is essential to align with the principles of fairness and accountability in public administration.

6.3 *Bank of Italy*

The Bank of Italy is the central bank of the Italian Republic, which has been an integral part of the European System of Central Banks (SEBC) since 1998. It has multiple functions aimed at ensuring monetary and financial stability. Among its different tasks, the Bank receives and analyzes complaints ("esposti"), namely written communications with which a customer or other interested parties may report behaviour that they consider irregular or improper on the part of banks and financial intermediaries or irregularities in the information recorded in the Risk Control Centre (Centrale dei Rischi) or in the Interbank Alarm Centre (Centrale di allarme interbancaria). Complaints are of utmost importance. Indeed, the analysis of the complaints received and the indications derived from them make it possible to intercept specific customer protection needs; enrich the information available to the supervisory authorities for the performance of their action; highlight gaps and aspects of the regulations that can be improved.

The Bank of Italy receives thousands of complaints, therefore since July 2021 it has been using a new procedure, called *EspTech*, that employs AI techniques to improve the analysis of complaints from users who report problems in their relations with banks and financial intermediaries.[140] More precisely, *EspTech* uses text mining and ML to analyse complaints and divide them into clusters based on their semantic content, as interpreted by the trained ML-model. The AI system allows the Bank to quickly understand which complaints are the most frequent and helps it to improve its advocacy. The model is periodically updated in order to achieve the best possible accuracy. The Bank points out that with *EspTech* it does not carry out any automated evaluation that may affect people's rights, nor does it create "profiling" of customers who send complaints. This is a clear example of the use of an AI system for auxiliary and specifically cognitive purposes by the public administration, which is extremely useful for making its action more efficient.

[139] See legislative decree no. 219/2023.

[140] See Banca d'Italia (2021).

Bank of Italy is an example of a virtuous public administration, as it is working on the transparency of results of *EspTech*, using explainability techniques (tagging) and running a dictionary for the ML-model. Furthermore, Bank of Italy established the group Citizens Data Scientist (CDS) which published the *Guidelines CDS*, highlighting the methodologies for the monitoring and re-training of ML-models in order to avoid risks of data drifts. Finally, the *Rules for the Processing of Personal Data in Complaints* was published, both on the administration's website and in the Official Journal.[141] Written in collaboration with the Italian DPA, they represent the first normative example of rules that regulate the use of AI-techniques by public authorities.[142] In addition to *EspTech*, many other use cases can be identified in the context of the Bank of Italy's activities.[143]

References

Agenzia delle Entrate (2023a) Gli Indici Sintetici di Affidabilità Fiscale. https://www.agenziaentrate.gov.it/portale/documents/20143/233439/Gli_indici_sintetici_di_affidabilita_fiscale_2023.pdf

Agenzia delle Entrate (2023b) Informativa sulla logica sottostante i modelli di analisi del rischio basati sui dati dell'Archivio dei rapporti finanziari. https://www.agenziaentrate.gov.it/portale/documents/20143/5316839/Documento+illustrativo+della+logica+degli+algoritmi.pdf

Albisinni FG, Peci K (2017) Il giudice e la regolazione. In: Torchia L (ed) La dinamica del diritto amministrativo. Dieci lezioni. il Mulino, Bologna, pp 295–299

Alti T, Barbieri C (2023) La trasparenza amministrativa come strumento di potere e di democrazia. Riv Trim Dir Pubblico 2:816

Armiento MB (2023) Prove di regolazione dell'intelligenza artificiale: il regolamento della banca d'Italia sulla gestione degli esposti. Giorn Dir Amm 1:105–115

Armiento MB (2024) Pubbliche amministrazioni e intelligenza artificiale. Strumenti, principi e garanzie. Editoriale Scientifica, Napoli

Auby JB (2019) Il diritto amministrativo di fronte alle sfide digitali. Istituzioni del Federalismo 3:619–641

Avanzini G (2019) Decisioni amministrative e algoritmi informatici. Predeterminazione, analisi predittiva e nuove forme di intelligibilità. Editoriale Scientifica, Napoli

Avanzini G (2024a) Art. 19. Della digitalizzazione del ciclo di vita dei contratti. In: Villata R, Ramajoli M (eds) Commentario al Codice dei Contratti pubblici D. Lgs. 31 marzo 2023, n. 36. Pacini Giuridica

Avanzini G (2024b) Art. 30. Uso di procedure automatizzate nel ciclo di vita dei contratti pubblici. In: Villata R, Ramajoli M (eds) Commentario al Codice dei Contratti pubblici D. Lgs. 31 marzo 2023, n. 36. Pacini Giuridica

Banca d'Italia (2021) Relazione sugli esposti dei clienti delle banche e delle finanziarie - anno 2021. https://www.bancaditalia.it/pubblicazioni/relazione-esposti/2022/index.html

Barberio M (2023) L'uso dell'intelligenza artificiale nell'art. 30 del d.lgs. 36/2023 alla prova dell'AI Act dell'Unione europea. Riv Ital Inform Diritto 2:253–264

Bassi N (2001) Principio di legalità e poteri amministrativi impliciti. Giuffrè, Milano

[141] See Official Journal of the Italian Republic General Series No. 75 of 30 March 2022.

[142] See Armiento (2023).

[143] See Federico (2021).

Benanti P (2022) Human in the loop. Decisioni umane e intelligenze artificiali. Mondadori Università, Milano
Benvenuti F (1996) Disegno della amministrazione italiana. Linee positive e prospettive. Padova, Cedam, p 52
Boeri T, Di Porto E, Naticchioni P, Scrutinio V (2021) Friday Morning Fever. Evidence from a randomized experiment on Sick Leave Monitoring in the Public Sector. WorkINPS Papers 37
Bombardelli M (2002) Informatica pubblica, e-government e sviluppo sostenibile. Riv Ital Dir Pubblico Comun 5:991
Bontempi V (2020) L'organizzazione dell'amministrazione centrale in materia di innovazione tecnologica e digitalizzazione. In: IRPA, Osservatorio sullo Stato Digitale
Bontempi V (2022) L'amministrazione finanziaria dello Stato. La gestione della finanza pubblica in un sistema di governo multilivello. FrancoAngeli, Milano, pp 217–223
Boscarino R, Di Porto E, Naticchioni P (2018) "SAVIO shut down": gli effetti sugli esiti delle visite mediche di controllo. https://www.bollettinoadapt.it/wp-content/uploads/2018/11/workInpsSAVIO_final.pdf
Bravo F (2020) Trasparenza del codice sorgente e decisioni automatizzate. Dir Inform Inform 4(5):693–724
Buono G, Bonanni P, Del Mondo G, Ciriello A (2022) Rapporto 4/2022 – Intelligenza artificiale e amministrazioni centrali. BioLaw J 1:261–274
Buratti V (2024) Art. 22. Ecosistema nazionale di approvvigionamento digitale (e-procurement). In: Villata R, Ramajoli M (eds) Commentario al Codice dei Contratti pubblici D. Lgs. 31 marzo 2023, n. 36. Pacini Giuridica
Burelli C (2024) Prime brevi considerazioni sul "ddl intelligenza artificiale": incompatibilità o inopportunità? In: Quaderni AISDUE - Riv Quadrim, Special Issue La nuova disciplina UE sull'intelligenza artificiale 2
Canalini V (2019) L'algoritmo come "atto amministrativo informatico" e il sindacato del giudice. Giorn Dir Amm 6:781–787
Canavesio G (1992) Il responsabile del procedimento. In: Alberti P, Azzariti G, Canavesio G et al (eds) Lezioni sul procedimento amministrativo. Giappichelli, Torino, pp 31–52
Cappai M (2024) Intelligenza artificiale e protezione dei dati personali nel d.d.l. n. 1146: quale governance nazionale? Federalismi.it 30:186–206
Cappai M (2025) Quale governance nazionale per l'Intelligenza Artificiale? Osservatorio sullo Stato digitale, 29 January 2025
Caranta R, Ferraris L (2000) La partecipazione al procedimento amministrativo. Giuffrè, Milano
Cardarelli F (2017) L'uso della telematica. In: Sandulli MA (ed) Codice dell'azione amministrativa. Giuffrè, Milano, p 509
Carloni E (ed) (2005) Codice dell'Amministrazione Digitale. Commento al D.Lgs. 7 marzo 2005, n. 82. Maggioli, Rimini
Carloni E (2011) La riforma del codice dell'amministrazione digitale. Giorn Dir Amm 5:469–476
Carloni E (2012) Amministrazione aperta e governance dell'Italia digitale. Giorn Dir Amm 11:1041–1046
Carloni E (2015) Tendenze recenti e nuovi principi della digitalizzazione pubblica. Giorn Dir Amm 2:148–157
Carloni E (2019) Algoritmi su carta. Politiche di digitalizzazione e trasformazione digitale delle amministrazioni. Dir Pubblico 2:363–391
Carloni E (2020) I principi della legalità algoritmica. Le decisioni automatizzate di fronte al giudice amministrativo. Dir Amm 2:273–304
Carloni E (2022) Il paradigma trasparenza. Amministrazione, informazione, democrazia. il Mulino, Bologna
Carotti B (2017) L'amministrazione digitale: le sfide culturali e politiche del nuovo codice. Giorn Dir Amm 1:7–18
Carotti B (2018) Il correttivo al codice dell'amministrazione digitale: una meta-riforma. Giorn Dir Amm 2:131–141

Carullo G (2021) Decisione amministrativa e intelligenza artificiale. Dir Inform Inform 3:434–440
Cassese S (1971) Il privato e il procedimento amministrativo. Una analisi della legislazione e della giurisprudenza. S.T.E.M.-Mucchi, Modena
Cassese S (1993) Il procedimento amministrativo tra modello partecipativo e modello "neo-classico". In: Torchia L (ed) Il procedimento amministrativo: profili comparati. Cedam, Padova, pp 1–6
Cassese S (2003) Le basi costituzionali. In: Cassese S (ed) Trattato di diritto amministrativo. Diritto amministrativo generale. Giuffrè, Milano, pp 213–222
Cavallo Perin R (2020) Ragionando come se la digitalizzazione fosse data. Dir Amm 2:305–328
Cavallo Perin R, Galetta DU (eds) (2020) Il diritto dell'amministrazione pubblica digitale. Giappichelli, Torino
Chiti MP (1977) Partecipazione popolare e pubblica amministrazione. Pacini, Pisa
Chiti E, Marchetti B, Rangone N, Togna T, Limosani A, Frega G, Deriu P, Ragucci G, Lo Schiavo L, Lazza L (2021a) Rapporto 1/2021 – L'impiego dell'intelligenza artificiale nell'attività di CONSOB, AGCOM e ARERA. BioLaw J 4:211–227
Chiti E, Marchetti B, Rangone N (2021b) Il progetto: L'uso dell'intelligenza artificiale nel sistema amministrativo italiano. BioLaw J 4:209–210
Chiti E, Marchetti B, Rangone N (2022a) L'impiego di sistemi di intelligenza artificiale nelle pubbliche amministrazioni italiane: prove generali. BioLaw J 2:489–507
Chiti E, Marchetti B, Rangone N (2022b) Smart cities e Amministrazioni centrali di fronte all'intelligenza artificiale: esperienze a confronto. BioLaw J 1:251–252
Civitarese Matteucci S (2005) La comunicazione di avvio del procedimento dopo la l. n. 15 del 2005. Potenziata nel procedimento, dequotata nel processo. Foro Amm C.d.S 6:1963–1973
Civitarese Matteucci S (2019) "Umano troppo umano". Decisioni amministrative automatizzate e principio di legalità. Dir Pubblico 1:5–41
Civitarese Matteucci S, Torchia L (2016) La tecnificazione. In: Ferrara L, Sorace D (eds) A 150 anni dall'unificazione amministrativa italiana. Studi, Vol. IV. Firenze University Press, Firenze
Clarich M (2005) Autorità indipendenti. Bilancio e prospettive di un modello. il Mulino, Bologna, pp 167–171
Coglianese C, Lehr D (2017) Regulating by robot: administrative decision making in the machine-learning era. Georgetown Law Rev 105:1147–1223
Coglianese C, Lehr D (2019) Transparency and algorithmic governance. Adm Law Rev 71:1–56
Cognetti S (2000) "Quantità" e "qualità" della partecipazione. Giuffrè, Milano
Colapietro C (2023) Gli algoritmi tra trasparenza e protezione dei dati personali. Federalismiit 5:151–174
Commissione parlamentare di inchiesta sul livello di digitalizzazione e innovazione delle pubbliche amministrazioni (2017) Relazione sull'attività svolta - La digitalizzazione nella pubblica amministrazione italiana: analisi degli errori e valutazione delle priorità, dall'efficacia degli strumenti all'importanza del capitale umano
Commissione speciale del Consiglio di Stato (2023) Relazione illustrativa al D.Lgs. No 36/2023
Corrado A (2023) I nuovi contratti pubblici, intelligenza artificiale e blockchain: le sfide del prossimo futuro. Federalismi.it 19:128–154
Costantino F (2016) L'uso della telematica nella pubblica amministrazione. In: Romano A (ed) L'azione amministrativa, Saggi sul procedimento amministrativo. Giappichelli, Torino, p 242
Data Protection Authority (2024) Parere su uno schema di disegno di legge recante disposizioni e deleghe in materia di intelligenza artificiale, 2 August 2024, No 477
De Giovanni E (2018) Il codice dell'Amministrazione digitale: genesi, evoluzione, principi costituzionali e linee generali. Rassegna dell'Avvocatura dello Stato 3:155–171
Del Gatto S (2021) I sistemi proprietari, l'open source e la pubblica amministrazione. Giornale di diritto amministrativo 5:571–577
Delgado IM (2017) La riforma dell'amministrazione digitale: un'opportunità per ripensare la pubblica amministrazione. In: Civitarese Matteucci S, Torchia L (eds) A 150 anni dall'unificazione amministrativa italiana. La tecnificazione. Firenze University Press, Firenze

Delgado IM (2019) Automazione, intelligenza artificiale e pubblica amministrazione: vecchie categorie concettuali per nuovi problemi? Istituzioni del federalismo 3:643–662
Di Nitto T (1999) La partecipazione al procedimento amministrativo. Rivista trimestrale di diritto pubblico 3:731–755
Duni G (2008) L'amministrazione digitale. Il diritto amministrativo nella evoluzione telematica. Giuffrè, Milano
European Commission (2019) Ethics Guidelines for Trustworthy AI. https://digital-strategy.ec.europa.eu/en/library/ethics-guidelines-trustworthy-ai
European Commission (2024) Digital Decade Country Report 2024: Italy
European Data Protection Board (2024) Statement 3/2024 on data protection authorities' role in the Artificial Intelligence Act framework
Federico F, Marcucci J, Bevilacqua M, Marchetti DJ (2021) Rapporto 2/2021 - L'impiego dell'intelligenza artificiale nell'attività di Banca d'Italia. BioLaw Journal 4:229–244
Fernández-Llorca D, Gómez E, Sánchez I, Mazzini G (2024) An interdisciplinary account of the terminological choices by EU policymakers ahead of the final agreement on the AI Act: AI system, general purpose AI system, foundation model, and generative AI. Artif Intell Law. https://doi.org/10.1007/s10506-024-09412-y
Finocchiaro G (2022) La proposta di regolamento sull'intelligenza artificiale: il modello europeo basato sulla gestione del rischio. Il diritto dell'informazione e dell'informatica 2:303–322
Fois S (1973) Legalità (principio di). In: Enciclopedia del diritto, vol. 23. Giuffrè, Milano
Forgione I (2018) Il caso dell'accesso al software MIUR per l'assegnazione dei docenti. Giornale di diritto amministrativo 5:647–662
FPA DATA INSIGHT (2024) L'impatto dell'intelligenza artificiale sul pubblico impiego
Gabanelli M, Marinelli A (2019) Tasse, ecco come un algoritmo difettoso ti fa pagare di più di quanto devi. Corriere della Sera. www.corriere.it/dataroom-milena-gabanelli/tasse-isa-ecco-come-algoritmo-difettoso-ti-fa-pagare-piu-quanto-dovi/77bbc760-03dd-11ea-a09d-144c1806035c-va.shtml
Galetta D-U (2020a) Algoritmi, procedimento amministrativo e garanzie: brevi riflessioni, anche alla luce degli ultimi arresti giurisprudenziali in materia. Rivista italiana di diritto pubblico comunitario 3:510–516
Galetta D-U (2020b) Digitalizzazione e diritto ad una buona amministrazione (il procedimento amministrativo, fra diritto Ue e tecnologie ICT). In: Cavallo Perin R, Galetta D-U (eds) Il diritto dell'amministrazione pubblica digitale. Giappichelli, Torino, pp 95–99
Galetta DU (2022) Transizione digitale e diritto ad una buona amministrazione: fra prospettive aperte per le Pubbliche Amministrazioni dal Piano Nazionale di Ripresa e Resilienza e problemi ancora da affrontare. federalismi.it 7:103–125
Galetta DU (2023) Digitalizzazione, Intelligenza artificiale e Pubbliche Amministrazioni: il nuovo Codice dei contratti pubblici e le sfide che ci attendono. federalismi.it 12:4–14
Gallone G (2023) Riserva di umanità e funzioni amministrative. CEDAM, Milano
Garapon A, Lassègue J (2021) La giustizia digitale. Determinismo tecnologico e libertà. il Mulino, Bologna
Giannini MS (2000) Istituzioni di diritto amministrativo. Milano, Giuffrè, p 271
Giglioni F, Lariccia S (2000) Partecipazione dei cittadini all'attività amministrativa. In: Enciclopedia del diritto, vol 4. Giuffrè, Milano
Giupponi TF (2024) Il governo nazionale della cybersicurezza. Quaderni costituzionali 2:277–303
Hacker P (2024) Comments on the Final Trilogue Version of the AI Act. Available at: https://doi.org/10.2139/ssrn.4757603
Impinna MA (2015) Il responsabile del procedimento amministrativo. In: Clarich M, Fonderico G (eds) Procedimento amministrativo. Wolters Kluwer, Milano, pp 116–159
INPS (2024) Linee guida per l'implementazione di sistemi di Intelligenza Artificiale - Direttiva del Direttore Generale n.8 del 8 aprile 2024
Laviola F (2020) Algoritmico, troppo algoritmico: decisioni amministrative automatizzate, protezione dei dati personali e tutela delle libertà dei cittadini alla luce della più recente giurisprudenza amministrativa. BioLaw journal 3:389–440

Levi F (1977) Partecipazione e organizzazione. Rivista trimestrale di diritto pubblico 4:1625–1647
Licata GF (2024) Intelligenza artificiale e contratti pubblici: problemi e prospettive. CERIDAP 2:30–63
Lo Sapio G (2021a) La black box: l'esplicabilità delle scelte algoritmiche quale garanzia di buona amministrazione. federalismi.it 16:114–127
Lo Sapio G (2021b) La trasparenza sul banco di prova dei modelli algoritmici. federalismi.it 11:243–244
Lo Sapio G (2024) L'Artificial Intelligence Act e la prova di resistenza per la legalità algoritmica. federalismiit 16:265–290
Macchia M (2020) Lo statuto giuridico dell'algoritmo amministrativo. Osservatorio sullo Stato digitale, Irpa. www.irpa.eu/lo-statuto-giuridico-dellalgoritmo-amministrativo/
Maddalena ML (2017) La digitalizzazione della vita dell'amministrazione e del processo. In: L'Italia che cambia: dalla riforma dei contratti pubblici alla riforma della Pubblica Amministrazione (Atti del 62° Convegno di studi di scienza dell'amministrazione Varenna-Villa Monastero, 22–23-24 settembre 2016). Giuffrè, Milano
Malgieri G, Comandè G (2017) Why a right to legibility of automated decision-making exists in the General Data Protection Regulation. Int Data Priv Law 7:243–265
Marchetti B (2021) La garanzia dello "human in the loop" alla prova della decisione amministrativa algoritmica. BioLaw J 2:367–385
Marchetti B (2022) Amministrazione digitale. In: Mattarella BG, Ramajoli M (eds) Enciclopedia del Diritto: funzioni amministrative. Giuffrè, Milano, pp 75–109
Marchetti B (2024a) Artificial intelligence and public authorities: Does the European AI act protect public values? Eur Rev Public Law 36:67–90
Marchetti B (2024b) L'esecuzione della regolazione digitale dell'Unione Europea e il ruolo della Commissione. Rivista trimestrale di diritto pubblico 4:1097–1120
Marchetti B (2024c) La regolazione europea del mercato dell'intelligenza artificiale. Rivista della Regolazione dei mercati 1:11
Martines F (2018) La digitalizzazione della pubblica amministrazione. Medialaws 2:146–157
Mascolo A (2021) Intelligenza artificiale e amministrazione fiscale: non tutti gli algoritmi sono uguali. Osservatorio sullo Stato digitale, Irpa. www.irpa.eu/intelligenza-artificiale-e-amministrazione-fiscale-non-tutti-gli-algoritmi-sono-uguali/
Masucci A (1993) L'atto amministrativo informatico. Primi lineamenti di una ricostruzione. Jovene, Napoli
Masucci A (2022) L'automatizzazione delle decisioni amministrative algoritmiche fra "big data" e "machine learning". Verso l'"algocratic governance"? Diritto e processo amministrativo 2:265–313
Meneghetti F, Rossi Chauvenet C, Fioroni G (2022) Rapporto 3/2022 – SMART cities e intelligenza artificiale. BioLaw J 1:253–259
Merloni F (ed) (2005) Introduzione all'e-government. Pubbliche amministrazioni e società dell'informazione. Giappichelli, Torino
Messina D (2022) La proposta di regolamento europeo in materia di Intelligenza Artificiale: verso una "discutibile" tutela individuale di tipo "consumer-centric" nella società dominata dal "pensiero artificiale". MediaLaws 2:196–231
Montessoro PL (2019) Cybersecurity: conoscenza e consapevolezza come prerequisiti per l'amministrazione digitale. Istituzioni del federalismo 3:783–800
Mosqueira-Rey E, Hernández-Pereira E, Alonso-Ríos D et al (2023) Human-in-the-loop machine learning: a state of the art. Artif Intell Rev 56:3005–3054
National Cybersecurity Agency (ACN) (2022) Strategia nazionale di cybersicurezza 2022–2026. https://www.acn.gov.it/portale/strategia-nazionale-di-cybersicurezza
Nigro M (1980) Il nodo della partecipazione. Riv Trimest Dirit Proced Civ 1:230
Notarmuzi C (2010) DigitPA: la terza riorganizzazione dell'informatica pubblica. Giornale di diritto amministrativo 10:1014–1020

Novelli C, Casolari F, Rotolo A, Taddeo M, Floridi L (2024a) AI risk assessment: a scenario-based, proportional methodology for the AI act. Digit Soc 3(1)
Novelli C, Hacker P, Morley J, Trondal J, Floridi L (2024b) A robust governance for the AI act: AI office, AI board, scientific panel, and national authorities. Available at: https://ssrn.com/abstract=4817755
Oddenino A (2020) Decisioni algoritmiche e prospettive internazionali di valorizzazione dell'intervento umano. DPCE online 1:199–217
Orofino AG, Gallone G (2020) L'intelligenza artificiale al servizio delle funzioni amministrative: profili problematici e spunti di riflessione. Giurisprudenza italiana 7
Otranto P (2021) Riflessioni in tema di decisione amministrativa, intelligenza artificiale e legalità. federalismi.it 7:204
Oxford Insights (2024) Government AI readiness index 2024
Palamoni GM (2024) Il paradigma digitale dell'evidenza pubblica. CERIDAP 2:64–100
Paolantonio N (2021) Il potere discrezionale della pubblica automazione. Sconcerto e stilemi. (Sul controllo giudiziario delle "decisioni algoritmiche"). Diritto amministrativo 4:824
Parona L (2021) L'istituzione dell'Agenzia per la cybersicurezza nazionale: prime osservazioni. Giornale di diritto amministrativo 6:709–719
Pasquale F (2015) Black box society. The secret algorithms that control money and information. Harvard University Press, Cambridge-London
Perfetti LR (ed) (2023) Codice dei contratti pubblici commentato. D. Lgs. 31 marzo 2023 n. 36. Wolters Kluwer, Milano
Pesce G (2018) Digital First. Amministrazione digitale: genesi, sviluppi, prospettive. Editoriale Scientifica, Napoli
Previti L (2022) La decisione amministrativa robotica. Editoriale Scientifica, Napoli
Prosperetti E (2019) Accesso al software e al relativo algoritmo nei procedimenti amministrativi e giudiziali. Un'analisi a partire da due pronunce del TAR Lazio. Il diritto dell'informazione e dell'informatica 4-5:979–1010
Rangone N (2022) Intelligenza artificiale e pubbliche amministrazioni: affrontare i numerosi rischi per trarne tutti i vantaggi. BioLaw J 2:473–488
Renzi A (2024) Proteggere le nuove frontiere del Paese, un'analisi della nuova legge sulla cybersicurezza nazionale italiana. Azienditalia 10:1110–1117
Resta G (2022) Cosa c'è di "europeo" nella Proposta di Regolamento UE sull'intelligenza artificiale? Il diritto dell'informazione e dell'informatica 2:323–342
Romano B (2024) Il DDL in materia di IA: l'utilizzo nell'attività giudiziaria e in ambito sanitario. Rivista italiana di Medicina Legale (e del Diritto in campo sanitario) 1-2:403–416
Rossa S (2023) Cybersicurezza e pubblica amministrazione. Editoriale Scientifica, Napoli
Saitta F (2000) L'omessa comunicazione dell'avvio del procedimento: profili sostanziali e processuali. Diritto amministrativo 3-4:449–504
Sandulli MA (1991) Art. 6, in V. Italia. In: Bassani M (ed) Procedimento amministrativo e diritto di accesso ai documenti (Legge 7 agosto 1990, n. 241). Giuffrè, Milano, pp 73–102
Sandulli MA (ed) (2000) Il procedimento amministrativo tra semplificazione e partecipazione. Modelli europei a confronto. Giuffrè, Milano
Sandulli MA (2004) La comunicazione di avvio del procedimento tra forma e sostanza (spunti dai recenti progetti di riforma). Foro amministrativo-TAR 5:1595–1608
Sartor G (2022) L'informatica giuridica e le tecnologie dell'informazione. Giappichelli, Torino
Satta F (1969) Principio di legalità e pubblica amministrazione nello Stato democratico. Cedam, Padova
Sgueo G (2016) L'amministrazione digitale. Giornale di diritto amministrativo 1:114–118
Tentoni F (2011) Organizzazione e nuove tecnologie nel "nuovo" codice dell'amministrazione digitale. Azienditalia 6:459–465
Terracciano G (1994) Sull'obbligo di comunicazione dell'avvio del procedimento. Il Foro amministrativo 9:2177–2179

Torchia L (2020) Il sistema amministrativo italiano e il Fondo di ripresa e resilienza. Astrid Rassegna 17
Torchia L (2021) L'amministrazione presa sul serio e l'attuazione del PNRR. Astrid Rassegna, pp 6–7
Torchia L (2023a) La giustizia amministrativa digitale. In: Ramajoli M (ed) Una giustizia amministrativa digitale? il Mulino, Bologna, pp 39–58
Torchia L (2023b) Lo Stato digitale. Una introduzione. il Mulino, Bologna
Traverso P (2022) Breve introduzione tecnica all'Intelligenza Artificiale. DPCE online 51(1):155–167
Tresca M (2018) I primi passi verso l'Intelligenza Artificiale al servizio del cittadino: brevi note sul Libro Bianco dell'Agenzia per l'Italia digitale. Rivista di diritto dei media 3:1–13
Troisi E (2022) Automated Decision Making and right to explanation. The right of access as ex post information. Eur J Priv Law Technol 1:181–202
Villata R (1992) Riflessioni in tema di partecipazione al procedimento amministrativo. Diritto processuale amministrativo 2:171–205
Virga G (1998) La partecipazione al procedimento amministrativo. Giuffrè, Milano
Wachter S, Mittelstadt B, Floridi L (2017) Why a right to explanation of automated decision-making does not exist in the General Data Protection Regulation. Int Data Priv Law 7(2):76–99
Zito A (1996) Le pretese partecipative del privato nel procedimento amministrativo. Giuffrè, Milano

Marianna Merler is a doctoral student in Comparative and European Legal Studies, curriculum in administrative, constitutional and international law, at the Faculty of Law, University of Trento. Her research interests include administrative law, digital administration and artificial intelligence.

Camilla Ramotti is adjunct professor in European administrative law at the University of Tuscia. Her research interests include administrative law, digital administration and the protection of the European Union's financial interests.

The EU Digital Regulation and Its Impact on Germany

Cristina Fraenkel-Haeberle

Contents

Abstract The contribution explores the digital regulation of the EU and its implications for administrative practices in Germany. It begins with a discussion of the evolving definition of AI, emphasizing its complexity and the challenges posed by biases in training data, which can affect the integrity of AI systems. The various application scenarios of AI in German administrations, including public safety, social benefits allocation and environmental monitoring are highlighted, illustrating

C. Fraenkel-Haeberle (✉)
University of Speyer and National Institute for Public Administration Germany, Speyer, Germany
e-mail: fraenkel-haeberle@foev-speyer.de

F. Decarolis et al. (eds.), *The EU Digital Regulation and its Impact on Member States*, European Union and its Neighbours in a Globalized World 27,
https://doi.org/10.1007/978-3-032-06490-5_3

the potential benefits and risks associated with these technologies. The essay also examines the legal framework governing use of AI in German public administrations, noting diverse procedural regulations across federal states and the implications of automated decision-making. It discusses recent legislative efforts to modernize tax procedures and to ensure transparency in automated processes while addressing concerns about citizen participation and data protection under GDPR. It emphasizes the need for robust guarantees to protect citizens' rights in an increasingly algorithm-driven administrative landscape, advocating balance between efficiency and participatory governance. This critical analysis of how EU digital regulations are shaping AI deployment in Germany highlights the opportunities and challenges for future governance.

1 Artificial Intelligence and Its Bias

The term artificial intelligence (AI) is not new. It was first used in a research project at Dartmouth College (NH, USA) in 1955.[1] However, defining AI is still challenging. It encompasses logical reasoning, decision-making under uncertainty, machine learning, adaptability, autonomy of technical systems, pattern recognition and modelling. A modern definition from Article 3, No. 1 of the AI Regulation[2] describes an "AI system" as a machine-based system designed to operate with varying levels of autonomy, capable of adapting after deployment. Such systems produce outputs—like predictions and recommendations—from the inputs they receive, potentially influencing both physical and virtual environments, and therefore also impacting social reality.[3] The 12th Recital of the EU AI Act explains what is meant by the term "AI system": "The capacity of an AI system to infer transcends basic data processing by enabling learning, reasoning or modelling", a definition often criticized as being excessively vague and overly broad.[4]

Notoriously, the quality of training data is closely linked to what AI applications can do, as expressed by the principle: "garbage in, garbage out".[5] If the training database is flawed or inadequate, the quality of the output will likewise suffer. Bias refers to distortions in survey results due to improper research methods. Avoiding such biases is crucial for the integrity of AI systems. Data bias is one form of

[1] Brockmann (2023), p. 287.

[2] Regulation (EU) 2024/1689 of the European Parliament and of the Council of 13 June 2024 laying down harmonised rules on artificial intelligence and amending Regulations (EC) No 300/2008, (EU) No 167/2013, (EU) No 168/2013, (EU) 2018/858, (EU) 2018/1139 and (EU) 2019/2144 and Directives 2014/90/EU, (EU) 2016/797 and (EU) 2020/1828 (Artificial Intelligence Act) (Text with EEA relevance), OJ L 2024/1689.

[3] Roth-Isigkeit (2024), p. 26.

[4] Seitz (2024), p. 838.

[5] Brockmann (2023), p. 289.

machine learning bias where data quality is distorted. For instance, crime statistics may suggest that long-term unemployment is correlated with an increased likelihood of crime; if employment status is treated as a variable, algorithms may generalize this correlation without a nuance.[6] Sample bias instead occurs when training data does not adequately represent the population of the area of application, leading to over- or under-representation of specific groups. For example, an algorithm trained on data from one U.S. state may not perform accurately when applied nationwide.[7]

Various challenges arise from these and other biases, especially since the learning processes of AI are not accessible to users. Since data-based systems may translate social stereotypes and even social inequality into apparently neutral systems, it is important to keep training data clean. Training hygiene should be a key principle, since whoever controls the training data also controls the otherwise incomprehensible decision-making process.[8]

Data protection issues may arise in relation to personal rights and privacy when AI technologies are used. Although the GDPR does not explicitly address AI, it remains relevant. In March 2023, Italy's data protection authority banned ChatGPT's data processing, prompting OpenAI to temporarily suspend its service there. A similar action was considered in Germany by the Federal Data Protection Commissioner (*Bundesbeauftragter für den Datenschutz*), due to concerns about the lack of legal basis for processing personal data without user consent—an argument supported by Article 6 of the GDPR. According to Article 5 of the GDPR, data processing must be comprehensible to individuals. Since this transparency is often lacking, it hinders effective acquisition of consent from users regarding use of their data for training purposes.[9]

2 The Use of AI Systems by German Administrations

There are many application scenarios for artificial intelligence in German administrations. The federal government has listed 79 fields of application[10] that range from "inauthentic mass proceedings" (*unechte Massenverfahren*),[11] where an indefinite number of identical or similar administrative acts are issued in a large number of

[6] Brockmann (2023), p. 294.

[7] Brockmann (2023), p. 294.

[8] Brockmann (2023), p. 295.

[9] Brockmann (2023), p. 288.

[10] Martini/Ruschmeier (2023), Mn. 10.

[11] According to Schmitz (2018), § 17, Mn. 6, the term "authentic mass proceedings" (*echte Massenverfahren*) covers proceedings in which a large number of people are involved in an administrative decision, usually an administrative act. However, if a larger number of people are the addressees of many identical or similar administrative acts, this constitutes so-called "inauthentic mass proceedings"; see also Lorse (2021a, b), p. 1659.

identical or similar administrative procedures,[12] and the acquisition and systematization of information in view of administrative decisions, to decisions concerning allocation and prioritization of social benefits, such as unemployment benefits and climate protection measures.[13]

Intelligent systems play a significant role in the federal administration, in the areas of public safety, where network analyses are conducted in the cyber domain, or fighting value-added tax fraud, which relies on web crawlers.[14] Intelligent video surveillance is increasingly used in danger prevention and law enforcement. Corresponding systems have been tested at Berlin Südkreuz station.[15] Customs administration also uses an analysis tool to identify low-risk and high-risk situations during customs clearance.[16] Other fields of deployment of artificial intelligence are fighting malware and the prediction of migration flows. Since 2017, the Federal Office for Migration and Refugees has been using AI to analyse speech samples of refugees to determine their origin.[17]

In the field of climate change and environmental protection, artificial intelligence can offer innovative solutions. The analysis of environmental data using intelligent systems not only helps to optimize waste, energy and transport but also enables rapid detection of environmental changes, such as air pollution.[18] Machine learning systems facilitate biological diversity monitoring, energy demand forecasting and renewable energy performance.[19]

Some federal states use predictive policing tools to identify crime hotspots. Police authorities have also long been using intelligent systems to collect and evaluate data from social media (so-called social media monitoring). In Hessen, a law was issued to permit data mining by the police using Palantir Technologies Inc. platforms.[20] The City of Hamburg and the state of North Rhine-Westphalia followed Hessen's example. Both states have introduced special standards for automated data comparison into their police laws.[21]

In North-Rhine-Westphalia, at the initiative of the *Westfälische Hochschule* and the Fraunhofer Institute, the programme URBAN.KI investigates and develops applications of artificial intelligence for municipalities and supports them in their effort to become smart cities.[22] Private companies are also involved in the

[12] Brockmann (2023) p. 291. This is the case with tax payments, pensions, fine notices, resident parking permits, child benefits, BAFöG (German Federal Education Assistance) benefits and "mass rejections" in the context of hiring procedures

[13] Lorse (2021a, b) p. 220 f.

[14] Martini/Ruschmeier (2023), Mn. 11.

[15] Busche (2024), p. 214.

[16] Busche (2024), p. 216.

[17] Martini/Ruschmeier (2023), Mn. 11.

[18] Martini/Ruschmeier (2023), Mn. 17.

[19] Martini/Ruschmeier (2023), Mn. 17.

[20] Martini/Ruschmeier (2023), Mn. 11.

[21] Martini/Ruschmeier (2023), Mn. 12.

[22] Die deutsche KI-Initiative für Kommunen (urban-ki.de).

development of algorithmic technologies for public administrations: in Baden-Württemberg Aleph Alpha, a start-up in Heidelberg, has developed a special KI based assistance program, called "F13" (an additional function on the computer keyboard), to support public servants in their document research and drafting activities.[23]

Many tasks of municipalities, especially mass proceedings, can be performed digitally. The "smart city" concept can enable better coordination of power generation and consumption, and intelligent traffic monitoring systems can avoid traffic jams. Weather sensors, street lighting based on usage time and parking guidance systems are also widespread.[24] In the field of communication with citizens, artificial intelligence can significantly relieve personnel. For instance, the city of Heidelberg is currently testing the generative AI-based chatbot Lumi, which is designed to respond reliably to all inquiries, much like a service employee.[25]

When combined with "Big Data", particularly in the context of learning data, AI offers a significant opportunity for enhancing problem-solving algorithms and decision-making processes. A primary challenge in this domain is ensuring the quality standards and the interoperability of the learning data. The use of blockchain technology as a decentralized database can enhance the integrity and transparency of this process.[26]

3 National Rules on the Use of AI by Administrations

In the German legal system, there are numerous laws on the use of automated administrative decisions. This is essentially due to two factors: on one hand, the federal structure entails different procedural regulations and laws on e-government (digital administration) in the *Länder* (federal states); on the other, the so-called "three column system", based on three different codes, namely the Tax Code (*Abgabenordnung—AO*) and the Social Code (*Zehntes Buch des Sozialgesetzgebuches*—SGB X), which coexist with the general Administrative Procedures Act (*Verwaltungsverfahrensgesetz*—VwVfG).[27] However, also in relation to this triple codification, the legislator is committed to ensuring uniformity of the rules of administrative procedure to facilitate interpretation of the three codes by administrations and judges. Because tax law is particularly suitable for digitization due to widespread use of routine measures, the starting point for fully automated (model-based) administrative procedures has come from tax assessment provisions

[23] Künstliche Intelligenz in der Verwaltung: Staatsministerium Baden-Württemberg (baden-wuerttemberg.de).

[24] Lorse (2021a, b), p. 222.

[25] Martini/Ruschmeier (2023), Mn. 21.

[26] Lorse (2021a, b), p. 220.

[27] See more extensively Fraenkel-Haeberle (2021), 525ff.; Fraenkel-Haeberle (2020), 105ff.

(§ 155 AO). Thus, when the federal government passed a law aimed at modernizing tax procedure (*Gesetz zur Modernisierung des Besteuerungsverfahrens*)[28] in 2016, stating that tax assessment (*Steuerfestsetzung*) had to be fully digitalized,[29] the innovation was extended in parallel to the other two codes. Since the regulations of the three codes have traditionally developed in parallel, § 35a on fully automated decisions was also enacted in the VwVfG and § 31a SGB X introduced a similar provision in the social sphere.[30]

The wording of § 35a VwVfG on electronic decisions is extremely terse. It envisages implementation of administrative acts (governed by the previous § 35 VwVfG) by fully automated procedures. To make that possible, a sectoral rule (*Rechtsvorschrift*) is required to ensure that only suitable procedures can be carried out in a fully automated manner and to comply with the requirements of Art. 22 DSGVO.[31] Briefly, the criteria set out in § 35a VwVfG are as follows: the administrative act must be suitable for issue in a fully automated format by electronic equipment; this must be envisaged by a legal provision; the administration cannot have discretionary power or a margin of appreciation (*Beurteilungsspielraum*).[32] The provision has been interpreted to mean that the aim of the legislator was to limit the scope of application of the rule to situations that could be managed easily by IT-systems and that allow full judicial review.[33] According to this interpretation, a fully automated decision not only depends on the absence of discretionary power, but also presupposes a simple measure.[34] So far there are only a few practical examples of fully automated decisions, namely the broadcasting fee notice and motor vehicle registration.[35] Scholars suggest the building permit process, provided no

---

[28] BGBl. I, p. 1679.

[29] So-called ELSTER-system (electronic tax declaration).

[30] Braun-Binder (2024), p. 437ff.

[31] Martini and Nink (2017), p. 8.

[32] Ziekow (2018), p. 1169 ff. The author investigates scholarly discussion on the legal nature of automated decisions, pointing out that due to the absence of human intervention, there is no declaration of intent, which is otherwise considered inherent to an administrative act. However, this approach does not take into account that even the discipline of silent assent (so-called "*Genehmigungsfiktion*"), referred to in § 42a VwVfG, does not depend on manifestation of intent by a public administration, since the administrative act is formed over time, pursuant to a specific legislative provision (p. 1170). Another example of a fully automated administrative act, cited in the literature, is algorithmic traffic regulation devices (for example traffic lights), framed in the German system as general administrative decrees (*Allgemeinverfügungen*), and referred to in § 35, second sentence VwVfG; see Augsberg (2019), p. 94; Kube (2019), p. 303.

[33] Buoso (2021), p. 507ff.

[34] Guckelberger (2019), p. 265.

[35] § 6 g (2) 1 *Straßenverkehrsgesetz* (StVG) in conjunction with §§ 15a ff. *Fahrzeug-Zulassungsverordnung* (FZV) of 3.2.2011, BGBl. I p. 139; since 2020, § 10a of the Interstate Treaty on Broadcasting Contributions (*Rundfunkbeitragsstaatsvertrags* - RBeitrStV) has legitimized the fully automated issuing of broadcasting contribution decisions; see additionally § 38a *Elektro- und Elektronikgerätegesetz* (ElektroG), § 3a *Bundesreisekostengesetz* (BRKG) and § 22 *Batteriegesetz* (BattG).

exceptions are requested, as well as the renewal of personal, disability and parking permits, and the granting of child benefits as additional areas of application.[36]

4 Guarantees to Protect Citizens and the Challenge of Algorithmic Administration

Traditional administrative procedural law is considered to lend itself to algorithmic decisions, even considering its very strong participatory approach. On one hand the administrative procedure is deemed an important point of reference for public servants to ensure transparency and effectiveness under the guidance of precise and detailed provisions.[37] Secondly, from the citizens' perspective, administrative procedure is a privileged occasion for participation in administrative decision-making, comparable to the Italian model of "shared administration"[38] (*amministrazione condivisa*), free from relationships of subordination.[39] Thirdly, with regard to judicial review by the administrative judge, it is always the law on the procedure that provides the tools indispensable for reconstructing the logical path followed by the administration, also thanks to the broad investigative powers explicitly provided by procedural law.[40]

In line with the architecture of German administrative procedure, which emphasizes strong investigative powers of public administrations and the inquisitorial principle, § 24 (1) of the Administrative Procedures Act (VwVfG) was amended in 2017 to accommodate automated decisions. This amendment added a new provision requiring administrations to consider any indications provided by parties that cannot be detected in digital format when using automated acts. This change was necessary because the highly participatory nature of the German procedural system is potentially threatened by automated decisions.[41] To address this, a specific obligation was introduced to ensure that all relevant information provided by the parties is

[36] Braun-Binder (2024), p. 443.

[37] In this area constitutional jurisprudence has developed the *Wesentlichkeitsprinzip* (principle of essentiality), as a derivation of the democratic principle and the rule of law. According to this principle, the fundamental rules governing the actions of public administrations must be established by the Parliament as representative of the people and not delegated to executive regulations, especially when these rules are essential for the protection of fundamental rights; see Maurer, Waldhoff (2024), § 6, Mn. 12. In this sense, the principle of essentiality is combined with the *Bestimmtheitsgebot* (requirement of determinateness), as stipulated in § 37 (1) VwVfG, which states that an administrative measure "must be sufficiently determined in its content" so that it can be easily and correctly understood by the recipients to whom it is addressed.

[38] Bombardelli (2011), p. 25 ss.

[39] See more extensively Jacquemet-Gauché, Stelkens (2016), p. 15ff.

[40] See § 86 (1) *VwGO* on the inquisitorial principle.

[41] This is demonstrated by the fact that § 24 (2) VwVfG obliges the administration to consider all relevant circumstances in individual cases, including "those favourable to the parties".

considered. A similar rule was introduced in the Social Code (SGB X, § 31a).[42] In tax procedures, a comparable approach was taken with the addition of § 88 (5) of the Tax Code (AO). This section allows the tax administration to use a computerized risk management system (*Risikomanagementsystem*) to identify anomalous cases, which must then be manually reviewed. This ensures that the requirement of cost-effectiveness in public administrations is maintained without compromising the inquisitorial principle.[43] Unlike tax procedures, the other two codes do not specify how non-digital examination of relevant elements should be requested. This inconsistency can be justified by the difficulty of matching the wide range of possible procedures with overly strict procedural rules outside of tax assessments.[44] Another aspect related to "end-to-end digitization" is the communication and publication of administrative acts in electronic form on virtual portals.[45] Initially envisaged by § 6 (4) of the Bavarian e-government law (BayEGovG), which came into force on 30 December 2015, this concept led to the addition of § 41 (2a) VwVfG at federal level.[46] This provision states that with the consent of the interested party, an administrative act can be made accessible to the addressee or his/her representative for download on a digital platform.[47] The administration is obliged to ensure that download of the authenticated administrative act is possible and that the act can be saved on an electronic medium by the party. Unlike postal transmission, the addressee must actively participate in this process. Electronic communication is voluntary due to the "digital divide" (the fact that not all citizens have access to electronic devices) and requires the party's consent, which can be revoked at any time.[48] The administration ensures that the electronic measure is deemed communicated the day after the download is made. If the download is not made within 10 days, the communication is deemed not to have taken place. However, the administration retains the option of repeating the communication in this or another form. Similar legislation was introduced in the social sphere by § 37 (2a) SGB X and in tax law by § 122a (4) AO. Publication on the website is independent of whether the procedure is fully or partially automated.[49]

Other provisions of the VwVfG have not been adapted to automated administrative decisions. This is the case of the *Auskunft und Beratungspflicht* (information and advisory obligation) under § 25 VwVfG, according to which administrative authorities have to provide citizens with necessary information and advice

[42] *Setzt die Behörde automatische Einrichtungen zum Erlass von Verwaltungsakten ein, muss sie für den Einzelfall bedeutsame tatsächliche Angaben des Beteiligten berücksichtigen, die im automatischen Verfahren nicht ermittelt würden.*

[43] Braun-Binder (2016c), p. 960.

[44] Braun Binder (2019), p. 315.

[45] Martini, Nink (2017), p. 3.

[46] *Gesetz über die elektronische Verwaltung in Bayern* (Bayerisches E-Government-Gesetz – BayEGovG) of 22.12.2015 (GVBl. p. 458).

[47] Braun-Binder (2016a), p. 342.

[48] Martini (2021), Mn. 39.

[49] Braun-Binder (2016b), p. 891.

regarding their rights and duties in administrative procedures. Since the law does not specify a particular form for fulfilling this obligation, it can be inferred that automated assistance systems, such as chatbots, may be used for this purpose.[50]

Before issuing an administrative act that affects the rights of a participant, according to § 28 VwVfG, the administration must provide the addressees with the opportunity to comment on facts relevant to the decision, outline their interests and provide relevant information. In contrast to § 25 VwVfG, the communication here is primarily from the citizen to the administration. Exceptions to this rule (urgent decisions, general administrative acts, etc.) established in 1976, based on the need to conserve personnel and hasten the procedure,[51] are not deemed suitable for fully automated administrative acts.[52]

The VwVfG mandates that administrative authorities grant participants in an administrative procedure the right to inspect files relevant to the procedure, in order to assert or defend their legal interests. The right to inspect files (*Akteneinsicht*) as outlined in § 29 VwVfG—a fundamental expression of the rule of law principle—raises the question of how this right can apply to fully automated administrative procedures and what the files are in such cases. However, the state does not necessarily have to publish the program code of all the software applications it uses for automated decision-making. This could only provide limited legal protection against measures taken by state authorities, since the codes of programming language are incomprehensible to the average addressee of administrative acts.[53] While disclosure of the entire algorithm may not be necessary, revealing the criteria that guide the decision-making process can help citizens understand how the data was processed and the decision reached, thereby enhancing transparency and trust in the automated system.[54]

Traditionally, the justification of an administrative act under § 39 (1) VwVfG aimed at disclosure of the decision criteria, including the essential factual and legal reasons that motivated the authority to make its decision, is deemed an expression of the rule of law principle. The requirement for a justification ensures transparency and accountability in administrative decision-making. According to the exceptions outlined in § 39 (2) VwVfG, under certain conditions, the administration is authorized to omit an individual justification.[55] However, lack of human involvement in an algorithmic decision-making process can even trigger an increased need for explanation, emphasizing the importance of transparent and justified administrative actions.[56]

[50] Eichenhofer (2023), p. 97.

[51] Ludwigs, Velling (2023), p. 90.

[52] Eichenhofer (2023), p. 97.

[53] Martini (2021), Mn. 48.

[54] Eichenhofer (2023), p. 98.

[55] Eichenhofer (2023), p. 98.

[56] Ludwigs, Velling (2023), p. 92.

Fully automated administrative acts may also enhance an appeal (*Widerspruch*) against the decision. This pre-trial procedure, foreseen in the administrative law of some federal states, gives the administration the opportunity to review both the lawfulness and the expediency of the contested decision before the matter is brought to court. This procedure has a quality assurance function, as the addressees of an administrative act can provide feedback, thereby influencing its implementation.[57] Even if the use of fully automated administrative acts does not automatically create a legal obligation to strengthen this remedy, it offers the affected parties the opportunity to express their views on an administrative decision.[58] Since this procedure also envisages a review of expediency, according to § 35a VwVfG it must be conducted in an analogue way, thus remaining inaccessible to automation.[59]

In administrative law, the question whether the behaviour of an AI system can be attributed as an administrative act to an administrative body in the sense of § 35 VwVfG may also arise, as well as under what conditions state liability exists, since this claim normally only concerns individuals or organizations.[60] Regarding civil liability for the behaviour of autonomous systems in contractual matters, similar application of § 278 BGB (debtor liability to third parties) is considered, assuming the autonomous system's actions can be attributed to culpable behaviour.[61] In the realm of tort law, the introduction of strict liability (*Gefährdungshaftung*), including insurance obligations or a general compensation fund, is being proposed to address the risks associated with autonomous systems.[62] In the context of financial compensation, claims for official liability (*Staatshaftung*) entail the requirement of fault under § 839 of the German Civil Code (BGB) in conjunction with Article 34 of the German Constitution (GG). The focus is on the culpability of the administrative decision to implement full automation in an unsuitable administrative procedure, or on refusal to "opt out" (*Aussteuerung*) of such automation, respectively.[63]

[57] Ludwigs, Velling (2023), p. 105.
[58] Ludwigs, Velling (2023), p. 105.
[59] Martini and Nink (2018) p. 1128ff.
[60] Brockmann (2023), p. 293.
[61] Brockmann (2023), p. 293.
[62] Brockmann (2023), p. 293.
[63] Ludwigs, Velling (2023), p. 85.

5 Relationship Between National Rules and the Provisions of the AI Act Concerning Administrations and Public Functions

The AI Regulation (AI Act) came into force on 1 August 2024, and has so far only partially taken effect. Nevertheless, the principles contained in it have already been tackled by German scholars and courts in the light of other European provisions, as the following examples illustrate.

5.1 Dealing with "Predictive Policing"

Predictive policing, which was extensively discussed in German literature long before implementation of the AI Act, revolves around identification of potential threats—such as through intelligent video surveillance—in the context of crime prevention.[64] In this field the Federal Constitutional Court issued a judgment in February 2023, declaring unconstitutional the application of HessenDATA,[65] a system based on the "Gotham" program of the US-American software company Palantir.[66]

With this judgment, the Federal Constitutional Court declared § 25a(1) first alternative of the Hessian Security and Public Order Act (HSOG) and § 49(1) first alternative of the Hamburg Act on Data Processing by the Police (HmbPolDVG) to be unconstitutional.[67] These provisions authorize the police to further process stored personal data by automated data analysis (Hesse) or automated data interpretation (Hamburg).

In this context, the Federal Constitutional Court (BVerfG) found a violation of the right to informational self-determination (*Recht auf informationelle Selbstbestimmung*) under Article 2 (1) in conjunction with Article 1 (1) of the German Basic Law (GG).[68] The BVerfG considered automated processing of stored data sets for preventively combatting certain crimes, without an adequate "threshold for intervention" (*Eingriffsschwelle*), to be disproportionate.[69] A violation of this fundamental right was seen not only in the further use of data but also in the acquisition of sensitive information through automated evaluation or analysis of personal

---

[64] Busche (2024), p. 209.

[65] BVerfG, judgement of the 16.2.2023 - 1 BvR 1547/19, 1 BvR 2634/20; English version under Bundesverfassungsgericht - Decisions search - Judgment of 16 February 2023

[66] Busche (2024), p. 214; Vasel (2023), p. 1174ff.; Wischmeyer (2023), p. 797 f.

[67] In Hesse, the authorities made repeated use of the powers granted under § 25a of the Hessian Police Act (HSOG) through the analysis platform "hessenDATA". In contrast, § 49 of the Hamburg Police Data Processing Act (HmbPolDVG) has not been applied to date.

[68] BVerfG (2023) Mn. 173.

[69] BVerfG (2023), Mn. 165ff.

data. This decision was made in spite of the rationale of these provisions, which is the threat of terrorist violence and organized crime, as well as the increasing use of digital media, requiring information which police authorities can hardly obtain manually and under time pressure.[70] Automated data analysis is therefore considered crucial for successful police action, although linking existing data can lead to new information that approaches "profiling".[71] The Federal Constitutional Court criticized the disproportionality of this regulation because the legislature had not specified what methods of analysis and evaluation were permitted, allowing data mining up to the use of self-learning systems, which can extend to risk assessments in the sense of "predictive policing".[72]

The judgment was made before the AI Act came into force. Now the prohibited practices outlined in Article 5 (1) letter d) are at stake. The following have to be considered: "placing on the market, putting into service for this specific purpose or using an AI system for making risk assessments of natural persons in order to assess or predict the risk of a natural person committing a criminal offence, based solely on profiling them or on assessing their personality traits and characteristics". This norm is directed against "person-based predictive policing", but may be unclear regarding the distinction between profiling and the assessment of personal characteristics.[73] Furthermore, the legitimacy of real-time biometric remote identification is questionable under Article 5(1) letter h) of the AI Act. According to this provision, real-time biometric remote identification in publicly accessible areas for law enforcement purposes is generally prohibited, as for instance, the use of video cameras with automatic face recognition for searching for individuals wanted by the police. However, there are three significant exceptions to this prohibition, which are the search for missing persons, the prevention of immediate and significant danger, and the identification of suspects of serious crimes.[74] This new regulatory framework will make it more complex to balance interests. There are also new procedural requirements under Article 5 (2) AI Act. The deployment of AI can be "authorised only if the law enforcement authority has completed a fundamental rights impact assessment as defined by Article 27 and has registered the system in the EU database according to Article 49".[75] A prior authorisation has to be granted by a judicial authority (Article 5, paragraph 3) or an independent administrative authority and "shall be notified to the relevant market surveillance authority and the national data protection authority."[76]

---

[70] BVerfG (2023), Mn. 167.

[71] BVerfG (2023), Mn. 69.

[72] BVerfG (2023), Mn. 98ff.

[73] Busche (2024), p. 246.

[74] Art. 5 (1) letters h) 1); h) 11); h) 111; Busche (2024), p. 247

[75] Art. 5 (3) AI Act.

[76] Art. 5 (4) AI Act; Busche (2024), p. 247.

5.2 *Schufa-Scoring and Its Comparison with Fully Automated Decisions*

AI systems can be employed as preliminary decision-making tools in various areas, such as the granting of credit. However, their opacity can lead to new forms of discrimination, which is why Article 22 GDPR provides protective mechanisms.[77] This provision is indeed seen as an expression of the regulator's "general unease" towards fully automated decisions.[78] Article 22 (1) GDPR establishes the right of the data subject not to be subject to a decision based solely on automated processing, including profiling. In this context, the 71th Recital explicitly mentions automatic rejection of a credit application "without human intervention".[71] The exceptions of Article 22 (2) GDPR include conclusion of a contract, relevant legal provisions of the Union or member states with appropriate safeguards in place, and explicit consent of the data subject. In the first and third cases, the right to human intervention by a controller and the right to express one's own point of view are specified.

The right to personal intervention by the controller (human in the loop) depends on the possibility of influencing essential aspects of the data processing process. The right to present one's own viewpoint is envisaged by German law at § 24 I 2 VwVfG.[79] It includes human case-by-case review and substantive re-evaluation.[80] Then there are the information and transparency obligations of Article 12 GDPR: the controller must inform the data subject that an automated decision is being made, and must also provide information about the logic involved, the scope, and the consequences of the processing. The data subject's corresponding right to information is stipulated in Article 15 GDPR.[81] The controller must document data processing activities by maintaining a comprehensive record according to Article 30 GDPR.[82]

Breach of these provisions was recently the subject of a case before the European Court of Justice (ECJ), albeit not in connection with an administrative act.[83] The ruling of the ECJ concerned the scoring assigned in Germany by Schufa Holding, a

---

[77] Seitz (2024), p. 841.

[78] Lorse (2021a, b), p. 219.

[79] Martini, Nink (2017), p. 8.

[80] Martini, Nink (2017), p. 4.

[81] Martini, Nink (2017), p. 5.

[82] Martini, Nink (2017), p. 6.

[83] Judgments of the Court of Justice in Case C-634/21|SCHUFA Holding (Scoring) and in Joined Cases C-26/22 and C-64/22| SCHUFA Holding (Discharge of remaining debt). In December 2023, the European Court of Justice (ECJ) handed down a decision on a preliminary ruling by the Administrative Court (VG) of Wiesbaden, at the latter's request. The plaintiff had been denied credit by his bank due to a low SCHUFA creditworthiness score. The plaintiff's request to SCHUFA for information under the General Data Protection Regulation (GDPR) was unsuccessful. A complaint filed with the Hessian Data Protection and Freedom of Information Commissioner was also rejected. The plaintiff subsequently took the decision to the VG. The VG then had to determine, among other things, whether the scoring procedure of SCHUFA constituted an "auto-

private company that provides information about people's credit-worthiness to clients such as banks and landlords. Schufa predicts the probability of future behaviour, such as repayment of a loan or mortgage, by a statistical method based on algorithms. In this context, the Court held that the scoring must be regarded as an "automated decision concerning an individual", prohibited in principle by Art. 22 GDPR if it significantly determines a bank's decision to deny credit, because Schufa's clients rely heavily on its recommendations. This substantive approach of the ECJ was surely inspired by the commendable intention of increasing the protection of interested parties. Nevertheless, as a commentator highlighted, since an objective criterion (whether or not there was any human intervention in the decision-making process) is replaced by more uncertain considerations (whether there is significant conditioning of a human decision), which may be difficult to demonstrate, legal protection is weakened in the absence of clear reference parameters.[84] Known as "automation bias", according to Art. 14 (4) letter b) AI Act, this interpretation demonstrates that even in cases where decisions are not fully automated, but rather where algorithm-based systems are used merely as tools for decision preparation, administrative action does not operate in a legal vacuum.[85]

5.3 ChatGPT and Academic Integrity

The use of AI in higher education, where levels of digitalization vary across universities, is a very controversial issue, not only in Germany. A first distinction concerns digital exams, that can be conducted on-site or online, while electronic examinations (e-exams) involve distribution and processing by information technology systems.[86] Due to their implications for fundamental rights, higher education laws in Germany typically set minimum content standards for examination regulations. Key considerations include occupational freedom under Article 12 and equality under Article 3 of the Basic Law.[87] These conditions are further detailed in the universities' examination regulations (*Prüfungsordnungen*).[88]

A real revolution occurred in November 2022, when OpenAI launched ChatGPT (Chat Generative Pre-Trained Transformer), a dialog-based chatbot that rapidly gained popularity, achieving over 100 million users shortly after its release.[89] Trained on a vast array of internet texts across different topics and styles, ChatGPT

---

mated decision concerning an individual" as intended by the GDPR. Cf. more recently, the Court of Justice in Case C-203/22| Dun & Bradstreet Austria of 27 February 2025.

[84] See more extensively Silvano (2024), p. 281.

[85] Lorse (2021a, b), p. 220.

[86] Ekardt and Bärenwaldt (2024), p. 295.

[87] Ekardt and Bärenwaldt (2024), p. 296 f.

[88] Ekardt and Klotz (2024), p. 545.

[89] Brockmann (2023), p. 288.

can answer factual questions quickly, provide recommendations, assist with creative writing tasks, summarize texts, translate languages, engage in discussions on various subjects and even write poems.[90] Its versatility includes adjusting language styles from formal to casual, from scientific to childish.[91] While ChatGPT has completely changed interactions between humans and algorithms by facilitating dialogue that serves as a training opportunity for applications, it lacks true cognitive understanding of causal relationships, because its operations are based solely on correlations derived from training data.[92]

Generative AI applications like ChatGPT offer substantial benefits as tools but also pose risks if misused—encouraging unethical practices that are difficult to monitor. Students can leverage AI tools to "outsource" portions or even all of their assignments or projects. These tools can optimize writing styles or even generate entire research proposals and analyses almost instantaneously.[93] This capability raises concerns about academic integrity in examinations—especially remote ones—prompting questions about what constitutes "independent" work when AI is involved.[94]

Determining when a piece of work has been prepared "independently", in spite of the use of AI, poses considerable challenges for educators. If AI-generated text passages are not clearly marked or defined in academic frameworks, assessing their originality becomes problematic.[95] To ensure fairness and clarity in academic evaluations, examination regulations should explicitly outline permissible uses of AI tools. Conversely, outright bans on tools like ChatGPT, are impractical, since legally secure proof of the use of AI is not yet possible.

Accordingly, Universities must implement measures to minimize the risk of cheating by clearly communicating acceptable aids during examinations and by considering how performance will be evaluated if AI tools are permitted. The question also arises regarding whether educators/examiners can use AI when grading student work—a practice that could alleviate (tiresome and time consuming) grading burdens and enhance objectivity.[96] However, most examination regulations require human evaluators to justify their grading decisions based on independent assessments. The deployment of AI in grading must therefore comply with existing regulations while ensuring it does not infringe on students' rights or lead to unequal treatment during evaluations.[97]

Unlike use of AI by students in the examination context, the AI Act has a significant impact on its deployment by examiners when grading examinations: use of AI

---

[90] Ekardt and Bärenwaldt (2024), p. 296.

[91] Brockmann (2023), p. 288.

[92] Brockmann (2023), p. 288.

[93] Ekardt and Bärenwaldt (2024), p. 298.

[94] Ekardt and Klotz (2024), p. 545.

[95] Ekardt and Klotz (2024), p. 545.

[96] Ekardt and Klotz (2024), p. 548.

[97] Ekardt and Bärenwaldt (2024), p. 299.

in examination assessment is not a prohibited practice covered by Title II. In particular, this is not a so-called "social scoring", in the context of which an "assessment of social behaviour for general purposes" takes place, a practice, which is generally prohibited under Article 5 (1) letter c) of the AI Regulation.[98] Rather, it is a performance assessment specifically related to professional suitability. Against this background, the use of AI in examination assessment under the AI Act appears to be permissible in principle. However, it follows from Article 6 (2) of the AI Regulation in conjunction with Annex III No. 3 that AI systems used to evaluate performance results in university entrance examinations (lit. b) and examination results in ongoing studies (lit. c), as well as to monitor and detect prohibited behaviour during examinations (lit. d) are high-risk AI systems, which must meet the requirements set out in Chapter 2 of Title III in accordance with Article 8 (1) of the AI Act.[99] Thus, when using AI, the AI Act requires universities to maintain, among other things, a risk management system as defined by Art. 9 AI Act, to prepare technical documentation pursuant to Art. 11 AI Act and to place the use of AI under human oversight as per Art. 14 AI Act.[100]

Rather than banning AI tools like ChatGPT in educational settings, universities should include them as teaching aids, while fostering critical engagement with these technologies among students. Progressive educators advocate integrating AI into curricula to better prepare students for a future where such technologies will play an essential role in various fields.[101]

6 Particular Rules for Public Procurement with Regard to AI Systems

In the field of public procurement it is necessary to differentiate between public contracts above and below the EU threshold. Above the threshold, the last package of public procurement directives of 2014 foresees binding requirements on the use of electronic communication. E-procurement was implemented in Germany by the 2016 Procurement Law Reform Act (*Gesetz zur Modernisierung des Vergaberechts*), which introduced the principle of electronic communication in § 97 (5) of the (federal) Act against Competition Restraints (*Gesetz gegen Wettbewerbsbeschränkungen—GWB*).[102] In October 2018, digital management of procurement procedures above

[98] Ekardt and Bärenwaldt (2024), p. 299.

[99] Ekardt and Bärenwaldt (2024), p. 300.

[100] Ekardt and Bärenwaldt (2024), p. 300.

[101] Furthermore, ChatGPT presents significant challenges regarding copyright law. Recent European legal findings suggest that copyright protection ceases when copied fragments are used in an unrecognizable manner. This raises questions about whether text generated by AI is eligible for copyright protection since German law stipulates that only works created by humans qualify for such protection (§ 2 Urheberrechtsgesetz – UrhG). See also Martini/Wiesenhofer (2024), p. 1ff.

[102] Reichling et al. (2020), p. 249; Reichling et al. (2020a), p. 308.

the EU threshold became mandatory in Germany for contracting authorities and bidders.[103] For procurement of supplies and services below the EU threshold, the relevant regulation (*Verfahrensordnung für die Vergabe öffentlicher Liefer- und Dienstleistungsaufträge unterhalb der EU-Schwelle—UVgO*) likewise prescribed digital management of tenders by 1 January 2020, although there is no full regulatory uniformity due to the federal organization of the German State.[104] For procurement of works below the EU threshold, electronic communication is not yet mandatory or "end to end" (*medienbruchfrei*).[105] Since without digitization the use of AI is inconceivable, the German doctrine highlights tackling this first challenge before contemplating automated solutions. The full potential of digital administrative processes can only be realized if the administration avoids a hybrid (partly electronic, partly analogue) approach.[106]

Public procurement is deemed crucial by the European Commission for the dissemination of Artificial Intelligence (AI) in the public sector. The European procurement directives 2004/18/EC and 2004/17/EC had already introduced electronic auctions and dynamic purchasing systems (DPS) as well as the possibility to use electronic communication devices.[107] Against this backdrop, the Commission is currently developing a program for the adoption of AI, known as the Adopt AI program, to promote automated public procurement contracts. This program aims to increase the demand for trustworthy AI, the public sector potentially serving as a pioneer in this area.[108]

There are numerous possible applications of artificial intelligence (AI) in the field of public procurement. AI models can automatically analyse contracts, identify relevant clauses, uncover risks, and assist in more precise error verification. AI-driven chatbots and virtual assistants can answer legal questions and provide information.[109]

A future obligation to implement artificial intelligence (AI) arising from European provisions cannot be excluded. Due to introduction of the mentioned digital solutions for various steps of the procurement cycle, the Commission believes that significant amounts of data will be generated.[110] The employment of automated decisions, introduced in Germany in other sectors, such as the tax and social fields, can be useful in the field of e-procurement. It can also prompt the use of modern data-mining techniques in proceedings that involve the transmission of huge amounts of data to contracting authorities, for example for the evaluation of bids, significantly improving the quality of assignments.

---

[103] Burgi et al. (2022), Mn. 6.

[104] Reichling et al. (2020), p. 250.

[105] Reichling et al. (2020), p. 249.

[106] Martini (2021), Mn. 52.

[107] Burgi et al. (2022), Mn. 3; Benvenuti (2024), p. 89.

[108] Braun (2023), p. 563.

[109] Braun (2023), p. 565.

[110] Braun (2023), p. 567.

7 What Has Been Done to Train Public Employees?

In the last few years various training programs have been run by the Federal Government and the *Länder* in the field of digitization of public administrations. For example, "eGovCampus" is a project supported by the IT Planning Council (the coordinating body of the Federation and the *Länder* in the field of digital technologies) to promote digital skills. It is complemented by "Qualifica Digitalis", a project initiated by the IT Planning Council and the State of Bremen, and also by "KommunalCampus" of the Rhine-Neckar metropolitan region and the Bergstrasse district.[111] The IT Planning Council, the Federal Ministry of the Interior and the Federal IT Cooperation (FITKO), which was established in January 2020 as a joint institution of the Federal Government and the *Länder*, are the stakeholder of Germany's digitization strategy. FITKO is the operational backbone of the IT Planning Council, coordinating and implementing digitalization projects across federal and state levels.[112] In accordance with the principle of subsidiarity, digital administrative services are initially developed by one or more federal states and then made available to other federal states and municipalities for joint or subsequent use, often against payment. This approach is guided by the "one for all principle" (*Einer für Alle-Prinzip—EfA-Prinzip*), which promotes nationwide coordination and avoids redundant development of online services in the same field.[113] In this context, a platform for online solutions at municipal level is being promoted by FITKO through GovDigital, a public enterprise in the legal form of a cooperative.[114] Nevertheless, the process of reuse is challenging due to differing technical standards and has so far been slow and iterative.[115]

According to the provisions of Article 4 AI Act (AI literacy), the necessary skills have to be trained by public administrations.[116] First attempts are being reported. For example, in October 2024, the Ministers of Education of the *Länder* agreed on recommendations for the use of AI in schools. They suggested "constructive-critical" use of these technologies. The training of teachers has to be adapted in this framework: besides active application and integration of AI into teaching, teachers must be made aware of the legal framework and enabled to understand the technical principles and to adequately assess the opportunities, limitations and risks of AI.[117]

---

[111] Seckelmann and Brunzel (2021); Catacli (2022), p. 71ff.

[112] Seckelmann and Berger (2020), p. 54.

[113] Richter (2021) p. VI; Seckelmann and Berger (2020), p. 54.

[114] Die Genossenschaft - govdigital

[115] Marktplatz (für EfA-Leistungen) - govdigital

[116] "*Providers and deployers of AI systems shall take measures to ensure, to their best of their possibilities, a sufficient level of AI literacy of their staff and other persons who deal with the operation and use of AI systems on their behalf, taking their technical knowledge, experience, education and training into account and the context the AI systems are to be used in, and considering the persons or groups of persons on whom the AI systems are to be used.*"

[117] www.kmk.org/fileadmin/veroeffentlichungen_beschluesse/2024/2024_10_10-Handlungsempfehlung-KI.pdf

In 2023, at federal level, the Ministry of the Interior (BMI) established a Consulting Centre for Artificial Intelligence (BeKI) designed to be a central point of contact and driving force for the federal administration to enhance coordination of AI deployment. Previously, each department had its own AI competence centre, an approach that was deemed inefficient. BeKI is currently developing an internal AI guideline for the BMI and initiating pilot implementation projects in four areas of activity (consulting, networking, competence building and knowledge management). It aims to ensure a coordinated approach by the federal administration in the utilization of AI technologies and the development of corresponding AI infrastructure and competence.[118]

In this context, the KIPITZ initiative (KI-Portal of the ITZ Bund) aims to support the "democratization of AI in public administration". Launched as a shared platform for AI applications in the federal administration, KIPITZ is designed to facilitate easy access to AI applications for federal administrative employees, integrate these applications into their work processes, and ensure legal certainty for public authorities.[119] KIPITZ has created a development environment to drive innovation based on the "one for all principle". It functions as a "marketplace of AI possibilities", a platform to promote the use of AI in administration and to generate subsequent utilization. The IT Planning Council can involve federal states and municipalities in the platform, enabling the entire public administration to be interconnected through KIPITZ. In line with Article 49 of the AI Act, the registration of high-risk AI systems is conducted in a publicly accessible database as stipulated by Article 71 of the AI Act.

The BeKI is also responsible, in joint leadership with the Data Lab of the Federal Chancellery, for building an overarching AI infrastructure for large language models and related applications. The federal administration in Germany is indeed developing open-source components with multiple AI language models through the AI portal KIPITZ.[120] This development reveals a substantial preference for in-house solutions and domestic AI capabilities in the German government's approach to generative AI in public administration.

As an additional example, the noteworthy Police AI Campus (*KI-Campus der Polizei*) was established to enhance security in the use of AI in the face of its increasing utilization by criminals (cybercrime). The objectives include enhancing knowledge transfer, facilitating networking, and providing concrete support for the deployment of AI. The AI Campus is an overarching collaborative initiative: it has been led by the Federal Ministry of the Interior (BMI) for 2 years and is now part of an IT consolidation project. In the framework of AI Campus, general information about AI and the specific needs of the police are both addressed. In line with Article 4 of the AI Act, a basic AI training program has been developed. An AI coaching

---

[118] https://www.digitale-verwaltung.de/SharedDocs/downloads/Webs/DV/DE/Transformation/akteurssteckbrief-beki.pdf?__blob=publicationFile&v=5

[119] https://egovernmentwettbewerb.de/wp-content/uploads/2024/06/ITZ_Bund_GPT4Gov_Kat_1.pdf

[120] CIO Bund - Daten und KI

program, which includes interdisciplinary evaluation involving ethicists, jurists, computer scientists and police experts, has also been introduced. The AI Campus platform (KI-Campus.org) has developed various general training formats as well as specific training programs for police officers.[121]

In accordance with Article 57 of the AI Act, national regulatory sandboxes are also developed as protected environments. This is another key point of German scholarly debate, namely the promotion of digital innovation, not only by administrative bodies, but also and especially by start-ups and SMEs, in the wake of the AI Act.[122] This goal is pursued through the obligation of member states to establish these sandboxes, according to Art. 57 (1) AI Act, that offer a controlled environment to foster innovation and facilitate the development, training and testing of AI systems before they are placed on the market. These simulations under real world conditions aim to reduce market access barriers under the oversight of the competent supervising authorities. The significance of this possibility is noteworthy, considering the obligations imposed on providers and suppliers of AI systems under Articles 16 (obligations of providers of high-risk AI systems), 26 (Obligations of deployers of high-risk AI systems) and 27 (fundamental rights impact assessment for high-risk AI systems) of the AI Act. It must also be considered that any modification or adaptation of commercially available AI systems for public administration purposes can transform an administrative body into a provider of AI solutions, thereby making it subject to the corresponding regulatory obligations.

8 Organizational Transformations Determined by AI Technology

Implementation of the AI Act notoriously requires establishment of new national authorities. According to Art. 70, member states have to designate "at least one notifying authority and at least one market surveillance authority", which are accorded comprehensive supervisory powers, including "full access to the documentation as well as the training, validation and testing data sets used for the development of high-risk AI systems" (Article 74, paragraph 12, AI Act) as well as to the source code of the high-risk AI.[123] Implementation of these provisions in the German federal system raises different questions. One is linked to inclusion of these authorities in ministerial organization and to possible involvement of the *Länder*, which—as the main actors of German executive federalism—deploy AI systems in their own administrations. Although according to the Constitution, the federal government can fulfil the tasks of AI supervision through its own authorities,[124] the AI Act also

[121] kikampus.pdf.

[122] Roth-Isigkeit (2024a), p. 20; Roth-Isigkeit (2024), p. 18.

[123] Art. 74 (12 and 13) AI Act.

[124] Art. 74 (1) No. 11 GG

imposes obligations on deployers of AI systems. This could imply centralization of competence at federal level and the exercise of sovereign authority over the states. In this regard, it is argued that a complete consolidation of regulatory tasks at federal level would require a state treaty.[125] Accordingly, compliance with EU regulations would imply a new balance of the powers enshrined in the German *Grundgesetz*.

The question of the authority best suited to fulfil the tasks outlined in the regulation is currently a topic of intense discussion. The preferred solution appears to be the centralization of these tasks in the Federal Network Agency (*Bundesnetzagentur*—BNetzA).[126] Data protection authorities are also an alternative being considered. This approach is supported by the fact that AI-related matters often overlap with data protection issues, potentially requiring coordination between the two domains.[127] On the other hand, the high demands on resources and competence make a centralized solution more preferable. The creation of an authority *sui generis* is also deemed conceivable.[128]

The second subject of discussion is related to the range of autonomous powers of these authorities and to whether they may enjoy full independence outside the sphere of traditional administration and outside the democratic circuit, in order to comply with the requirements of Art. 70 (1) AI Act: independence, impartiality and objectivity.[129] In this context, German legal scholarship points out that unlike the Digital Services Act (DSA), the AI Act does not require complete independence of the acting authorities. A high degree of independence from the state is necessary for the neutrality of democratic will-formation in areas such as those covered by the DSA, but does not appear necessary in the case of the AI Act.[130]

9 Conclusions

In December 2023, the President of the European Commission, Ursula von der Leyen, announced that the AI Act was the "first-ever comprehensive legal framework on Artificial Intelligence worldwide".[131] The EU is not however the only entity that has created a horizontal legal framework. China has been pursuing a "New Generation AI Plan" since 2017, aiming to become the world's leading AI power by 2035, and the United States invested $47.4 billion in this field alone in 2023.[132] It is also worth noting that, almost simultaneously to the AI Act, in May 2024 the

[125] Roth-Isigkeit (2024a), p. 19.
[126] Roth-Isigkeit (2024a), p. 19.
[127] Vasel (2024), p. 833.
[128] Vasel (2024), p. 833.
[129] Korte (2024), p. 773; Roth-Isigkeit (2024a), p. 19.
[130] Korte (2024), p. 773.
[131] Vasel (2024), p. 829.
[132] Vasel (2024), p. 833.

Committee of Ministers of the Council of Europe adopted a Framework Convention on Artificial Intelligence and Human Rights, Democracy and the Rule of Law, which is also open to signature by non-European states.[133] In this context, the question arises whether a "Brussels Effect" can be expected and whether the global AI industry will indeed align itself with the European AI Act.[134]

These pages indicate that there is no EU regulation obliging member states to automate administrative acts, or conversely prohibiting them.[135] In general, German administrative procedure is cautious of algorithms, equating them with "black boxes".[136] Mostly conditionally programmed, deterministic algorithms (known as "explainable AI") are therefore in use.[137]

Despite efforts to standardize administrative actions in order to achieve more economical and expedient processing, in line with European law, the general intention is to apply AI without compromising justice in individual cases.[138] At the same time, the immense benefits of automated processing are to be fully exploited. Following this approach, AI has to be used to provide an information basis and a "knowledge repository" for preparing administrative decisions, to facilitate their communication to third parties, and to design administrative proceedings better,[139] always bearing in mind the principles of the rule of law and the social state, as well as the procedural dimension of fundamental rights.

As scholars have noted in ongoing discussions, the AI regulation appears to offer limited flexibility for member states (in contrast to the GDPR).[140] It seems to restrict national discretion, with the exception of the mentioned provisions on notifying and surveillance authorities. Germany faces a dual challenge in early 2025 with the federal election on February 23 and the ongoing implementation of the EU AI Act. The public administration needs to engage intensively with this complex situation, as the AI Act implementation law is not expected to be enacted in the immediate future. Many areas classified as high-risk AI systems by the AI Regulation concern the activities of public authorities. For instance, according to Annex III No. 2, "AI systems intended to be used as safety components in the management and operation of critical digital infrastructure, road traffic, or in the supply of water, gas, heating or electricity" are considered high-risk. The same can be said of AI systems in the field of education and vocational training (No. 3), as well as in personnel recruitment and management (No. 4). According to No. 5 lit. a, high-risk also includes governmental AI systems for assessing whether natural persons are entitled to public support services and benefits, including healthcare services.[141] Many other exam-

[133] Seitz (2024), p. 837.

[134] Vasel (2024), p. 829.

[135] Ludwigs, Velling (2023), p. 85.

[136] Eichenhofer (2023), p. 99.

[137] Eichenhofer (2023), p. 96.

[138] Eichenhofer (2023), p. 99.

[139] Eichenhofer (2023), p. 93.

[140] Marchetti (2023), p. 88.

[141] Guckelberger (2025), p. 48.

ples could be cited. Actually, AI opens up a significant challenge for public administration. It underscores the need to align AI implementation with core public values. This alignment necessitates the development of strong ethical frameworks to ensure that AI deployment serves and protects the public interest.

References

Augsberg I (2019) Herausforderungen und Innovationen im Verwaltungsverfahrensrecht. In: De Lucia L, Wollenschläger F (eds) Sfide e innovazioni nel diritto pubblico. Nomos, Baden-Baden, pp 85–100

Benvenuti M (2024) Le prime esperienze Consip in materia di digitalizzazione. In: Marchetti B, Mattarella BG (eds) La digitalizzazione dei contratti pubblici nel nuovo codice. Giappichelli, Torino, pp 89–95

Bombardelli M (2011) Democrazia partecipativa e assetto policentrico dell'organizzazione amministrativa. In: Arena G, Cortese F (eds) Per governare insieme: il federalismo come metodo. Cedam, Padova, pp 17–39

Braun C (2023) Künstliche Intelligenz im Vergabeverfahren NzBau 563-568

Braun-Binder N (2016a) Elektronische Bekanntgabe von Verwaltungsakten über Behördenportale. NVwZ:342–347

Braun-Binder N (2016b) Vollständig automatisierter Erlass von Verwaltungsakten und Bekanntgabe über Behördenportale. DÖV:891–898

Braun-Binder N (2016c) Vollautomatisierte Verwaltungsverfahren im allgemeinen Verwaltungsverfahrensrecht? NVwZ:960–965

Braun-Binder N (2019) Vollautomatisierte Verwaltungsverfahren, voll automatisiert erlassene Verwaltungsakte und elektronische Aktenführung. In: Seckelmann M (ed) Digitalisierte Verwaltung - Vernetztes E-Government, 2nd edn. Erich Schmidt Verlag, Berlin, pp 311–326

Braun-Binder N (2024) Vollautomatisierte Verwaltungsverfahren, vollautomatisiert erlassene Verwaltungsakte und elektronische Aktenführung. In: Seckelmann M (ed) Digitalisierte Verwaltung – Vernetztes E-Government, 3rd edn. Erich Schmidt Verlag, Berlin, pp 435–452

Brockmann T (2023) ChatGPT, die Lehre und die Verwaltung – wie verändert KI unsere Institutionen? VBl 287–295

Buoso E (2021) La pubblica Amministrazione in Germania nell'era dell'Intelligenza Artificiale: procedimenti completamente automatizzati e decisioni amministrative robotiche. Persona e Amministrazione 495–524

Burgi M, Dreher M, Opitz M (2022) Beck'scher Vergaberechtskommentar, 4th edn. C.H. Beck, München

Busche D (2024) Algorithmenbasierte Risikoerkennung – Potenzial und Grenzen des staatlichen Einsatzes. VerwArch 149:207–258

Catacli D (2022) Verwaltung im digitalen Zeitalter. Springer Fachmedien, Wiesbaden

Eichenhofer J (2023) Der vollautomatisierte Verwaltungsakt zwischen Effizienz und Rechtsschutzgebot. DÖV:93–100

Ekardt F, Bärenwaldt M (2024) Digitalisiertes Hochschulrecht: Online-Prüfungen, Benotungen, ChatGPT und Anwesenheitspflicht NJ 295–301

Ekardt F, Klotz PC (2024) Nutzung von KI-Systemen in der Hochschulprüfung. MMR:545–548

Fraenkel-Haeberle C (2020) Fully digitalized administrative procedures in the German legal system. European Review of Digital Administration and Law:105–112

Fraenkel-Haeberle C (2021) Procedimenti amministrativi algoritmici: la risposta tedesca. Persona e Amministrazione:525–550

Guckelberger A (2019) E-Government: Ein Paradigmenwechsel in Verwaltung und Verwaltungsrecht? VVDStRL 78:235–282

Guckelberger A (2025) Hochrisiko-KI-Systeme in der Verwaltung. DÖV:45–56
Jacquemet-Gauché A, Stelkens U (2016) Caractères essentiels du droit allemand de la procédure administrative. In: Auby JB (ed) Droit comparé de la procédure administrative. bruylant, Paris, pp 15–35
Korte S (2024) Verfassungsrechtliche Regelungsaufträge im Bereich der Digitalisierung der Verwaltung. DÖV:770–776
Kube H (2019) E-Government: Ein Paradigmenwechsel in Verwaltung und Verwaltungsrecht? VVDStRL 78:289–332
Lorse J (2021a) Entscheidungsfindung durch künstliche Intelligenz – Zukunft der öffentlichen Verwaltung? NVwZ:1657–1661
Lorse J (2021b) Künstliche Intelligenz im Dienstrecht – bauen wir Windmühlen oder Mauern. ZBR:217–226
Ludwigs M, Velling A (2023) Der vollständig automatisierte Verwaltungsakt in den Grenzen des Europa- und Verfassungsrechts. VerwArch:71--106.
Marchetti B (2023) Artificial intelligence and public authorities: Does the European AI act protect public values? ERPL/REDP 36:67–90
Martini M (2021) Digitalisierung der Verwaltung. In: Kahl W, Ludwigs M (eds) Handbuch des Verwaltungsrechts, vol I. C.F. Müller, Heidelberg, pp 1105–1150
Martini M, Nink D (2017) Wenn Maschinen entscheiden… – vollautomatisierte Verwaltungsverfahren und der Persönlichkeitsschutz. NVwZ:1–14
Martini M, Nink D (2018) Subsumtionsautomaten ante portas? Zu den Grenzen der Automatisierung in verwaltungsrechtlichen (Rechtsbehelfs-)verfahren. DVBl:1128–1138
Martini M, Ruschemeier H (2023) KI und öffentliches Recht. In: Hoeren T, Sieber U, Holznagel B (eds) Handbuch Multimediarecht. Beck, München, pp 1–48
Martini M, Wiesenhofer C (2024) Auf dem Weg zur Regulierung von General-Purpose-AI – eine erste Bestandsaufnahme und Kritik der Regelungsentwürfe. NVwZ:1–19
Maurer H, Waldhoff C (2024) Allgemeines Verwaltungsrecht, 21th edn. C.H. Beck, München
Reichling I, Scheumann NK, Lampe O (2020) e-Vergabe – Ist das Vergaberecht im Zeitalter der Digitalisierung angekommen? (part I). GewArch 248–251
Reichling I, Scheumann NK, Lampe O (2020a) e-Vergabe – Ist das Vergaberecht im Zeitalter der Digitalisierung angekommen? (part II). GewArch 308–313
Richter M (2021) Geleitwort. In: Seckelmann M, Brunzel M (eds) Handbuch Onlinezugangsgesetz – Potentiale – Synergien – Herausforderungen. Springer, Berlin, pp V–VI
Roth-Isigkeit D (2024) Stellungnahme im Rahmen der öffentlichen mündlichen Anhörung am 15. Mai 2024 des Digitalausschusses des Bundestages
Roth-Isigkeit D (2024a) Der neue Rechtsrahmen für künstliche Intelligenz in der Europäischen Union. Künstliche Intelligenz und Recht:15–20
Schmitz H (2018) § 1 VwVfG. In: Stelkens P, Bonk HJ, Sachs M (eds) Verwaltungsverfahrensgesetz, Kommentar, 9th edn. C.H. Beck, München
Seckelmann M, Berger C (2020) Die Nutzerkommune und das Bürgerkonto – partizipative Gestaltungsoptionen nach dem Onlinezugangsgesetz. In: Braun Binder N, Feld LP, Huber PM, Poier K, Wittreck F (eds) Jahrbuch für direkte Demokratie 2019. Nomos, Baden-Baden, pp 38–62
Seckelmann M, Brunzel M (2021) Das Onlinezugangsgesetz im Kontext einer digital vernetzten Gesellschaft und datengetriebenen Wirtschaft: Zur Einleitung. In: Seckelmann M, Brunzel M (eds) Handbuch Onlinezugangsgesetz – Potentiale – Synergien – Herausforderungen. Beck, Heidelberg, pp 1–13
Seitz C (2024) Grundrechtsschutz und künstliche Intelligenz – Das KI-Gesetz der EU und die KI-Konvention des Europarats. EuZW:836–846
Silvano C (2024) La nozione di "decisione completamente automatizzata" sotto la lente della Corte di Giustizia: il caso Schufa. CERIDAP:270–306
Vasel JJ (2023) Verfassungsrechtliche Fesseln? – Karlsruher Urteil zur automatisierten Datenanalyse. NJW:1174–1178

Vasel JJ (2024) Sieben Sünden und Defizite europäischer KI-Regulierung. EuZW:829–835
Wischmeyer T (2023) Grundrechte: automatisierte Datenanalyse durch die Polizei. JuS:797–798
Ziekow J (2018) Das Verwaltungsverfahrensrecht in der Digitalisierung der Verwaltung. NVwZ:1169–1172

Cristina Fraenkel-Haeberle is Professor of Public Law at the German University of Administrative Sciences Speyer (Germany) and Senior Researcher at the National Institute for Public Administration Germany. Her main research interests include European and comparative administrative law, university law, digitalization, and civil service.

AI Systems in French Public Administration: Implementation, Legal Safeguards, and Organizational Evolution in the Context of EU Regulation

Lucie Cluzel-Métayer and Nina Lasbleiz

Contents

Abstract The integration of artificial intelligence (AI) into the French public administration is part of a digital transformation initiated in the 1970s. While AI has the potential to enhance key functions such as personal identification, fraud detection, and access to public services, its use raises significant legal and ethical concerns, particularly regarding transparency and data protection. Projects such as

L. Cluzel-Métayer (✉) · N. Lasbleiz
Nanterre University, Law Department, Nanterre, France
e-mail: lucie.cluzelmetayer@parisnanterre.fr; nina.lasbleiz@parisnanterre.fr

F. Decarolis et al. (eds.), *The EU Digital Regulation and its Impact on Member States*, European Union and its Neighbours in a Globalized World 27,
https://doi.org/10.1007/978-3-032-06490-5_4

Parcoursup, ALICEM, and the scoring algorithm implemented by the National Family Allowance Fund (CNAF) have sparked controversies over surveillance and algorithmic fairness. Despite the existing legal framework (French Data Protection Act and GDPR), France lacks specific AI regulations, a gap partially filled by the European AI Act. The adoption of AI in France also requires an organisational overhaul of the administration, upskilling of public officials, and the strengthening of the CNIL's role to ensure effective oversight of AI algorithms used by public authorities.

1 Introduction

As the European Union advances its ambitious regulatory framework for artificial intelligence, the French administration's use of AI systems has yet to be accompanied by a thorough analysis or reflection on the critical legal issues involved. However, the integration of AI systems in the French public sector is not just a technological breakthrough, but a profound transformation that calls administrative law into question, for example by affecting the definition of an administrative decision, the rules governing administrative decision-making, the administrative trial or even judicial review. It also has an impact on the relationship between public officials and citizens, who are increasingly confronted with online administrative procedures or chatbots to answer their questions, as well as on the internal organization of the administration.

The French administration's use of AI systems, which has become more widespread thanks to the deployment of the National Strategy for Artificial Intelligence launched in 2018,[1] is part of a broader process of digital transformation of the State that began in the 1970s.[2] This long-term evolution has progressively integrated various digital tools to enhance the efficiency and effectiveness of public services. The SAFARI[3] file scandal in France during the early 1970s served as a starting point of awareness on the potential dangers of digital technologies and privacy awareness. The SAFARI project aimed to establish a centralized computer database of the population, using social security numbers as a universal identifier across all administrative files. This initiative, however, faced intense criticism from journalist Philippe Boucher, who denounced the project's potentially repressive implications in a 1974 press article titled "SAFARI ou la chasse aux Français" published in *Le Monde*.[4] Boucher's article highlighted the risk of granting the administration excessive

[1] Ministry of the Economy, Finance and Industrial and Digital Sovereignty, *La stratégie nationale pour l'intelligence artificielle*, online: https://www.entreprises.gouv.fr/fr/numerique/enjeux/la-strategie-nationale-pour-l-ia

[2] See Nora and Minc (1978)

[3] Automated system for administrative files and individual directories.

[4] See Boucher (1974).

centralized access to personal information, leading to widespread public concern. The controversy surrounding SAFARI ultimately compelled the Prime Minister to stop the project. In response, the government established a Commission about IT and freedom to develop safeguards ensuring that information technology advances in a manner that upholds privacy and individual freedoms. The Commission's recommendations culminated in the 1978 Data Protection Act,[5] which established the independent administrative authority known as the *Commission Nationale de l'Informatique et des Libertés* (CNIL) to oversee the protection of personal data.

The 1990s marked a decisive turning point in the integration of digital technologies within public administrations, notably through the introduction of teleservices for citizens[6] and the expansion of video surveillance systems in public spaces.[7] Since then, the digitization of administration has continued at a steady pace, accompanied by the implementation of specific legislation to govern these new practices. For example, in 2016, France adopted the Law for a Digital Republic (*Loi pour une République numérique*),[8] which requires public or private entities entrusted with a public service mission to open their data free of charge to enable reuse and provides a legal framework for individual decision-making based on algorithms. However, it is important to note that France has not yet adopted specific regulations for artificial intelligence systems, despite the increasing integration of these technologies into administrative processes. The COVID-19 crisis further accelerated this evolution, forcing the administration to rapidly adapt in order to fulfill its public service missions. Nevertheless, the crisis also highlighted the absence of a clear legislative framework for AI, highlighting the growing need for regulation in this emerging field.

Three key factors contribute to this substantial expansion in France. First, it seeks to enhance the performance of public action by making processes simpler, more efficient, and more secure, while optimizing human and financial resources. Digital technology is primarily seen as a tool to improve the services provided to citizens, for example, by reducing response times to inquiries and minimizing human errors. Second, the fact that AI systems are deployed to help decision-making is anticipated to improve decision-making quality by harnessing large datasets for optimal adaptation to individual requirements and ensuring impartiality through algorithmic neutrality. Moreover, the automation of processes is expected to significantly speed up decision times. Finally, efficiency gains are a major driver; automation enables a more effective allocation of human and material resources, allowing these to focus on tasks that cannot be handled by algorithms. Indeed, in a speech on the transformation of public action, French Prime Minister Gabriel Attal

---

[5] Loi n° 78-17 du 6 janv. 1978 *relative à l'informatique, aux fichiers et aux libertés*, JORF du 7 janv. 1978.

[6] See Cluzel-Métayer (2013).

[7] See Darras and Deharbe (1996), pp. 79–90.

[8] Loi n° 2016-1321 du 7 octobre 2016 *pour une République numérique*, JORF du 8 oct. 2016.

emphasized this point with a striking phrase: "Leave the tedious tasks to AI, and the connection with our citizens to public agents".[9]

In France, digital technologies are primarily employed by the administration within the scope of public service missions. These technologies are particularly used to serve traditional administrative purposes, such as algorithmic video surveillance to maintain public order or scoring algorithms to combat fraud. Other traditional administrative objectives are also addressed: digital tools can be used to allocate students to higher education programs, prevent public order disturbances, and preliminarily review administrative files. The areas of application are numerous and are expected to increase in the coming years.

Therefore, this study provides an overview of the use of AI systems in French public administration. First, by analyzing the purposes for which such systems are used, we will highlight the contested and debated cases that have emerged (I). Next, we will identify the French legal rules that can be applied to AI systems, despite not being specific to AI, and examine how these rules are complemented by the European AI Act (II). Finally, we will analyze the consequences of implementing AI systems on the organization of public administration. While these impacts are significant, not all of the consequences are fully understood in France at this time (III). This study will offer a preliminary assessment of the extent of the digital transformation driven by AI in France and the responses it has prompted.

2 Controversial Use Cases of AI in French Public Administration

AI systems are employed in French public administration for five main purposes,[10] each sparking significant debate. Firstly, AI is employed for identification purposes (1). Secondly, AI aids in determining access to rights or public services (2). Thirdly, AI systems are instrumental in fraud detection (3). Fourthly, risk identification is another critical application, where predictive analytics anticipate potential public safety threats or health crises (4). Lastly, AI enhances communication with citizens through chatbots and virtual assistants that provide information and support to citizens (5).

[9] See Attal (2024).

[10] We use the classification made by the 2019 UN Special Rapporteur on Extreme Poverty and Human Rights applying it to the French case. See: Report of the Special Rapporteur on Extreme Poverty and Human Rights (2019), p 5 and Cluzel-Métayer (2022).

2.1 AI Systems for Identification Purposes

The verification of personal identity is an interesting area for the introduction of digital technologies. In 2015, a teleservice called "FranceConnect" was established, enabling users to authenticate themselves with various teleservice providers using an existing account (such as a tax account) for which their identity has already been verified, thus eliminating the need to create a new account. FranceConnect does not generate a digital identity but associates a verified identity from one online account with several others. Since 2021, this teleservice has been qualified as "high security level" by ANSSI (the National Agency for Information Systems Security), allowing for cross-border electronic authentication in accordance with the European eIDAS regulation.[11]

In 2017, the initiative to establish a secure digital identity was highlighted in a roadmap by the French Ministry of the Interior.[12] As the national identity card allows individuals to prove their identity in the physical world, digital identity aims to meet the need for a simple and secure way to verify one's identity online. Digital identity was thus presented as a "crucial tool for accessing rights" with a dual purpose: to mitigate the risk of online fraud for citizens and to establish digital identity standards that would streamline administrative processes. The ALICEM (*Authentification en Ligne Certifiée sur Mobile* - Certified Online Authentication on Mobile) project was born out of the desire to simplify access to online administrative services, while guaranteeing a high level of security. This project represented an important step towards the verification of digital identity using biometric technology. Developed by the French government, ALICEM was designed to enable secure online authentication for citizens using facial recognition, which compares a live video selfie with the biometric data stored in the user's identity document.[13]

While ALICEM aimed to simplify access to online public services by providing a convenient method of identity verification, it has sparked controversy and debate, particularly regarding privacy protection. Critics argued that the use of facial recognition technology could lead to wider surveillance implications and potential violations of individual freedoms—including the freedom to come and go anonymously. The association La Quadrature du Net had challenged before the Conseil d'État, France's highest administrative court, the decree authorizing the creation of ALICEM on the grounds that users' consent to the processing of their biometric data was not valid, in line with the CNIL's deliberation on the draft decree.[14]

---

[11] Regulation (EU) n° 910/2014 of the European parliament and of the Council of 23 July 2014 on electronic identification and trust services for electronic transactions in the internal market and repealing Directive 1999/93/EC.

[12] See Ministère de l'Intérieur (2017), p 32.

[13] Décret n° 2019-452 du 13 mai 2019 *autorisant la création d'un moyen d'identification électronique dénommé "Authentification en ligne certifiée sur mobile"*.

[14] CNIL, Délibération n° 2018-342 du 18 octobre 2018 *portant avis sur projet de décret autorisant la création d'un traitement automatisé permettant d'authentifier une identité numérique par voie électronique dénommé "Application de lecture de l'identité d'un citoyen en mobilité" (ALICEM)*

However, this appeal was dismissed by the Conseil d'État[15] but the project was abandoned a few months later by the government. It was replaced by a more conventional service that does not utilize facial recognition. This new service, known as the Digital Identity Guarantee Service (*Service de garantie de l'identité numérique*—SGIN), is designed to enable holders of a national identity card to verify and authenticate their identity to public or private organizations. This is achieved through an application installed on their electronic devices, which facilitates contactless reading of the identity component.[16]

2.2 AI Systems for Determining Access to Rights or Public Services

Algorithms used to determine whether individuals can access rights—particularly social rights—and public services are becoming increasingly numerous. The one that has gathered the most attention in France is undoubtedly the Parcoursup algorithm.

The "Parcoursup" case in France traces its roots to the controversies surrounding its predecessor, the "Admission Post-Bac" (APB) system. Established in 2009, APB was an algorithm-based platform designed to manage the allocation of university seats to high school graduates. Over time, however, the opacity of APB's algorithm drew increasing scrutiny. Specifically, in 2016, an association sought access to the algorithm's source code, invoking the right to access administrative documents and personal data under French law.[17] This request highlighted concerns regarding the fairness and transparency of the admissions process, particularly due to the use of a random draw (*tirage au sort*) in cases where demand exceeded supply in certain academic programs. In response to the growing dissatisfaction with APB, the French government decided to replace it with a new platform—Parcoursup—in 2018. Parcoursup was designed not only to improve transparency and fairness in the allocation of university places but also to better align with the educational aspirations and academic records of students. Unlike its predecessor, Parcoursup does not rely on random selection but instead incorporates multiple criteria to evaluate applicants. The operation of Parcoursup is based on a central algorithm that manages the overall allocation process. However, a significant innovation lies in the existence of local algorithms used by individual universities. These local algorithms are designed

et modifiant le code de l'entrée et du séjour des étrangers et du droit d'asile, demande d'avis n° 18008244.

[15] CE, 4 nov. 2020, *ALICEM*, n° 432656.

[16] Décret n° 2022-676 du 26 avril 2022 *autorisant la création d'un moyen d'identification électronique dénommé "Service de garantie de l'identité numérique" (SGIN) et abrogeant le décret n° 2019-452 du 13 mai 2019 autorisant la création d'un moyen d'identification électronique dénommé "Authentification en ligne certifiée sur mobile"*.

[17] See Crouzet J (2017), p 46; Graveleau S (2016).

to assess candidates based on specific criteria determined by each institution, such as academic performance, extracurricular activities, and motivation letters.[18] While this system allows for greater flexibility and tailored admissions, it has also raised concerns about consistency and equity in the selection of candidates.

One of the primary challenges faced by Parcoursup has been ensuring transparency in the admissions process. French law mandates that administrative algorithms principal characteristics be accessible to the public,[19] a principle reinforced by the controversies surrounding APB. However, the complexity of these algorithms and the decentralized nature of decision-making have led to debates over the adequacy of the information provided to applicants and the public. While the government has published general explanations of how Parcoursup works and his source code,[20] the specific criteria used by individual universities often remain opaque.

Thus, the implementation of Parcoursup has led to a series of legal disputes, as applicants and advocacy groups have sought greater transparency and fairness in the admissions process. Several cases have been brought before administrative courts, requesting access to universities' local algorithms.[21] The difficulty lay in striking a balance between the need for transparency, the autonomy of universities and the protection of sensitive data. A compromise was finally reached to set up a dual-track system. This system distinguishes between the national Parcoursup platform, and the procedures employed by universities and higher education establishments. While Parcoursup operates under a transparent system, as required by French law, some institutions benefit from a special status that allows them to bypass the national procedure. These establishments are not subject to the general system of access to administrative documents and source codes, in order to guarantee the secrecy of educational deliberations. The implementation of this dual-track system has been legally validated by both the Conseil d'État[22] and the Conseil Constitutionnel.[23] Both courts have affirmed that the system provides adequate access to the decision-making criteria for candidates, ensuring transparency both before and after decisions are made.

---

[18] The explanation of how the Parcoursup algorithm works is taken from the "Document de présentation des algorithmes de Parcoursup" put online by the Ministry of Higher Education and Research in July 2022, online.

[19] Art. L. 312-1-3 *Code des relations entre le public et l'administration.*

[20] The Parcoursup source code was published on May 21, 2018 and can be viewed online. See https://www.enseignementsup-recherche.gouv.fr/fr/parcoursup-publication-du-code-informatique-des-algorithmes-46680; https://framagit.org/parcoursup/algorithmes-de-parcoursup

[21] For example, see Tribunal administratif de Guadeloupe, 4 févr. 2019, *Union nationale des étudiants de France (UNEF)*, n° 1801094.

[22] CE, 12 juin 2019, *Université des Antilles*, n° 427916: *JCP A* 2019. 2238, concl. F. Dieux, note P. Fressoz; *AJDA* 2019.1192; *D.* 2019.1673, obs. W. Maxwell et C. Zolynski; *Dalloz IP/IT* 2019. 700, obs. T. Douville.

[23] CC, QPC, 3 avril 2020, déc. n° 2020-834, *Union nationale des étudiants de France.*

2.3 AI Systems for Fraud Detection

Data mining algorithms are also used by tax authorities to detect potential fraud. In the field of taxation, data mining is integrated into tax auditing. Its purpose is to help identify individuals or entities engaged in fraudulent activities. To achieve this, the administration provides the algorithm with a theoretical model of the fraudster. The algorithm then performs correlations between this model and the data available in the administration's processing operations. Agents can guide them to narrow the search to specific taxpayers. In addition, the algorithm has a predictive dimension: it can attempt to model the behavior of fraudsters based on the data it processes to detect possible fraud risks. This practice was tested in France in 2013 and then perpetuated with the implementation of the "Targeting of fraud and valuation of requests" (*Ciblage des fraudes et valorisation des requêtes*—CFVR) processing.[24]

But the development of algorithms aimed at detecting fraud is not limited to tax matters. In social matters too, the National Family Allowance Fund (CNAF) which has set up a data mining tool supposed to help detect family allowance fraud, such as in other countries.[25] Since 2012, the CNAF has employed a data mining model[26] to detect cases where beneficiaries are at high risk of overpayments,[27] prioritizing these cases for further scrutiny. The algorithm had given rise to debates about the transparency of its operation, especially given the potentially significant impact on the individuals involved. In response to concerns about the opacity of the CNAF's data mining practices, La Quadrature du Net association requested access to the source code of the algorithm.[28] This request was grounded in the belief that transparency is crucial for ensuring that the algorithm operates fairly and does not unduly target certain groups of beneficiaries. The association argued that access to the source code would allow for a better understanding of how decisions are made. To comply with the request, the CNAF did provide the association with access to the algorithm's source code. However, the organization took the precaution of obfuscating the names of all variables used within the algorithm. As a result, the disclosed source code was largely unintelligible and did not provide meaningful insight on how the algorithm works. The CNAF justified this action by arguing that revealing the variables and their weightings would compromise the effectiveness of fraud detection and prevention efforts. They claimed that such disclosure could enable individuals to circumvent the algorithm's checks, thereby undermining its purpose.

---

[24] On this subject, see Lequesne-Roth (2021).

[25] The fight against social benefit fraud is also the subject of algorithmic processing in the Netherlands with the SyRI tool (Meuwese A (2020) p 209) or in Belgium with the OASIS tool (Degrave 2022, p 269).

[26] See CNAF (2022).

[27] See CADA, Avis n° 20226179 of Dec. 15, 2022.

[28] See the CADA request made by the La Quadrature du Net association: https://www.laquadrature.net/wp-content/uploads/sites/8/2022/12/demande.pdf

The CNAF's decision to hide the variables was further validated by the Commission for Access to Administrative Documents (CADA).[29] The CADA accepted the CNAF's argument that full transparency could impede the detection and prevention of various types of infractions. The commission recognized that revealing the inner workings of the algorithm could facilitate attempts to manipulate the system, thus justifying the CNAF's limited disclosure as a necessary measure to protect public interests. This case exemplifies the broader tension between the need for transparency in government operations made by AI systems and the imperative to protect the efficacy of administrative processes. As such, it highlights the ongoing challenge for public institutions to navigate these competing demands in a way that upholds both public trust and the integrity of their digital operations.

However, criticisms of this algorithm are far from over. In October 2024, 15 civil society organizations filed an appeal with the Council of State against this algorithm, in the name of the right to personal data protection and the principle of non-discrimination. Among the factors that increase the suspicion score are low income, unemployment, receiving the Active Solidarity Income (RSA) or the Disabled Adult Allowance (AAH). As a result, people in difficulty are subjected to excessive scrutiny compared to the rest of the population. The appeal challenges both the extent of the ongoing surveillance and the discrimination carried out by this algorithm against beneficiaries who are already vulnerable in their life trajectories. By equating precariousness with suspicion of fraud, this algorithm contributes to a policy of stigmatization and institutional mistreatment of the most disadvantaged. In France, this type of discrimination is expressly prohibited under Article 225-1 of the Penal Code.

2.4 AI Systems for Risk Identification

AI systems have increasingly been recognized as valuable tools for risk identification, particularly in the context of public safety and security, but also to prevent natural or health risks. These systems are capable of reliably identifying potential threats by analyzing vast amounts of data. Their ability to process complex patterns and trends allows them to detect early warning signs of possible risks, thereby enabling proactive measures to mitigate such dangers.[30]

Historically, digital technologies have played in France a significant role in maintaining public order. One of the most notable examples is the use of surveillance cameras, which have long been employed since the '80 s to monitor public spaces and deter criminal activities.[31] These technologies have provided law

[29] CADA, Avis n° 20226179 du 15 déc. 2022; CADA, Conseil n° 20225787 du 15 déc. 2022.

[30] See Conseil d'État (2022) p 279.

[31] For example, in 1988, the French Data Protection Authority (CNIL) received a complaint against the city of Hyères, which had installed five surveillance cameras throughout the city. The CNIL, deeming itself not competent to handle the matter, referred the case to the Ministries of Justice and Interior (as per Deliberation n° 88-86 dated July 8, 1988, regarding complaints filed against the

enforcement agencies with crucial data to manage and prevent disturbances. However, while traditional surveillance methods are reactive and rely on human interpretation, AI systems offer a more advanced approach by not only identifying existing threats but also predicting future ones. Today, AI systems are increasingly utilized in various applications to enhance public safety. For example, emerging initiatives are now combining video surveillance, geolocation, and biometrics to enhance threat prevention, improve event detection, and reduce response times for mobilizing available forces. This approach is often referred to as "intelligent video surveillance" which involves image analysis to detect abnormal signals. In some cases, this technology comes together with facial recognition algorithms for identification purposes.

Although American companies such as PredPol and Palantir have made attempts to establish a presence in France, the country is focused on developing its own predictive tools. For example, the Gendarmerie Nationale employs software like Paved to anticipate burglaries and vehicle vandalism, and PredVol for predicting car thefts.[32] However, it is in Marseille that the first fully predictive algorithm dedicated to general administrative policing was introduced. In 2016, the city launched the "Big Data for Public Safety" (*Big Data de la tranquillité publique*) project, marking a significant milestone in the application of predictive analytics to urban security. This project features a platform that integrates Big Data and machine learning methods. The system is designed to analyze past events, assess the current situation, and anticipate future or likely scenarios.[33]

Like the surveillance of public spaces through drones, which now has a legal basis,[34] these "intelligent surveillance" systems used for mass monitoring significantly increase the risks of infringing on individual freedoms. The potential violations are numerous, particularly concerning privacy, as these systems involve the capture, viewing, and sometimes recording of images that can identify individuals, as well as the collection of sounds—including conversations—and biometric data such as body heat. Additionally, these surveillance practices pose threats to fundamental liberties, including freedom of expression, opinion, conscience, movement, and the right to protest. Despite these concerns, the French government has signaled its intention to expand the use of AI for public safety.

Moreover, Article 10 of the law of May 19, 2023,[35] related to the Olympic and Paralympic Games of 2024, authorized the experimentation of algorithmic video surveillance in public spaces for public security purposes. The experiment was

city hall of Hyères). The city contested this decision by appealing to the Conseil d'État. However, before the case could be adjudicated, the city withdrew its appeal (Conseil d'État, October 23, 1992, Case n° 101764).

[32] See Gauthier F (2017).

[33] See Création d'un outil Big Data de la Tranquillité Publique et prestations d'accompagnement, 2018, p 12, as cited by La Quadrature du Net (2018).

[34] Loi n° 2022-52 du 24 janvier 2022 relative à la responsabilité pénale et à la sécurité intérieure.

[35] Loi n° 2023-380 du 19 mai 2023 relative aux jeux Olympiques et Paralympiques de 2024 et portant diverses autres dispositions

approved by the Constitutional Court because it included certain safeguards. First, no biometric data can be processed, which means facial recognition is excluded. Second, the systems can only be used to alert law enforcement to the occurrence of predefined "abnormal" events (abandoned package, fire outbreak, person collapsing, etc.). This means that AI does not make decisions; instead, the authorized officer is responsible for doing so. Finally, it is only an experiment running until March 2025, under the supervision of public authorities (the prefect—the State representative in the department- in particular).[36]

These precautions were taken to allow for a future extension and expansion of the experiment, in compliance with the European AI regulation. It will even be possible to activate the "facial recognition" function on these devices if the conditions of the AI Act are met (for example, in the search for serious offenders or the prevention of a terrorist threat). Apparently, this function has already been activated several times in several municipalities in France, a practice that the administrative judge recently sanctioned.[37]

This initiative underscores the government's commitment to integrating advanced technologies into public administration. However, it also raises further questions about the potential for these technologies to encroach on civil liberties and the adequacy of the legal frameworks governing their use.

2.5 AI Systems for Communication with Citizens

Finally, the drive to digitize administrative procedures has led to the development of technological solutions aimed at improving communication between public services and citizens. In an effort to make these processes more efficient, AI-powered tools, such as chatbots and virtual assistants, have been created to assist citizens in navigating the complexities of administrative tasks. These innovations are integral to the broader digital transformation of public services, as they help streamline interactions and make services more accessible.

In France, several AI-driven solutions have been implemented to achieve these goals. For instance, "Lisa" the chatbot on the "toutemesaides.fr" website, provides personalized guidance to citizens seeking information on available social aids. Similarly, "Amelibot" developed by the French Health Insurance (*Assurance Maladie*), assists users with inquiries related to health coverage and benefits. Another example is "NOA" ("*Nous Orienter dans l'Administration*"), a virtual assistant designed specifically to facilitate administrative procedures for start-ups. These tools ensure that citizens can access necessary information and support without the need for physical visits to government offices. However, while these digital

[36] Décision n°2023-850 DC du 17 mai 2023 sur la loi relative aux jeux Olympiques et Paralympiques de 2024 (C. Crichton, « Vidéosurveillance intelligente aux JO: validation sous réserve par le Conseil constitutionnel », *D. IP/IT* 24 mai 2023.

[37] Tribunal administratif de Grenoble, 24 janvier 2025, n°2105328.

services offer benefits, it is crucial to ensure that they are not exclusive. There remains a significant portion of the population that may be uncomfortable with or unable to access digital platforms due to lack of internet access, digital literacy, or other barriers. To avoid excluding these individuals from essential public services, it is important that physical access points and traditional modes of communication remain available as complementary options.[38]

The use cases of AI systems in public administration in France are becoming increasingly prevalent, giving rise to debates and disputes. Despite this, the current legal framework does not include specific regulations for AI systems. However, certain legal rules may still be applicable to these technologies and the European AI regulation further complements the existing legal landscape.

3 The Lack of Specific Regulation Governing AI Use in Public Administration

France has established a robust legal framework for the protection of personal data. In 1978, the *Loi Informatique et Libertés* was enacted, leading to the creation of the *Commission Nationale de l'Informatique et des Libertés* (CNIL), an independent administrative authority responsible for data protection. This foundational piece of legislation applies to the processing of personal data through AI systems and introduced rules on transparency and algorithmic decision-making, applicable to both the private and public sectors (1). Over time, this law has undergone several amendments, with a major revision following the implementation of the GDPR.[39] Additionally, in 2016, France adopted the *Loi pour une République Numérique*, which further clarified the transparency rules governing automated decision-making by public administration (2). Complementing this framework, the European AI Regulation has recently been introduced, bringing a risk-based approach that was previously absent in France and imposing new requirements for public sector entities (3).

[38] Regarding access to public services, the Council of State has authorized the implementation of mandatory online services, provided that support measures, or even an alternative solution, are put in place. With this decision, it endorses the 'Digital first' approach and likely only postpones the move to 'Digital only'. CE 3 juin 2022, *Conseil National des barreaux, La Cimade et autres*, n°452798.

[39] Regulation (EU) 2016/679 of the European Parliament and of the Council of 27 April 2016 on the protection of natural persons with regard to the processing of personal data and on the free movement of such data, and repealing Directive 95/46/EC.

3.1 The Establishment of a Legal Framework for the Processing of Personal Data

When an AI system involves one or more processing of personal data, it falls under the scope of the *Loi Informatique et Libertés*. Consequently, several obligations must be fulfilled. First, certain data processing activities carried out by the State require the completion of preliminary formalities (a). Additionally, individuals whose data is processed by such systems have specific rights (b), which are further extended in cases where automated decisions are made (c).

3.1.1 Preliminary Formalities for Implementing the Processing of Personal Data

In accordance with the *Loi Informatique et Libertés*, certain data processing activities carried out on behalf of the State are subject to preliminary formalities. For instance, processing operations conducted on behalf of the State that "concern state security, defense, or public safety, or are intended to be used for the prevention, investigation, detection, or prosecution of criminal offenses, or the execution of criminal sentences or security measures" must be submitted for review by the CNIL, whose opinion will be published.[40] Even though this formality applies only to data processing related to public security, it enables the CNIL to control data protection prior to the implementation of sensitive processing activities. The CNIL is also consulted when processing activities involve "new mechanisms, technologies, or procedures that present high risks to the rights and freedoms of the individuals concerned".[41] This provision could apply to high-risk AI systems, as classified by the AI Act. For example, when the municipality of Valenciennes implemented an automated video surveillance system, the CNIL determined that it posed a high risk to rights and freedoms and that such an algorithmic system constituted a new technology. Consequently, this processing "could not be implemented without prior consultation with the CNIL".[42]

In addition to the CNIL's oversight of specific processing activities, other formalities are required: Articles 31 and 32 of the *Loi Informatique et Libertés* mandate that certain processing activities be authorized by a regulatory act. For example, processing activities conducted on behalf of the State that concern state security, defense, or public safety, or are intended for the prevention, investigation, detection, or prosecution of criminal offenses must be authorized by a ministerial order issued after the CNIL's motivated and published opinion.

[40] Art. 31 *Loi informatique et libertés.*

[41] Art. 90 *Loi informatique et libertés.*

[42] See CNIL (2021), a warning issued following an on-site inspection.

3.1.2 The Rights of Individuals Subject to Personal Data Processing

The regulations governing the protection of personal data grant specific rights to individuals whose data is being processed. Firstly, individuals must be provided with clear, understandable, and easily accessible information regarding the use of their data and their corresponding rights.[43] This right to information imposes a duty on data controllers to inform individuals at the time of data collection, or subsequently if the data was not directly collected from the individual concerned.

In addition to the right to accessible and comprehensible information, individuals whose personal data is being processed also have the right to access this information after data processing. This right to access can take two forms: the right to know whether personal data concerning them is being processed, and the right to obtain a copy of that data.

The rights to information and access, as guaranteed by personal data protection regulations, ensure that individuals can obtain information both before and after the automated processing of their data. However, these obligations apply solely to the processing of personal data and are afforded only to the individuals concerned. When an AI system processes personal data, the data controller must ensure that these rights are effectively upheld.

Additionally, individuals have other rights, such as the right to object to the processing of their personal data, the right to rectify inaccuracies in their data, the right to have their data erased, and the right to effective legal remedies.

3.1.3 The Rights of Recipients of an Algorithmic Decision

The concept of automated decision-making, whether in the public or private sector, is not a new one in France. It originates from the first version of the *Loi Informatique et Libertés*. The Article 2 planned that no judicial decision could be based, in whole or in part, on an algorithm, while the second paragraph prohibited the exclusive use of algorithms to make decisions involving an assessment of human behaviour. Therefore, there was a general prohibition against making decisions based on an algorithm: a total ban for judicial decisions and a partial ban for public or private decisions, as only those decisions made exclusively on the basis of an algorithm were prohibited. However, this has evolved, particularly with the introduction of the GDPR, which allowed Member States to regulate automated decision-making through specific legislation. France has taken advantage of this opportunity by permitting the use of algorithms as the sole basis for making individual administrative decisions. This provision is now enshrined in Article 47 of the law, which reminds us that a decision can be made solely on the basis of an algorithm in the cases specified in points (a) and (c) of Article 22, Section 2 of the GDPR.

[43] Pursuant to Articles 13 and 14 of the GDPR and Article 48 *Loi informatique et libertés*.

The rights established by the *Loi Informatique et Libertés* and the GDPR apply to all data processing activities, whether automated or not. Consequently, automated processing that lead to an individual administrative decision are concerned. Articles 13 and 14 of the GDPR require that individuals must be informed, at the time their data is collected, of "the existence of automated decision-making (...) referred to in Article 22 [of the GDPR] and (...) useful information regarding the underlying logic, as well as the significance and anticipated consequences of this processing for the data subject". Additionally, individuals have a right of access. Upon request, the data subject has the right to obtain from the data controller information about "the existence of automated decision-making, including profiling, referred to in Article 22, paragraphs 1 and 4, and, at least in such cases, useful information regarding the underlying logic, as well as the significance and anticipated consequences of this processing for the data subject".

In addition, Article 22 of the GDPR establishes the right of individuals not to be subjected to decisions solely based on automated processing, including profiling, that produce legal effects or significantly affect them. However, this right is not absolute. Exceptions are allowed when such decisions are necessary for the performance of a contract between the individual and the data controller, when authorized by Union or Member State law with appropriate safeguards for the individual's rights and freedoms, or when the individual has given explicit consent.[44] In cases where exceptions apply, the data controller must implement measures to protect the individual's rights, such as the right to human intervention, the opportunity to express their viewpoint, and the ability to contest the decision.[45] Additionally, decisions involving special categories of personal data, as outlined in Article 9 of the GDPR, are further restricted unless specific conditions are met, ensuring that any automated processing of sensitive data is accompanied by stringent safeguards to protect the individual's rights and legitimate interests.

3.2 The Impacts of the *Loi pour une République Numérique* on Automated Decision-Making in Public Administration

The *Loi pour une République Numérique* of 2016, now codified in the *Code des relations entre le public et l'administration* (CRPA), established the framework for transparency regarding algorithmic administrative decisions in France.[46]

Firstly, pursuant to Article L. 312-1-3 of the CRPA, administrations with at least 50 employees are required to publish online the rules defining the primary algorithmic processes used in their functions when these processes underpin individual decisions.

---

[44] Art 22, (2) a), b), c), GDPR.

[45] Art. 22, (3), GDPR.

[46] For a detailed analysis of the law, see Cluzel-Métayer L (2017).

Furthermore, Article L. 311-3-1 mandates that recipients of an individual administrative decision based on an algorithm must be personally informed through a statement on the decision received. The administration is thus obligated, under penalty of invalidity of the decision, to indicate that the decision was made based on an algorithm, specify its purpose, and provide the right to access the rules defining the processing and its main characteristics.[47] Once the decision has been made and communicated to the recipient, the individual may request additional information that was not provided spontaneously. Upon request, the administration must provide details including the degree and manner of the algorithmic processing's contribution to the decision, the data processed and its sources, the processing parameters and, where applicable, their weighting as applied to the individual's situation, and the operations performed by the processing.[48] If the administration remains silent for a month following a request for the rules defining the processing and its main characteristics, this is considered a rejection. The individual then has 2 months to refer the matter to the Commission for Access to Administrative Documents (*Commission d'Accès aux Documents Administratifs* - CADA), a prerequisite for any subsequent legal recourse.[49]

3.3 The European AI Act: Introducing a Risk-Based Approach to Public Sector AI Systems

Although provisions concerning the processing of personal data and those related to automated decision-making may apply to AI systems, France has not yet established a specific legal framework governing the development of AI systems. Thus, the AI Act provides an essential complement to the existing legal framework and the many existing legislative blind spots will largely be closed. In line with the risk-based approach that has been adopted, the AI Act does not impose obligations on all AI systems. Apart from the general prohibitions it provides for, only "high-risk" AI systems are subject to a comprehensive legal framework. For the administration, this has significant consequences, as most of its AI systems would fall into this category due to their involvement in sovereign activities.

Administration is particularly affected by Articles 5 and 6 of the AI Act, which respectively prohibits certain practices or categorizes them as high-risk. Indeed, the practices in question largely fall within the traditional public powers assigned to the State. For instance, Article 5 prohibits the prediction of criminal risk based solely on individual profiling. It also prohibits AI systems that infer the emotions of employees or civil servants in the workplace, as well as those involved in biometric recognition and categorization that make automatic inferences or affiliations regarding

[47] Art. L.311-3-1 and R.311-3-1-1 *Code des relations entre le public et l'administration.*

[48] Art. R.311-3-1-2 *Code des relations entre le public et l'administration.*

[49] Art. L. 342-1 *Code des relations entre le public et l'administration.*

union membership, sexual orientation, religious beliefs or political opinions on the basis of biometric data. This also excludes systems that condition access to social and civic services on "good" behavior.

Nevertheless, certain uses of AI systems that are otherwise prohibited may be permitted provided that they meet specific cumulative conditions. This includes, for example, the legal use of real-time or remote biometric identification systems in public spaces, provided that the search's purpose is to combat incidents of abduction, sexual trafficking, search for missing persons, prevent a specific and imminent threat to individuals' lives, or locate a person under criminal investigation. In cases of imperative necessity, such as searching for kidnapping victims or preventing imminent threats, these technologies can only be used after obtaining judicial or administrative authorization[50] and must adhere to stringent conditions of use and oversight.[51] Additionally, the article imposes monitoring and reporting obligations on the use of biometric identification systems, including the requirement for national authorities to submit annual reports to the European Commission and for the Commission to publish consolidated reports.[52] Despite the relative complexity of the article, it helps to clarify the rules concerning biometric data processing, a legal framework that was previously unclear in France and open to various interpretations, leading to the adoption of tools that could potentially infringe upon the rights and freedoms of citizens.

Concerning Article 6 and the related Annex III, it outlines a number of high-risk AI systems that predominantly relate to sovereign matters. Public administrations will need to map these systems and ensure their compliance with European regulation. Certainly, the rules regarding transparency for high-risk AI systems are the most compelling to compare with the existing legal framework in France.

We have observed that there are already several regulations in France ensuring that individuals affected by personal data processing can access information, and that recipients of automated decisions are informed and understand how such decisions are made. Articles 13 and 14 of the AI Act specifically address transparency and human oversight in addition to French requirements. Article 13 stipulates that, for high-risk AI systems only, a user manual must be provided to AI systems' deployers. This manual must intelligibly detail a series of information regarding the system's characteristics, capabilities, and performance limitations, including its purpose, accuracy level, robustness, cybersecurity, performance, and the datasets used for training. This complements our national legislation by imposing transparency requirements on AI system providers towards deployers (who will most often be public administrations). Furthermore, it will enable administrations to have clear information about the systems they deploy.

In addition, Article 14 mandates that effective human oversight be maintained over high-risk AI systems during their operation. Specifically, the provider of the

---

[50] Art. 5 (3), AI Act.

[51] Art 5 (2), (4), AI Act.

[52] Art 5 (6), (7), AI Act.

system must ensure that the deployer can understand how the system operates, be aware of any tendency to overly rely on machine results and have the capability to intervene in the system's functioning or halt it in case of issues. This article necessarily implies that administrative personnel must be trained to oversee such AI systems.[53] Internal training programs will need to be established and that a reorganization of services may be required.

The implementation of a regulatory framework adapted to AI systems must now be accompanied by a reorganization of state services to effectively execute an AI strategy.

4 The Consequences of Implementing AI Systems on Administrative Organization

The implementation of AI systems within the French public administration has significant organizational implications, influenced by several key factors. A central issue is the multiplicity of actors involved in leading the AI strategy, which raises concerns about the coherence and effectiveness of these efforts (1). Additionally, the operational implementation of AI systems varies considerably across different parts of the administration, reflecting diverse approaches and structures (2). The role of the French data protection authority (CNIL) is also evolving, especially in the context of the AI Act, which could redefine its responsibilities (3). Moreover, there is a pressing need to address the lack of training and capacity-building for public-sector employees, as effective engagement with AI technologies requires a workforce with the appropriate skills and knowledge (4).

4.1 The Multiplicity of Actors Responsible for Leading the AI Strategy

In France, the strategic governance of artificial intelligence (AI) within public administration is currently dispersed across multiple actors operating at different levels, including ministerial, inter-ministerial, and local authorities. The primary entities responsible for this governance include the Interministerial Directorate for Digital Affairs (DINUM), the Interministerial Directorate for Public Transformation (DITP), and the National Coordinator for AI. The DINUM, established in its current form in 2019, is a service under the authority of the Prime Minister and reports to the Minister for Public Transformation and the Civil Service. Its mission is to develop the digital strategy of the state, oversee its implementation, and support the government's digital projects. Within DINUM, the Etalab department, which

[53] It is an obligation under Article 4, AI Act.

coordinates the state's open data policy, supports the administration in the use of public algorithms. DITP plays a complementary role by steering the public transformation program defined by the Government, notably through the integration of AI technologies. The National Coordinator for AI, on the other hand, serves as a liaison between various stakeholders, including government bodies, private sectors, and academia, to ensure the coherent deployment of AI strategies.

Despite these efforts, the current structure lacks a unified approach to AI governance, leading to questions about whether a single entity should be established to streamline and enhance the impact of France's AI strategy. The lack of formalized coordination among these actors contributes to fragmentation, potentially limiting the effectiveness of AI implementation across the public sector. A centralized structure could potentially offer clearer leadership, more coherent policy implementation, and enhanced accountability, thereby strengthening France's position in the global AI landscape.

4.2 *Different Approaches to the Operational Implementation of AI Systems Within the Administration*

The operational implementation of AI systems in the French public administration is characterized by significant variability across different organizations. According to the Conseil d'État's report on AI and public action, there is no standardized organizational structure for executing AI projects within public institutions.[54] Typically, the digital departments within each organization are responsible for overseeing the deployment of AI systems, although their capabilities and approaches can differ widely.

At the ministerial level, some ministries have developed specialized structures to manage AI implementation more effectively. For instance, certain ministries have established "LabIA"[55] and "digital factories" (*fabrique numérique*) to incubate and accelerate AI projects, fostering innovation and experimentation.[56] The French Ministry of Armed Forces has created a dedicated national service, the Defense Innovation Agency, which focuses on leveraging AI to enhance national defense

[54] See Conseil d'État (2022), p 198.

[55] For example, in 2015, the French Ministry of Defence set up a digital laboratory (Labo Big Data et AI) which conducts studies, research and experiments in the field of massive data processing and artificial intelligence. The Ministry of Ecological Transition has also set up "Ecolab", an innovation laboratory for the ecological transition of the ministerial pole. It includes a data-driven innovation and artificial intelligence unit. For an overview of existing innovation labs, see Direction interministérielle de la transformation publique (2024).

[56] For instance, the social ministries have created a digital factory, an incubator for state startups. It aims to encourage digital innovation and digital transformation within ministries and social services.

capabilities.[57] These tailored approaches allow ministries to address specific operational needs and challenges, although the absence of a uniform model across the administration may lead to inconsistencies in AI systems deployment.

4.3 The Evolving Role of CNIL

The French data protection authority (CNIL) is poised to play a crucial role in the oversight of AI technologies in France, particularly in the context of the European AI Act. The AI Act, which seeks to establish a comprehensive regulatory framework for AI across the European Union, emphasizes the need for robust oversight to ensure that AI systems are developed and deployed in a manner that is ethical, transparent, and aligned with fundamental rights.

If CNIL was designated as the national supervisory authority under the AI Act, it would bear significant responsibilities, including the monitoring of AI systems for compliance with the regulation, assessing the risks associated with high-risk AI applications, and enforcing sanctions in cases of non-compliance. This would require CNIL to expand its expertise and resources to address the complexities associated with AI technologies, beyond its traditional focus on data protection. The designation of CNIL as the national authority could also reinforce the legal and ethical safeguards surrounding AI in France, providing a critical check against potential abuses and ensuring that AI development aligns with European values and standards. To initiate these changes, the CNIL established a dedicated AI department in January 2023.[58] This department, consisting of five members, is tasked with strengthening the CNIL's expertise in AI systems by working collaboratively across all divisions.

4.4 The Lack of Training and Capacity-Building for Public-Sector Employees

In its 2017 annual report titled *Public Authority and Digital Platforms: Supporting the Uberization Process*, the Conseil d'État recommended incorporating a mandatory requirement into the continuous training of public servants to periodically update their knowledge of the digital aspects of their profession.[59] The goal was to ensure that all public officials develop a cross-cutting competence in digital technologies and language. However, this recommendation was not implemented with

[57] See the agency's presentation on its website: https://www.defense.gouv.fr/aid/mieux-nous-connaitre/presentation-lagence

[58] See CNIL (2023).

[59] See Conseil d'État (2017), proposition 16, p 134.

great rigor. In its 2022 report on AI and Public Action, the Conseil d'État acknowledged that "AI literacy is weak, if not nonexistent, among most public servants, including those in senior positions".[60] This observation underscores the importance of Article 4 of the AI Act, which mandates that personnel receive adequate training in AI literacy.

The introduction of AI systems into the public administration underscores the need for extensive training and capacity building among public sector employees. There is a growing recognition that public officials, particularly those in leadership positions, require a deep understanding of AI and digital technologies to effectively navigate the challenges and opportunities presented by AI. This need extends beyond senior management to include all levels of public sector employees, who must be equipped with the skills and knowledge necessary to interact with AI tools and incorporate them into their daily work.

In response, a Human Resources Department for the digital sector of the state (RHN) was established within DINUM to support the development of digital skills across the state. Its purpose is to facilitate the emergence of an interministerial professional digital sector. Also, from 2016, there is an increasing emphasis on recruiting data experts and AI specialists into the public sector. Nevertheless, these efforts remain insufficient. According to a joint report by INSEE and DINUM,[61] state administrations, excluding intelligence services and operators, employ over 2000 data experts. This includes approximately 1150 data analysts, 290 data scientists, and 220 data engineers.

However, the current shortage of such experts, a situation that is also reflected in the private sector, poses a significant challenge to the effective implementation of AI initiatives. To address this gap, the French government must prioritize the development of comprehensive training programs that not only raise awareness about AI but also foster technical expertise among public sector employees. By building a more AI-literate workforce, the public administration can better harness the potential of AI technologies to enhance service delivery, policy-making, and public sector innovation. This is even more necessary as the AI Act emphasizes the need for specific training for the individual responsible for deploying an AI system, as part of human oversight.[62]

References

Attal G (2024) Speech on the transformation of public action. Sceaux, France, 23 April 2024

Boucher P (1974) SAFARI ou la chasse aux Français. Le Monde, 21 March 1974

Cluzel-Métayer L (2013) Les téléservices publics face au droit à la confidentialité des données. Revue française d'administration publique 146(2):405–418

[60] See Conseil d'État (2022), p 162.

[61] See DINUM and INSEE (2021), p 31.

[62] See Art 4 and 14, AI Act.

Cluzel-Métayer L (2017) La loi pour une République numérique: l'écosystème de la donnée saisi par le droit. Actualité juridique Droit administratif
Cluzel-Métayer L (2022) Intelligence artificielle et décision administrative. In: Droit de l'intelligence artificielle, 2nd edn. LGDJ 505
CNAF (2022) Aide à la détermination des dossiers allocataires nécessitant une vérification à l'aide d'un procédé de datamining. Press release, 27 January 2022. https://www.caf.fr/sites/default/files/medias/cnaf/DCOM/mentions_legales/informatique_libertes/Communique-Datamining-score.pdf
CNIL (2021) Warning to Commune de Valenciennes, 12 May 2021
CNIL (2023) Création d'un service de l'intelligence artificielle à la CNIL. https://www.cnil.fr/fr/creation-dun-service-de-lintelligence-artificielle-la-cnil-et-lancement-des-travaux-sur-les-bases-de
Conseil d'État (2017) Puissance publique et plateformes numériques: accompagner l'"ubérisation". Les rapports du Conseil d'État, Paris
Conseil d'État (2022) IA et Action publique: construire la confiance, servir la performance. Les rapports du Conseil d'État, Paris
Création d'un outil Big Data de la Tranquillité Publique et prestations d'accompagnement (2018) Cahier des Clauses Techniques Particulières, Marseille
Crouzet J (2017) Déchiffrer l'algorithme. La saga Admission post-bac (APB) se poursuit. RLDI 142:46
Darras E, Deharbe D (1996) La politique du regard. Remarques sur la légalisation de la vidéosurveillance. In: Curapp (ed) La Gouvernabilité. PUF, Paris, pp 79–90
Degrave E (2022) La mutation de l'administration en Belgique: le système OASIS. In: Cluzel-Métayer L, Prébissy-Schnall C, Sée A (eds) La transformation numérique du service public, une nouvelle crise? Mare et Martin, Paris, p 269
DINUM and INSEE (2021) Évaluation des besoins de l'État en compétences et expertises en matière de donnée. Report
Direction interministérielle de la transformation publique (2024) L'Atlas des laboratoires d'innovation publique. Ministère de la Transformation et de la Fonction publiques, Paris
Gauthier F (2017) Prédire les vols de voitures? Revue de la Gendarmerie nationale 260
Graveleau S (2016) APB: les questions que soulève le code source. Le Monde, 26 October 2016
La Quadrature du Net (2018) La surveillance policière dopée aux Big Data arrive près de chez vous! 20 March 2018. https://www.laquadrature.net/2018/03/20/surveillance_big_data_marseille/
Lequesne-Roth C (2021) La lutte contre la fraude à l'ère digitale. Revue de droit fiscal 5
Meuwese A (2020) Regulating Algorithmic Decision-making One Case at the Time: a Note on the Dutch 'SyRI' Judgment. ERDAL 1(1):209
Ministère de l'Intérieur (2017) Protéger, garantir et servir. Feuille de route
Nora S, Minc A (1978) L'informatisation de la société. Report to the French President. La documentation française, Paris
Report of the Special Rapporteur on Extreme Poverty and Human Rights (2019) Uses of digital technologies in the welfare state. Document A/74/48037, 11 October 2019

Lucie Cluzel-Métayer is a Professor of Law at Paris-Nanterre University. Her research focuses on digital law, particularly data law and public algorithms. She is the co-author of the "Law and AI" column in La Semaine Juridique (LexisNexis), and co-directs the Digital Law Master's program at Paris-Nanterre University.

Nina Lasbleiz is a PhD candidate in Public and Digital Law at the University of Paris Nanterre. Her research focuses on how public algorithms are controlled to ensure compliance with the law, through judicial or non-judicial mechanisms.

AI in the Spanish Public Sector

Susana de la Sierra

Contents

This chapter has been prepared in the framework of two research projects, of which the author is Principal Investigator (together with Prof. Juana Morcillo Moreno): "Protección jurídica y oportunidades de los colectivos vulnerables ante la digitalización y la inteligencia artificial" [Legal protection and opportunities of vulnerable groups vis à vis digitalisation and artificial intelligence] (PRODIGIA: PID2021-124967OB-I00, funded by MICIN/AEI/10.13039/501100011033/ and the EU) and "Digitalización y colectivos vulnerables: protección, garantías y propuestas para su implantación en Castilla-La Mancha" [Digitalisation and vulnerable groups: protection, guarantees and proposals for its implementation in Castilla-La Mancha] (PRODIGITAL: SBPLY/21/180501/000089, funded by Junta de Comunidades de Castilla-La Mancha and the EU).

S. de la Sierra (✉)
University of Castilla-La Mancha, Toledo, Spain
e-mail: Susana.Sierra@uclm.es

F. Decarolis et al. (eds.), *The EU Digital Regulation and its Impact on Member States*, European Union and its Neighbours in a Globalized World 27,
https://doi.org/10.1007/978-3-032-06490-5_5

Abstract In Spain, there are accredited uses of artificial intelligence systems by public administrations. However, access to information remains challenging due to the absence of public inventories or registries. In this regard, legal scholarship advocates for the application of the principle of algorithmic transparency as an essential element for safeguarding citizens' rights and ensuring administrative oversight. This principle has been included in regional legislation (such as in Comunitat Valenciana). Some regions (Comunidades Autónomas/*Autonomous Communities*) have established their own governance frameworks (Castilla-La Mancha, Catalonia, Galicia, Madrid), and some have even promoted the adoption of a comprehensive artificial intelligence act (Galicia and, to a lesser extent, Extremadura). At the national level, notable developments include the drafting of the Digital Rights Charter in 2021, the creation of a regulatory sandbox for artificial intelligence and the establishment of the Spanish Agency for the Supervision of Artificial Intelligence (AESIA) in 2023. Nevertheless, no adaptation of the legal framework governing public administrations has been undertaken to address this new reality, and as a result, the general legal framework remains applicable.

1 Introduction

It can be argued that Spain is a pioneer in the regulation of digitalisation processes and the use of artificial intelligence (AI). This applies not only in general but also specifically to the public sector. Indeed, the Spanish Government initiated the drafting of a Digital Rights Charter in 2020, which was developed by a group of experts—both academic and non-academic—and was made public on 14 July 2021 by the Prime Minister (De la Sierra 2022).[1] The Charter itself does not possess legal force but is intended to serve as the basis for future legislation. Moreover, as it will be later explained, some recently adopted norms have incorporated references to the Charter, thus conferring legal value on some of its contents. The Charter, which was taken into consideration by the European Commission in the process of drafting the European Declaration on Digital Rights and Principles,[2] is now undergoing analysis with the aim of being translated into specific norms and public policies.

[1] The text of the Charter can be found at the site https://espanadigital.gob.es/en.

[2] Communication from the Commission to the European Parliament, the Council, the European Economic and Social Committee and the Committee of the Regions Establishing a European Declaration on Digital rights and principles for the Digital Decade, COM (2022) 27 final, 26

It should be noted that Spain has a decentralized territorial structure, resembling a federation, and the regions (*Comunidades Autónomas/Autonomous Communities*) possess significant legislative competences. For instance, regarding this chapter's topic, Extremadura adopted a Decree-Statute in 2021 to partially regulate the use of artificial intelligence within its territory, while Galicia's Parliament has passed a Statute in April 2025, being the first attempt to comprehensively regulate the use of AI in Spain. Other regions may soon follow this example as is the case of Castilla-La Mancha.

The practical use of AI in Spain is highly diverse. Local and regional authorities, as well as the central government, employ AI for different purposes, generally with a lack of transparency. In fact, it is particularly difficult to determine when and how public administrations utilise AI. There are currently at State level no public registers of AI algorithms used in Spanish administrations, although some local and regional cases are worth discussing. Moreover, the legal standing of specific AI systems in administrative procedures is also often unclear. Spanish legal scholarship is unanimous in demanding greater transparency in this regard, and the Digital Rights Charter, which will be discussed later, includes a corresponding legal mandate in heading XVIII, 6, b).

From an institutional perspective, Spain was also a pioneer in establishing a dedicated public body to supervise the use of AI. In 2023, the *Agencia Estatal para la Supervisión de la Inteligencia Artificial* (AESIA/State Agency for the Supervision of Artificial Intelligence) was founded. So far, no regional authorities exclusively dedicated to AI have been created, yet various regional agencies include AI within their competences. This is the case of the Agency of Digital Administration (*Agencia para la Administración Digital*) in Madrid or the more recent and ambitious Agency of Digital Transformation (*Agencia de Transformación Digital*) in Castilla-La Mancha, which will be discussed later.

In the following sections, the aforementioned considerations will be further developed to provide an overview of the situation in Spain.

January 2022. And Declaration on Digital rights and principles for the Digital Decade, COM (2022) 28 final, 26 January 2022. See in particular the Commission Staff Working Document "Report on the stakeholder consultation and engagement activities" accompanying the Communication, where the Spanish Charter is included in Annex III as one of the analysed initiatives on digital rights and principles.

2 The Effective Use of AI Systems by Spanish Public Administrations and the Lack of Legal Basis and Transparency

Artificial intelligence tools have countless applications in administrative activity.[3] Different uses call for different legal frameworks as well, depending on the public functions which are to be fulfilled, as well as the public goods and interests involved therein. In the following lines some of these uses will be presented, according to a classification that distinguishes between (1) communication and engagement with the administration; (2) and other uses across various areas of administrative action which go beyond mere communication. Finally, some insights on the need to create registries of algorithms will be provided.

2.1 Communication and Engagement with the Administration. A Focus on Vulnerability and the Digital Social State

AI tools to allow and foster communication with citizens are proliferating. They are useful for providing information to citizens in relation to all areas of public action. Besides classical chatbots, specific instruments have been designed, such as those intended to make phone calls to schedule appointments (for vaccinations, for example), sending deadline reminders, or notifying individuals about the availability of financial aid. In the region of Cantabria, a robot *Jano* made phone calls and set dates for vaccination during the COVID-29 pandemic and the regional government is assessing whether to use it again for similar purposes beyond the pandemic and, in general, for organising the doctors' schedule. Furthermore, various examples of chatbots used in the Spanish public sector are discussed in Cerrillo i Martínez 2021. Also, again during the pandemic a "COVID radar" was created, so as to detect infected people and inform those people in the surroundings potentially affected by them. Yet the practical effectiveness of this system unfortunately does not seem to provide very optimistic results.

Speech recognition systems allow for the transcription of dictated texts, improving efficiency for public employees or individuals with reading and writing difficulties. They can support efforts to bridge the technological or digital divide, such as transcribing spoken words into written text for blind individuals, just as text-to-speech systems serve the reverse function. Associations defending the rights of people with disabilities in Spain as well as public administrations have thoroughly studied how AI can improve their lives, also in the particular aspects of the relations between them and public administrations.[4] The report mentioned in the footnote

[3] In general, on the uses of AI in the Spanish public sector see Cotino Hueso (2023).

[4] Carcedo Yllera and Hernández Galán (2023).

does not discuss specific uses in the public sector, yet it correctly highlights where and how AI tools may be useful to enhance personal experience of these people in their relations with public administrations, something which could furthermore be of help to all the population.[5]

The report mentions voice assistants as tools that enhance self-sufficiency, something that, logically, can also be used in general in the public sector. In this way, people with disabilities would reduce their dependence on third parties for carrying out administrative procedures. Intelligent translation systems, as well as voice transcription systems and document recognition systems, similarly promote autonomy. In this regard, an appropriate legal framework for the protection of citizens, particularly this group, would require adjustments to the general legal framework. For example, the concept of error[6] in administrative procedures could be reconsidered to the extent that a citizen has used one of these systems to enhance their self-sufficiency, and, as a result, a communication or transcription error has occurred, leading to a legally adverse outcome for the individual.

The report is based on interviews conducted with the affected group and does not analyse specific use cases, including in the public sector. However, it is highly relevant for identifying needs and, if necessary, for developing an integrative artificial intelligence model from the perspective of the Digital Social State.[7] In particular, the document highlights that home automation systems and smartwatches or smart bracelets are useful for purposes such as health preservation and caregiving. However, it also points out that in this field, economic factors represent a significant barrier to use, with approximately 60% of the sample indicating that they cannot afford these technologies.[8]

Such data is relevant for shaping public policies on healthcare, social assistance, and caregiving—key sectors within the Social State, distinct from those that have traditionally shaped the classical categories of Administrative Law.

Clearly, the use of AI systems may cause or strengthen the digital divide among groups of population and affect negatively people with disabilities. This could be added to other grounds of discrimination. Yet it is also necessary to strengthen the view of positive uses of AI in order to fulfil a so-called Digital Social State, where public powers use AI tools to foster integration. This would go beyond a general "digital *Daseinsvorsorge*",[9] applicable to the population irrespective of their particularities or of their belonging to a specific group.

[5] On the impact of digital Administration in certain vulnerable groups, see Costas et al. (2022).

[6] On the concept of error in the digital Administration, see Boto Álvarez (2023).

[7] De la Sierra et al. (2025).

[8] Yllera and Galán (2023), p. 119.

[9] De la Sierra (2023).

2.2 Uses Accross Various Areas of Administrative Action

Beyond simple conversational tasks (which, in some cases, may potentially have legal effects), artificial intelligence is widely used in many public administrations to perform routine or repetitive tasks, such as sending automated emails or text messages (for example, to schedule medical appointments). As it will further developed, lack of transparency and of specific regulation leaves the research question still a highly exploratory one.

Additionally, basic artificial intelligence programs accessible to any user can assist public employees in drafting resolution templates. This practice is not legally regulated in Spain for administrative activity, but it is in the field of the judiciary. Specifically, Royal Decree-Law 6/2023, of December 19,[10] introduced urgent amendments concerning certain aspects of digital efficiency in the justice system. In particular, it incorporated provisions from a draft bill on the digital efficiency of the public justice service, which was left unapproved in Parliament in July 2023 due to the early call for general elections. Among other provisions, Royal Decree-Law 6/2023 includes a First Book on measures for digital and procedural efficiency in the justice system and introduces Chapter VII on automated, proactive, and assisted actions in Title III, which regulates the electronic processing of judicial procedures.

Of particular relevance is Article 57, which addresses so-called "assisted actions" and is regulated as follows:

Article 57. Assisted Actions

1. An assisted action is defined as one in which the information system of the Administration of Justice generates a complete or partial draft of a complex document based on data, which may be produced by algorithms and can serve as the basis or support for a judicial or procedural decision.

2. Under no circumstances shall the generated draft document, on its own, constitute a judicial or procedural decision without validation by the competent authority. The systems of the Administration of Justice shall ensure that the draft document is generated solely at the user's request and can be freely and entirely modified by them.
3. The issuance of a judicial or procedural decision shall always require the validation of the final text by a judge, magistrate, prosecutor, or legal counsel of the Administration of Justice, within their respective competencies and under their responsibility. Additionally, the identification, authentication, or electronic sig-

[10] Real Decreto-ley 6/2023, de 19 de diciembre, por el que se aprueban medidas urgentes para la ejecución del Plan de Recuperación, Transformación y Resiliencia en materia de servicio público de justicia, función pública, régimen local y mecenazgo (Royal Decree-Law 6/2023, of December 19, approving urgent measures for the implementation of the Recovery, Transformation, and Resilience Plan in matters of public justice service, civil service, local governance, and patronage). The urgency arises from the need to fulfill the commitments made with the European Commission for the execution of the Next Generation Funds.

nature required by law must be provided, alongside any procedural requirements established by the applicable legal framework.

As in other fields, both the judicial body, when using artificial intelligence to produce a draft, and the public administration, when applying similar tools within their respective competencies, may be subject to the so-called "automation bias,"[11] whereby individuals tend to accept the results provided by the machine uncritically.

Equivalent systems may be available for citizens to complete forms or other documents relevant to administrative actions. These systems are particularly useful for individuals with disabilities or those who, in general, face difficulties in drafting or interacting with the administration through documentation.

In the realm of control and supervision, there are some well-documented cases of artificial intelligence applications in Spain.[12] These include monitoring beach occupancy,[13] particularly in the post-pandemic period, traffic control and the issuance of penalties,[14] as well as detecting behaviours contrary to competition regulations.[15]

Finally, proactive systems can even be developed to function without prior requests, based on available public administration data, one example of this being the potential pre-approval of grants and subsidies (Cerrillo i Martínez and Velasco Rico 2023).

This brief overview of artificial intelligence applications in the public sector ties into established governmental powers: sanctioning, taxation and inspection, as well as activities related to public spending, such as grants and procurement. Public management, planning authority, regulatory authority, and organizational autonomy are also impacted.

---

[11] Ruschmeier and Hondrich (2024).

[12] Some of them are discussed in Digital Future Society (2023). In particular, this report analyses BOSCO (a tool to determine if a person has the right to benefit from national aid on the electricity bill), RisCanvi (a system that calculates the risk of recidivism among inmates in Catalonia), VioGen (a mechanism of the National Police that predicts the risk of reoffending in cases of gender-based violence), and SALER (a system that forecasts potential cases of corruption in the Autonomous Community of Valencia).

[13] This and other examples in the city of Barcelona can be found in the project "Global Observatory of Urban Artificial Intelligence" (https://gouai.cidob.org/).

[14] Some existing experiences can be found under https://media.uc3m.es/video/643fb8978f4208da2f8b456d, a link that hosts a seminar hold at the University Carlos III in Madrid where this question was discussed.

[15] The Spanish National Markets and Competition Commission (*Comisión Nacional de los Mercados y de la Competencia*) has an Economic Intelligence Unit, which uses artificial intelligence (among other tools) to ensure the proper functioning of markets and to analyse anti-competitive behaviour. Among its tasks, it plays a key role in improving inspections and handling the referral of anti-competitive indications detected in public procurement procedures that come to its attention in the exercise of its duties (Articles 69.2, 132.3, and 150.1 of Statute 9/2017 on Public Sector Contracts). Additionally, the Commission itself states that these tools can be useful in detecting cases of algorithmic collusion. See https://www.cnmc.es/vigilamos-la-competencia/unidad-de-inteligencia-economica.

2.3 Lack of Transparency and of a Specific Legal Framework

The role of artificial intelligence, as in the rest of society, is to integrate into public action as an additional tool at its disposal. However, as demonstrated, its applications are highly diverse, necessitating regulatory clarification from lawmakers that aligns with the evolving circumstances. Since artificial intelligence is being used in the exercise of public powers, the principle of legality established in Article 103.1 of the Spanish Constitution—just as valid now as before—requires that such use (or rather, such uses) be explicitly provided for in a legal instrument with sufficient regulatory density, adapted to each case. Additional legal or para-legal instruments may then further refine the regulatory framework as needed.

Yet in order to assess whether public administrations are using AI tools in a legally appropriate way and in conformity also with ethical standards, transparency is required. So far there are at State level no public registries of AI tools being used by public administrations in Spain. Only in scarce cases does a public administration make public that such a tool is being used. It happens regularly when the AI tool is being used for communication or information purposes (chatbots), but there is much obscurity when those instruments are used in decision-making processes. Furthermore, even if the information concerning the effective use of an AI instrument by administrations is provided to the general public, its functioning usually remains hidden. There has been some litigation in Spain concerning this aspect and the Supreme Court has recently issued a judgment on 11 September 2011 addressing this question.[16]

The matter in question is the so-called "Bosco case," which originates from a software application of the same name developed at the request of the Ministry for Ecological Transition. The purpose of this application is to determine whether individuals meet the requirements to qualify for the social bonus and, consequently, be eligible for a reduction in their electricity bill.

The CIVIO Foundation requested information about this software program under the Transparency Law[17] and, among other things, sought access to its source code. The Ministry denied the request, leading CIVIO to appeal to the Council for Transparency and Good Governance (CTBG). The Council refused the request for access to the source code (a stance it later corrected in subsequent rulings), prompting CIVIO to take the matter to court (Ponce Solé 2024).

Both the first and second instance courts dismissed CIVIO's claims, which led to the filing of an administrative cassation appeal before the Third Chamber of the Supreme Court, namely the one in charge of judicial review of administrative action. The Supreme Court considered that under these circumstances the plaintiff had a right to get access to the source code of the algorithm.

---

[16] Judgment 1119/2025 of the Supreme Court (Third Chamber, competent for administrative law issues).

[17] Law 19/2013, of December 9, on Transparency, Access to Public Information, and Good Governance.

Together with courts, the role of the Spanish Council of Transparency and Good Governance has been relevant. Indeed, various requests of information have reached the CTGG after the Bosco case, in particular, in order to have access to the source code of algorithms being used by administrations (both national and regional) in decision-making processes.

2.4 *Transparency, Public Registries and a Regulatory Sandbox*

As stated above, there is a claim of a lack of transparency regarding the use of AI systems in the Spanish public sector. The use of AI varies, as does its impact on citizens' rights. However, it is important to know whether public administrations are making decisions using AI algorithms and to understand exactly how these operate. Transparency is key in this regard, and public registries providing such information are useful tools for ensuring legal protection.

At State level, a registry of AI algorithms has been announced as part of the National Strategy on Artificial Intelligence 2024. Yet so far such a registry does not exist. Additionally, this Strategy includes as an action line the creation of a repository of use cases, so that they may serve as examples for other bodies within the same administration or for other administrations. This will be carried out under the GovTech program.

These and other issues must also be considered in relation to Royal Decree 817/2023 of November 8, which establishes a controlled testing environment for assessing compliance with the European Parliament and Council's proposed Artificial Intelligence Regulation (AI Sandbox). In practice, AI systems participating in the controlled testing environment serve as a preliminary step before being registered. This applies to public administrations, institutional public sector entities, and selected private entities (article 2 of Royal Decree 817/2023).

To participate in the controlled testing environment, an application must be submitted once the call for participation is published on the corresponding web portal by the Secretary of State for Digitalisation and Artificial Intelligence, within the Ministry for Digital Transformation and Public Service (article 6 of Royal Decree 817/2023). According to paragraph 2 of Article 6:

> The call for participation in the controlled testing environment will specify the number of AI systems selected, the duration of the controlled testing environment, the conditions for participation in accordance with the requirements of the royal decree, the criteria for evaluating applications as well as their weighting, the deadline for submission, communication channels, the standardized application model, and the necessary documentation to submit the application.

To develop this initiative, collaboration is expected with other public administrations, institutional public sector entities, international organisations, and authorities from other EU member states with competence in matters related to the various cases being developed within this controlled testing environment. The goal is to ensure its proper functioning and facilitate its progress, regardless of the territorial scope it affects (article 26 of Royal Decree 817/2023).

Back to transparency and registries, some regional initiatives should also be noted. A registry has been created in the Autonomous Community of Valencia, derived from the pioneering Law 1/2022 of April 13 on Transparency and Good Governance of the Valencian Community. Such a register was announced in 2023 in the Community of Madrid and a similar registry is also expected to be created in Castilla-La Mancha in the near future.

At the local level, some initiatives are also emerging. Notably, the Barcelona City Council is participating in the Eurocities' Digital Forum Lab, a network that includes the city councils of Amsterdam, Brussels, Eindhoven, Mannheim, Rotterdam, and Sofia. Within this framework, the Algorithmic Transparency Standard project has been launched, proposing a Guidance for European Cities. As described in the document:

> This standard presents a fairly comprehensive set of categories of information for cities to provide about their algorithms. By using the same 'standard' categories across many cities, information on the algorithms can be more easily compared and understood. Both making the information publicly available and making it comparable contribute to making it transparent. At the basis for any interoperable algorithm register is a data schema that determines the scope of information on algorithms and describes the dataset to support common understanding.[18]

However, the project does not include a consensus definition of what constitutes an algorithm for registry purposes, which remains an open issue to be clarified later.

Another noteworthy public initiative is led by the *Consorcio Administración Abierta de Cataluña* (AOC/Catalonian Open Administration Consortium), an entity originating from an agreement in the Parliament of Catalonia between various political groups and public administrations in 2001. Its legal framework is defined by Law 29/2010 of August 3 on the Use of Electronic Means in the Public Sector of Catalonia. Article 7 establishes a duty of cooperation between administrations within the Autonomous Community of Catalonia, stating that collaboration will be concretized through the following actions: (a) Promoting and developing the use of electronic means by entities in the Catalan public sector; (b) Coordinating their strategies and actions concerning the use of electronic means; and (c) Defining and implementing common strategies to be developed in [specific areas].

Additionally, article 7 references necessary cooperation with two agencies that complement Catalonia's governance model: The Catalan Certification Agency, which oversees electronic signatures in the Catalan public sector, and the Cybersecurity Agency of Catalonia.

The AOC Consortium has launched a transparency initiative within its jurisdiction, providing an online space that reports on the AI algorithms effectively used by some Catalan administrations. However, at present, the system is limited to

[18] https://www.algorithmregister.org/guidance.

chatbots, distinguishing between conversational chatbots and those using generative AI.[19]

3 Regulatory Framework

3.1 Spain's Compromise with Digitalisation and Digital Rights as a Starting Point for the Regulation of AI

3.1.1 Introduction: Institutional Context and Strategies

In January 2020, the then new Government included a Ministry of Economic Issues and Digital Transformation (the Minister was also Vicepresident of the Government). This was the first time that digitalisation was part of a Ministry's label, thus placing digitalisation at the top of the public agenda as one of the Government's priorities. In the Ministery a new position of Secretary of State for Digitalisation and Artificial Intelligence was created and this sent also a clear message in this field.

Various public policy documents and soft law instruments have been adopted in the meantime regarding both digitalisation and AI. Besides the Digital Rights Charter, which will be discussed in detail further down, one document should be singled out, namely the already mentioned Strategy on Artificial Intelligence [*Estrategia Nacional de Inteligencia Artificial*/ENIA] 2020 (of barely 10 pages) and the new Strategy 2024 (of almost 70 pages).[20]

The Strategy on AI follows the path of the previous and more general Strategy on Digital Spain [*España Digital*] 2025, launched in July 2020 and then completed with *España Digital 2026*. Back then, the Government appointed a group of 18 experts (among which the author of this chapter) to draft a Digital Rights Charter, which was accomplished in July 2021. Both the Strategy on Digital Spain 2026 and the Digital Rights Charter, albeit being generally referred to digitalisation, include specific references to AI. Thus, Axis number 4 of the Strategy on Digital Spain 2026 referred to the Data Economy and AI. Among the main outcomes of the Strategy in the field of AI so far, it is to be stressed the creation of the already mentioned regulatory sandbox of AI, an initiative led together with the European Commission, which is meant to be the place in which guides and operative tools will be designed to implement the Artificial Intelligence Act.[21]

---

[19] Document available at the website of the AOC: https://www.aoc.cat/en.

[20] As with other references to public policy documents and other texts alike, they can be easily found on the web through the usual research tools. Therefore, I have expressly avoided the use of (many) long host addresses, which might excessively alter the features of what is an academic work. I have introduced some references, where the text might present some difficulties to be found.

[21] Regulation (EU) 2024/1689 of the European Parliament and of the Council of 13 June 2024 laying down harmonised rules on artificial intelligence and amending Regulations (EC) No 300/2008, (EU) No 167/2013, (EU) No 168/2013, (EU) 2018/858, (EU) 2018/1139 and (EU) 2019/2144 and

3.1.2 The Digital Rights Charter

The discussion on the protection of rights in the digital environment did not exactly begin with the Spanish Digital Rights Charter of 2021. Rather, the Charter can be considered the culmination of a broader process that has taken place both in Spain and beyond, in response to challenges affecting all aspects of life across different regions of the world. It was also framed within the European Commission's strategy *"A Europe Fit for the Digital Age"* and Spain's Digital Spain 2025 Strategy.

Some members of the Experts' Group appointed to draft the Charter had previously participated in another group formed in 2017, whose report led to the introduction of Title X in Organic Law 3/2018, of December 5, on the Protection of Personal Data and the Guarantee of Digital Rights. Prior to this, a Citizen Digital Rights Forum had been held at the Reina Sofía Museum on May 30, 2017.

There are precedents in other countries, as well as early texts that emerged beyond state structures. However, the Spanish Charter has distinct characteristics. A particularly relevant reference—due to its connections with the Spanish text—is the Italian Declaration of Internet Rights, developed within the Parliamentary Commission on Internet Rights and Duties and promoted by Laura Boldrini, then President of the Chamber of Deputies.

The Italian text was drafted within Parliament, not from he Government, and resulted from a public consultation process and expert hearings. Professor Stefano Rodotà led the work and delivered a speech to Parliament titled *Verso una dichiarazione dei diritti di Internet* (Towards a Declaration of Internet Rights), in which he explained the underlying purpose of the proposal.

The Spanish Charter classifies rights and freedoms from a substantive perspective (rather than, for example, from the standpoint of protection or guarantees, as is the case with the Spanish Constitution). In this regard, it follows the model of the Charter of Fundamental Rights of the European Union, clearly aiming to connect both instruments, given that the purpose of the Digital Rights Charter is to complement the existing fundamental rights framework and link it to the digital environment.

In drafting the Charter, two main objectives were pursued. On the one hand, the text was formulated with technical precision, as its conceptual framework is based on the protection of rights, regardless of the fate of the document—whether or not it ultimately becomes a legal norm. On the other hand, the specific mandate was also considered: the creation of a document that would serve as a basis for broad debate, not only among specialists but also among the general public. In this sense, efforts were made to give visibility to the rights and to detail the content of some of them—sometimes with an educational intent for those less familiar with the subject, and in other cases with more specific and technical references to aspects that, in the opinion of the Expert Group, require detailed consideration by the relevant public authorities.

Directives 2014/90/EU, (EU) 2016/797 and (EU) 2020/1828 (Artificial Intelligence Act). Hereinafter, AI Act.

The Charter is not necessarily drafted in broad terms, as many sections (not articles in the strict sense) include a certain level of detail, aligning with the invitation to develop public policies. As in the Italian Declaration, the first section refers to existing international and national legal texts. This aims to emphasise that the digital environment is not separate from the classical fundamental rights discourse and that the fundamental rights we have known so far do not disappear in this new context. Human dignity remains the central axis around which any reflection on the challenges of disruptive technologies—and their legal framework—must be structured. In this regard, the Charter also highlights the need to ensure compliance with legal norms from the design phase, which will apply to the development of all digital processes.

The rights are then presented in five blocks, inspired by the Charter of Fundamental Rights of the European Union but with some particularities. The blocks are as follows: (1) freedom rights; (2) equality rights; (3) rights of participation and the structuring of public space; (4) rights in the labour and business environment; and (5) digital rights in specific contexts. As a closing clause, a section on guarantees and the effectiveness of rights is included.

Artificial intelligence is mentioned multiple times throughout the text. Specifically, Section XXV (in block 5, concerning digital rights in specific contexts) refers to rights related to artificial intelligence and states the following:

1. Artificial intelligence must ensure a human-centered approach that respects inalienable human dignity, pursues the common good, and adheres to the principle of non-maleficence.
2. In the development and lifecycle of artificial intelligence systems:

(a) The right to non-discrimination must be guaranteed, regardless of its origin, cause, or nature, in relation to decisions, data usage, and processes based on artificial intelligence.
(b) Conditions of transparency, auditability, explainability, traceability, human oversight, and governance must be established. In all cases, the information provided must be accessible and understandable.
(c) Accessibility, usability, and reliability must be ensured.

3. Individuals have the right to request human oversight and intervention and to challenge automated decisions made by artificial intelligence systems that affect their personal or financial sphere.

Meanwhile, Section XVIII, concerning the digital rights of citizens in their interactions with public administrations (in block 3, on rights of participation and the structuring of public space), includes a subsection specifically addressing the use of artificial intelligence tools by public administrations:

(6) The rights of citizens concerning artificial intelligence recognised in this Charter will be promoted within the framework of administrative action, ensuring in all cases the right to:

(a) Ensure that decisions and activities in the digital environment respect the principles of good governance and the right to good digital administration, as well as the ethical principles guiding the design and use of artificial intelligence.
(b) Transparency regarding the use of artificial intelligence tools, their functioning, and their scope within each specific procedure, particularly concerning the data used, their margin of error, their scope of application, and whether they are decision-making or non-decision-

making tools. The law may regulate the conditions of transparency and access to the source code, especially to verify that the system does not produce discriminatory outcomes.

(c) Receive a comprehensible explanation in natural language of decisions made in the digital environment, including justification based on relevant legal norms, the technology used, and the criteria applied to the case. Individuals shall have the right to an explanation when an administrative decision deviates from the recommendation proposed by an automated or intelligent system.

(d) Ensure that discretionary decision-making remains reserved for humans unless regulations explicitly allow automated decision-making with appropriate safeguards.

The Digital Rights Charter is not positive law but can be considered a public policy or soft law document intended to inspire the interpretation of existing regulations. However, recent legal reforms have included references to the Charter, suggesting that its content has been at least partially codified.[22]

One notable example is Law 15/2022, of July 12, on comprehensive equality of treatment and non-discrimination, whose Article 23 addresses artificial intelligence and automated decision-making mechanisms. This provision states the following:

1. Within the framework of the National Artificial Intelligence Strategy, the Digital Rights Charter, and European initiatives on Artificial Intelligence, public administrations will promote mechanisms to ensure that the algorithms involved in decision-making processes used by public administrations take into account bias minimisation, transparency, and accountability criteria, whenever technically feasible. These mechanisms will include considerations regarding their design and training data and will address their potential discriminatory impact. To achieve this, impact assessments will be encouraged to determine possible discriminatory biases.
2. Public administrations, within their competencies related to algorithms involved in decision-making processes, will prioritise transparency in their design and implementation, as well as the interpretability of the decisions they produce.
3. Public administrations and companies will promote the use of ethical, reliable artificial intelligence that respects fundamental rights, particularly following the recommendations of the European Union in this regard.
4. A quality seal for algorithms will be promoted.

Finally, the public entity Red.es is currently funding an ambitious reform program for the development of the Digital Rights Charter, highlighting the creation of the Digital Rights Observatory.

3.2 A Legal Framework Still under Construction

The laws 39/2015, of October 1, on the Common Administrative Procedure of Public Administrations, and 40/2015, of October 1, on the Legal Regime of the Public Sector, along with other complementary and sector-specific regulations, are insufficient in the context of digital administration. In this regard, their revision

[22] In addition to Law 15/2022, which is explained later in the text, the following laws should also be mentioned: Law 11/2022, of June 28, the General Telecommunications Law, whose Preamble states that the law is aligned with the Digital Rights Charter; as well as Law 13/2022, of July 7, the General Audiovisual Communication Law, whose Article 10—regarding media literacy—refers to the application of the provisions of the Digital Rights Charter on this matter.

should be undertaken, as already envisioned in the Spain Digital 2025 Strategy and later specified in the Public Administration Digitalisation Plan.

Regulation must achieve a certain degree of sophistication while balancing three principles of modern administrative law: legality, equality and transparency. The legal and para-legal instruments currently in place could perhaps be considered "experimental," pending verification of evolving needs and the development of the most appropriate regulatory framework. In fact, this experimentation is particularly taking place at the regional and local levels, suggesting that national regulation will likely follow once these decentralised experiments reach maturity.

The key (but still insufficient) provision today at State level is article 41 of Law 40/2015, of October 1, on the Legal Regime of the Public Sector, which addresses automated administrative action and has been referenced earlier. This provision refers to "automated" administrative action (with and without AI) within the framework of an administrative procedure, establishing general criteria that define its legal framework. This article, together with Article 42 of the same law, constitutes today the most evident legal basis—albeit a concise one—for the exercise of administrative powers through artificial intelligence.

As for public procurements, no specific provisions of the existing legal framework in Spain at State level deal in particular with artificial intelligence, but certain Autonomous Communities are particularly active in this realm, such is the case of Aragón or Castilla-La Mancha.[23]

In the absence of a clear legal framework in general, again regional and local authorities have promoted interesting initiatives. One such example is the Protocol of the Barcelona City Council for defining work methodologies and protocols for the implementation of algorithmic systems, adopted as part of the Municipal Strategy on Algorithms and Data for the Ethical Promotion of Artificial Intelligence, which was implemented in 2021.

Based on a broad definition of artificial intelligence in Annex I, the protocol adopts a very specific concept of intelligent systems, understood here as "automated decision-making algorithms capable of making decisions without human intervention. The only requirement is that the algorithm analyses the given scenario based on data and makes a decision accordingly." The protocol aims to establish common guidelines for public procurement or the acceptance of pilot tests of reliable algorithmic systems within the framework of the Municipal Strategy on Algorithms and Data for the Ethical Promotion of Artificial Intelligence, which includes a specific section on the legal framework.

On the regional front, mention should be made of the pioneering Law 1/2022, of April 13, on Transparency and Good Governance of the Valencian Community. Its Article 16 regulates proactive disclosure and mandates that obligated entities publish, among other things, "[t]he list of algorithmic or artificial intelligence systems that impact administrative procedures or the provision of public services, with a

[23] Mention should be made of the Observatory of Public Procurement (*Observatorio de Contratación Pública*), one of the best sources in order to follow up the state of the art of public procurements in Spain.

comprehensible description of their design and functioning, the level of risk they entail, and the contact point for inquiries, in accordance with the principles of transparency and explainability."

And, from a more general perspective, Royal Decree-Law 2/2023, of March 8, on urgent measures to promote artificial intelligence in Extremadura stands out, particularly two articles:

Article 11. Artificial intelligence systems in decision-making.

1. The regional public administration may adopt administrative acts using artificial intelligence systems within the framework of an administrative procedure, in accordance with the Digital Rights of citizens in their relations with Public Administrations, as described in the Digital Rights Charter of the Government of Spain and the European Declaration on Digital Rights and Principles for the Digital Decade (2023/C 23/01).
2. To this end, in addition to the requirements established in Article 41 of Law 40/2015, of October 1, on the Legal Regime of the Public Sector, due publicity will be given to the decision-making mechanism, the priorities assigned in the evaluation process, and all data that may impact its content.

Article 12. Guarantees for the use of artificial intelligence in administrative procedures.

1. Regulations governing administrative procedures must explicitly refer to the impact of artificial intelligence systems on the provision of public services, including their role in assisting with applications, responsible declarations, or communications, verifying the requirements of interested parties, and making decisions.
2. The Administrative Information Inventory must document the validations carried out by the body responsible for administrative procedures regarding the logical process designed for decision-making, the associated risks, and any other aspects ensuring the rights of the concerned parties.

Meanwhile, a Statute on artificial intelligence has been passed on 2 April, 2025 by the Parliament of Galicia (the Autonomous Community where the Spanish Agency for the Supervision of Artificial Intelligence is located). The Galician initiative is ambitious, proposing a comprehensive regulation of artificial intelligence, starting with the identification of a set of general principles and citizens' rights, as well as a sophisticated governance system. It also establishes the legal framework for the use of artificial intelligence systems and general-purpose AI models, including a provision on strategic public procurement of artificial intelligence (Article 68).

One notable aspect of the Galician law is that it includes the training and capacity-building of public employees in artificial intelligence (Article 69), granting this matter the highest regulatory status. The law states:

1. The General Administration of the Autonomous Community of Galicia and its public sector shall provide the necessary resources to ensure public employees have access to initial training and continuous education, tailored to the characteristics of their job positions, for the development of their competencies related to artificial intelligence systems and their efficient use in public service delivery.
2. Initial training and continuous education in artificial intelligence for public employees must cover not only technical aspects but also the ethical and legal dimensions of its use.

This responsibility will primarily fall to the Galician School of Public Administration (*Escola Galega de Administración Pública*/EGAP), in collaboration with other entities such as the Agency for the Technological Modernization of Galicia (*Axencia para a modernización tecnolóxica de Galicia*/AMTEGA).

At the national level, there is no explicit mandate of this kind yet, but the National Institute of Public Administration (*Instituto Nacional de Administración Pública*/INAP) has been offering courses on this subject for some time.

Spanish public administrations are, in general, not prone to change and adaptation. Spain follows the French system of public service, where public exams (*concours*) are organized for different categories (the so-called "bodies" or *Cuerpos*) of public servants. Besides specific groups such as judges, teachers, doctors, there are no less specific groups such as Finance inspectors, social security inspectors, and more general groups such as technicians of the public administration and State lawyers, both high-rank officials with good reputation. More recently, STEM positions have been created, but there is still a deficit in number, in order to face all the challenges public administrations are subject to.

4 Governance at the Central and Regional Level

4.1 The Proliferation of Independent Bodies in the States and in the European Union

In recent years, a phenomenon has emerged that affects both national administrations and the European administration. This concerns the proliferation of various bodies created specifically for the development of public policies or the achievement of objectives of general interest. Particularly noteworthy for the purposes of this discussion are the bodies responsible for supervising specific areas of reality, especially those originating from European Union regulations to ensure their effective implementation and enforcement.

In the context of digital transformation processes, the emergence of these bodies has been particularly significant. Currently, there is an extensive governance system in which data protection authorities, market and digital services supervisory bodies, and authorities promoting digital transformation in public administrations coexist. Additionally, regarding this chapter, there are authorities responsible for regulating and supervising artificial intelligence.

It is not appropriate to conduct here an exhaustive evaluation of this new reality,[24] but it is relevant to briefly highlight some of its significant characteristics for the purposes of this chapter. A networked system such as the one described offers certain advantages, such as the technical expertise of the bodies and, consequently, better management of each concerned sector. Moreover, these bodies should exercise oversight functions in an ostensibly independent manner, so their actions can

---

[24] See on this De la Sierra (2024).

positively contribute to the protection of rights. At the same time, this could reduce the burden on the judiciary if it results in a decrease in subsequent litigation.

On the other hand, even when a case reaches the courts, the existence of a prior resolution by a highly qualified and, in principle, neutral body should ensure a higher quality procedural debate, as qualified material is available.

However, it is advisable to strengthen cooperation mechanisms between bodies (Sola 2023), as the organisational inflation described may become ineffective, generate duplications, and ultimately hinder proper sector management, as well as affect the legal standing of individuals or businesses.

4.2 The Spanish State Agency for the Supervision of Artificial Intelligence and a Brief Note on the Spanish Agency of Digital Administration

Following these considerations, we will now outline the governance model developed in Spain to date concerning artificial intelligence. However, this is a constantly evolving field, and it is likely that the framework will undergo notable changes in the coming months.

Spain has also been a pioneer in this area, as the creation of a governance body for artificial intelligence was part of a set of initiatives by the Ministry of Economic Affairs and Digital Transformation between 2020 and 2024. Indeed, the government that began working a few weeks before the pandemic established a new Secretariat of State for Digitalisation and Artificial Intelligence within the aforementioned Ministry. At the head of this Secretariat of State was a professional from the sector trained in Spain and the United States, Carme Artigas, who, after completing their tenure in 2023, continued in the private sector while also serving as co-Chair of the UN AI Advisory Board.

The Secretariat of State proposed an ambitious agenda and, among other initiatives, promoted the aforementioned Digital Rights Charter, as well as the creation of the Spanish State Agency for the Supervision of Artificial Intelligence (*Agencia Estatal de Supervisión de la Inteligencia Artificial*/AESIA).

The creation of AESIA was foreseen in Law 22/2021, of December 28, on the General State Budget for 2022, which authorised the government to promote a law for its effective establishment. The proposed legal structure for this agency was that of a "state agency". These entities possess legal public personality, their own assets, and management autonomy. Additionally, they may be granted administrative powers. The effective creation of such entities must be established by a specific law, according to Article 91 of Law 40/2015, of October 1, on the Legal Regime of the Public Sector. This specific law was Law 28/2022, of December 21, on fostering the startup ecosystem, whose Seventh Additional Provision states:

> One. In accordance with the provisions of Article 91 of Law 40/2015, of October 1, on the Legal Regime of the Public Sector, the creation of the Spanish Agency for the Supervision

of Artificial Intelligence is authorized as a public body with legal personality, its own assets, full operational capacity, and administrative, inspection, and sanctioning powers as attributed by national and European regulations regarding the safe and reliable use of artificial intelligence systems.

Two. The Agency's activities shall serve the following purposes:

(a) Raising awareness, disseminating information, and promoting training, as well as the responsible, sustainable, and reliable development and use of artificial intelligence.
(b) Defining advisory and support mechanisms for society and other actors involved in the development and use of artificial intelligence.
(c) Collaborating and coordinating with national and supranational authorities responsible for AI supervision.
(d) Promoting real-world testing environments for artificial intelligence systems to enhance user protection.
(e) Supervising the deployment, use, and commercialisation of AI-based systems, especially those that may pose significant risks to health, safety, and fundamental rights.

Three. The Agency shall be attached to the State Secretariat for Digitalisation and Artificial Intelligence within the Ministry of Economic Affairs and Digital Transformation. It shall be governed by its organic statute and by the provisions of Law 40/2015, of October 1, on the Legal Regime of the Public Sector.

Four. The Agency's legal assistance, including advisory services, legal representation, and defence in court, shall be provided by State Attorneys integrated into the State Legal Service.

The legal framework for the agency was established by Royal Decree 729/2023, of August 22, which approved the Statute of the Spanish State Agency for the Supervision of Artificial Intelligence. As can be seen, this body was created long before the approval of the EU Regulation. However, the Royal Decree states that "the creation of the Agency is based on the obligation [set forth by the AI Act proposal] for Member States to designate a 'national supervisory authority' responsible for monitoring the implementation and enforcement of the AI Law, coordinating the activities assigned to Member States, acting as the single contact point for the Commission, and representing the respective Member State before the European Artificial Intelligence Board." Additionally, it is stated that the establishment of this agency aligns with Spain's commitments to the European Commission for the reception of Next Generation Funds, as outlined in the Recovery, Transformation, and Resilience Plan. Specifically, the sixth driving policy of the Plan is the Pact for Science and Innovation, which includes the National Artificial Intelligence Strategy.

The Agency is headquartered in the city of A Coruña, in the Autonomous Community of Galicia, as part of the decentralisation process of public bodies promoted in past years. While a comprehensive analysis of the Agency's legal framework is not possible here, we will focus on two aspects: its structure and some specific functions.

AESIA is attached to the Ministry of Digital Transformation and Public Function through the Secretariat of State for Digitalisation and Artificial Intelligence. This attachment is formal and should not necessarily undermine the agency's independence. However, from an independence standpoint, its organisational structure is striking. It is divided into governing bodies and executive bodies. According to

Article 12 of its Statute, the Presidency of the agency is assigned to the holder of the Secretariat of State for Digitalisation and Artificial Intelligence, which is the second level in the ministerial hierarchy, a position freely appointed at the Minister's discretion. The Presidency, together with the Governing Council, constitute the governing bodies, and the Governing Council also oversees the Control Commission. The Governing Council is composed as follows, according to Article 15 of its Statute:

1. The Governing Council shall be composed of the holder of the Presidency of the Agency, who shall preside over it, and the following members:

(a) The holder of the Agency's Directorate.
(b) Four representatives from the Ministry of Economic Affairs and Digital Transformation, with a rank of at least Deputy Director General.
(c) One representative from the Ministry of Finance and Public Administration, with a rank of at least Deputy Director General.
(d) One representative from the Ministry of Industry, Trade, and Tourism, with a rank of at least Deputy Director General.
(e) One expert representing the artificial intelligence ecosystem, proposed jointly by the Advisory Council on Artificial Intelligence and the Permanent Commission for the Digitalisation of the Economy, Administration, and Citizenship.

2. The members shall be appointed by the holder of the Ministry of Economic Affairs and Digital Transformation.

Regardless of the individuals ultimately appointed—who may, of course, be highly competent—the formal configuration of the Governing Council raises concerns regarding independence. The majority of the appointed members represent specific ministries, while only one individual represents the AI ecosystem. Furthermore, the structure lacks representation from civil society, particularly from areas such as disability, equality, environmental concerns (given the environmental impact of AI tools), or labour rights.

According to article 70.1 of the AI Act market surveillance authorities shall exercise their powers *independently, impartially and without bias* so as to safeguard the objectivity of their activities and tasks, and to ensure the application and implementation of this Regulation. The members of those authorities shall refrain from any action incompatible with their duties. In this regard, as mentioned earlier, it can be argued that the current configuration of AESIA's governing bodies does not fully meet the requirements of the Regulation.[25]

Beyond the governing bodies, one of the most notable executive bodies is the General Directorate, a position that was filled through a public selection process with over one hundred applications. The selected candidate, Ignasi Belda, is a computer engineer with a double PhD in Artificial Intelligence and Technology Law. His professional career to date has spanned both the private sector and, in a broad sense, the public sector.[26] In addition to the General Director, the executive structure is

[25] Also in Cotino Hueso (2024). See further on the AESIA Barrio Andrés (2023), Gil Franco (2025) and Artero Muñoz et al. (2023).

[26] https://digital.gob.es/dam/es/portalmtdfp/comunicacion/notas-de-prensa/comunicacion_SEDIA/20240611_NdP_DGAESIA.pdf.

completed by the following bodies: General Secretariat; Sub-Directorate for Reports and Testing Infrastructures; Sub-Directorate for Certification, Trend Evaluation, Coordination, and Training in Artificial Intelligence.

Among the Agency's competencies, the following stands out: "The supervision of artificial intelligence systems to ensure compliance with national and European regulations related to the use of this technology, where the Agency has jurisdiction. Specifically, the Agency will be responsible for oversight and, where applicable, sanctioning in accordance with European regulations concerning the supervision of artificial intelligence systems. The design, execution, and evaluation of this supervisory function will incorporate a gender perspective." (Article 10.1.k of the Agency's Statute).

Beyond this competence directly linked to the implementation of the European AI Regulation, the Agency's scope of action is broad: promoting testing environments, fostering market dynamisation, encouraging the environmentally sustainable use of artificial intelligence, and strengthening public-private collaboration, among other competences.

Additionally, the Deputy Directorate for Certification, Trend Evaluation, Coordination, and Training in AI has been assigned, among others, the following functions (Article 26 of the Statute):

1. Proactive supervision of AI systems used by public administrations, as well as issuing binding reports and decisions regarding the continuation or deployment of these systems.
2. Providing technical support and/or advisory services to judges and courts in cases involving artificial intelligence, upon request.

It is important to highlight that the Agency is a body of the General State Administration, with authority to exercise administrative powers for the implementation of public policies within its competencies. As a result, given the Agency's wide-ranging objectives, some of its responsibilities will extend across the entire national territory, while others will depend on regional competencies and require coordination with the relevant administrations.

A brief reference should also be made to the State Agency for Digital Administration (*Agencia Estatal de Administración Digital*/AEAD), created by Law 22/2021, of December 28, on the General State Budget for 2022. This law stipulates that the AEAD will not only promote the digitalisation of the General State Administration but also coordinate digital transformation efforts across different levels of government.

Furthermore, Royal Decree 1118/2024, of November 5, approved the Statute of the AEAD. According to this decree, the AEAD is attached to the Ministry of Digital Transformation and Public Service, but unlike AESIA (Spanish AI Supervision Agency), it reports not to the State Secretariat for Digitalisation and Artificial Intelligence but to the State Secretariat for Public Service, emphasizing its role in transforming internal government operations.

The AEAD's scope is extensive, covering all aspects of public sector digitalisation, including specific references to artificial intelligence. For example, among the functions of the Directorate-General for Digital Administration, section 16.b), numbers 2° and 10°, includes:

1. "Managing the intelligent automation service (RPA), integrating AI processes and business management workflows in a centralized manner, facilitating the adoption of this technology by entities within the General State Administration and its dependent public organizations."
2. "Promoting the use of AI capabilities to maintain a proactive relationship between the government and both citizens and businesses."

Consequently, the AEAD is responsible for centralizing the integration of AI tools within the General State Administration, a measure that could contribute to greater transparency and clarity in this field.

As previously mentioned, coordination is an essential aspect of the expanding landscape of agencies forming Spain's AI governance model. The AEAD Statute specifically addresses cooperation in Article 5. Following a general mention of inter-administrative collaboration, the text includes a specific provision on cooperation among key regulatory bodies. In this regard, it urges the adoption of measures to enhance collaboration between AEAD and the Spanish Data Protection Agency (AEPD), ensuring early advisory input on relevant matters. Additionally, coordination with both the AEPD and AESIA is explicitly encouraged concerning AI systems.

4.3 Regional and Local AI Governance

The regional and local landscape regarding AI regulation varies significantly. While digitalisation is a key focus in most regional policies, artificial intelligence is still emerging as a major public policy area. Spanish Autonomous Communities (regional governments) enjoy a high degree of autonomy, with their own legislative and executive powers and extensive competencies. Occasionally, a particular region takes a pioneering role in a specific policy area, leading to early regulations that later serve as models for other administrations.

Currently, there are no autonomous AI agencies in Spain. However, AI governance is integrated into regional government structures and, in some cases, falls under independent agencies responsible for digital transformation.

Strictly speaking, there are no regional artificial intelligence agencies, but AI is included in some cases within the organizational structure of the Administration or is considered a responsibility of certain independent bodies tasked with digitalisation.

For example, in Castilla-La Mancha, a Directorate-General for Digitalisation and Artificial Intelligence was created, operating within the ordinary structure of the Administration under what is now the regional Ministry of Finance, Public Administration, and Digital Transformation. Recently, in 2023, the Digital Transformation Agency was established, granted autonomy, and integrating the Directorate-General, which now exercises leadership functions in the relevant field. Additionally, this same Agency houses a Directorate-General for Digital Health, whose functions include implementing software applications and information systems related to data analytics, big data, and artificial intelligence within the public healthcare system.

Other regional entities relevant to this matter include, among others, the following, even though most do not explicitly include the term "artificial intelligence" in their titles:

- The Andalusian Digital Agency, which oversees the implementation of the Andalusian Artificial Intelligence Strategy 2030, approved by Government Council Agreement on June 20, 2023.
- The Agency for Digital Administration of the Community of Madrid, as well as the Cybersecurity Agency in the same Autonomous Community.
- The AI Observatory for Public Administration, part of the Valencian Government, which compiles and publicises various AI applications in Public Administration.
- The previously mentioned Agency for Technological Modernisation of Galicia, responsible, among other things, for implementing the Galician Artificial Intelligence Strategy 2030.

In Extremadura, the Directorate-General for Digitalisation of the Administration, under the regional Ministry of Economy, Employment, and Digital Transformation of the Regional Government of Extremadura, is responsible for driving digitalisation in the region. This Directorate-General aims to modernize and optimize administrative processes through the implementation of digital technologies.

Additionally, other Autonomous Communities, such as Murcia, have announced future artificial intelligence strategies or other initiatives along similar lines.

Spain's AI governance landscape is evolving, with regional governments playing an increasingly important role in digital transformation and AI regulation. While there are no dedicated regional AI agencies, AI-related functions are often embedded in digitalisation authorities, technology modernisation agencies, or sector-specific entities (such as digital health departments).

Moreover, certain regions (e.g., Galicia) are taking a leading role in AI legislation, which could serve as a model for future national and regional regulations. Meanwhile, coordination remains a crucial challenge, particularly given the interplay between state-level and regional-level competencies in AI governance.

References

Artero Muñoz A, Ruiz de Toledo Rodríguez CF, Mairat Medina P (2023) Agencia Española de Supervisión de la Inteligencia Artificial, la clave para un desarrollo tecnológico ético, justo y sostenible. Revista española de control externo (25, n. 74–75: "Inteligencia artificial. Gestión y control público"): 32–45

Barrio Andrés M (2023) Sobre la Agencia Española de Supervisión de la Inteligencia Artificial (AESIA). Diario La Ley (10349)

Boto Álvarez A (2023) Nuevas barreras burocráticas: la Administración defensiva digital. Documentación Administrativa 10:40–58

Carcedo Yllera V, Hernández Galán J (eds) (2023) Estudio del impacto de la inteligencia artificial en los derechos de las personas con discapacidad, Real Patronato sobre Discapacidad/ Ministerio de Derechos Sociales y Agenda 2030, Madrid
Cerrillo i Martínez A (2021) Robots, asistentes virtuales y automatización de las administraciones públicas. Revista Galega de Administración Pública 61:271–309
Cerrillo i Martínez A, Velasco Rico CI (2023) Una persona como Usted ha recibido esta subvención. Proceso subvencional, personalización e inteligencia artificial. In: Gamero Casado E, Alarcón Sotomayor L (eds) 20 años de la Ley General de Subvenciones. INAP, Madrid, pp 243–252
Costas E, Ferrer C, Ponce J. (2022) El impacto de los trámites administrativos en el acceso a las prestaciones sociales. Una perspectiva conductual, Taula del Tercer Sector, Barcelona
Cotino Hueso L (2023) Los usos de la inteligencia artificial en el sector público, su variable impacto y categorización jurídica. Revista canaria de Administración pública 1:211–242
Cotino Hueso L (2024) La supervisión del cumplimiento del Reglamento de inteligencia artificial por las autoridades de vigilancia del mercado. Revista Canaria de Administración Pública 4:159–186
De la Sierra S (2022) Una introducción a la Carta de derechos digitales. In: Cotino L (ed) La Carta de Derechos Digitales. Tirant lo Blanch, Valencia, pp 27–52
De la Sierra S (2023) Los procesos de transformación digital, las brechas y la lucha contra la despoblación: ¿hacia una procura existencial digital? In: Navarro C, Ruiz A, Velasco F (eds) Despoblación, territorio y gobiernos locales. Marcial Pons, Madrid, pp 120–143
De la Sierra S (2024) Taming the smart cyber beast: A network of courts and other authorities. Eur Rev Digital Adm Law 5/1:83–95
De la Sierra S, Morcillo J, Meix P (eds) (forthcoming 2025) El Estado Social Digital, Aranzadi, Cizur Menor (Navarra)
Digital Future Society (2023) El uso de algoritmos en el sector público en España: cuatro estudios de caso sobre ADMS
Gil Franco AJ (2025) ¿Por qué la Agencia Española de Supervisión de la Inteligencia Artificial (AESIA) debe ser un organismo incluido dentro de la categoría "Administración independiente"? In: P. Valcárcel, F.L. Hernández (eds.) El Derecho Administrativo en la era de la inteligencia artificial: Actas del XVIII Congreso de la Asociación de Profesores de Derecho Administrativo. Vigo 25 a 27 de enero de 2024, pp 177–186
Ponce Solé J (2024) La transparencia algorítmica y los entes localeslecciones de las sentencias recaídas en el caso BOSCO, con especial atención a la de la Audiencia Nacional de 30 de abril de 2024. Consultor de los ayuntamientos y de los juzgados (3 extra: "Las entidades locales ante el reto de la inteligencia artificial")
Ruschmeier H, Hondrich J (2024) Automation bias in public administration – an interdisciplinary perspective from law and psychology. Government Information Quartely (41)
Sola A (2023), Il coordinamento amministrativo nelle funzioni di regolazione di fenomeni complessi: le economie dei dati. PhD Thesis, LUISS University, Rome

Susana de la Sierra is Professor of Administrative Law at University of Castilla-La Mancha (Spain). LL.M. (Bayreuth), Ph.D. (EUI, Florence). Former law clerk at the Spanish Supreme Court. Her research interests include administrative justice, public comparative law, law & culture, digital society and artificial intelligence.

Automated Decision-Making in Estonia's Public Sector: Innovation, Regulation, and Challenges About Non-Discrimination

Tanel Kerikmäe, Kristi Joamets, and Ebru Metin

Contents

This book chapter is written by the support of the European Commission funded project, "EquiTech – improving response to risks of discrimination, bias and intolerance in automated decision-making systems to promote equality (01.05.2024-30.04.2026)", which seeks to enhance responses to discrimination and bias in automated decision-making systems within the Estonian public sector. The project is undertaken in collaboration with the Gender Equality and Equal Treatment Commissioner's Office of Estonia, the Office of the Equal Opportunities Ombudsperson of Lithuania, the Ministry of Economic Affairs and Communications of Estonia, the Ministry of Justice of Estonia, and Tallinn University of Technology. See also; https://www.volinik.ee/en/interested/ec-projects.html.

"Prof. Tanel Kerikmäe passed away during the final stages of this publication. The remaining authors and editors honour his contribution to this article.".

T. Kerikmäe (✉) · K. Joamets · E. Metin
Tallinn University of Technology, Tallinn, Estonia
e-mail: kristi.joamets@taltech.ee; ebru.metin@taltech.ee

F. Decarolis et al. (eds.), *The EU Digital Regulation and its Impact on Member States*, European Union and its Neighbours in a Globalized World 27,
https://doi.org/10.1007/978-3-032-06490-5_6

Abstract The integration of Automated Decision-Making (ADM) systems in Estonia's public sector reflects the country's continued leadership in digital governance. This chapter examines the current state of ADM implementation, highlighting key applications such as *Bürokratt*, *OTT*, and *ABC Gates*. It analyses the legal dimensions of these systems while identifying challenges related to algorithmic bias, transparency, and regulatory compliance. The discussion also explores strategies for mitigating biases in ADM applications without compromising operational efficiency. Th chapter provides insights into the evolving regulatory framework, including the impact of the EU AI Act and Estonia's national AI strategy. The findings contribute to a better understanding of Estonia's innovative use of ADM in public administration and offer practical recommendations for policymakers and practitioners alike.

1 Introduction

Estonia is renowned for its advanced digital society.[1] As a strategic decision, Estonian e-governance focuses on enhancing the country's competitiveness and improving the well-being of its citizens. The goal is to ensure seamless, 24/7 government operations, supported by digital identity, secure data exchange, and reliable, high-quality databases.[2] One part of this is user-friendly public e-services. The use of artificial intelligence (AI) in the Estonian public sector is a growing trend, with solutions being implemented across various domains.[3] AI has been a key priority for Estonian e-governance since 2018, when the first expert group, established by the Ministry of Economic Affairs and Communications (MKM) and the Government Office, published a report on the potential adoption of AI in Estonia and introduced the country's first AI strategy.[4] Since then, the development and implementation of AI solutions in the public sector have gained momentum, with

[1] See Kerikmäe and Pärn-Lee (2021).
[2] See e-Estonia (2025).
[3] See Kratid.ee (2025).
[4] See Pilving and Mikiver (2020), AI Watch (2025).

agencies actively adopting new technologies to automate routine processes. As a result, Estonia now has over 140 AI use cases in the public sector,[5] with the number steadily increasing. Furthermore Estonia's Digital Agenda 2030 sets the vision of the creation of an AI-powered government system[6] that increases its efficiency in the public sector by means of AI and other modern routine automation technologies, with AI applications deployed being trustworthy.[7]

A key component of this transformation is the use of automated decision-making (ADM) systems—tools designed to streamline operations, enhance efficiency, and improve service delivery. Estonia's experience with ADM systems provides valuable insights into the opportunities and challenges associated with integrating AI into public administration. The Estonian public administration's early adoption of digital governance laid the foundation for its ADM innovations. The implementation of the X-Road infrastructure was a significant step toward building interconnected and data-driven systems.[8] This digital backbone enables secure and efficient data exchange across government agencies, reducing redundancy and facilitating decision-making processes. Subsequent developments, such as *Bürokratt*—a conversational AI interface—demonstrate Estonia's application of AI to improve public services.[9]

However, the implementation of ADM systems comes with challenges. Algorithmic systems can perpetuate biases, undermine procedural fairness, and erode public trust if not carefully implemented.[10] For instance, Clarke[11] illustrates the detrimental impact of algorithmic bias when welfare decisions are automated without adequate safeguards, highlighting how systemic errors in data processing led to unjustified debt claims and emphasizing the need for accuracy, transparency, and human oversight. Similarly, Zolkin[12] discusses how the Estonian Unemployment Insurance Fund relies on algorithmic decisions, emphasizing the importance of clear legal grounds, state accountability, and the need to regulate automated decisions beyond data protection. In Estonia, initiatives like the 'Kratt' project showcase the potential of algorithmic tools in administrative processes but also illustrate the need for careful implementation to avoid infringements on procedural rights.[13] Additionally, Paes[14] highlights the growing use of AI in Estonia's public services

[5] See Equitech(a) (2024).

[6] See Paes (2023).

[7] See Ministry of Economic Affairs and Communications (a) (2024).

[8] See Pilving and Mikiver (2020).

[9] See Kratid.ee (2025).

[10] See Clarke et al. (2024).

[11] See Clarke et al. (2024).

[12] See Zolkin et al. (2023).

[13] See Pilving and Mikiver (2020).

[14] See Paes (2023).

and stresses the significance of a human-centric approach to AI, ensuring that algorithmic systems respect fundamental rights and democratic principles.

Public perceptions of ADM systems also vary significantly based on trust and transparency, as shown by Kaun,[15] who found that citizens in Estonia, Sweden, and Germany have differing attitudes towards the use of automated decisions in welfare services, shaped by their historical experiences with administrative practices. Therefore, while ADM systems offer efficiency gains, their deployment requires robust legal frameworks, ethical considerations, and public engagement to maintain trust and fairness in administrative practices.

The regulatory landscape surrounding ADM is complex and continuously evolving. Ensuring compliance while supporting technological innovation requires ongoing regulatory adaptation—a task that Estonian policymakers have addressed with systematic efforts and regular updates to legal frameworks.[16] Technical challenges also persist, as highlighted by Zolkin,[17] who emphasizes the need for continuous algorithmic auditing to mitigate bias and maintain system reliability, particularly in public welfare systems where fairness and accuracy are paramount. Estonia's response to these challenges includes the development of fairness-aware algorithms, robust data governance frameworks, and collaborations with academic and industry stakeholders to share best practices, as seen in their AI strategy.[18] Looking ahead, Estonia's ADM strategy reflects a commitment to responsible innovation, with the government's AI roadmap outlining the planned expansion of ADM systems across various sectors while emphasizing ethical considerations, particularly in high-impact areas like welfare administration and law enforcement.[19]

This chapter provides a structured analysis of Estonia's ADM experience. First, it presents an overview of current implementations, examining key applications such as *Bürokratt*, *OTT*, and *ABC Gates*. Next, it analyses the legal and regulatory frameworks guiding these implementations, with particular attention to the EU AI Act's influence. The discussion then shifts to the challenges Estonia has encountered, including algorithmic bias and operational issues. In the subsequent section, the chapter explores the strategies adopted to mitigate these biases, such as algorithmic audits and fairness-aware design principles. Finally, the chapter concludes with practical recommendations for policymakers and a forward-looking assessment of Estonia's ADM development.

[15] See Kaun et al. (2024).

[16] See Cantero Gamito and Gentile (2023).

[17] See Zolkin et al. (2023).

[18] See Kerikmäe and Pärn-Lee (2021).

[19] See Paes (2023).

2 Overview of Current ADM Implementations

As of 2024, over 140 AI projects have been implemented across various sectors of Estonia's public administration.[20] These projects include innovative applications, such as the development of risk models by the State Agency of Medicines to manage medicinal product price agreements, the risk-based selection of claims for VAT refunds by the Tax and Customs Board, and the use of decision-making support systems by the Unemployment Insurance Fund (UIF) to assess the likelihood of an unemployed individual returning to work.[21] Other notable projects include the analysis of customer calls to the National Social Insurance Board, a risk assessment assistant for the Emergency Response Centre, and the detection of hay cutting using satellite imagery. Estonia is also aiming to provide proactive, invisible, and human-centric public services through efficient data utilization. These proactive government services are designed to automatically deliver services across multiple authorities, enabling individuals to access their rights and meet responsibilities without the need to request each service separately.

This chapter adopts the selection criteria of the AI use-cases for analysis which was established to ensure that the most relevant and impactful systems were included. These criteria focused on the system's importance and significance, especially in relation to its potential impact on public rights and obligations. The data processing involved, the system's operational status, and the availability of results on the system's functioning were also considered. Additionally, systems that had a higher likelihood of causing discrimination due to direct interactions with individuals and the nature of the data processed were prioritized. Based on these criteria, three AI systems were selected for closer examination: *Bürokratt, OTT*, and *ABC Gates*.[22]

Bürokratt is a virtual assistant developed by the Ministry of Economic Affairs and Communications to improve public sector communication.[23] The assistant functions as an interoperable network of chatbots, offering Estonian citizens and residents easy access to public services and information from various governmental agencies. This project, which started in 2017, aims to build a proactive relationship between citizens and the government by providing a unified gateway for interactions and has been gradually implemented. *Bürokratt* utilizes RASA software, a natural language processing tool, to continuously improve through machine learning. It is designed to direct user queries to specific chatbots associated with individual ministries, ensuring that interactions remain private and that data is handled

[20] See Equitech(a) (2024).

[21] See Kratid.ee (2025).

[22] See Equitech(a) (2024).

[23] See Dreyling III et al. (2024).

in accordance with Estonia's data protection laws, which require data to be stored at the source of capture.

OTT, a machine learning-based data analysis tool developed by the Estonian Unemployment Insurance Fund (EUIF), forecasts the likelihood that registered unemployed individuals will find employment again and identifies the factors influencing these probabilities. Initiated in 2018, *OTT* aids EUIF consultants by providing decision support that enhances the quality and efficiency of job matching services. The system processes a range of personal data, including gender, education, employment history, and health conditions, as well as market data about job availability. The tool's predictions assist counsellors in offering tailored services to individuals, allowing for more personalized support in the job search process.

ABC Gates, introduced in 2020 by the Police and Border Guard Board in collaboration with Information Technology and Development Centre of the Ministry of the Interior of Estonia, represent a leap in the automation of border control procedures. These biometric-based gates streamline the border crossing process by verifying travellers' identities through facial recognition and fingerprint scanning. The system, which is fully operational at Tallinn Airport and certain border points, automates the process of checking documents and verifying entry rights based on predefined rules. It enhances security by preventing unauthorized crossings and speeds up the process for those using biometric passports. However, the system has limitations, including its inability to accommodate travellers with special needs or items such as large luggage or strollers, who must go through manual border control.

These three AI systems—*Bürokratt, OTT,* and *ABC Gates*—represent a significant part of Estonia's public sector AI initiatives, showcasing the country's commitment to utilizing technology for improving service delivery, enhancing efficiency, and ensuring security. By focusing on systems that have a broad impact on public rights and obligations, process large amounts of personal data, and operate in fields with higher risks of discrimination, Estonia is taking steps toward more transparent, efficient, and equitable governance. These projects not only highlight the potential of AI in public services but also underscore the need for careful consideration of the ethical, legal, and social implications of AI deployment.

3 Regulatory Landscape in Estonia

The use of Automated Decision-Making (ADM) systems in public administration raises significant legal questions, particularly with respect to non-discrimination and equality.[24] ADM systems, powered by algorithms, have the potential to reproduce or exacerbate biases that exist within the data they are trained on. In the public sector, these systems may impact vital decisions such as the allocation of public services, social benefits, and access to justice.

[24] See EquiTech(a) (2024), EquiTech(b) (2024).

Recognized as a frontrunner in public sector digital innovation, the government remains committed to expanding automation in public decision-making to enhance efficiency, reduce administrative burdens, and improve accessibility. Estonia's legal framework on non-discrimination is largely shaped by international and EU regulations. The country ratified the European Convention on Human Rights in 1996, establishing anti-discrimination obligations. It is also a party to several key international treaties, including those addressing racial and gender-based discrimination, children's rights, and protections for persons with disabilities. As being part of the European Union, Estonia also complies with the Charter of Fundamental Rights of the European Union. The EU legal framework on non-discrimination, further influences Estonia's approach. While Estonia's equality laws apply to algorithmic decision-making, they do not explicitly address it. This section will explore the specific national regulations that ensure equality and non-discrimination in the context of algorithmic systems used in the public sector.

Estonia's non-discrimination framework is primarily rooted in the Constitution of the Republic of Estonia,[25] which prohibits discrimination and guarantees equality before the law. Two key legal acts—the Equal Treatment Act[26] and the Gender Equality Act[27]—define what constitutes unlawful discrimination. However, a proposed Gender Equality and Equal Opportunities Act is set to replace both, refining the country's anti-discrimination framework. Additional legislation relevant to non-discrimination includes the Employment Contracts Act,[28] which embeds anti-discrimination principles within employment, and the Administrative Procedure Act (2002), which governs public sector procedures, including the use of algorithmic systems, ensuring fairness and transparency.

The chapter also explores enforcement mechanisms available to individuals who experience algorithmic discrimination. This includes the adjudication process, burden of proof, available remedies, and the role of public institutions, such as equality bodies, in upholding non-discrimination rights. Finally, the chapter identifies regulatory gaps and proposes recommendations to strengthen Estonia's legal framework in response to the growing challenges posed by algorithmic decision-making.

3.1 *Constitution of the Republic of Estonia*

The principle of equality is enshrined in Section 12 of the Constitution of the Republic of Estonia, affirming that all individuals are equal before the law. It explicitly prohibits discrimination based on nationality, race, colour, sex, language, origin, religion, political or other beliefs, property, social status, or any other grounds. The

[25] See the Constitution of the Republic of Estonia (1992).

[26] See Equal Treatment Act (2008).

[27] See Gender Equality Act (2004).

[28] See Employment Contracts Act (2009).

Constitution also explicitly prohibits incitement to hatred. It criminalizes actions that promote national, racial, religious, or political hatred, violence, or discrimination. Additionally, it extends this prohibition to incitement of hatred, violence, or discrimination between social groups, ensuring legal consequences for such offenses.

The principle of equal treatment, as established in law, ensures that individuals in similar situations are not treated differently without justification, while also recognizing that those in different circumstances should not be treated identically if doing so would result in unfairness.[29] A violation of this principle constitutes discrimination when unequal treatment lacks an objective, reasonable, and legally justifiable basis. However, this means that not all instances of unequal treatment are inherently unlawful.[30]

The Supreme Court has interpreted the phrase 'on other grounds' in Section 12 to indicate that the grounds for discrimination are not confined to those explicitly listed but instead form an open-ended category.[31] For instance, discrimination could also occur based on factors such as disability, field of work, or age, even though these are not explicitly mentioned in Section 12 of the Constitution.[32] Moreover, the general principle of equality applies universally across all domains, which explicitly includes algorithmic discrimination.

The prohibition of discrimination outlined in Section 12 of the Constitution does not directly govern relationships between private individuals. However, this does not imply that private persons have unrestricted freedom to discriminate. Instead, Section 19 of the Constitution establishes that everyone must respect the rights and freedoms of others while exercising their own rights and fulfilling their duties. To enforce this principle, the Estonian legislator has enacted the Gender Equality Act and the Equal Treatment Act, which explicitly extend anti-discrimination protections to private-law relationships.

The Estonian Supreme Court has interpreted the principle of equality in ways that are also applicable to the automation of public sector tasks using algorithmic systems: Firstly, Section 12 of the Constitution mandates that laws must be applied equally to all individuals.[33] The Supreme Court has emphasized that this primarily means equality in the application of the law, requiring that laws in force be enforced impartially and consistently for everyone. Given that many public sector algorithmic systems are designed to apply laws to specific cases, this constitutional requirement implies that such systems must be robust and designed to ensure consistency in legal application across all cases.

The Supreme Court has also clarified that the right to equality is not violated if the state does not correct an error in favor of a person simply because a similar

[29] See Estonian Supreme Court (2002).

[30] See Aaviksoo et al. (2020).

[31] See Estonian Supreme Court (2007).

[32] See Meiorg and Grossthal (2022).

[33] See Estonian Supreme Court (2002).

mistake was made in another case (Estonian Supreme Court 2022). This principle extends to algorithmic errors—if a programming error in an algorithm erroneously benefits a person, it does not create a right for others to demand the same advantageous treatment in future cases. Such errors, while common, do not establish a legal precedent for similar outcome.

Although Section 12 does not explicitly mention it, the principle of equality also applies to the drafting and enactment of laws. This means that lawmakers must ensure that legislation does not create unjustified disparities or discriminatory effects. (Estonian Supreme Court 2007; Estonian Supreme Court 2008) Consequently, if generative AI solutions are integrated into the legislative drafting process or if algorithmic systems are used to assess the impacts of proposed laws and identify optimal legislative solutions, the principle of equality must be upheld throughout. This ensures that automated tools used in legislative processes do not introduce or reinforce biases that could lead to unequal treatment.

Section 12 may also apply when discrimination is not based on a single characteristic but rather results from a combination of multiple intertwined factors. This is particularly relevant in the context of algorithmic discrimination, where biases can emerge from the interaction of different characteristics, leading to unique and compounded disadvantages.[34] Many commentators emphasize the intersectional nature of algorithmic discrimination, meaning that individuals may face discrimination based on a combination of attributes—such as gender, race, disability, or socioeconomic status—rather than a single factor. This principle ensures that courts can recognize and address intersectional discrimination, preventing automated systems from reinforcing or exacerbating existing inequalities.

Legal equality does not automatically translate into substantive or real equality. For instance, while everyone has the right to apply for public sector jobs, this right is undermined if job postings are only available online, effectively excluding individuals without internet access.[35] This issue is especially relevant to the automation of public services. While automation can increase accessibility, streamline processes, and improve efficiency, it also poses challenges in ensuring equitable access. Even basic digitalization of public services raises equality concerns for individuals who lack digital literacy, access to devices, or an internet connection. To achieve real equality, automated systems must be designed inclusively, ensuring they are: (i) accessible to all users, regardless of technological limitations, (ii) transparent, so individuals understand how decisions affecting them are made, and (iii) adaptable, taking into account the diverse needs and capabilities of different population groups. Thus, the principle of equality in Section 12 requires that automated public services be implemented in a way that does not reinforce existing inequalities but rather promotes genuine inclusion.

According to the Estonian Supreme Court, the state is not prohibited from using legal measures to reduce or eliminate factual inequalities that result from formal

[34] See Gerards and Xenidis (2021).

[35] See Estonian Supreme Court (2002, 2007).

legal equality—and in some cases, the state is even required to do so.[36] This aligns with the concept of substantive (or real) equality, where the state has a positive obligation to take proactive steps to mitigate inequalities that persist despite formal legal protections. In the context of automating administrative decisions that affect individuals' rights or obligations, this principle suggests that automation should not only maintain equality but, where necessary, actively work to improve it for vulnerable or disadvantaged groups. This could mean that: (i) automated public sector systems must include safeguards to prevent discrimination, (ii) fairness assessments and bias audits should be conducted to ensure equitable outcomes, and (iii) special accommodations or alternative access methods should be available for those who might be disadvantaged by automation, such as individuals with disabilities, limited digital access, or low technological literacy. Thus, the introduction of algorithmic decision-making in public administration should not just preserve equality but, where necessary, enhance it through targeted interventions to ensure fair and inclusive outcomes.

3.2 *Equal Treatment Act (2009)*

The Equal Treatment Act was adopted on 11 December 2008 and entered into force on 1 January 2009. Its primary objective is to protect individuals from discrimination and ensure that their rights are equally safeguarded, regardless of their personal characteristics. The Equal Treatment Act[37] covers discrimination based on gender, race, nationality, age, disability, religion, beliefs, sexual orientation, and, in some cases, other characteristics. It applies to both the public and private sectors in areas that affect individuals' rights and obligations, including employment, education, social protection, healthcare, and access to goods and services. However, certain areas, such as family and private life, fall outside the scope of the Act.

The Equal Treatment Act establishes that all individuals must be treated equally and ensures that they have equal access to employment, education, healthcare, and other essential services without the risk of discrimination. At the same time, different characteristics are protected to varying degrees. Discrimination based on a person's nationality (ethnicity), race, or colour is prohibited in multiple areas, including employment, working conditions, remuneration, termination of contracts, vocational training, professional organization membership, social welfare, healthcare, education, and access to goods and services offered to the public. In contrast, discrimination based on a person's religion or beliefs, age, disability, or sexual orientation is specifically prohibited in employment-related areas, such as hiring, working conditions, remuneration, termination of contracts, vocational training, and professional organization membership.

[36] See Estonian Supreme Court (2008).

[37] See Equal Treatment Act (2008).

Through these provisions, the Equal Treatment Act ensures that individuals are safeguarded against discrimination in key areas of social and economic life while also recognizing that some forms of discrimination require stronger legal protection.

The Equal Treatment Act also extends the principle of equal treatment to employment relationships based on characteristics that are not explicitly mentioned in the law. In particular, it protects individuals from discrimination related to the fulfilment of family obligations, social status, the representation of employees' interests, membership in employee associations, language skills, or military service obligations. This ensures that various aspects of employment and professional life remain free from unjustified discrimination.

The Act explicitly prohibits all forms of discrimination, including direct and indirect discrimination, harassment, and the act of giving instructions to discriminate. Discrimination is defined as an instance where a person is treated unfavourably due to their legally protected personal characteristics. Indirect discrimination occurs when a seemingly neutral rule or practice disproportionately disadvantages a particular group, even if it is not explicitly targeted at them.

Both public and private sector employers, educational institutions, healthcare providers, goods and services providers, and other organizations and individuals operating within the scope of the Act are required to uphold the principle of equal treatment and actively prevent discrimination. This obligation extends beyond simply refraining from discriminatory practices, as it also requires these entities to take proactive steps to ensure equal treatment. Employers and service providers must create suitable working and service conditions that take into account the diverse needs and rights of individuals. Additionally, they must ensure that their policies and practices do not create barriers to equal access to services, employment, or opportunities.

In summary, the Equal Treatment Act plays a crucial role in safeguarding individuals from discrimination and ensuring equal opportunities for all. By establishing clear legal protections, it helps prevent and reduce discrimination in society while promoting fairness and inclusion in various aspects of public and private life.

3.3 Gender Equality Act

The Gender Equality Act[38] was enacted on 7 April 2004 and came into effect on 1 May 2004. This law aims to advance equality between women and men while addressing gender-based discrimination. It serves as a complement to the Equal Treatment Act, with a specific focus on gender equality matters.

The Gender Equality Act aims to guarantee equal rights and opportunities for women and men across all areas of society. It seeks to promote gender balance while preventing and eliminating gender discrimination. The Act addresses both

[38] See Gender Equality Act (2004).

direct and indirect gender-based discrimination and applies to various aspects of life, including the labour market, education, public services, and social protection. However, it does not regulate gender equality within the private sphere. Both public sector institutions and private sector employers, as well as educational institutions, healthcare providers, and other organizations, are required to uphold and promote gender equality by implementing appropriate measures.

The level of gender equality is assessed by comparing the status of women and men in different areas of life. Gender inequalities are evident in varying degrees of participation in decision-making processes, disparities in employment and economic status, differences in family responsibilities, distinct educational choices, and unequal access to resources such as time, information, and networks. These inequalities highlight the structural and societal factors that influence gender-based disparities in different domains, particularly in leadership and decision-making roles.[39]

The key obligations set out in the Gender Equality Act include the prevention and avoidance of discrimination, as well as the active promotion of gender equality. Employers and other responsible parties must implement measures to prevent both direct and indirect gender-based discrimination. This includes ensuring that job offers, positions, and promotion opportunities are equally accessible to both men and women. Additionally, employers and public sector institutions are required to integrate gender equality into their policies and activities. This involves maintaining fair employment and salary policies within organizations and providing equal career development and educational opportunities for both genders.

Gender Equality Act strictly prohibits gender-based harassment and sexual harassment in the workplace and other areas of life. Employers and other obligated entities must ensure that such incidents do not occur within their organizations and must take appropriate measures if harassment does take place.

The obligations outlined in the Act also extend to public sector algorithms. Authorities using algorithmic systems must ensure that these technologies operate in alignment with the general principles and obligations of the Act. This is particularly important because algorithmic decision-making, especially when based on historical data, can unintentionally reinforce gender-based stereotypes and biases, potentially leading to unequal outcomes for men and women.

Together with the Equal Treatment Act, the Gender Equality Act helps ensure that Estonia remains a fair, safe, and discrimination-free society, where everyone has equal opportunities to reach their full potential. Compliance with the Act is monitored by several national authorities, including the Gender Equality and Equal Treatment Commissioner, who provides assistance and advice in discrimination cases and intervenes when necessary.

[39] See Meiorg and Grossthal (2022).

3.4 *Draft Gender Equality and Equal Opportunities Act*

3.4.1 General Overview

The proposed Gender Equality and Equal Opportunities Act aims to address some of the limitations of the Equal Treatment Act and the Gender Equality Act by consolidating and expanding their scope.[40] According to its Explanatory Memorandum, the primary objective of the draft Act is to promote gender equality as a fundamental human right and a universal good across all areas of society. Additionally, the Act seeks to eliminate social barriers that prevent equal opportunities for minorities and to ensure the equal treatment of individuals based on protected characteristics under the law. By consolidating the protection and promotion of equality rights into a single legal framework, the new Act aims to enhance legal clarity and strengthen anti-discrimination protections.

The draft Act removes the hierarchy of protections based on different characteristics, meaning that all protected characteristics will be equally covered across all areas of society, with the exception of family and private life. In line with § 12 of the Constitution, the list of protected grounds remains open-ended, allowing flexibility in addressing emerging forms of discrimination.

The proposed amendment will significantly enhance protection against discrimination for individuals based on religion or belief, age, disability, and sexual orientation, as the Equal Treatment Act currently limits protection for these characteristics to employment and vocational training. The draft Gender Equality and Equal Opportunities Act will expand the scope of protection, ensuring that these characteristics are safeguarded in a broader range of societal contexts. Additionally, it will extend protections in the workplace, further strengthening legal safeguards against discrimination in employment settings.

A key focus of the draft Act is the promotion of equal opportunities for people with disabilities. Public institutions, employers, and providers of goods and services will be legally required to take active measures to prevent discrimination against persons with disabilities and to ensure equal access to rights and freedoms. This effectively expands non-discrimination obligations for private entities, requiring them to take steps to accommodate individuals with disabilities in employment, education, and service provision.

The draft Act also proposes an expansion of the powers of the Gender Equality and Equal Treatment Commissioner, ensuring that more individuals facing discrimination can access legal assistance and protection.

The new Act is expected to enter into force on 1 January 2026. This transition period is designed to provide sufficient time for raising awareness about the new regulations among obligated parties, developing supporting tools where necessary, and ensuring that employers, service providers, and institutions have adequate time to prepare for compliance with the new legal requirements.

---

[40] See Government of Estonia (2024).

3.4.2 Impact of the Draft Act on Algorithmic Discrimination

A particularly relevant aspect of the draft Gender Equality and Equal Opportunities Act is its explicit recognition of algorithmic discrimination as a distinct form of discrimination. The draft Act defines algorithmic discrimination as a situation in which a person is subjected to a decision that is partly or wholly based on the output of an automated system, leading to an unjustified difference in treatment or having an adverse effect on them due to a protected characteristic.

While algorithmic discrimination would still be unlawful even without an explicit legal provision, the draft Act introduces a more impactful obligation by requiring state and local authorities to ensure that the algorithmic systems they use are designed and developed in compliance with the principle of equal treatment and the objectives of gender equality and equal opportunities. Moreover, authorities must ensure that these systems do not disadvantage individuals based on protected characteristics or reinforce social inequalities. This marks a shift from merely holding authorities accountable for discriminatory outcomes to requiring proactive measures that integrate anti-discrimination safeguards at the design and development stages of algorithmic systems.

By embedding these principles early in the process, the law aims to prevent discriminatory biases from taking root, reflecting a similar logic to that of the EU AI Act. The Explanatory Memorandum[41] suggests several concrete measures to fulfil this commitment, including ensuring that machine-readable datasets are representative, excluding discriminatory data, conducting regular testing, involving representatives from diverse social groups in the design, development, and testing of algorithms, carrying out impact analyses on the risks of discrimination and bias in sectoral policymaking, and commissioning external audits to assess fairness and compliance.

3.5 *Employment Contracts Act*

Employment relations are particularly significant in the context of algorithmic discrimination, as algorithms are increasingly employed in processes such as recruitment, task allocation, and performance evaluation. These relationships are primarily governed by the Employment Contracts Act,[42] which mandates that employers must protect employees from discrimination, uphold the principle of equal treatment, and promote equality in accordance with the Equal Treatment Act and the Gender Equality Act. These laws establish the grounds and general scope of discrimination in the workplace.

[41] See Government of Estonia (2024).

[42] See Employment Contracts Act (2009).

It is important to note that while the Equal Treatment Act generally prohibits discrimination only on specific grounds, in the context of employment relations, it extends protection to additional characteristics not explicitly listed in the Act. Potential grounds for discrimination in employment may include, among other factors, family-related responsibilities, social status, employee representation, membership in employee organizations, language proficiency, and military service obligations.

Discrimination in employment relations is prohibited in various aspects of employment, including the conclusion of employment contracts, appointment or election to office, conditions for access to employment, working conditions, giving instructions, remuneration, termination or cancellation of contracts, and dismissal from office.

In the context of gender equality, the Gender Equality Act not only prohibits direct and indirect discrimination but also specifies particular situations in employment that are considered discriminatory. These include practices related to recruitment, promotion, access to training, employment conditions, remuneration, benefits, work management, task allocation, and workplace conditions, as well as gender-based and sexual harassment.

Additionally, the Employment Contracts Act stipulates that when an employer extraordinarily cancels an employment contract, they must adhere to the principle of equal treatment. Moreover, an employer cannot terminate an employment contract on the basis that an employee has requested flexible working arrangements as provided for under the Gender Equality Act.

Once the draft Gender Equality and Equal Opportunities Act comes into force, the Employment Contracts Act will be amended to reference the provisions of the new law when determining discrimination in employment relationships. The draft Act introduces broader grounds for discrimination and imposes additional obligations on employers within the employment context.

One of the key proposals is a clear and enforceable duty for employers to actively, systematically, and purposefully promote gender equality and equal opportunities in the workplace. The draft Act also specifies various practices that would constitute discriminatory behaviour, including the unequal application of selection criteria during recruitment, task assignment, and the allocation of remuneration or benefits. These provisions aim to strengthen protections against discrimination and ensure that employers take proactive steps to foster a fair and inclusive work environment.

Once the draft Gender Equality and Equal Opportunities Act comes into force, the legal framework addressing algorithmic discrimination in employment relations will be significantly strengthened and more comprehensive. The grounds for discrimination will be open-ended and will include a wide range of concrete examples of discriminatory practices, ensuring greater legal clarity and protection.

Employers will be required to undertake proactive measures to promote gender equality and equal opportunities, a responsibility that will extend to algorithmic decision-making, supervision, and other automated systems that could contribute to discrimination. They will also need to provide oversight on equality measures and data, ensuring transparency regarding the impact of algorithmic systems in the workplace.

Although Estonian law—both currently and under the draft Act—does not impose a direct obligation on private sector entities to audit or mitigate discrimination in their algorithmic systems, it is important to note that various AI systems used for employment, employee management, and access to self-employment are classified as high-risk under the AI Act. The AI Act regulates the development and use of such systems, requiring them to meet stringent data quality standards, integrate risk management practices, and implement safeguards to mitigate the risk of algorithmic discrimination in employment relations.

3.6 Administrative Procedure Act

An essential component of the legal framework for ensuring equality in public sector algorithmic systems is the Administrative Procedure Act,[43] which establishes the rules and principles governing administrative procedures. Public authorities must comply with the the Act when issuing administrative decisions and implementing administrative measures, including those executed through algorithmic systems.

Under this Act, all administrative acts must be lawful, meaning they must adhere to non-discrimination rules as outlined in relevant legal provisions. Additionally, when carrying out administrative measures, public authorities are explicitly required to observe the principle of equal treatment.

As the Administrative Procedure Actcodifies principles of good administration and due process, it plays a crucial role in establishing safeguards to protect individuals' rights. An administrative act that affects a person's rights or obligations must be clear, unambiguous, and include written reasoning. This requirement underpins the transparency and explainability of administrative decisions, ensuring that individuals understand the basis for decisions that affect them. Additionally, this Act mandates that public authorities must provide concerned individuals with the opportunity to express their opinions and contest decisions that impact them.

When ADM systems are used in administrative processes, the Administrative Procedure Act serves as a legal framework to ensure that these systems operate with sufficient transparency and provide clear explanations. This enables individuals to assess whether the automated decision complies with legal principles, particularly regarding equality. By requiring transparency and explanation, this Act facilitates meaningful human participation in public procedures, reducing the risk of arbitrary state actions in algorithmic decision-making.[44] This ensures fairness and enhances accountability in cases of wrongful or biased decisions.

[43] See Administrative Procedure Act (2002).

[44] See Ebers and Trasberg (2023).

The Estonian Government is currently in the early stages of developing additional rules for the automation of administrative acts and measures. These forthcoming regulations could further define transparency standards, ensuring that algorithmic systems used in public administration are sufficiently monitored for potential discriminatory effects and that their decision-making processes remain fair, accountable, and legally sound.

3.7 The Government AI and Data Policies

This subsection provides a brief analysis of the Estonian Government's AI and data policies in relation to the protection of the principle of equality. Although these policies do not form part of the formal regulatory framework, they influence how algorithmic fairness is incorporated into Estonian digital policies. Additionally, they outline the non-regulatory measures the government may adopt to promote and facilitate fairness in algorithmic systems, complementing existing legal protections and guiding the responsible development and deployment of AI technologies.

Two key digital policy documents shaping Estonia's approach to AI and data governance are the Estonia 2035 Development Strategy[45] and Estonia's Digital Agenda 2030. Both strategies share the overarching goal of fostering a smart, caring, collaborative, and innovative society, with digitalization and the adoption of new technologies identified as essential tools for achieving this vision. These policy frameworks guide Estonia's long-term digital transformation, emphasizing the role of emerging technologies in enhancing public services, economic growth, and societal well-being.

A concrete roadmap for Estonia's AI and data governance is outlined in the 2024–2026 AI Action Plan and the 2024–2025 Data Action Plan. While both plans primarily focus on fostering an innovative, knowledge-based economy and public sector, they also emphasize the trustworthy and human-centric use of technology. One of the key goals of the AI Action Plan explicitly states the need to ensure that digital solutions are secure, protect people's rights, and maintain public trust in Estonia's digital state.

To achieve this, the action plans set out several concrete initiatives, including establishing standards and guidance for assessing the impacts of algorithmic solutions, developing an algorithmic transparency standard for public sector algorithms, providing training for institutions on the lawful and human-centric use of AI, and creating regulatory sandbox environments to test algorithmic solutions before large-scale implementation. Additionally, the EquiTech project and its deliverables are considered part of the AI Action Plan's activities, further reinforcing Estonia's commitment to responsible AI deployment.

[45] See Government of Estonia (2020).

Meanwhile, the Data Action Plan promotes responsible data management, emphasizing the importance of high-quality and unbiased data in algorithmic systems and broader public sector processes. By ensuring the integrity of the data used in decision-making, this plan aims to reduce algorithmic bias and discrimination in automated systems.

Through these initiatives, both public and private entities are expected to gain the knowledge and skills necessary to implement measures that uphold the fairness and reliability of algorithmic systems while mitigating potential risks. Given the cross-sectoral nature of these measures, they are designed to address and minimize the risk of algorithmic discrimination. However, ongoing efforts will be essential to adapt these policies to emerging technological challenges and ensure they remain sufficiently focused on promoting fairness and equality in public sector algorithms and data processing.

3.8 Enforcement of Rights in Cases of Discrimination

This subsection outlines the legal framework in Estonia for enforcing individuals' rights in cases of discrimination. Various institutions and enforcement mechanisms are available to address discrimination claims and provide legal remedies. First the resolution of discrimination cases through the courts and the labour dispute committee are examined, which serve as key legal avenues for individuals seeking redress. Then an overview of the roles of the two primary public institutions responsible for protecting equality rights: the Chancellor of Justice and the Gender Equality and Equal Treatment Commissioner is provided. These institutions play a crucial role in monitoring compliance with anti-discrimination laws, handling complaints, and promoting fairness and equal treatment across different sectors of society.

3.8.1 Adjudication

Discrimination disputes can be resolved through either the courts or the labour dispute committee. Victims of discrimination have the right to file a lawsuit in either civil or administrative court, depending on whether the infringement occurred in a private or public context. In cases involving employment discrimination, individuals can seek resolution through the labour dispute committee, which mediates and adjudicates conflicts between employees and employers.

However, many instances of discriminatory use of public sector algorithms would typically be classified as unlawful actions by a public authority in the exercise of executive power. As such, these cases fall within the jurisdiction of the administrative court. The court has the authority to grant remedies, including compensation for damages and orders to cease discriminatory practices, ensuring legal accountability for algorithmic decision-making in the public sector.

It is important to note that certain discriminatory behaviors may constitute criminal offenses, such as incitement to hatred and specific violations of equality. In such cases, individuals can report the offense to the police and seek prosecution under the Penal Code. This ensures that particularly severe forms of discrimination, which go beyond civil or administrative violations, are addressed through criminal proceedings.

3.8.2 Burden of Proof

A crucial aspect of enforcing equality rights, particularly in cases involving complex and often opaque algorithmic systems, is the allocation of the burden of proof in discrimination cases. The way this burden is distributed depends on whether the case is adjudicated as a civil, administrative, or criminal proceeding.

In civil court and before the labour dispute committee, neither the plaintiff nor the respondent is required to prove that the victim belongs to a specific protected group. Instead, the burden of proof is shared between the parties. The plaintiff must present facts that create a presumption of discrimination. Once such a presumption is established, the respondent must then demonstrate that there has been no violation of the principle of equal treatment. If the respondent refuses to provide proof, this refusal is treated as an acknowledgment of discrimination, effectively shifting the legal advantage to the plaintiff.

In the context of algorithmic discrimination, the shared burden of proof is particularly significant. Establishing whether an automated system considers discriminatory parameters or produces discriminatory outcomes often requires a detailed review of the system's functioning. This may necessitate access to source code, data, or documentation from the respondent, as algorithmic processes tend to be complex and opaque. Without transparency regarding the underlying mechanisms, it becomes difficult to determine whether discrimination has occurred. Therefore, enforcement mechanisms must be robust enough to ensure that such information is disclosed when necessary.

In administrative cases, a judicial review is conducted during the proceedings to determine if an infringement has occurred. The court is responsible for actively ensuring that all material facts relevant to resolving the case are identified. If needed, the court may gather evidence itself or require the parties to provide it. As part of this process, public authorities may also be required to disclose relevant information about the functioning of an algorithm, ensuring that the principle of equal treatment is upheld in automated decision-making.

3.8.3 Remedies

If a person's rights are violated due to discrimination, they have the right to demand that the discriminatory act be discontinued and to seek compensation for the damages suffered. Compensation may cover both material damages, such as financial losses, and non-patrimonial damages, including emotional distress or harm to dignity resulting from the violation. When determining the amount of compensation, the court or labour dispute committee will consider several factors, including the scope, duration, and nature of the discrimination. These elements help assess the impact of the violation and ensure that the awarded compensation is appropriate to the harm suffered.

3.8.4 Public and Private Institutions Protecting Equality Rights

In addition to adjudication, several public institutions play a crucial role in protecting fundamental rights, including equality rights. One of the most significant institutions in Estonia is the Gender Equality and Equal Treatment Commissioner (hereafter referred to as the Commissioner), an independent and impartial body responsible for promoting equality and combating discrimination. Operating autonomously, the Commissioner provides guidance and support to individuals who experience discrimination.

The Commissioner works to increase public awareness of equality issues, provides recommendations for improving legislation and policies, and encourages equality and diversity in both the public and private sectors. Furthermore, the Commissioner offers legal advice and consultations to both individuals and organizations, helping them understand and apply the principles of equality and non-discrimination. Additionally, they assist employers and institutions in developing policies that prevent discrimination and promote equal opportunities. The Commissioner plays a key role in handling discrimination cases, offering legal advice to individuals who believe they have been discriminated against on the basis of gender or other protected characteristics. By reviewing complaints, the Commissioner helps ensure that equality rights are upheld and provides a non-judicial avenue for addressing discrimination.

The Commissioner's role in oversight and complaint resolution involves several key functions to ensure that cases of discrimination are properly assessed and addressed. Individuals who believe they have experienced discrimination can submit a complaint to the Commissioner. Upon receiving a complaint, the Commissioner conducts an initial assessment to determine whether the case falls within their jurisdiction and whether there is sufficient basis to initiate an investigation. If the complaint is deemed valid, the Commissioner launches an investigation. This process involves gathering facts, hearing both parties, and collecting relevant documents and evidence. The Commissioner may collaborate with the complainant, the alleged discriminator, and other institutions to obtain the necessary information and establish whether discrimination has occurred. Based on the findings of the investigation, the Commissioner determines whether discrimination has taken place. If discrimination is identified, the Commissioner issues an official opinion or provides recommendations for improving the situation. These recommendations may include measures to stop the discrimination and prevent future occurrences. Although the Commissioner does not have the authority to impose sanctions or fines, they may suggest compensation for the victim. The Commissioner may continue to monitor the implementation of their recommendations and take further action if the discriminatory practices persist or if no improvements are made. If the complainant is not satisfied with the outcome or seeks compensation, they have the right to take the case to court. In such cases, the Commissioner may provide the court with an expert opinion on the matter to support the enforcement of equality rights.

The new draft Gender Equality and Equal Opportunities Act would expand the Commissioner's authority by granting broader powers to investigate and provide expert opinions in discrimination cases. The Commissioner's opinion serves as a valuable tool for complainants, helping them determine their next legal steps and obtain support in defending their rights. In addition to the extended scope of application—which directly enhances the Commissioner's competences—and the expansion of protected grounds, the draft Act would also grant the Commissioner the power to take legal action on behalf of a complainant, with their consent, to defend their rights in court.

Beyond the Commissioner, the Chancellor of Justice also plays a role in resolving discrimination disputes through conciliation. In cases involving administrative procedures—which cover most algorithmic decisions made by public authorities—the Chancellor of Justice may conduct a supervision procedure to assess whether a public authority has complied with the principle of equal treatment. Based on their findings, the Chancellor may issue criticism, recommendations, or formal opinions and propose corrective measures to address violations.

Additionally, non-governmental organizations such as the Estonian Human Rights Centre contribute to promoting and monitoring human rights in Estonia. These organizations offer resources, guidance, and legal assistance in discrimination cases, further strengthening the protection and enforcement of equality rights across society.

3.9 *Regulatory Gaps and Recommendations*

The scope of discrimination addressed by existing regulations may not fully capture all potential biases, particularly as AI systems evolve and new forms of discrimination emerge. A key issue discussed in academic literature is the intersectional nature of discrimination, which refers to how multiple forms of discrimination can intersect and compound one another, leading to unique and often more severe disadvantages.[46]

This issue is particularly significant in the context of algorithmic decision-making. For instance, an AI system used in healthcare might disproportionately underdiagnose medical conditions for older women of certain ethnic backgrounds due to age-related and ethnic biases embedded in the data. This results in a

[46] See Gerards and Xenidis (2021).

compounded disadvantage that cannot be explained by either age or ethnicity alone. The way in which gender and ethnicity interact to create unique disadvantages highlights how algorithms can reinforce and exacerbate existing inequalities.

These compounding effects emphasize the importance of considering intersectionality in the design, development, and regulation of algorithmic systems. This has sparked an ongoing debate about whether a static list of prohibited grounds for discrimination is sufficient to identify unfair treatment that may limit the realization of fundamental rights.[47] While EU law does not explicitly prohibit intersectional discrimination, it does not prevent the Court of Justice of the European Union (CJEU) from addressing it. However, the CJEU has yet to fully develop its approach to intersectional discrimination.[48]

A major challenge in enforcing equality rights arises from the lack of transparency in algorithmic decision-making processes, particularly due to the opaque nature of many AI systems. Individuals often struggle to fully understand which conditions or parameters influenced a decision and whether any of these factors were driven by discriminatory logic. This lack of transparency creates a significant barrier to effective enforcement of anti-discrimination protections.

For instance, if an AI-powered job recruitment platform systematically filters out resumes containing certain cultural references or names associated with particular ethnic groups, affected applicants may be unaware that their applications were rejected based on biased criteria. Without knowledge of how the decision was made, proving discrimination and seeking legal redress becomes extremely difficult.

For individuals, the ability to challenge discriminatory practices effectively depends on their access to information about how a decision was made. Ensuring that algorithmic systems operate with transparency and that their decision-making processes are accessible for review is essential for upholding the principle of equality. This raises the question of whether Estonian law provides sufficient procedural tools to address opacity in discrimination cases involving algorithmic systems.

In the context of administrative decisions and measures, the Administrative Procedure Act requires authorities to ensure transparency in their decision-making processes, including those automated by algorithms. It also mandates that administrative decisions must be sufficiently explained. In administrative court proceedings, the court has the power to compel authorities to provide all relevant data and information for assessing potential discrimination.

In civil cases, where a discrimination claim has been initiated, the principle of shared burden of proof plays a crucial role. This principle ensures that once a plaintiff presents facts suggesting discrimination, the burden shifts to the respondent to prove that no discrimination occurred. This is particularly significant in cases involving complex algorithmic systems, where the plaintiff may lack direct access to the internal workings of the algorithm.

---

[47] See Weerts et al. (2023).

[48] See Weerts et al. (2023).

However, these measures have a limited effect on resolving the problem. In many cases, it is challenging to even recognize that discrimination may have occurred.[49] Even when there is a suspicion, cases involving algorithmic systems can take a long time to resolve, potentially discouraging individuals from pursuing claims. The technical complexity of these cases requires expert analysis and auditing, which can be expensive. Moreover, if the algorithmic systems are poorly documented or if the respondent does not provide comprehensive information, it becomes extremely difficult to assess them effectively. The situation is further complicated when AI components are involved, particularly machine learning models that often operate as 'black boxes'—even their developers may not fully understand or explain how a specific output was generated. Consequently, it may remain challenging to identify or produce evidence of discrimination, even when the required standard of proof is relatively low.

While non-discrimination law focuses on outcomes, meaning that an infringement occurs when a decision or action results in unjustified unequal treatment, there is an increasing shift toward *ex ante* requirements. These requirements aim to assess risks and introduce preventive measures during the development and deployment of algorithmic systems to mitigate discriminatory outcomes.

A key regulatory step in this direction is the EU AI Act, which mandates that training, validation, and testing datasets must be relevant, representative, free of errors as much as possible, and complete in relation to their intended use. This requirement is further reinforced by quality and risk management processes. Similarly, the draft Gender Equality and Equal Opportunities Act requires public authorities to ensure that the algorithmic systems they use are designed and developed in accordance with the principle of equal treatment and the objectives of gender equality and equal opportunities. Legal compliance in this context depends on whether the authority has implemented adequate processes to identify and mitigate discrimination risks within the system.

While these regulatory developments are a step forward, determining the substance and extent of these requirements remains highly complex. A major issue is how to define fairness and equality when setting the parameters and decision logic of algorithmic systems.[50] Various standards and benchmarks have been proposed to measure fairness, but their effectiveness has been limited.[51] Ideally, fairness should be grounded in legal principles, but in reality, non-discrimination law serves multiple social functions, including: (i) recognizing historical injustices and protecting disadvantaged social groups, (ii) redistributing opportunities and valuable resources, (iii) safeguarding dignity and autonomy, (iv) accommodating diverse lifestyles, and (v) facilitating equal access to key social institutions such as the labor market, education, and healthcare.[52]

---

[49] See Wachter et al. (2021).

[50] See Hacker (2018).

[51] See Wachter et al. (2021).

[52] See Weerts et al. (2023).

Given these varied functions, the concept of equality is dynamic and context-dependent, shaped by socio-economic developments. As a result, defining a single benchmark or technical standard that an algorithm could consistently follow is highly challenging.

It is widely recognized that no single fairness metric can fully satisfy all fairness conditions, as fairness assessments often depend on assumptions about what constitutes just treatment. As Weerts and colleagues argue, while many fairness metrics have drawn inspiration from non-discrimination law, legal compliance cannot be reduced to a single fairness threshold or mathematical formula. Instead, ensuring compliance with non-discrimination law requires a deliberate reflection on the normative goals behind both legal and technical fairness interventions.[53]

To address this, Weert and colleagues suggest that instead of simply asking what should be equal, fairness assessments should focus on determining the correct distribution of burdens and benefits in a given context. However, this issue has yet to be adequately addressed within the current legislative framework.[54]

Another significant gap in the current legal framework is the lack of specific obligations to identify and mitigate bias and discrimination risks during the design, development, and operation of algorithmic systems. At present, no comprehensive legal requirements exist to ensure that public sector algorithms are systematically assessed for their potential discriminatory impact before deployment. The EU AI Act partially addresses this issue by requiring a risk management process throughout the AI system's lifecycle, including oversight mechanisms and measures to detect and mitigate biases. However, the scope of the EU AI Act remains limited, meaning that many public sector algorithmic systems will not be subject to these requirements.

Moreover, existing non-discrimination laws do not impose specific obligations to integrate bias detection and prevention measures into the development or deployment of public sector algorithms. This presents a regulatory gap, as many algorithmic systems used in the public sector—even those not classified as AI-based under the EU AI Act—can still pose significant discrimination risks. For instance, an algorithm used to allocate social welfare benefits may not fall under the AI Act if it does not meet the criteria for AI-based decision-making. However, such a system could still introduce bias by inadvertently favoring applicants from certain socio-economic backgrounds, leading to unequal treatment. Despite posing clear discrimination risks, these systems currently lack regulatory oversight under both AI-specific and non-discrimination laws. To ensure that all public sector algorithmic systems are developed and operated with robust safeguards against bias and discrimination, it is essential to close this regulatory gap. Future legislative efforts should establish clear and enforceable obligations requiring systematic risk assessments, fairness evaluations, and transparency measures in all public sector algorithmic systems, regardless of whether they fall within the AI Act's scope.

---

[53] See Weerts et al. (2023).

[54] See Weerts et al. (2023).

4 Challenges in ADM Implementation

The integration of Automated Decision-Making (ADM) systems in Estonia's public administration has introduced significant advancements in efficiency and service delivery. However, their deployment also presents critical challenges related to algorithmic bias, transparency, and the balance between operational efficiency and ethical concerns. This section explores these challenges in detail, drawing on insights from Estonia's experience and broader global discussions on AI governance.

4.1 Identification of Major Challenges: Algorithmic Bias and Transparency

One of the primary challenges in ADM systems is algorithmic bias. Bias in ADM can lead to discriminatory outcomes, particularly in public services such as welfare distribution, employment recommendations, and border control. Bias can emerge from multiple sources, including historical discrimination embedded in training data, biases introduced during algorithmic design, and disparities in how the system is tested and deployed. These biases can manifest as selection bias, where certain groups are disproportionately affected, or proxy discrimination, where seemingly neutral variables correlate with protected characteristics, leading to indirect but harmful discriminatory effects[55] highlight that algorithmic bias in ADM can result in unequal treatment of different demographic groups, particularly in welfare administration across Estonia and Sweden.

In Estonia, algorithmic fairness has been a focal point of discussions regarding ADM governance, particularly in high-impact areas like unemployment insurance and social benefits allocation. The Estonian Unemployment Insurance Fund (EUIF) utilizes machine learning models to assess individuals' likelihood of returning to work. However, as Zolkin and colleagues[56] discusses, these systems operate without comprehensive legal safeguards, making it difficult to challenge biased decisions that affect people's access to social benefits. Similarly, Estonia's *ABC Gates*, which automate border control using biometric verification, have raised concerns about accuracy discrepancies across demographic groups. According to Pilving and Mikiver,[57] reliance on biometric recognition introduces risks of discrimination, particularly against individuals whose features are underrepresented in training datasets.

A related concern is transparency, often referred to as the "black box problem." Many ADM models, especially those using deep learning techniques, lack interpretability, making it difficult to explain how specific decisions are reached.

[55] See Equitech(a) (2024), Kaun et al. (2024).

[56] See Zolkin et al. (2023).

[57] See Pilving and Mikiver (2020).

According to Palmiotto,[58] this opacity can undermine public trust and create legal challenges, particularly when ADM affects individuals' fundamental rights. Estonia's efforts to address this issue include integrating explainable AI (XAI) principles into decision-making frameworks; however, challenges remain in ensuring that ADM-generated decisions are understandable to both public officials and citizens. This issue is particularly relevant in Estonia, where automated systems such as *Bürokratt* and *OTT* rely on complex machine learning models that remain difficult for the public to scrutinize.[59] Gamito and Gentile[60] argue that without enforceable transparency requirements, ADM risks becoming a tool of opaque governance rather than a means of improving administrative efficiency.

Furthermore, the issue of algorithmic fairness remains contentious, as different fairness metrics (e.g., group fairness vs. individual fairness) can yield conflicting results. Fairness-aware algorithms are needed to balance these competing metrics while ensuring regulatory compliance. The EU AI Act aims to address these concerns by mandating bias audits and requiring high-risk ADM systems to undergo rigorous impact assessments to prevent discriminatory outcomes.[61]

Moreover, the challenge of explainability is exacerbated by the increasing complexity of ADM systems. According to Rizk and Lindgren,[62] lack of transparency in algorithmic decision-making prevents affected individuals from effectively contesting decisions, thereby undermining procedural fairness. In Estonia, regulatory efforts have aimed to improve algorithmic explainability, yet achieving meaningful transparency remains a work in progress.

4.2 Balancing Operational Efficiency and Ethical Concerns

ADM systems are often deployed with the goal of improving operational efficiency by automating routine administrative processes and reducing human workload. In Estonia, projects like *Bürokratt* and *ABC Gates* illustrate how AI-driven automation enhances service delivery by streamlining interactions between citizens and public authorities. However, these efficiency gains must be weighed against ethical considerations, particularly regarding individual rights, data protection, and procedural fairness.

A key concern is the right to contest automated decisions. The General Data Protection Regulation (GDPR) Article 22 provides individuals with protections against being subjected to solely automated decisions that have significant effects

[58] See Palmiotto (2024).

[59] See Equitech(b) (2024).

[60] See Gamito and Gentile (2023).

[61] See Equitech(a) (2024).

[62] See Rizk and Lindgren (2024).

on them. However, as Mac[63] points out, not all ADM systems fall within the scope of GDPR protections, particularly those that process non-personal data. This regulatory gap presents challenges in ensuring adequate human oversight in automated administrative decisions.

Another critical issue is accountability. When ADM systems make erroneous or unjust decisions, determining responsibility can be complex, particularly if the decision-making process lacks human oversight. Hirvonen[64] argues that the current accountability structures in Estonia's ADM framework require further refinement to clarify the role of human decision-makers and ensure that public authorities remain answerable for ADM-generated outcomes.

Finally, public perception and trust in ADM systems remain significant hurdles. According to Kaun and colleagues,[65] public acceptance of ADM in Estonia is relatively high compared to other European countries, largely due to the country's long history of digital governance. However, concerns persist regarding bias, fairness, and the right to appeal decisions, particularly in high-impact areas like social welfare and law enforcement.

These challenges are further complicated by constitutional constraints on decision-making authority in public administration. As Langer explains, the principle of non-delegation places strict legal boundaries on how much decision-making power public entities can transfer to automated systems and external developers. The delegation of decisions affecting citizens' rights must remain within legally permissible limits, ensuring accountability, contestability, and reviewability. Notably, cases such as the Robodebt scheme in Australia illustrate how flawed ADM implementations, lacking proper oversight, can lead to large-scale legal and social failures, undermining public trust in automated governance.[66]

The challenges associated with ADM implementation in Estonia underscore the importance of ongoing policy development, regulatory adaptation, and technical advancements. Ensuring fair, transparent, and accountable ADM systems requires a multifaceted approach, including stronger regulatory oversight, increased public engagement, and the continuous improvement of AI fairness and explainability mechanisms. While Estonia has made significant progress in this field, addressing these challenges will be crucial to maintaining the integrity and effectiveness of its digital governance model.

---

63 See Mac (2024).

64 See Hirvonen (2024).

65 See Kaun et al. (2024).

66 See Langer (2024).

5 Mitigation Strategies for Biases

5.1 Strategies and Methodologies Adopted to Mitigate Biases in ADM Applications

One of the primary methods for mitigating bias in ADM systems is conducting systematic algorithmic audits, as they help identify sources of bias in AI-driven decision-making processes.[67] Regular audits enable the identification of discriminatory patterns and allow for adjustments to reduce biases in automated decision-making.[68] Algorithmic audits are essential in ensuring that models do not reinforce historical discrimination embedded in data sources. Continuous assessment of AI-based public services is needed to ensure that algorithms do not disproportionately disadvantage specific groups. Regular audits allow policymakers to assess the impact of ADM applications and make necessary adjustments to reduce discriminatory outcomes.

Developing fairness-aware machine learning algorithms is another crucial strategy for mitigating bias. Estonia's AI regulatory framework mandates that training datasets used in ADM systems must be representative and free from systemic biases to the greatest extent possible. Bias can emerge from data imbalances, reinforcing existing inequalities. To address this, developers of high-risk ADM systems are encouraged to use re-weighting, re-sampling, and adversarial debiasing techniques to improve fairness.

Lack of transparency, often referred to as the "black-box problem," has been identified as a significant challenge in Estonia's ADM systems.[69] To counter this, efforts have been made to incorporate Explainable AI (XAI) frameworks. *Bürokratt*, Estonia's virtual public service assistant, is designed with mechanisms that ensure users are aware when interacting with an AI system. Future improvements for *Bürokratt* are needed such as a standardized fairness framework, dedicated audit tools for detecting bias and implementing structured documentation to explain the decision-making logic behind ADM models.

Transparency standards play a key role in making ADM systems accountable. It is not clear if all the Estonian ADM applications currently lacking formal transparency measures, leading to concerns over public trust. Research has shown that public acceptance of ADM is highly dependent on how transparent and explainable these systems are to citizens, particularly in decision-making areas affecting fundamental rights.[70] Estonia is piloting an AI transparency tool within the Unemployment Insurance Fund (EUIF) to disclose key information about AI-supported decisions,

[67] See Mac (2024).

[68] See Rizk and Lindgren (2024).

[69] See Equitech(a) (2024).

[70] See Kaun et al. (2024).

ensuring affected individuals understand the reasoning behind automated recommendations. These efforts align with the EU AI Act's provisions on high-risk AI systems, which require detailed documentation and human oversight.

Human oversight remains a critical safeguard against biased automated decisions, particularly in high-stakes administrative processes where AI-generated outcomes influence fundamental rights.[71] Studies suggest that maintaining human-in-the-loop mechanisms is essential for mitigating unintended discriminatory effects in automated decision-making systems. Estonia's approach to ADM ensures that AI-generated decisions are subject to human review in cases involving significant rights or obligations. For instance, *OTT* (the AI-driven decision-support tool used by EUIF) does not make final decisions regarding unemployment benefits; instead, human consultants interpret and validate AI-generated recommendations. While this mitigates the risk of unchecked algorithmic discrimination, the audit report suggests enhancing human oversight by providing additional training to decision-makers on algorithmic bias detection.

While fairness in ADM is often framed in technical terms—such as statistical parity or algorithmic bias mitigation—public perceptions of fairness are shaped by broader social and ethical concerns.[72] A study on subjective fairness perceptions in Germany found that citizens prioritize human oversight, the contextualization of decisions, and the ability to challenge automated outcomes over purely technical fairness metrics.[73] Respondents expressed concerns about the dehumanization of decision-making processes and emphasized the importance of human elements, such as empathy and individual assessment, in ensuring just outcomes. These findings underscore the need for citizen-centered ADM governance frameworks that incorporate public perceptions of fairness alongside regulatory compliance and technical accuracy.

Estonian policymakers recognize that public engagement is essential for building trust in ADM systems. Research suggests that incorporating participatory governance mechanisms—such as co-design workshops and citizen feedback channels—enhances the legitimacy and fairness of AI-driven public services.[74] Additionally, recent experimental research by Locci and Massoni[75] found that individuals were more likely to accept ADM outcomes when provided with clear explanations about algorithmic decision-making processes. This supports the argument that Estonia's AI governance framework should prioritize explainability as a key principle, ensuring that ADM-generated decisions are accompanied by transparent reasoning accessible to the public. Integrating participatory governance mechanisms are recommended allowing affected individuals to provide feedback on algo-

---

[71] Mac (2024).

[72] See Szafran and Bach (2024).

[73] See Szafran and Bach (2024).

[74] See Rizk and Lindgren (2024).

[75] See Locci and Massoni (2024).

rithmic decisions.[76] In Estonia's welfare sector, research suggests that the inclusion of citizens in ADM governance improves both fairness and system legitimacy (Kaun et al. 2023). Estonia's forthcoming *AI Action Plan 2024–2026* (2024) envisions co-design workshops, where stakeholders—including civil society organizations and digital rights advocates—can influence the development and deployment of ADM tools.

5.2 Examples of Successful Bias Reduction in Estonia's ADM Applications

Bürokratt, Estonia's AI-driven virtual assistant, represents a significant step toward AI-enabled public services. To ensure inclusivity, a planned update in 2025 will introduce English and Ukrainian language support, improving accessibility for non-Estonian speakers. The expansion of language capabilities is expected to mitigate linguistic bias, addressing concerns that the current Estonian-only model may inadvertently exclude foreign residents.

The AI-powered decision-support system used by EUIF, *OTT*, has undergone enhancements to improve transparency. The ongoing pilot project for an AI transparency tool seeks to provide clear explanations for AI-generated recommendations. This initiative reflects broader efforts within the Estonian government to align ADM practices with the EU AI Act's transparency requirements.

ABC Gates, Estonia's biometric-based border control system, has faced criticism for potential bias in facial recognition accuracy, particularly concerning demographic disparities. In response, Estonia has implemented algorithmic adjustments to enhance recognition rates across diverse populations. The Equitech Audit Report (2024) notes that ongoing testing and recalibration efforts have reduced error rates, improving fairness in automated border security.

Estonia has made significant strides in mitigating algorithmic bias within its ADM systems. The adoption of algorithmic audits, fairness-aware AI models, transparency standards, and human oversight mechanisms reflects a commitment to responsible AI governance. However, challenges remain in ensuring that these measures are effectively implemented across all public sector ADM applications. The forthcoming AI Action Plan and regulatory alignment with the EU AI Act are expected to further strengthen Estonia's approach to AI fairness and accountability. Future efforts should focus on expanding participatory governance models, enhancing algorithmic transparency, and refining fairness metrics to ensure equitable outcomes in ADM systems.

[76] See Equitech(b) (2024).

6 Recommendations and Future Directions

The implementation of Automated Decision-Making (ADM) systems in Estonia has introduced significant efficiencies in public administration but has also raised legal, ethical, and technical challenges. As ADM technologies continue to evolve, policymakers, regulators, and practitioners must take a proactive approach to ensuring transparency, fairness, and accountability in these systems. This section outlines key recommendations and explores potential future directions for ADM in Estonia's public sector.

6.1 Practical Recommendations for Policymakers and Practitioners to Enhance ADM Implementation

6.1.1 Legal Safeguards Against Algorithmic Discrimination

Estonia should explicitly recognize algorithmic discrimination within its legal framework, particularly in the forthcoming Gender Equality and Equal Opportunities Act. Public institutions using ADM systems should be mandated to demonstrate compliance with non-discrimination obligations, ensuring that algorithms do not disproportionately impact protected groups.

To enhance accountability, Estonia should create a publicly accessible registry of ADM systems used in government decision-making. This registry should include: (i) the purpose of each ADM system, (ii) information on data sources, bias mitigation strategies, and oversight mechanisms, and (iii) contact points for citizens to challenge or request explanations regarding ADM-driven decisions. This initiative aligns with the AI Act's transparency requirements and reinforces public trust in AI-driven governance.

Before deploying ADM systems, public authorities should conduct Algorithmic Impact Assessments (AIAs) to systematically evaluate the potential risks associated with algorithmic decision-making. These assessments should identify and mitigate risks of discrimination and unfair outcomes, ensuring that ADM systems do not disproportionately disadvantage any group. Additionally, AIAs should assess the explainability and interpretability of automated decisions, providing clear justifications for outcomes and enabling affected individuals to understand and challenge decisions when necessary. To uphold accountability, AIAs must also establish mechanisms for human oversight, ensuring that automated processes remain subject to meaningful human review and intervention. To maintain transparency and adaptability, AIAs should be publicly available and periodically reviewed, allowing for continuous monitoring and improvement in compliance with Estonia's legal and ethical AI governance framework.

Moreover, The Gender Equality and Equal Treatment Commissioner's Office is considered with explicit powers to investigate algorithmic discrimination in public sector ADM systems. This would be followed by requesting documentation on high-risk ADM models, as permitted under Article 77 of the AI Act and mandating corrective actions when ADM systems are found to cause discriminatory outcomes. This approach would align Estonia's ADM governance with EU best practices and ensure stronger enforcement of equality rights.

Victims of algorithmic discrimination often struggle to prove bias due to the opaque nature of ADM systems. Estonia should consider shifting the burden of proof in such cases, requiring public institutions and companies deploying ADM to demonstrate non-discrimination. In addition to this, ADM system providers should be required to disclose algorithmic logic and conduct fairness audits when discrimination claims arise. This reform would make it easier for affected individuals to seek redress under Estonia's non-discrimination laws.

6.1.2 Refining the AI Toolkit for Public Decision-Making

One of the core challenges in ADM implementation is the gap between machine learning (ML) models and the realities of public sector decision-making. Standard predictive models often fail to account for key complexities such as distribution shifts, label bias, and the long-term impact of past decision-making.[77] Estonia should move beyond traditional ML techniques and adopt more sophisticated causal modeling and policy-learning approaches. Counterfactual prediction methods can be integrated into ADM systems to ensure that decisions are not based on historical biases but on reliable estimations of intervention effects.

6.1.3 Developing a Framework for Algorithmic Fairness and Bias Audits

Algorithmic audits must be systematically conducted to identify and mitigate biases in ADM applications, as bias can emerge at multiple stages, including historical data collection, model training, and real-world implementation.[78] Given Estonia's increasing reliance on ADM in border control, welfare, and tax administration, it is essential to develop sector-specific fairness auditing frameworks tailored to the unique risks and challenges of each domain.[79] While compliance with the EU AI Act sets a foundational standard, Estonia should go further by integrating context-sensitive fairness assessments that address localized disparities in data and policy implementation.

To enhance trust and accountability, public-sector AI systems should be designed with explainability at their core, ensuring that individuals affected by

[77] See Fischer-Abaigar et al. (2024).

[78] See Mac (2024).

[79] See Palmiotto (2024).

ADM decisions can understand the rationale behind automated outcomes and effectively challenge unfair determinations.[80] Implementing algorithmic transparency tools, interactive decision explanations, and user-accessible impact assessments will help bridge the gap between regulatory compliance and meaningful AI oversight, fostering a more equitable and accountable digital governance ecosystem.

6.1.4 Strengthening Human Oversight in AI-Driven Decisions

While Estonia has taken steps to integrate AI into public administration, the effectiveness of human oversight remains a key challenge. Research shows that merely having a human in the loop does not guarantee meaningful oversight, as automation bias can lead human reviewers to over-rely on AI outputs.[81] Estonia should develop training programs focused on critical algorithmic assessment skills to ensure that human decision-makers can effectively challenge AI recommendations.

Moreover, research highlights that timing plays a critical role in human-AI interaction—if human oversight occurs too late in the decision-making process, it is less effective in correcting AI errors.[82] Estonia should implement tiered oversight mechanisms, where AI-driven decisions are flagged at multiple checkpoints before finalization.

6.1.5 Enhancing AI Literacy and Public Awareness

The importance of increasing AI literacy among policymakers, public officials, and citizens is also highlighted by the European Commission's Competence Center of Foresight. According to their analysis, governments should develop AI literacy programs to educate key stakeholders about ADM systems, including their opportunities, risks, and limitations. Furthermore, public engagement initiatives should focus on demystifying AI decision-making and empowering individuals to exercise their rights regarding ADM-based decisions. Incorporating citizen feedback mechanisms in AI-driven public services was also found to help enhance transparency and accountability.[83]

[80] See Jakubek-Lalik (2024).

[81] See Agudo et al. (2024).

[82] See Agudo et al. (2024).

[83] See European Commission (2025).

6.2 *Forecasting on Future Trends in ADM Applications within the Estonian Public Sector*

Estonia is at the forefront of developing proactive, invisible, and human-centric public services through AI and automated decision-making.[84] The country's Digital Agenda 2030 envisions a future where AI automates routine bureaucratic processes while ensuring compliance with fundamental rights.[85] Future applications will likely involve more predictive AI models in areas such as healthcare, taxation, and welfare distribution.

With the continued use of ADM in border control through *ABC Gates*, Estonia is expected to further integrate AI-driven security measures.[86] However, concerns about biometric bias and the potential for discriminatory outcomes will require ongoing adjustments in algorithmic fairness.[87] Future developments should focus on improving the accuracy of facial recognition systems while ensuring that privacy and human rights considerations remain central.[88]

As ADM systems become more complex, Estonia will need to refine its legal and regulatory framework to keep pace with AI developments. The EU AI Act (Regulation (EU) 2024/1689) provides a foundation, but Estonia must develop national legislation that incorporates AI ethics principles into law.[89] This may include stricter requirements for AI procurement, expanded legal remedies for individuals affected by ADM decisions, and increased regulatory scrutiny of high-risk AI applications.[90]

As Estonia continues to lead in digital innovation, fostering collaboration between academia, government, and industry will be essential for sustainable ADM governance. Initiatives such as the AI Sandbox proposed in Estonia's AI Action Plan 2024–2026 should be expanded to allow for continuous experimentation, testing, and regulatory adaptation.[91]

ADM systems will continue to shape Estonia's public administration, providing efficiency gains while introducing new legal and ethical challenges. The recommendations outlined in this section highlight the need for stronger transparency measures, enhanced algorithmic audits, improved human oversight, and increased citizen engagement. By proactively addressing these issues, Estonia can maintain its position as a global leader in digital governance while ensuring that ADM applications align with human rights and democratic values. The next phase of Estonia's AI strategy must focus on aligning national regulations with EU legal frameworks,

---

[84] See Paes (2023).

[85] See Ministry of Economic Affairs and Communications (a) (2024).

[86] See Pilving and Mikiver (2020).

[87] See Equitech(a) (2024).

[88] See Kerikmäe and Pärn-Lee (2021).

[89] See Gamito and Gentile (2023).

[90] See Zolkin et al. (2023).

[91] See Ministry of Economic Affairs and Communications (b) (2024).

expanding fairness-aware AI policies, and fostering collaboration across sectors to build more responsible and trustworthy ADM systems.

7 Conclusion

Estonia's approach to Automated Decision-Making (ADM) in public administration reflects its broader digital governance ambitions, blending efficiency with innovation while grappling with legal and ethical challenges. The implementation of ADM systems such as *Bürokratt*, *OTT*, and *ABC Gates* demonstrates how AI can enhance service delivery, streamline administrative processes, and support decision-making. However, Estonia's experience also highlights the complexities associated with algorithmic bias, transparency, and regulatory compliance.

The analysis of Estonia's regulatory framework, particularly in the context of the EU AI Act, underscores the evolving nature of AI governance. While Estonia has established legal safeguards to mitigate discrimination and ensure fairness in automated decisions, challenges persist, particularly in areas such as algorithmic explainability and accountability. The discussion of algorithmic bias in ADM applications reveals the necessity for fairness-aware AI models, systematic bias audits, and improved transparency mechanisms. Estonia's efforts, including the integration of Explainable AI (XAI) and participatory governance mechanisms, represent important steps toward ensuring that ADM systems align with fundamental rights and democratic values.

Looking forward, Estonia must refine its ADM strategies by strengthening human oversight, expanding regulatory tools for bias detection, and fostering greater public engagement in AI governance. The country's Digital Agenda 2030 and AI Action Plan 2024–2026 indicate a commitment to responsible AI deployment, but their success will depend on continuous regulatory adaptation, interdisciplinary collaboration, and investment in fairness-aware AI methodologies.

As Estonia continues to lead in digital transformation, its ADM experience offers valuable lessons for other nations seeking to integrate AI into public administration. By maintaining a focus on transparency, accountability, and inclusivity, Estonia can balance technological advancement with ethical AI governance, ensuring that ADM systems serve public interests while upholding legal and human rights standards.

References

Aaviksoo B, Kalmo H, Mälksoo L et al (2020) In: Madise Ü (ed) Eesti Vabariigi põhiseadus: kommenteeritud väljaanne. Iuridicum, Tallinn

Administrative Procedure Act (Estonia) (2002) RT I 2001, 58, 354

Agudo U, Liberal KG, Arrese M, Matute H (2024) The impact of AI errors in a human-in-the-loop process. Cogn Res Princ Implic 9(1):1

AI Watch (2025) Estonia AI Strategy Report. AI Watch – European Commission. https://ai-watch.ec.europa.eu/countries/estonia/estonia-ai-strategy-report_en
Cantero Gamito M, Gentile G (2023) Algorithms, rule of law, and the future of justice: implications in the Estonian justice system. Report. European University Institute, Florence
Clarke R, Michael K, Abbas R (2024) Robodebt: a socio-technical case study of public sector information systems failure. Australas J Inf Syst 28
Constitution of the Republic of Estonia (1992) RT 1992, 26, 349
Dreyling R III, Tammet T, Pappel I (2024) Technology push in AI-enabled services: how to master technology integration in case of Bürokratt. SN Comput Sci 5(6):738
Ebers M, Trasberg H (2023) Due process, fair trial, transparency, and explainability. In: Artificial intelligence and machine learning powered public service delivery in Estonia: opportunities and legal challenges. Springer, Cham, pp 103–128
e-Estonia (2025) e-Governance: e-services and registries. e-Estonia – The Digital Society. https://e-estonia.com/solutions/e-governance/e-services-registries/.
Employment Contracts Act (Estonia) (2009) RT I 2009, 5, 35
Equal Treatment Act (Estonia) (2008) RT I 2008, 56, 315
EquiTech(a) (2024) Report on auditing discrimination and bias within Estonian public sector ADM systems. Report. Tallinn University of Technology, Tallinn
EquiTech(b) (2024) Legal analysis on non-discrimination regulation and regulatory gaps concerning algorithmic systems in Estonia and Lithuania. Report. Tallinn University of Technology, Tallinn
Estonian Supreme Court (2002) Case No. 3-4-1-2-02. Riigikohus (Supreme Court of Estonia). https://www.riigikohus.ee/et/lahendid?asjaNr=3-4-1-2-02
Estonian Supreme Court (2007) Case No. 3-4-1-14-07. Riigikohus (Supreme Court of Estonia). https://rikos.rik.ee/LahendiOtsingEriVaade?asjaNr=3-4-1-14-07
Estonian Supreme Court (2008) Case No. 3-4-1-8-08. Riigikohus (Supreme Court of Estonia). https://www.riigikohus.ee/et/lahendid?asjaNr=3-4-1-8-08
Estonian Supreme Court (2022) Case No. 5-17-22/10. Riigikohus (Supreme Court of Estonia). https://www.riigikohus.ee/et/lahendid/?asjaNr=5-17-22/10
European Commission (2025) Automated decision-making impacting society. Knowledge for Policy – European Commission. https://knowledge4policy.ec.europa.eu/foresight/automated-decision-making-impacting-society_en
Fischer-Abaigar U, Kern C, Barda N, Kreuter F (2024) Bridging the gap: towards an expanded toolkit for AI-driven decision-making in the public sector. Gov Inf Q 41(4):101976
Gender Equality Act (Estonia) (2004) RT I 2004, 27, 181
Gerards J, Xenidis R (2021) Algorithmic discrimination in Europe: challenges and opportunities for gender equality and non-discrimination law. European Commission
Government of Estonia (2020) Estonia 2035 development strategy: strategic goals. Government of Estonia. https://valitsus.ee/en/estonia-2035-development-strategy/strategy/strategic-goals
Government of Estonia (2024) Draft Gender Equality and Equal Opportunities Act. Eelnõud – Government of Estonia. https://eelnoud.valitsus.ee/main/mount/docList/389a2753-fc8e-4e10-9912-469b6fc2acf8
Hacker P (2018) Teaching fairness to artificial intelligence: existing and novel strategies against algorithmic discrimination under EU law. Common Mark Law Rev 55(4):1143–1185
Hirvonen H (2024) Just accountability structures – a way to promote the safe use of automated decision-making in the public sector
Jakubek-Lalik J (2024) The challenges of AI in administrative law and the need for specific legal remedies: analysis of Polish regulations and practice. Cent Eur Public Adm Rev 22:109
Kaun A, Männiste M, Liminga A (2023) Mapping the automated decision-making landscape in Swedish and Estonian welfare states
Kaun A, Larsson AO, Masso A (2024) Automating public administration: citizens' attitudes towards automated decision-making across Estonia, Sweden, and Germany. Inf Commun Soc 27(2):314–332

Kerikmäe T, Pärn-Lee E (2021) Legal dilemmas of Estonian artificial intelligence strategy: in between e-society and global race. AI Soc 36:561–572

Kratid.ee (2025) AI use cases in Estonia. Kratid – The AI Register. https://www.kratid.ee/en/ai-use-cases

Langer C (2024) Decision-making power and responsibility in an automated administration. Discov Artif Intell 4(1):59

Locci I, Massoni S (2024) Judged by robots: preferences and perceived fairness of algorithmic versus human punishments. Rev Law Econ (forthcoming)

Mac TA (2024) Bias and discrimination in ML-based systems of administrative decision-making and support. Comput Law Secur Rev 55:106070

Meiorg M, Grossthal K (2022) Võrdse kohtlemise seadus, Käsiraamat. Tallinn, p 16

Ministry of Economic Affairs and Communications (2024) Tehisintellekti tegevuskava 2024–2026. https://www.mkm.ee/media/10157/download.

Ministry of Economic Affairs and Communications (a) (2024) Digital Agenda 2030. Republic of Estonia – Ministry of Economic Affairs and Communications. https://www.mkm.ee/en/e-state-and-connectivity/digital-agenda-2030

Ministry of Economic Affairs and Communications (b) (2024) Andmete tegevuskava 2024–2025. Government of Estonia. https://www.mkm.ee/sites/default/files/documents/2024-02/Andmete%20tegevuskava%202024-2025.pdf

Paes S (2023) From ethics to action: a study of human-centric AI implementation in public services, comparing the Estonian approach with approaches used in other countries. Master's thesis, TalTech University, Tallinn

Palmiotto F (2024) When is a decision automated? A taxonomy for a fundamental rights analysis. Ger Law J 25(2):210–236

Pilving I, Mikiver M (2020) A Kratt as an administrative body: algorithmic decisions and principles of administrative law. Jurid Int 29:47

Regulation (EU) 2016/679 of the European Parliament and of the Council (2016) On the protection of natural persons with regard to the processing of personal data and on the free movement of such data (General Data Protection Regulation). OJ L 119

Regulation (EU) 2024/1689 of the European Parliament and of the Council (2024) Laying down harmonised rules on artificial intelligence (Artificial Intelligence Act) and amending various regulations and directives. OJ L 2024/1689

Rizk A, Lindgren I (2024) Automated decision-making in the public sector: a multidisciplinary literature review. In: Proceedings of the international conference on electronic government. Springer, Cham, pp 237–253

Szafran D, Bach RL (2024) "The human must remain the central focus": subjective fairness perceptions in automated decision-making. Minds Mach 34(3):24

Wachter S, Mittelstadt B, Russell C (2021) Why fairness cannot be automated: bridging the gap between EU non-discrimination law and AI. Comput Law Secur Rev 41:105567

Weerts H, Xenidis R, Tarissan F et al (2023) Algorithmic unfairness through the lens of EU non-discrimination law: or why the law is not a decision tree. In: Proceedings of the 2023 ACM Conference on Fairness, Accountability, and Transparency. ACM, pp 805–816

Zolkin V, Chochia A, Hoffmann T (2023) Automated decision-making in the EU member state's public administration: the compliance of automated decisions of the Estonian Unemployment Insurance Fund with Estonian Administrative Procedure Law. Eur Stud Rev Eur Law Econ Polit 10(2):178–202

Tanel Kerikmäe is a law professor of at Tallinn University of Technology (TalTech), having a worldwide experience in teaching and research. He is a designer of new type of legal education whose research activities are related to law & technology.

Kristi Joamets (PhD) is a senior lecturer at the Tallinn University of Technology (TalTech). Her main areas of research include labour law and equality law in the context of fundamental rights and technology development.

Ebru Metin is an early-stage researcher at Tallinn University of Technology. Her interdisciplinary research explores how legal design can reduce regulatory complexity, making corporate sustainability frameworks more accessible, actionable, and effective for businesses, policymakers, and stakeholders.

DSA, DMA and Their Interaction with How Member States Regulate Their Digital Markets

Implementing the DMA and DSA: Comparing National Approaches in the EU

Alexandre de Streel and Francesco Decarolis

Contents

Abstract Part II of this volume presents a comprehensive analysis of the national-level implementation of the Digital Markets Act (DMA) and Digital Services Act (DSA) across five European Union member states: Estonia, France, Germany, Italy, and Spain. By examining the institutional arrangements, regulatory responses, and challenges faced by these countries, the chapter reveals the complex landscape of digital regulation implementation. The research highlights variations in national approaches, demonstrating how different member states are adapting to the new EU digital rulebook. The analysis uncovers critical challenges in implementing these regulations, including potential regulatory fragmentation, overlapping national and EU-level enforcement mechanisms, and inherent difficulties in monitoring and enforcing digital markets and services rules. The comparative study provides

A. de Streel
University of Namur, Namur, Belgium
e-mail: alexandre.destreel@unamur.be

F. Decarolis (✉)
Bocconi University, Milano, Italy
e-mail: francesco.decarolis@unibocconi.it

F. Decarolis et al. (eds.), *The EU Digital Regulation and its Impact on Member States*, European Union and its Neighbours in a Globalized World 27,
https://doi.org/10.1007/978-3-032-06490-5_7

insights into how different countries are balancing national regulatory autonomy with European harmonization, offering valuable lessons for policymakers and researchers interested in the evolving landscape of digital market governance. Ultimately, the research underscores the importance of adaptive, nuanced approaches to implementing comprehensive digital regulations across diverse European contexts.

1 Introduction

This second part of the volume delves into the complex landscape of the newly introduced Digital Markets Act (DMA) and Digital Services Act (DSA). It focuses on the implementation of these regulations at the national level in Estonia, France, Germany, Italy, and Spain.[1] Specifically, it examines the institutional arrangements needed to support this new EU legal regime. This analysis reveals different and relatively unexplored aspects of the DMA and DSA. It also complements the first part of the book in a crucial way.

The aim of each chapter in this second part is to provide a comprehensive and detailed understanding of the national-level implementation of the DMA and the DSA to reason on the associated implications, highlighting the institutional interplay and the complexities of what is effective regulation in the digital economy and society. Indeed, the effectiveness of the DMA and DSA in the coming years will largely depend on how well the EU and national institutions will implement these regulations. This part of the book thus examines the responses of the European Commission and national competent administrations—particularly National Competition Authorities and Digital Services Coordinators—to the new digital rulebook and whether domestic regulations were amended to align with the DSA or DMA, either by merely extending the scope of existing digital rules or by requiring more significant remedies.

2 DMA and DSA: A Brief Recap

Digital intermediaries have become indispensable in modern society, fundamentally shaping how European citizens live and how EU businesses operate. For years, these services operated under minimal formal oversight, with general horizontal laws (such as competition law, consumer protection law or data protection law) and self-regulation being the primary mechanism for addressing societal concerns. This

[1] For an interesting comprehensive analysis of the implementation of the DSA and DMA in the EU Member States, see also FIDE (2025).

light-touch approach has proven inadequate as the power of digital platforms has grown to unprecedented levels, creating risks that extend far beyond traditional markets dynamics.

The light regulatory approach has created multiple challenges. The control of the dominant digital platforms on innovation has kept rising, as they exploited their scale, financial resources and data dominance to foreclose the tech innovation space to new entrants. These problems have been exacerbated by inherent features of digital markets. Network effects, data-linked scale economies and limited consumer attention have driven a tendency of digital markets toward concentration, leading to the emergence of a few tech giants that are now in control of vast swaths of the digital economy. Their economic, innovation and informational power enables them to exclude emerging competitors, creating a self-reinforcing cycle of market concentration. Businesses, particularly small and medium enterprises, have faced increasingly unfair terms and conditions imposed by dominant platforms, hampering their ability to compete effectively.[2] Moreover, citizens have fallen victim to manipulation through false content and misinformation, posing serious threats to democratic processes.[3]

To address these challenges, the European response has evolved from fragmented national initiatives to comprehensive EU-wide regulation. Initially, some Member States attempted to address these issues through national legislation. However, this fragmented approach risked undermining the Digital Single Market and proved insufficient to regulate digital platforms operating across borders. The EU has therefore adopted in 2022 two landmark regulations: the Digital Markets Act[4] the Digital Services Act,[5] creating the most ambitious and comprehensive rulebook yet for governing digital platforms.

The DMA and DSA establish complementary but distinct regulatory frameworks to 'Make the Cyberspace Great Again' and regain the early promises of the cyberspace so well explained by John-Perry Barlow in his famous Declaration of the independence of the Cyberspace given in Davos in 1996. On the one hand, the DMA

---

[2] Impact Assessment Report of the Commission Services of 15 December 2020 on the Proposal for a Regulation of the European Parliament and of the Council on contestable and fair markets in the digital sector (Digital Markets Act), SWD(2020) 363. Several reports done by or for competition authorities also shows the economic issues raised by the biggest digital platforms: Lancieri and Morita Sakowski (2021). For a recent overview of how the intricate web of EU regulations could be turned into an engine for innovations see Decarolis et al. (2025b) Rules That Empower - Turning EU Digital Regulation into a Catalyst for Innovation, IEP Bocconi technical report.

[3] Impact Assessment Report of the Commission Services of 15 December 2020 on the Proposal for a Regulation of the European Parliament and of the Council on a Single Market For Digital Services (Digital Services Act), SWD(2020) 348.

[4] Regulation 2022/1925 of the European Parliament and of the Council of 14 September 2022 on contestable and fair markets in the digital sector and amending Directives 2019/1937 and 2020/1828 (Digital Markets Act), OJ [2022] L 265/1.

[5] Regulation 2022/2065 of the European Parliament and of the Council of 19 October 2022 on a Single Market for Digital Services (Digital Services Act) and amending Directive 2000/31, OJ [2022] L 277/1.

regulates the *systemic gatekeeper power* by opening the largest tech ecosystems in order to increase digital markets contestability and fairness and, ultimately, increase innovation and users' choices.[6] On the other hand, the DSA regulates digital intermediaries, and in particular those with *systemic influence power*, by changing their internal governance to create a safer digital space where users' fundamental rights are protected.[7]

2.1 DMA: Opening the Big Tech Ecosystems

The DMA targets the largest digital platforms—the so called "gatekeepers"—through an innovative, ex-ante, regulatory approach. To qualify as a gatekeeper, a platform must meet specific thresholds regarding economic significance and users base in the EU, serve as a critical intermediary, and maintain an entrenched market position. The regulation marks a significant shift toward centralized oversight, with the European Commission as sole enforcer, though national authorities can assist in investigations.[8]

The designation of gatekeepers follows a clear procedure based on both quantitative and qualitative criteria. Companies must meet specific thresholds regarding their economic turnover or market value, their presence across EU Member States, and their user base among both consumers and businesses. Qualitatively, these platforms must constitute an important gateway for business users to reach end users.[9] This designation process serves two crucial purposes: it creates legal certainty by clearly identifying which platforms must comply with DMA obligations and it ensures that smaller platforms and new market entrants are not burdened with complex regulatory requirements. By targeting only the largest digital platforms, the DMA aims to promote innovation and competition while avoiding the creation of entry barriers for emerging digital companies.

The DMA ex-ante approach allows preventive intervention, contrasting with traditional competition law's lengthy ex-post investigations.[10] The DMA contains a long list of obligations which may be clustered into four categories: (i) preventing anti-competitive leveraging practices within the digital ecosystem of the gatekeepers with the prohibition of bundling or self-preferencing, (ii) reducing entry barriers on the supply side and opening up the platforms and the data of the gatekeepers with vertical and horizontal interoperability obligations or data portability mandates, (iii) reducing entry barriers on the demand side and facilitating users switching and

[6] Bania and Geradin (2024), Podszun (2024).

[7] Husovec (2024), Wilman et al. (2024).

[8] Larouche and de Streel (2021).

[9] For analysis of the first designation decisions: Bostoen and Monti (2024).

[10] Chirico (2021). This crucial feature of the DMA is well understood by the EU Courts: Case T-1077/23 Bytedance v Commission, EU:T:2024:478.

multi-homing with the prohibition of price parity or anti-steering clauses, and (iv) increasing transparency in the online advertising value chain.

Another innovation is the DMA is the requirements to disclose all mergers. Gatekeepers must inform the Commission of all digital sector acquisitions, even below traditional notification thresholds. This requirement aims to prevent "killer acquisitions"—where dominant platforms eliminate potential competitors by acquiring promising startups before they can scale up, a practice that may reduce competition in digital markets.[11]

The DMA's implementation faces several critical challenges. First, fundamental information asymmetries between regulators and gatekeepers hamper enforcement. Despite its role as sole enforcer, the Commission is likely to struggle verifying gatekeepers' claims about technical feasibility and compliance costs. These firms possess exclusive knowledge of their systems and technologies that regulators cannot easily evaluate, creating opportunities for strategic behavior. Gatekeepers can claim technical impossibility or excessive implementation costs, while regulators lack the expertise to effectively challenge these claims. This problem is compounded by the Commission's limited technical resources and digital markets' rapid evolution.

Moreover, the prevalence of antitrust-style enforcement also creates tensions within the Commission itself, where two departments with distinctly different cultures are involved in implementing the DMA. DG Competition, drawing from its antitrust experience, primarily operates through bilateral relationships with individual parties, particularly the platforms under investigation. DG Connect, by contrast, favors a more inclusive approach based on simultaneous consultation with multiple stakeholders. The resulting enforcement culture—based on the antitrust model—produces predominantly bilateral relationships between the Commission and gatekeepers, marginalizing other stakeholders. Small and medium-sized businesses, though primary DMA beneficiaries, often lack meaningful input in enforcement decisions. Some avoid active participation, fearing retaliation from gatekeepers they depend on. This dynamic undermines the DMA's goal of rebalancing digital market power.[12]

Formal compliance mechanisms have proven similarly problematic. Gatekeepers' transparency reports lack standardization and meaningful insight. Critical contextual information about changes between reporting periods is often omitted, hampering compliance monitoring. The Commission's failure to establish clear reporting guidelines has resulted in inconsistent and superficial disclosure practices.[13]

Second, as some DMA provisions were inspired by past antitrust remedies that proved insufficiently bold to be effective, the Commission should learn from past mistakes. The regulation of browsers and search engines illustrates this point.[14]

---

[11] Motta and Peitz (2021).

[12] de Streel et al. (2025).

[13] Ibidem.

[14] For a comprehensive discussion of how the economic regulation of internet search in Europe see Decarolis and Li (2023).

These DMA provisions were modeled on the Commission's Google Android antitrust case, where Google had secured its near-monopoly in search by paying mobile device manufacturers to pre-install Google Search as the default search engine.[15]

The Commission's antitrust remedy in that case—requiring Google to implement a choice screen allowing users to select their preferred search engine during device setup—proved inadequate, failing to account for behavioral realities: users rarely deviate from pre-selected options when faced with complex choices. This "status quo bias" effectively maintained Google's dominance despite the formal presence of alternatives. Turkey's competition authority, by contrast, demonstrated the effectiveness of bolder intervention by prohibiting Google's revenue-sharing agreements with manufacturers. This direct approach prevented Google from using its financial power to secure default positions and led to meaningful increases in alternative search engine usage.[16]

This comparison is particularly relevant for DMA enforcement: while the regulation's provisions may mirror past antitrust remedies, its enforcement should embrace more innovative and decisive approaches rather than following the historically conservative patterns of antitrust enforcement. The Commission must avoid repeating the mistakes of past antitrust enforcement when implementing these new digital regulations.

More generally, the limited effectiveness of the Google Android antitrust case highlights the critical importance of using quantitative metrics to assess the impact of the DMA obligations. Relying solely on a process-based approach to verify compliance, based on the assumption that compliant processes guarantee compliant behavior, risks implementing remedies that fail to be sufficiently effective and achieve their intended goals. This could trap the European Commission in a Sisyphean task, endlessly expending resources on ineffective interventions. To avoid this, the Commission should integrate quantitative measures into its monitoring of remedy efficacy, alongside process evaluation. For instance, to measure the effectiveness of the DMA obligations, the Commission could develop market output indicators which measure how much the business and end-users of the gatekeepers seize the opportunities brought by the DMA[17] While the interpretation of these metrics may remain subject to debate, they would provide a common factual foundation, allowing the Commission to make timely and informed adjustments.

Third, the DMA's foundation in Article 114 TFEU—regulating the harmonization of the single market—rather than in competition law articles, has created complications. This approach has led to an overlap between the DMA and competition law frameworks, as both can be applied to the same conducts by the same companies. While the DMA designates the Commission as sole enforcer, national authorities retain full power to apply competition law to gatekeepers. This creates a complex

[15] Commission Decision of 18 July 2018, Case 40,099 *Google Android* which has been upheld (in part) by the General Court in Case T-604/18 *Google v. Commission*, EU:T:2022:541.

[16] Decarolis et al. (2025a).

[17] See de Streel et al. (2024).

scenario where the same conduct could be subject to both DMA obligations and competition law provisions, potentially leading to divergent interpretations and enforcement approaches between EU and national levels.

2.2 *DSA: Changing the Internal Governance of the Digital Intermediaries*

The Digital Services Act focuses on the interaction between digital platforms and users. The DSA regulates a broad range of online intermediaries including social networks and marketplaces. The regulation introduces a graduated set of obligations that increase with platform size and potential impact, with Very Large Online Platforms (VLOPs) and Search Engines (VLOSEs) facing the most stringent requirements, reflecting their outsized influence on information dissemination and commerce.

Under the DSA, platforms must implement comprehensive systems for content moderation, user protection, and transparency. These requirements include establishing clear procedures for handling illegal content, and maintaining effective complaint handling systems. The regulation places particular emphasis on advertising transparency and protecting minors online. VLOPs and VLOSEs must additionally conduct annual risk assessments of their societal impact and take measures to mitigate identified risks. The DSA backs these obligations with significant enforcement powers, including fines up to 6% of annual turnover for violations.

The regulation establishes a multi-level enforcement mechanism where the Commission directly oversees the stricter obligations imposed to VLOPs and VLOSEs, while national Digital Services Coordinators supervise the others, less stringent, obligations. This structure aims to ensure consistent enforcement across the EU while maintaining flexibility for national contexts. The DSA also establishes, notably with the European Board of Digital Services (EBDS) a sophisticated cooperation mechanism between national authorities and the Commission, coordinating enforcement across the EU while respecting national competencies.

3 The Responses at National Level

By analysing the implementation strategies and institutional framework in Estonia, France, Germany, Italy, and Spain, the following chapters aim to shed light on the diverse approaches and challenges faced by Member States in implementing adapting to the DMA and DSA. This comparative analysis will not only highlight best practices but also identify potential pitfalls, thereby contributing to a more informed and effective application of these ground-breaking regulations across Europe.

Despite a shared objective, each chapter presents a distinct analytical approach, tailored to the unique challenges faced by its focal Member State. For instance, some chapters prioritize an in-depth analysis of the Competition Authorities and scrutinize whether the legislature has granted investigative powers to the national antitrust authorities to ensure DMA compliance or if their role is limited to enforcing competition rules for gatekeepers. Others focus more of different features, such as the application of new merger review powers assigned to antitrust authorities by Article 14 of the DMA, or how the European Competition Network—as envisaged by the DMA—will facilitate cooperation and coordination between the European Commission and antitrust authorities. All chapters discuss the specific complexities of the DSA enforcement, with some specifically investigating the relationship between the national digital services coordinators, the post-market AI Act supervisory authorities, and the antitrust authorities.

The Estonian case presents a novel and insightful approach to digital regulation due to its advanced digital infrastructure and proactive governance, which make it a unique testing ground for EU regulations like the DMA and the DSA. Estonia's extensive experience with e-governance, digital identity, and cybersecurity has positioned it as a leader in digital policy within the EU, influencing the design and implementation of these regulations. The country has successfully integrated national regulatory bodies, such as the Consumer Protection and Technical Regulatory Authority (TTJA) and the Estonian Competition Authority (ECA), into the broader European framework, ensuring compliance while maintaining its leadership in digital governance. Estonia's experience highlights both the opportunities and challenges of aligning national innovation-driven digital policies with EU-wide regulatory frameworks, offering valuable insights into the balance between national sovereignty and European integration in digital markets.

Spain's regulatory trajectory is characterized by how national laws, such as the Law on Information Society Services and Electronic Commerce (LSSI), required significant adaptation to comply with the DSA's transparency and accountability mandates. Additionally, Spain's regulatory institutions, particularly the Comisión Nacional de los Mercados y la Competencia (CNMC), have had to adjust to a diminished role in competition oversight, as enforcement of digital platform rules is now centralized at the EU level. The Spanish case highlights the challenges of balancing national regulatory autonomy with European harmonization, illustrating the complexities of integrating digital services and market governance into a unified EU framework.

France's approach to implementing the DMA and DSA underscores the complexities of balancing national regulatory structures with EU-wide enforcement. The French regulatory framework distributes enforcement responsibilities among multiple authorities: the Autorité de la concurrence oversees competition-related matters, particularly in coordination with the European Commission; Arcom, the national audiovisual and platform content regulator, acts as the digital services coordinator responsible for overseeing compliance with the DSA; and the CNIL enforces data protection rules. This multi-agency structure necessitates extensive coordination, formalized through agreements among regulators. While this division of responsibilities ensures sector-specific expertise, it also raises concerns about fragmentation and the efficiency of enforcement. Additionally, the French legal framework goes beyond the DMA and DSA, incorporating new oversight powers over cloud computing markets and self-preferencing practices. The French case exemplifies the challenge of reconciling national regulatory autonomy with the harmonization goals of EU law, illustrating the potential risks of parallel enforcement and the administrative complexity of coordinating multiple agencies at both national and EU levels.

Germany provides another striking example of regulatory overlap through Section 19a of its Competition Act. This provision establishes a special abuse control regime for companies of "paramount significance for competition across markets," targeting essentially the same digital platforms designated as gatekeepers under the DMA. The Bundeskartellamt has already designated several major platforms under this provision, including Alphabet, Amazon, Apple, Meta and Microsoft. While the German framework technically complements the DMA by allowing for "further obligations" on gatekeepers, in practice it risks creating a parallel enforcement regime with potentially divergent standards.

Similarly, in recent legislation, Italy has modified its economic dependence law to introduce a presumption of dependence when businesses rely on digital platforms that play a decisive role in reaching end users or suppliers. While the law does not automatically apply to DMA-designated gatekeepers, there is significant potential overlap, as platforms meeting the DMA's gatekeeper criteria are likely to fall under this national definition as well. The Italian Competition Authority retains the power to investigate and sanction these platforms independently of DMA enforcement, creating a dual-track system that could lead to inconsistent standards and increased compliance burdens.

The insights from the different chapters highlight that the cooperation mechanism between national and EU authorities may at times suffer from incentive problems. For instance, national authorities lack motivation to invest resources in DMA investigations when they cannot lead enforcement actions. Germany's case is instructive: despite sophisticated digital market expertise, its competition authority has yet to refer cases to the Commission. This highlights broader challenges in creating effective multilevel enforcement mechanisms.

Moreover, the national legislation developed by some member states—partially overlapping with the DMA or the DSA—risks creating regulatory fragmentation, precisely the outcome the EU rulebook sought to prevent through the harmonization efforts. To mitigate this risk, the Commission may have powerful tools at its disposal. For instance, Article 38(7) of the DMA allows the Commission to preempt potential fragmentation by initiating its own investigation into a matter already under national scrutiny. When the Commission begins an investigation, it effectively suspends or precludes national authorities from conducting parallel investigations, thereby ensuring a unified and consistent approach to digital market regulation across the EU.

Overall, the implementation of the DMA and the DSA reveals fundamental challenges in establishing effective digital market regulation at the European level. The tension between, on the one hand, harmonization of rules and sometimes centralized enforcement and, on the other hand, national regulatory traditions creates practical difficulties that extend beyond simple coordination problems. The experiences documented in this book's subsequent chapters illuminate how different Member States navigate these challenges. Through detailed analysis of national responses in Estonia, France, Germany, Italy, and Spain, the following chapters provide crucial insights into emerging best practices and potential pitfalls in digital markets and services regulation. This comparative perspective offers valuable lessons for policymakers and regulators as they continue to refine and adapt the European framework for digital governance.

To conclude, we hope that this comparative study will provide valuable insights into best practices and common challenges that Member States are now facing, offering a balanced assessment from expert contributors that is essential for the ongoing evolution and refinement of these regulations. The insights from expert contributors across different jurisdictions and fields, from economics to law, enrich the nuanced understanding of the impacts of the DMA and DSA in Europe offering an interdisciplinary perspective and a well-rounded analysis.

References

Bania K, Geradin D (2024) The digital markets act: a guide to the regulation of big tech in the EU. Oxford University Press, Oxford
Bostoen F, Monti G (2024) The Rhyme and Reason of Gatekeeper Designation under the Digital Markets Act. TILEC Discussion Paper 2024-16
Chirico F (2021) Digital markets act: a regulatory perspective. J Eur Compet Law Pract 12(7):493
de Streel A, Bourreau M, Feasey R et al (2024) Implementing the DMA: substantive and procedural principles. Centre on Regulation in Europe (CERRE)
de Streel A, Feasey R, Monti G (2025) DMA@1: looking back and forward. CERRE
Decarolis F, Li M (2023) Regulating online search in the EU: from the android case to the digital markets act and digital services act. Int J Ind Organ 90
Decarolis F, Li M, Paternollo F (2025a) Competition and defaults in online search. American Economic Journal: Microeconomics 17(3):369–414.
Decarolis F, De Gregorio G, Fumagalli C et al (2025b) Rules that empower - turning EU digital regulation into a catalyst for innovation. IEP Bocconi technical report
Fédération Internationale de Droit Européen (2025) EU Digital Economy: general framework (DSA/DMA) and specialised regimes
Husovec M (2024) Principles of the digital services act. Oxford University Press, Oxford
Lancieri F, Morita Sakowski P (2021) Competition in digital markets: a review of expert reports. Stanford J Law Bus Finance 26(1):65
Larouche P, de Streel A (2021) The European digital markets act: a revolution grounded on traditions. J Eur Compet Law Pract 12(7):542–560
Motta M, Peitz M (2021) Big Tech Mergers. Inf Econ Policy 54:100868
Podszun R (2024) Digital markets act: article-by-article commentary. Beck/Hart/Nomos, Munich
Wilman F, Kaleda S, Loewenthal P (2024) The EU digital services act. Oxford University Press, Oxford

Alexandre de Streel is Professor of European law at the University of Namur and visiting professor at the College of Europe (Bruges) and SciencesPo Paris. He is also academic director of the digital research programme at the Brussels think-tank Centre on Regulation in Europe (CERRE) and member of decision panel at the Belgian Competition Authority.

Francesco Decarolis is Professor of Economics at Bocconi University - Milan. He is a CEPR Research Affiliate, he held editorial roles in leading scientific journals including Econometrica, The Review of Economic Studies and Econometrica.

Implementing the Digital Service Act and the Digital Market Act in Italy

Mariateresa Maggiolino

Contents

Abstract This chapter examines the implementation of the Digital Services Act (DSA) and Digital Markets Act (DMA) within the Italian legal and institutional framework, exploring the complex interactions between European and national regulatory mechanisms. By analyzing the roles of key national authorities—specifically the Italian Communications Regulatory Authority (ICRA) and the Italian Competition Authority (ICA)—the chapter reveals the nuanced approaches adopted to integrate these European regulations into Italy's existing legal landscape. The research highlights the intricate institutional frameworks established by the DSA and DMA, demonstrating how national authorities are empowered to collaborate with European institutions while maintaining distinct investigative and enforcement capabilities. Notably, the chapter explores how Italy has strategically positioned its national authorities to retain regulatory influence, particularly through innovative

M. Maggiolino (✉)
Bocconi University, Department of Law, Milan, Italy
e-mail: mariateresa.maggiolino@unibocconi.it

F. Decarolis et al. (eds.), *The EU Digital Regulation and its Impact on Member States*, European Union and its Neighbours in a Globalized World 27,
https://doi.org/10.1007/978-3-032-06490-5_8

legislative measures like the reform of rules on abuse of economic dependence. The analysis ultimately underscores the challenges of regulatory layering and the critical importance of effective cooperation between different regulatory levels. By examining the potential overlaps and complementarities between EU and national regulations, the chapter argues that streamlined regulatory processes can reduce compliance costs, foster innovation, and maintain the attractiveness of European digital markets. The research suggests that national adaptations play a crucial role in ensuring the practical effectiveness of supranational digital regulations.

1 Introduction

The adoption of the Digital Services Act (DSA)[1] and the Digital Markets Act (DMA) represents a milestone in the European Union's effort to regulate the unprecedented power of large digital platforms, which have become central to the exchange of goods and dissemination of content on a global scale. The DSA aims to ensure that the goods shared across these platforms are authentic and that the content disseminated is lawful, fostering an environment of trust and accountability. At the same time, the DMA addresses the competitive dynamics of the digital economy, seeking to preserve market contestability and fairness in the relationships between platforms and other stakeholders.

Therefore, these regulations play a crucial role in ensuring a safe and dignified digital environment. They protect fundamental individuals, a core value of the European Union, safeguard consumers through transparency and fairness, and support smaller businesses in their interactions with dominant platforms. Furthermore, by leveling the playing field, the DSA and DMA aim to foster a more inclusive and balanced digital economy, where innovation and competition can thrive without compromising equity and justice.

But equally important is the legal harmonization that these regulations aim to achieve, ensuring their consistent application across the Union. This uniformity prevents the fragmentation of the single market, which could arise from divergent national regulations and inconsistent obligations imposed on platforms. By eliminating such barriers, the DSA and DMA facilitate the free movement of goods and content, strengthening the integrity of the internal market and enabling seamless cross-border innovation and commerce, with the final goal of spurring economic growth.

However, to this end, the DSA and DMA establish two distinct institutional frameworks. The DSA introduces a multi-level enforcement system, distinguishing between the vertically centralized regulation of VLOPs and VLOSEs, overseen

[1] Regulation (EU) 2022/2065 of the European Parliament and of the Council of 19 October 2022 on a Single Market For Digital Services and amending Directive 2000/31/EC (Digital Services Act), OJ L 277, 27.10.2022, pp. 1–102.

exclusively by the European Commission, and the horizontally decentralized regulation of other platforms and intermediary services, managed by national authorities.[2] In contrast, the DMA designates the European Commission as the sole enforcer, while allowing national competition authorities to contribute during investigations.

The chapter examines these institutional frameworks, focusing on their implementation in Italy. Specifically, paragraph 2 addresses the enforcement system established by the DSA, while paragraph 3 explores the enforcement system outlined by the DMA. Each paragraph begins by briefly outlining the primary objectives of the DSA and DMA, before analyzing the national regulations governing the enforcement and sanctioning powers of the Italian authorities responsible for applying, or collaborating in the application of, the DSA and DMA. Paragraph 4, by contrast, takes a different approach. It focuses on the interplay between the DMA and national rules on the abuse of economic dependence—laws adopted by the Italian legislature at a time when the institutional framework outlined by the DMA was known but had not yet been definitively approved. These laws were designed to ensure that the Italian Competition Authority (ICA) retained the power to intervene in matters involving large digital platforms despite the European Commission's exclusive competence under the DMA. Paragraph 5 concludes.

2 The DSA and the Italian Communications Regulatory Authority

The **DSA** introduces a comprehensive legal framework for digital services within the EU, tackling new challenges posed by online intermediaries and platforms, including those offering goods, services, and content to EU consumers from outside the EU.

The DSA encompasses a wide range of entities, such as online marketplaces, app stores, gig economy platforms, social networks, hosting providers (e.g., cloud storage services), and intermediary infrastructure providers (e.g., internet service providers). It is a differentiated regulation, imposing obligations that vary based on the role and size of the entity, reflecting the risks they pose and their influence on users and market dynamics. All intermediaries must meet basic requirements, such as appointing contact points, publishing transparency reports, cooperating with legal authorities, and maintaining clear terms of service. Hosting providers must also enable third parties to report suspected illegal content, facilitate the reporting of criminal activities, and provide "notice and action" mechanisms, including explanations of their actions. Additionally, online platforms must establish internal systems for handling complaints, offer access to out-of-court dispute resolution, ensure

[2] In addition, many other bodies are involved: the digital services committee; the European Board for digital services people from providers; and external expertise (such as trusted flaggers).

protections against misuse, increase advertising transparency, and implement safeguards for minors. Very large online platforms (VLOPs) and search engines (VLOSEs), given their significant role in amplifying illegal content and societal risks, face stricter requirements. These include risk management obligations, crisis response protocols, independent audits, data-sharing mandates, and restrictions on recommendation systems based on user profiling.

This way, the DSA recognizes the diverse and complex nature of intermediary services and their providers, aiming to resolve the ambiguities that arose in national legal systems under the e-Commerce Directive.[3] Furthermore, this new regulation extends beyond the scope of the Directive, which primarily addressed intermediaries' liability for illegal third-party content. In contrast, the DSA aligns more closely with the significant transformations in the digital services landscape over the past two decades. It acknowledges the societal influence of certain intermediaries, particularly very large online platforms, and considers their impact on fundamental rights and democratic principles. The DSA's transparency requirements reflect a more nuanced understanding of the broader societal implications of digital services for individuals, organizations, and society as a whole.

Therefore, The DSA is expected to deliver significant protections and advantages across various societal groups, catering to the needs of individuals, digital service providers, business users, and society at large. For individuals, the DSA seeks to enhance the protection of fundamental rights, empowering citizens with greater control over their online experiences. This includes streamlined mechanisms for reporting illegal content and reducing exposure to harmful material. Moreover, the regulation emphasizes online safety for minors by banning targeted advertising aimed at children and ensuring greater transparency in content moderation practices. For digital service providers, the DSA promises increased legal clarity by establishing a unified legal framework across the EU,[4] simplifying compliance requirements, and supporting startups and companies in scaling more effectively within the European market. Business users of digital platforms are also set to benefit from expanded access to EU-wide markets and a fairer competitive environment, where illegal content providers cannot gain an unfair advantage. On a broader societal level, the DSA introduces stronger democratic oversight and accountability measures for large, systemic platforms, ensuring they take responsibility for their influence on public discourse and access to information. The regulation also tackles

---

[3] For an overview of the uncertainties emerged over the past decades concerning the correct interpretation of Directive 2000/31/EC, see Dinwoodie (2017). The fact that the EU lawmakers chose to replace a Directive with a Regulation, as in the case of the GDPR, is telling of the need to bring to an end the legal uncertainty sparked by the existence of 27 different pieces of legislation across the EU Member States. In particular, significant divergences emerged in the interpretation and enforcement of the liability exemptions by courts, leading to discrepancies among the various jurisdictions and, ultimately, to a decrease in the trust of consumers and organizations.

[4] But the DSA is supposed to have a significant impact also beyond the European Union: see among others Tourkochoriti (2023) and Nunziato (2023).

systemic risks, such as manipulation and disinformation, which threaten democratic integrity and social stability.[5]

At the institutional level, the DSA has introduced a sophisticated governance framework aimed at fostering close collaboration between the European Commission and national authorities to ensure the effective enforcement, monitoring, and oversight of its provisions. Specifically, while the European Commission is entrusted with the exclusive authority to enforce the DSA in relation to Very Large Online Platforms (VLOPs) and Very Large Online Search Engines (VLOSEs), as well as to supervise the additional obligations specifically assigned to them, the DSA designates National Digital Services Coordinators (DSCs) to oversee its implementation and enforcement within their respective Member States. These coordinators are also responsible for coordinating the activities of other competent national authorities. Moreover, the DSA establishes the European Board for Digital Services, an independent network comprising the European Commission and the national DSCs. This body is tasked with providing guidance, promoting the consistent application of the Regulation, and facilitating effective cooperation between the DSCs and the Commission.

In response to this framework, national legislatures have been working in recent months to designate their respective DSCs. In Italy, Article 15 of Law Decree No. 123/2003 assigns the role of DSC to the Italian Communications Regulatory Authority (ICRA), entrusting it with the responsibility to carry out its duties in a fair, transparent, and timely manner. The ICRA is charged with enforcing the rights and obligations outlined in the DSA, ensuring rigorous oversight, and achieving the Regulation's objectives. In practice, this includes safeguarding minors from online pornography, addressing illegal or prohibited content disseminated by online platforms and intermediary service providers, and fostering the creation of a secure digital environment.[6]

Moreover, Article 15 requires that the ICA, the Italian Privacy Authority, and any other relevant national bodies collaborate fully with ICRA, within their respective areas of competence, to assist in carrying out its duties. These authorities can formalize their cooperation through memoranda of understanding, defining the operational and procedural aspects of their collaboration.

The ICRA itself is also empowered to establish, through its own regulations, the conditions, procedures, and methods for exercising its powers and functions as the DSC under the DSA. To date, the ICRA has indeed adopted two key regulations: one concerning the verification process for granting the status of a trusted notifier (under Article 22(2) DSA),[7] and another related to the certification process for out-

[5] For some overviews on the advantages of the DSA, see Hoboken et al. (2023); Husovec (2024); Savin (2021); Davola (2022); Turillazzi et al. (2023).

[6] Official Journal, n. 216, 15 September 2023. Today, this Law-Decree has been converted, with amendments, by Law No. 159 of November 13, 2023.

[7] Resolution no. 283/24/CONS – Procedural regulation for the recognition of the status of trusted flagger pursuant to article 22 of the DSA, available at https://www.agcom.it/sites/default/files/provvedimenti/delibera/2024/Delibera%20283_24_CONS.pdf.

of-court dispute resolution bodies between online platform providers and service recipients (under Article 21 DSA).[8]

To ensure the consistent and effective enforcement of the DSA across the European Union, national authorities must be equipped with the necessary tools to act against digital service providers that violate or fail to comply with its provisions. In particular, to uphold the effectiveness of EU law, the powers of national authorities should align with those of the European Commission.

Under the DSA, the Commission may impose fines of up to 6% of a provider's global annual turnover for violations of DSA obligations, non-compliance with interim measures, or breaches of commitments. Additionally, the Commission may inflict daily penalties of up to 5% of the provider's average daily global turnover for each day of non-compliance with remedies, interim measures, or commitments, following a College decision imposing such obligations. Finally, the Commission may impose a fine up to 1% of the global turnover of the service provider if it gives inaccurate, incomplete, or misleading information, failing to respond or correct such information, or not complying with an inspection requirement.

Therefore, Article 15 of Decree-Law no. 123/2003 creates an equally robust sanctions framework to support ICRA in fulfilling its role, whether under Articles 51 and 52 of the DSA or in its broader capacity as the DSC. Specifically, the decree grants the ICRA the authority to impose financial penalties, ensuring they are fair, proportionate, and in line with due process, as outlined in its own regulations. More generally, it stresses that when applying sanctions, the ICRA must take into account the severity of the violation, its consequences, and whether the offense is recurring or ongoing. Importantly, the decree also rules out any possibility of reduced payment terms for these penalties. More in details, as for the Commission, these penalties first include a fine of up to 6% of the global turnover in the year prior to the commencement of proceedings for violations of the specific obligations related to transparency, user protection, removal of illegal content, and the management of risks and responsibilities of online platforms—namely, the obligations outlined in Articles 9, 14, 15, 23, 24, 26, 27, 28, 30, 45, 46, 47, and 48 of the DSA. Furthermore, the Law-Decree stipulates that the maximum daily penalty the ICRA may impose is 5% of the average daily global turnover of the relevant intermediary service provider in the preceding financial year, calculated from the date specified in the decision. Finally, also the Law-Decree no. 123/2003 enables the ICRA to impose a fine of up to 1% of the global turnover in the previous year for providing inaccurate, incomplete, or misleading information, failing to respond or correct such information, or not complying with an inspection requirement.

In conclusion, the governance and enforcement framework established by the DSA, supported by national measures such as Italy's Decree-Law No. 123/2003, reflects the will to craft a robust and coordinated approach to regulating the digital landscape across the EU. By empowering both the European Commission and

[8] Resolution 282/24/CONS – Regulation on the procedure for certifying extrajudicial dispute resolution bodies between online platform providers and service recipients pursuant to Article 21 of the DSA, available at https://www.agcom.it/provvedimenti/delibera-282-24-cons.

national authorities like the ICRA with clear roles, significant enforcement tools, and a shared commitment to transparency and accountability, the DSA aims to create a safer and more transparent online environment, ensuring compliance while addressing the challenges posed by rapid technological advancement. It is clear that, in such a context, cooperation will be key to ensuring the achievement of these goals.

3 The DMA and the Italian Competition Authority

The DMA aims to foster fair and competitive digital markets by addressing the power of large online platforms. These companies, known as 'gatekeepers,' hold considerable influence as intermediaries between businesses and consumers, controlling access to key digital services and holding entrenched market positions across several scenarios. The objective of the DMA is hence to ensure that gatekeepers operate fairly, creating an online environment where both users and smaller companies can succeed without facing unfair competitive barriers, and allowing them, where possible, to challenge gatekeepers' market positions.

Under the DMA, gatekeepers are defined as large digital platforms providing specific 'core platform services,' which include online search engines, app stores, messaging services, and social networks. To qualify as a gatekeeper, a company must meet several well-defined criteria: (*i*) it must have a substantial economic presence across the EU and operate in multiple member states; (*ii*) it must connect a large user base with a wide range of businesses, highlighting its intermediary role; and (*iii*) its market position must be longstanding, demonstrating that its influence has become entrenched over time.

To regulate gatekeepers' behavior, the DMA specifies (or would like to specify) clear obligations and prohibitions, setting a framework for acceptable conduct and curbing practices that could undermine market contestability and be unfair. Among the key obligations, gatekeepers are required to: (*i*) allow third-party platforms to interoperate with their services in certain cases, which fosters a more interconnected digital ecosystem and enhances user choice; (*ii*) grant business users on their platform access to their own data, enabling better business decisions and optimized strategies based on accurate data; (*iii*) equip advertisers and publishers with tools and data to independently verify the performance of their advertisements, which promotes fair competition by preventing gatekeepers from manipulating ad metrics; and (*iv*) allow business users to promote their services and enter into contracts with customers outside the gatekeeper's platform, giving businesses greater control over their customer interactions.

The DMA also tries to outline specific prohibitions for gatekeepers. For example, they are (*i*) prohibited from favoring their own products and services over those of third parties in rankings or other visibility methods, levelling the playing field and allowing competitors fair access to consumers; (*ii*) restricted from blocking consumers from connecting with businesses outside the platform's ecosystem, thus supporting consumer choice; (*iii*) prevented from pre-installing or restricting the removal of software on users' devices, safeguarding user autonomy and device customization; and (*iv*) barred from tracking users outside of their platform without explicit consent, which protects user privacy and curtails opaque targeted advertising practices.

Thus, through these provisions, the DMA is intended to bring substantial benefits to consumers, businesses, and the EU's digital ecosystem as a whole. According to EU institutions, business users dependent on gatekeepers will find a more equitable environment in which to operate. Previously, smaller companies faced restrictive conditions that stifled their growth potential. With the DMA, these companies could conduct business on more balanced terms, giving them a fair opportunity to compete. For innovators and technology start-ups, the DMA is said to offer relief from the barriers to entry and growth traditionally imposed by dominant platforms. Without restrictive conditions, start-ups are free to experiment, innovate, and bring new services to market without fear of being unfairly restricted. In the view of EU institutions, consumers also stand to gain significantly, enjoying a broader range of services, more options to switch providers, and fairer pricing. The DMA obligates gatekeepers to make it easier for consumers to explore alternatives, fostering competition and improving service quality across the market. Furthermore, from the perspective of the drafters of the DMA, while gatekeepers are restricted from certain monopolistic practices, they are encouraged to continue innovating—though without using unfair practices that disadvantage their business users or customers. Additionally, the DMA aimed to introduce new levels of legal clarity for these platforms because, for the first time, gatekeepers should face clearly defined obligations they must adhere to, so that non-compliance could even result in significant penalties or even structural changes within the company, such as asset divestiture.

With regard to the institutional framework outlined by the DMA, it was noted how the Regulation entrusts the European Commission alone with the task of designating companies as gatekeepers and ensuring their compliance with the newly established obligations and prohibitions. Nonetheless, the DMA allows for a certain degree of collaboration with national authorities. Therefore, following the enactment of the DMA, the Italian Parliament has taken decisive steps to ensure its operationalization within the national legal framework. Namely, Article 18 of Law No. 214/2023—commonly referred to as the 2022 Annual Market and Competition Law[9]—designates the Italian Competition Authority ("ICA") as the principal body tasked with enforcing the DMA. At the same time, the Italian Data Protection Authority ("IDPA") retains its pivotal role in overseeing and supervising matters specifically addressed by Articles 5(2), 5(6), 5(10), 7(8), 8(1), and 13(5) of the DMA, which deal with topics such as data access, data portability, interoperability, and mergers. In practical terms, this allocation of competences delineates a need for effective collaboration between the ICA and the IDPA, particularly in relation to issues that intersect their respective domains.

[9] Official Journal No. 303, 30 December 2023.

Moreover, Article 18 establishes a robust framework empowering the ICA to execute its mandate under the DMA, mirroring the investigative powers granted under the Italian Antitrust Law ("IAL"). Namely, to augment the efficacy of these powers, the ICA is authorized to enlist the support of law enforcement agencies (see "*guarda di finanza*"), thereby enhancing the overall enforcement capabilities of the DMA. Additionally, these investigative powers are fortified by the punitive measures inherent in the IAL, including sanctions and penalties for non-compliance.

On a broader scale, Article 18 obliges the ICA to engage in all forms of cooperation and coordination as envisioned by the DMA. In this regard, the ICA is empowered to issue its own regulatory provisions, provided they remain aligned with the procedural frameworks established under national competition law. These measures collectively position the ICA as a central and indispensable actor in ensuring the effective implementation and enforcement of the DMA within Italy's legal and institutional context. In line with this mandate, on 23 July 2024, the ICA formally enacted a dedicated regulation titled "Measures for the Implementation of Regulation (EU) 2022/1925 of the European Parliament and of the Council of 14 September 2022" (hereinafter, the "Cooperation Regulation").[10]

3.1 The Cooperation Regulation

To ensure a consistent, effective, and complementary application of the DMA, the Cooperation Regulation aims to establish the procedural framework for investigations conducted under Article 38(7) of the DMA. Furthermore, this Regulation extends, where compatible, to all other forms of collaboration and cooperation envisaged by the DMA, thereby providing a coherent and systematic approach to its enforcement. In this way, the ICA seeks to leverage all available legal instruments applicable to the designated gatekeepers.

Regarding the ICA's activities under Article 38(7) of the DMA, the Cooperation Regulation establishes detailed procedural timelines and modalities for its implementation. Furthermore, it outlines the ICA's investigative and sanctioning powers, which mirror those granted under the IAL.

Therefore, when it comes to initiating investigations, the ICA, upon assessing proposals from the relevant offices, may decide to launch an inquiry under Article 38(7) of the DMA, notifying the European Commission of its intention to investigate before proceeding. In particular, the decision to initiate an investigation must specify the following: the essential elements related to the potential non-compliance with the DMA; the deadline for concluding the investigation before the ICA; the officer responsible for the investigation; and the office to which the investigation is assigned. The decision to initiate the investigation must be notified to the undertakings concerned, as well as to individuals who, having a direct, immediate, and

[10] Official Journal No. 191, 16 August 2024.

current interest, have submitted complaints or requests relevant to the initiation of the investigation. Finally, notice of the investigation's initiation must be published in the ICA's Bulletin.

The Cooperation Regulation also specifies who can be involved in the investigations run under the DMA. It includes: (*a*) those formally notified of the decision to initiate the investigation, and (*b*) individuals, entities, or consumer representative associations with public or private interests who could face direct, immediate, and current harm from the alleged regulatory infringements. As it happens under the IAL in relation to antitrust proceedings, to participate, these parties must submit a reasoned request within thirty days of the investigation's announcement in the Bulletin. Furthermore, eligible participants are entitled to submit written statements, documents, arguments, and opinions, as well as access the relevant investigation materials. They may be represented by legally authorized agents or specially appointed proxies, provided they present documentation verifying their authority. Additionally, participants can seek assistance from trusted consultants throughout the investigation process.

Similarly, as said before, the Cooperation Regulation expands the scope of powers conferred upon the ICA under the IAL to encompass cases initiated pursuant to Article 38(7) of the DMA; and provides detailed guidelines for handling requests for information, document submission,[11] and hearing convocations, ensuring clarity and procedural fairness throughout the investigation process.

Thus, starting from the notification of the decision to initiate the investigation, the ICA will be permitted to use the investigatory powers set out in Article 14, paragraphs 2 to 2-quinquies, of IAL, with the help of of law enforcement agencies (see "*guardia di finanza*").

Furthermore, the ICA will be allowed to issue requests for information or document submission to any party holding information pertinent to the investigation. These requests will be communicated in accordance with Article 16, paragraph 2, of the IAL and must adhere to principles of proportionality. Each request must succinctly outline: a) the facts and circumstances requiring clarification; b) the purpose of the request, linked to the subject of the investigation; c) a reasonable deadline for compliance, factoring in the urgency of the case and the complexity of the requested information; d) the format and recipient of the submission; and e) the penalties for non-compliance, including refusal, omission, or unjustified delays, as well as for providing false, incomplete, or misleading information. To be sure, requests may also be made orally during hearings or inspections, in which case the same details must be recorded, excluding the deadline if the requested information or documents are not immediately available. In such cases, parties may submit a reasoned request for an extension before the original deadline, and if granted, a new deadline is set. In addition, the ICA retains the authority to summon any individual who may

[11] The term "document" refers to any graphical, photographic, cinematographic, electromagnetic, or any other form of representation of the content of acts, including internal and informal ones, created and used for business activity, regardless of the level of responsibility and representativeness of the author of the document, on any form of support or device.

possess relevant information at any stage of the investigation. Hearing notices, communicated to the parties, explicitly state the penalties for non-compliance. During hearings, a formal record is prepared, documenting the submission of information or documents and the proceedings. Should any party fail to appear, a record of non-appearance is likewise drawn up, ensuring transparency and accountability throughout the process.

With regard to inspections, the ICA, upon a proposal from the relevant offices, may authorize inspections, which are carried out by its officials following notification of their inspection orders. Each order specifies the scope of the investigation and outlines the sanctions and penalties applicable for violations, omissions, or unjustified delays in providing information or presenting documents requested during the inspection. It also covers penalties for providing false or misleading information or documents. During inspections, officials also notify the parties of the reasoned decree issued by the public prosecutor with jurisdiction over the location where the inspection is conducted. For the purposes of these sanctions, the following cannot be invoked as grounds for non-compliance: a) confidentiality or restrictions imposed by company regulations or internal instructions, even if conveyed orally; b) self-protection concerns related to potential fiscal or administrative penalties; and c) the need to safeguard business or industrial secrets. Parties subject to inspection may be assisted by consultants of their choice, though their presence does not suspend the inspection. A detailed record of all activities conducted during the inspection, including statements made and documents collected, is prepared in accordance with the procedures set out in the Cooperation Regulation.

In relation to the results of the investigation under Article 38(7) DMA, the Cooperation Regulation clarifies that ICA must send the results of the investigation conducted to the Commission and informs the parties that participated in the investigation. The closure of the investigation and the submission of its results to the Commission may be announced through the publication of a notice in the Bulletin.

The Cooperation Regulation also addresses various other procedural aspects, such as the involvement of experts, the formal requirements for documents (including notifications, communications, requests, document transmissions, convocations, and verbatim records), the right of access, and the confidentiality of documents.

For instance, the regulation grants individuals or entities involved in investigations the right to access documents created or permanently held by the ICA, provided they submit a written and reasoned request. However, access is excluded for documents whose disclosure could undermine the Commission's investigative powers or the enforcement measures established by the regulation. Similarly, notes, proposals, and other materials prepared by the ICA's offices for the purpose of drafting or analyzing acts are not accessible. Documents relating to communications between the ICA and European Union institutions, as well as between the ICA and competition authorities of other Member States, are also excluded unless specifically authorized for disclosure. Additionally, minutes of ICA meetings and documents concerning interactions between the ICA and other administrations or state bodies may be withheld, either partially or entirely, unless authorization is granted.

Furthermore, documents containing trade secrets or other confidential information about individuals or legal entities are protected from disclosure. Interested parties can request confidentiality at the time of submission or within a specified deadline, providing reasons and a non-confidential version of the documents in question. On the other hand, information collected under Article 38(7) of the DMA is safeguarded by confidentiality with respect to other public administrations, except where disclosure is required under Article 331 of the Italian Criminal Procedure Code or under cooperation obligations with European Union institutions.

Notably, the Cooperation Regulation allows the ICA to use documents and information gathered during investigations under Article 38(7) of the DMA for its broader enforcement powers, in compliance with European Union law. This includes oversight of digital markets covered by the DMA, as well as matters related to anti-competitive agreements, abuses of dominant positions, economic dependence, and merger control operations.

As the following paragraph will illustrate, the ICA also retains the authority to pursue gatekeepers independently of the DMA, addressing abuses of economic dependence and violations of EU and Italian competition laws.

4 The Italian Rule on the "Abuse of Economic Dependence" for Digital Platforms and the Imposition of Further Obligations on Gatekeepers (Article 1(6)(b))

Article 18 of Law No. 214/2023 provides that the findings of investigations carried out under the DMA may be utilized by the ICA, in compliance with EU law, to exercise its authority in digital markets regulated by the DMA. This includes areas such as restrictive agreements, abuses of dominant position, abuses of economic dependence, and merger control. Consequently, this provision raises significant challenges, particularly concerning the potential overlap between the DMA and these regulatory frameworks, as well as the resulting need for effective coordination.

However, thus far, the ICA has provided no indication of the criteria it will adopt to determine whether to apply: *i*) EU or Italian competition law to gatekeepers already subject to the DMA; and/or *ii*) the recently revised legislation on abuses of economic dependence, specifically tailored to facilitate the prosecution of digital platforms.

Since the overlap—or perhaps, more accurately, the continuity—between the DMA and EU or national antitrust laws is almost encouraged by the European Commission, which expects competition rules to address new anti-competitive practices that the DMA has not yet identified, this paragraph focuses on the intersection between the DMA and the new Italian legislation on the abuse of economic dependence. This choice stems from the fact that such a recent legislative change was introduced precisely to ensure that the ICA retains its ability to intervene against gatekeepers—and, consequently, the visibility and influence such interventions bring. In other words, it was a response to the bold decision to designate the European Commission as the sole regulator of gatekeepers—a response that was not blocked by the drafters of the DMA. Indeed, under its Article 1(6)(b) gatekeepers can still be prosecuted for abuses of economic dependence, provided that such conduct is "additional" to the practices addressed by the DMA.

Thus, turning to the Italian reform, consider that in October 2022 the Italian Parliament amended Article 9 of Law No. 192/1998 on the abuse of economic dependence by introducing, under Article 33 of Law No. 118/2022, the following provision which reads: "[u]nless proven otherwise, economic dependence is presumed when a business relies on the intermediation services provided by a digital platform that plays a decisive role in reaching end users or suppliers, including through network effects or data availability". Furthermore, the same provision offered illustrative examples, stating: "abusive practices carried out by digital platforms [...] may include providing insufficient information or data regarding the scope or quality of the service provided, demanding unjustified unilateral performance unrelated to the nature or content of the activity performed, or adopting practices that inhibit or obstruct the use of alternative providers for the same service. This could involve the imposition of unilateral conditions or additional costs not provided for in the existing contractual agreements or licenses". In other words, the reform introduced a rebuttable presumption. It assumes, unless proven otherwise, that the counterparts of digital platforms—particularly those benefiting from network effects or data advantages and playing a decisive role in reaching end users or suppliers—are in a position of economic dependence.

If we examine the rationale behind this legislative change, it seems evident that the 2022 legislator aimed to reduce and redistribute the burden of proof in cases of abuse of economic dependence involving such platforms. Typically, the weaker party or the ICA alleging the abuse must prove the existence of economic dependence. However, as a result of the reform, it is now the responsibility of the digital platform to "defend itself" by proving that its commercial counterpart possesses sufficient contractual power to exclude any inherent subordination.

To be sure, this reform does not absolve the weaker party or the ICA from demonstrating the abusive nature of the conduct under scrutiny, nor does it exempt the ICA from proving the market impact of such conduct. Therefore, one should approach with caution any enthusiasm over the so-called "evidentiary advantage" introduced by the reform. This is particularly true because the presumption applies only to digital platforms that play a "decisive role" in reaching end users or suppliers. The weaker party must still provide evidence of this decisive role before an ordinary court, or the ICA must do so within its own proceedings. Put more plainly, the evidentiary advantage that justifies the introduction of this new rule might, in practice, turn out to be rather limited.

That said, it is important to delve further into this point.

The reform appears to link the "decisive role" required for the presumption to apply to the network effects and informational advantages enjoyed by digital platforms. It further defines this "decisive role" in relation to the ability of platforms to facilitate access to end users and suppliers, positioning the platform as either a crucial meeting point or an intermediary between businesses and consumers.

Given the description of gatekeepers as companies with extremely high numbers of business and end users that function as gateways for certain core platform services—marked by network effects and informational advantages—it is worth questioning whether there is any overlap between the companies subject to the DMA and those benefiting from the presumption introduced by the Italian reform of the abuse of economic dependence.

However, nothing in the legal text explicitly suggests such an overlap. In practice, this coincidence may or may not occur. More precisely, it is reasonable to expect that companies meeting the quantitative and qualitative thresholds outlined in Article 3 of the DMA might also fulfill the "decisive role" in mediating the interaction between businesses and consumers, as described in the reform. Nonetheless, the Italian Council of State has rightly clarified that no automatic link exists between the designation of a company as a gatekeeper under the DMA and its qualification under the "decisive role" criterion.[12]

Therefore, on the one hand, it must be acknowledged that the presumption has a subjective scope of application that does not necessarily overlap with that of the DMA. As a result, companies other than those designated as gatekeepers at the European level may also fall within its ambit. On the other hand—as already mentioned—one should resist the temptation to indulge in undue optimism. Even with the entry into force of the DMA and the designation of certain companies as gatekeepers, those alleging an abuse of economic dependence are still required to independently prove, on a case-by-case basis, the platform's "decisive role."

Regarding the presumption established by the reform, two further and final considerations must be made, relating respectively to its fairness and its justification.

From the first perspective, the reform clearly introduces a distinction in the treatment of weaker businesses, suggesting that those interacting with the mentioned digital platforms should benefit from a privilege not extended to other businesses that, while potentially subject to abuse, interact with powerful but "analog," traditional, or even digital firms that do not play a decisive role in connecting with end users and suppliers. However, it remains unclear what grounds this distinction as fair.

From the second perspective, it could be argued that a platform acting as a meeting point—or intermediary—between businesses and consumers, thereby controlling the access of the former to the latter, often ends up enjoying significant bargaining power over these businesses. This would make the presumption, though rebuttable, grounded in the traditional principle of *id quod plerumque accidit* (what generally happens). However, a business is considered to be in a state of economic dependence not merely because it holds less bargaining power than its counterpart but because it is tied to the counterpart in such a way that it lacks viable market alternatives to recover its investments or sustain its operations. Ideally, the reform

[12] Consiglio di Stato, Sez. VI, *Meta/SIAE*, n. 05827/2024, 2 July 2024.

should address scenarios where a business, having engaged with a platform, incurs expenses or develops specific activities that would either be unrecoverable or unfeasible outside that platform.

Yet, the reform does not explicitly address this.

To clarify: the described scenario could indeed occur—for instance, a business developing an application might make non-recoverable investments to ensure its app's interoperability exclusively with the platform in question. Nevertheless, there is no logical or factual link between this state of economic dependence, rooted in the absence of viable alternatives, and the fact that a platform plays a "decisive role in reaching users and suppliers." This is unless such a role implies a market condition—perhaps dominance?—in which businesses (like our hypothetical app developer) cannot avoid interacting with the platform as an unavoidable contractual partner, regardless of their specific investments or activities tied to it.

If this were the case, however, the reform would effectively reduce the burden of proof not only—if not primarily?—for cases of economic dependence abuse but also—perhaps especially?—for cases of abuse of dominance. It would appear as though the true aim were to provide the ICA with a more flexible tool—seemingly more flexible, given the caveats above—than the competition rules on abuses o dominance to pursue the "web giants".

A final set of reflections concerns the practices that may now be considered abusive under the amended Italian rule on abuse of economic dependence. The examples provided by the legislature are not particularly revealing, as they largely rely on the familiar principles of transparency and proportionality. However, one aspect deserves attention: the legislature identifies as a possible abuse of economic dependence the scenario where the dominant business prevents the weaker business from "using a different provider for the same service." While this assessment is certainly accurate, it is striking that such behavior typically has a broader impact on the market—precisely the kind of conduct the ICA could challenge under its remit.

In sum, where the European level opted to strip national authorities of the power to enforce European rules—particularly in the case of the DMA—national legislators have found alternative mechanisms to ensure that national (competition) authorities can still play a role in regulating web giants. And this, for sure, brings to light challenges of overlap between different sets of rules affecting the same actors.

5 Concluding Remarks

This brief analysis has highlighted how the DSA and DMA shape institutional frameworks, engaging national authorities through distinct mechanisms. Furthermore, it has demonstrated that these diverse frameworks not only emphasize the need for effective cooperation between the European Commission and national authorities but also reveal the complexities of regulatory layering—not only among various pieces of EU legislation but also between EU and national laws.

Ensuring effective cooperation and minimizing overlaps between different regulatory frameworks serve not only to reduce enforcement costs for public administrations but also to alleviate compliance costs for businesses. By streamlining regulatory processes and avoiding unnecessary duplication, businesses can allocate fewer resources to navigating complex legal requirements and focus instead on their core operations.

Reducing compliance costs is essential for enabling companies to continue investing in innovation and maintaining their competitive edge. This is particularly crucial in the context of European markets, where regulatory attractiveness plays a key role in fostering business growth. By creating a regulatory environment that is efficient and predictable, European markets remain appealing to businesses, ultimately benefiting consumers through access to higher-quality goods and services.

References

Davola A (2022) The Digital Services Act, Published: A Good Start And – Yet – Just A Start. Kluwer Competition Law Blog. https://competitionlawblog.kluwercompetitionlaw.com/2022/10/19/the-digital-services-act-published-a-good-start-and-yet-just-a-start/

Dinwoodie GB (2017) Secondary liability of internet service providers. Springer, Heidelberg

Hoboken J, Buri I, Quintais JP, Fahy R, Appelman N, Straub M (eds) (2023) Putting the DSA into Practice : Enforcement, Access to Justice, and Global Implications. Verfassungsblog. https://verfassungsblog.de/category/debates/dsa-practice/

Husovec M (2024) Principles of the Digital Services Act. Oxford University Press, Oxford

Nunziato DC (2023) The Digital Services Act and the Brussels Effect on Platform Content Moderation. Chic J Int Law 24:115

Savin A (2021) The EU Digital Services Act: Towards a More Responsible Internet. Copenhagen Business School Law Research Paper. CBS LAW Research Paper 21-04

Tourkochoriti I (2023) The Digital Services Act and the EU as the Global Regulator of the Internet. Chic J Int Law 24:129

Turillazzi A, Taddeo M, Floridi L, Casolari F (2023) The Digital Services Act: an analysis of its ethical. Leg Soc Implications 15(1):83–106

Mariateresa Maggiolino is a professor of antitrust law at Bocconi University, where she directs the five-year Master's program in Law. She has published extensively in both international and national journals on competition law and related topics.

Implementing and Enforcing the EU's Digital Gatekeeper Regulation: A German Perspective on the Role of National Authorities

Jens-Uwe Franck

Contents

The author gratefully acknowledges support from the Deutsche Forschungsgemeinschaft (DFG) through CRC TR 224 (Project B05).

J.-U. Franck (✉)
University of Mannheim, Department of Law, and Mannheim Centre for Competition and Innovation (MaCCI), Mannheim, Germany
e-mail: franck@uni-mannheim.de

F. Decarolis et al. (eds.), *The EU Digital Regulation and its Impact on Member States*, European Union and its Neighbours in a Globalized World 27,
https://doi.org/10.1007/978-3-032-06490-5_9

Abstract In this chapter I review the measures taken in Germany to implement and publicly enforce the Digital Markets Act (DMA) and the Digital Services Act (DSA). A focus is on the institutional design aspects of these measures, their impact on and interaction with existing national instruments, and their interplay with the new EU rules. I describe the Bundeskartellamt's powers to investigate infringements of the DMA and discuss the complementary role that the special abuse regime for digital gatekeepers under section 19a of the German Competition Act can play. Moreover, I explain why Germany has not yet played the role that the Commission would like it to play in referring merger cases to Brussels via the 'Article 22 EUMR route', as envisaged in Article 14 of the DMA, as well as the legal sticking points for the emerging restrictive interpretation of the transaction value-based threshold. I also outline the institutional arrangements intended to ensure the administrative enforcement of the DSA. Finally, I show that the DSA required the repeal of national digital gatekeeper regulation and the enactment of new substantive law to maintain the legal status quo ante, taking into account the scope for national specifications and for national supplementary regulation left by the DSA.

1 Introduction

The EU's Digital Markets Act (DMA) and the Digital Services Act (DSA) stand out in the regulatory landscape: two pieces of regulation that are globally visible, highly controversial, and certain to have a lasting impact on the digital economy in Europe and beyond. Both legal instruments are perceived as the EU's footprint in the field of digital gatekeeper regulation. This is of course justified, as they are the result of political initiatives, processes and compromises at EU level. But it is also correct from a legal point of view, as they have been adopted as regulations and therefore apply directly without the need for transposition through national legislation. Nevertheless, their practical effectiveness depends on the cooperation of Member States, in particular on the adaptation of substantive law and the provision of capable enforcement mechanisms. The EU has taken on a Herculean task that cannot be accomplished with the resources of its institutions alone.

Against this background, this chapter examines and illustrates German measures to implement the DMA and the DSA in the context of public enforcement of digital gatekeeper regulation. The focus is on aspects of institutional design, the impact on existing national instruments regulating digital gatekeepers and their interplay with the new EU regulation. This seems particularly fruitful for a comparative perspective, as Germany has in some respects played a pioneering role in addressing the challenges posed by digital gatekeepers. On the one hand, this means that public authorities already have some experience of enforcement against digital gatekeepers. On the other hand, it also means that there is a need to adapt legislation, or at least to limit the application of national instruments, to take account of the primacy of the new EU instruments.

Below, I will examine these DMA- and DSA-related national adjustments, new institutional arrangements and interactions between EU and German law in five main parts. First, in Sect. 2.1, I will first describe the powers of the Bundeskartellamt to investigate possible infringements of the DMA by which the German legislature has made use of the option provided by Article 38(7) of the DMA. I will point out the (dubious) power to publish the results of investigations and the incentive problems that may prove to be a decisive obstacle to the effective use of these powers. Second, in Sect. 2.2, I will briefly introduce the '19a tool', which, although embodied in competition law, should be seen as the German (functional) equivalent of the DMA. The section will analyse the role that this instrument can play as a complement to the DMA, which in its Article 1(6)(b) leaves room for the use of such a national instrument. Third, in Sect. 3, after briefly outlining how Article 14 of the DMA is intended to extend the reach of EU merger control via the 'Article 22 EUMR route', I will discuss why Germany has so far not played the role in procuring merger cases for the Commission that Brussels would like to see. The legal sticking points for the restrictive handling of the transaction value-based threshold, which is currently emerging but which is still contested, are explained. Fourth, in Sect. 4, I will discuss the institutional arrangements by which the German legislature intends to ensure the administrative implementation of the DSA, the challenge being that this is in an area where public enforcement in Germany has traditionally not been very strong and where, in addition, there is a tendency for competences to be fragmented, particularly owing to the federal system. Finally, in Sect. 5 I will explain and illustrate, on the one hand, how the DSA required the repeal of national digital gatekeeper regulation and, on the other hand, the enactment of new substantive law in order to maintain the (German) legal status quo ante, taking into account the scope for national specifications and for national supplementary regulation left by the DSA.

2 The Bundeskartellamt's Twofold Complementary Role Under the DMA Framework

The Bundeskartellamt was one of the first competition authorities to turn its attention to the digital gatekeepers. The authority's antitrust practice inspired various obligations that are now embodied in the DMA:[1] Its Facebook decision, based on section 19 of the German Competition Act,[2] laid the foundations for the rule that only freely given user consent can allow the combination and cross-use of data in

[1] For an overview of DMA obligations and related antitrust cases, see Crémer et al. (2023), p. 331, Table 1.

[2] Bundeskartellamt, 6 February 2019, B6-22/16, Facebook Data Processing. An appeal against this decision was pending before the Düsseldorf Higher Regional Court (Kart 2/19 (V)). The court referred questions to the ECJ on the relationship between the GDPR and antitrust enforcement, which the ECJ decided in its preliminary ruling of 4 July 2023, Case C-252/21, Meta Platforms,

digital ecosystems, which is now enshrined in Article 5(2) of the DMA. The Bundeskartellamt's prohibition of the use of narrow (price) parity clauses by Booking.com[3] (together with corresponding legislative interventions in four Member States including France and Italy[4]) laid the groundwork for the strict ban on parity policies in Article 5(3) of the DMA. Indeed, as far as can be seen, prior to the DMA, the German competition authority was the only national competition authority within the EU to prohibit Booking.com (or any other online travel agency) from using the narrow form of (price) parity clauses, i.e. a parity policy that only prevented hotels from offering favourable conditions on their direct channel but allowed better conditions on competing online travel agencies.[5] The Bundeskartellamt's investigation into various practices related to Amazon Marketplace was closed without a formal decision after the company announced that it would address the concerns. Among other things, Amazon abandoned plans to oblige sellers to inform the platform if public authorities are contacted.[6] The case thus inspired Article 5(6) of the DMA, which states that digital gatekeepers should not prevent users from raising issues with public authorities.

In addition, Germany has been at the forefront of countries that have provided competition authorities with new instruments to address competition concerns related to large digital platforms. The new instrument came into force on 19 January 2021 and is enshrined in section 19a of the German Competition Act (the '19a tool'). It is a functional equivalent of the EU's DMA. As it was adopted when the DMA proposal was only a few weeks old, it can be seen as a catalyst for the adoption of the DMA and Amazon, Meta, Alphabet, Apple and Microsoft have been designated as '19a undertakings'. By December 2024, the authority had initiated seven abuse proceedings under this special regime. Three proceedings have been

---

ECLI:EU:C:2023:357. The case ended when Meta withdrew its appeal in October 2024. See Bundeskartartellamt, Case Summary of 10 October 2024, Case B6-22/16, p. 14.

[3] Bundeskartellamt, 22 December 2015, B9-121/13, Booking.com. The decision was initially successfully challenged by Booking before the Düsseldorf Higher Regional Court (4 June 2018, Kart 2/16(V)), but was ultimately upheld by the Bundesgerichtshof, the Federal Court of Justice (19 May 2021, KVR 54/20).

[4] European Commission, Impact Assessment Report, SWD(2020) 363 final, Part 2/2, 111. For an overview of these legislative interventions and their motivation see Franck and Stock (2020), pp. 362–370.

[5] In 2015, the Swedish, French and Italian competition authorities had accepted Booking.com's commitment to reduce its wide parity clause to a narrow parity clause. In Sweden, private litigation against Booking's use of narrow parity clauses was also ultimately unsuccessful. See Franck and Stock (2020), pp. 359–360 (text accompanying notes 149–151 and 160–161). In 2024, the Spanish competition authority considered Booking.com's use of narrow (price) policy clauses (combined with a policy of 'undercutting', i.e. reserving the possibility of unilaterally reducing prices at the expense of its commission) to be an exploitative abuse. See Comisión Nacional de los Mercados y la Competencia, 29 July 2024, S/0005/21, Booking, para. 498.

[6] Bundeskartellamt, Case Summary of 17 July 2019, B2-88/18, p. 6.

fully or partially closed as a result of commitments or changes in the behaviour of the gatekeepers.[7]

Against this background, it is apparent that the Bundeskartellamt had to redefine its role in the protection of competition with regard to digital gatekeepers when the DMA came into force. Two facets of this new role will be examined in this section.

First, it has been sobering for the Bundeskartellamt to learn that in enforcing the DMA it can only play the role of an assistant investigator to the Commission. After all, the German legislature has granted the authority all the investigative powers necessary for this purpose.

Second, the authority may continue to enforce EU or national competition law against the digital gatekeepers. However, enforcement of national competition law in respect of unilateral conduct is only possible under the restrictions of Article 1(6)(b) of the DMA. The implications of this for the application of the special abuse control regime under section 19a of the Competition Act will be the subject of the second part of this section.

2.1 *The Bundeskartellamt as the Commission's 'Assistant Investigator' for DMA Infringements (Article 38(7) of the DMA)*

Public enforcement of the DMA is monopolised at the EU level: only the Commission can establish that an infringement has occurred and impose sanctions on the designated gatekeepers.[8] Given that the enforcement powers of national authorities are limited to their jurisdiction, this appears to be a sound institutional choice in principle, as it allows the Commission to establish consistent, EU-wide solutions for EU-wide digital gatekeeper activities. On the other hand, the administrative challenges associated with the implementation of the DMA are so immense that it is impossible to see how it can be managed even halfway with the Commission's resources alone. In addition, it seems reasonable to pave the way for the use of the intimate knowledge that competition authorities have of national markets and their established relationships with market players and stakeholders.[9]

---

[7] See Sect. 2.2.

[8] See Article 38(7) of the DMA ('to support the Commission in its role as sole enforcer of this Regulation'); see also recital 91 to the DMA ('The Commission is the sole authority empowered to enforce this Regulation'). It is true that national authorities are given a supporting role in various contexts, for example in dawn raids and interviews (Article 22 of the DMA) or in the conduct of market investigations (Article 38(6) of the DMA). However, supportive involvement of national authorities in these contexts requires a request from the Commission. They are not allowed to act on their own initiative. See MPI Innovation and Competition (2023), para. 55; Gappa and Käseberg (2024), paras 23–24.

[9] See MPI Innovation and Innovation (2023), para. 54.

With this in mind, the German government, together with France and the Netherlands, had argued in the DMA legislative process for a stronger role for national competition authorities in enforcing the DMA. In a position paper of 8 September 2021, the three governments ('Friends of an effective DMA') had proposed that, while the Commission should remain primarily responsible for the enforcement of the DMA, it should have the option to refer cases to national competition authorities. This could ensure, so it was argued,

> that the DMA can be swiftly and effectively enforced, the workload is optimally allocated at European and national levels, and that Commission and national competition authorities have adequate leeway to set own enforcement priorities.[10]

As we know, things turned out differently: according to Article 38(7) of the DMA, national authorities may—if they have been granted the relevant powers under national law—investigate on their own territory whether infringements of Articles 5, 6 and 7 of the DMA have been committed. However, national authorities do not have any further enforcement powers. The Commission must be notified prior to taking the first formal investigative measure and must be informed of the results of the investigation. When the Commission initiates proceedings under Article 20 of the DMA, all investigative powers of the national authorities cease.[11] In contrast to EU antitrust proceedings,[12] the Commission does not have to consult the national authorities in order to 'take over' an investigation.[13]

2.1.1 Investigation Powers Under Section 32g of the Competition Act

The German legislature has made use of the option provided in Article 38(7) of the DMA[14] in the course of the 11th amendment to the Competition Act and stipulated in section 32g(1) of the German Competition Act that,

> In the event of possible non-compliance with Articles 5, 6 or 7 of [the DMA] by an undertaking designated pursuant to Article 3 of the [DMA], the Bundeskartellamt may carry out an investigation.

---

[10] Federal Ministry for Economic Affairs and Energy, Ministère de l'économie, des finances et de la relance, and [Dutch] Ministry of Economic Affairs and Climate Policy (2021), p. 2 and Annex 2.

[11] In its opening decisions, the Commission explicitly refers to Article 38(7) of the DMA and the fact that national competition authorities are deprived of any investigative powers. See, e.g., Commission, 25.3.2024, DMA.100193 - *Alphabet Online Search Engine - Google Search* - Article 6(5).

[12] See Article 11(6) of Regulation 1/2003.

[13] Gappa and Käseberg (2024), para. 29.

[14] Prior to this, as of 1 January 2023, the Hungarian legislature had already granted its national competition authority the right to investigate possible violations of the DMA. See Hungarian Competition Authority (GVH) (2023). In the Netherlands, a corresponding bill has been drafted. See MPI Competition and Innovation (2023), para. 57. The Italian competition authority was granted powers to investigate DMA violations by a regulation dated 23 July 2024 ('Measures for the Implementation of Regulation (EU) 2022/1925 of the European Parliament and of the Council of 14 September 2022'). See Maggiolino (in this volume), sub 3.1 The Cooperation Regulation.

This first of all clarifies that these powers of investigation only apply after the Commission has designated a gatekeeper and its core platform services (CPSs). This already follows from Article 38(7) of the DMA, because a case of possible non-compliance can only exist after a designation decision has been made.

Section 32g(2) of the Competition Act further states that for these investigations the Bundeskartellamt 'may conduct all inquiries necessary'. The powers and instruments that apply to the investigation of infringements of competition law under sections 57 to 59b and section 61 of the Competition Act therefore also apply to these investigations into infringements of the DMA: the authority may collect all necessary evidence, question witnesses, seize objects, request information, examine business documents, and carry out searches.

The restriction of investigations to the national territory required by Article 38(7) of the DMA naturally follows from the limits of enforcement jurisdiction as recognised under international law. It does therefore not require an explicit provision in national law. Some authors refer to section 185(2) of the Competition Act.[15] On the basis of its wording,[16] however, this provision seems to regulate only the scope of legislative jurisdiction.

The obligation to inform the Commission prior to the first formal investigation measure is not explicitly provided for in section 32g of the Competition Act. This is entirely natural because this obligation applies directly under Article 38(7) of the DMA. A declaratory reproduction in national law would have entailed the risk of blurring the Union law nature of this obligation and, in particular, concealing the fact that the relevant concepts are subject to autonomous interpretation under EU law.

As to possible violations of Article 7 of the DMA, the rules on the interconnection of communications services, during the proceedings, the Federal Network Agency (the Bundesnetzagentur) must be given the opportunity to comment on a case.[17] The aim is to make use of the specific expertise of this authority. Under section 21(2) of the German Telecommunications Act, the authority already has the right to require providers of messenger services to ensure interoperability.[18]

Although the wording of section 32g(1) of the Competition Act refers only to 'possible violations of Articles 5, 6 or 7' of the DMA, this reference must be understood as also giving the Bundeskartellamt the power to investigate possible violations of the anti-circumvention provisions of Article 13(4) and (6) of the DMA. When analysing the concept of public enforcement under the DMA, it is clear that Articles 29, 30 and 31 of the DMA in particular apply without distinction as to whether the conduct of a gatekeeper is directly covered by Articles 5, 6 or 7 of the DMA or (only) in conjunction with Article 13(4) or (6) of DMA. Against this background, it is more than reasonable to interpret the ancillary enforcement competence under German law as also including investigations into circumvention. Indeed, Article

---

[15] Wirtz (2024), para. 3.

[16] Section 185(2) of the Competition Act reads: 'The provisions of Parts 1 to 3 of this Act shall be applied to all restraints of competition having an effect within the area of application of this Act, even if they were caused outside the area of application of this Act.'

[17] Section 32g(2), 3rd sentence of the Competition Act.

[18] Wirtz (2024), para. 4.

13(4) and (6) of the DMA should generally be understood as an extension of the scope of the obligations under Articles 5, 6 and 7 of the DMA.[19]

2.1.2 The (Dubious) Authorisation to Publish Investigation Results

Section 32g(3) of the Competition Act provides that 'the Bundeskartellamt will report the results of the investigation … to the European Commission', followed by conferral of the power to 'publish a report on the results of the investigation'. While the first statement is a mere acknowledgement of what is already required under Article 38(7) of the DMA, the second statement is indeed quite remarkable. Under German law, the publication of the results of an investigation requires explicit legal authorisation as it interferes with the fundamental rights of the companies under investigation. It is therefore crucial that they are given a fair hearing.[20] But is this publishing permitted under EU law? The German legislature seems to have assumed that the issue of publication of the results of the investigation is neither positively nor negatively regulated by Article 38(7) of the DMA[21] and that there is therefore scope for national regulation. Certainly, if the Bundeskartellamt were to publicly announce that it had found evidence of a violation of the DMA, this could have a detrimental effect on the investigated company, in particular on its reputation, even if it is clear that these are only preliminary findings, the publication of which has no immediate legal consequences. Therefore, such activities may well be seen as having an enforcement element—which could amount to a 'naming and shaming' mechanism—that could undermine the Commission's role as the sole enforcer of the DMA. Irrespective of these fundamental concerns about compatibility with EU law, publication is at the discretion of the Bundeskartellamt, which in exercising its powers must also take account of the interests of the European Commission, to which it has delegated the powers of investigation. The publication of preliminary results has to be omitted if the publication is likely to hamper the further investigation of the Commission.[22]

2.1.3 The Incentive Problem to Actually Use the Powers to Investigate

Investigations into possible DMA infringements under section 32g of the Competition Act are conducted at the Bundeskartellamt's discretion.[23] To date, no results from such investigations are known. A possible starting point could be proceedings under section 19a of the Competition Act, as all addressees designated so far under this provision are also gatekeepers under the DMA. If, in the course of a 19a procedure, the Bundeskartellamt becomes aware of a suspected infringement of

[19] Franck and Peitz (2024a), pp. 303–305.

[20] Wirtz (2024), para. 6.

[21] Kumkar (2024), para. 49.

[22] Kumkar (2024), para. 50.

[23] Kumkar (2024), paras 34–35.

the DMA,[24] it may suspend the 19a procedure and first investigate whether this suspicion is substantiated and, if so, forward its findings to the Commission. Ideally, an efficient division of tasks between national authorities and the European Commission could be achieved and national, and thus potentially internal market-dividing, interventions avoided.

From the Commission's point of view, it is indeed essential to mobilise national resources to monitor the compliance of digital gatekeepers with their obligations under the DMA. However, it is unclear whether the Bundeskartellamt will ever carry out such investigations: the current incentive mechanisms seem too unfavourable as the national authority does not receive any visible credit for the (successful) use of its resources.[25] One way to improve this would be to prominently acknowledge where national authorities have contributed to the enforcement of the DMA in a particular case. A more ambitious and sophisticated way forward, inspired by the Single Supervisory Mechanism for the largest banks in the Eurozone, could be the creation of 'joint supervisory teams' staffed by the Commission and national competition authorities.[26]

2.2 *The German '19a Tool' and the Imposition of 'Further Obligations' on DMA Gatekeepers (Article 1(6)(b) of the DMA)*

National competition law may impose 'further obligations' on DMA gatekeepers by way of rules that prohibit other forms of unilateral conduct than abuses of dominant positions.[27] In this section, I will elaborate on the Bundeskartellamt's use of this regulatory leeway, focusing on the use of section 19a of the Competition Act as this instrument was introduced specifically to combat possible abuses by digital gatekeepers, and because the Bundeskartellamt appears to channel abuse cases against companies designated as '19a undertakings' (which are all also designated as DMA gatekeepers) into abuse proceedings under this special abuse regime.

---

[24] See Recital 91, 3rd sentence, to the DMA ('[Investigatory powers by national competition authorities] could in particular be relevant for cases where it cannot be determined from the outset whether a gatekeeper's behaviour is capable of infringing this Regulation, the competition rules which the national competent authority is empowered to enforce, or both').

[25] See Monti (2022), p. 26 ('The incentive for this step [by the German legislature to adopt section 32g of the Competition Act] is that the national authority can then contribute to shaping the DMA'); MPI Innovation and Competition (2023), para. 56 ('[National authorities] will only be willing to participate in the Commission's investigations if they benefit from this cooperation, for instance by gaining specialised knowledge that could be relevant for their own (related) national cases').

[26] Crémer et al. (2023), p. 346.

[27] Article 1(6)(b) DMA.

2.2.1 Key Features of the '19a Tool', Revealing Its Conceptual Overlap with the DMA

Section 19a of the Competition Act[28] is characterised by a 'two-step activation' design.[29] First, the Bundeskartellamt must declare that a platform operator is an undertaking of 'paramount significance for competition across markets' ('designation decision'). Second, the authority can prohibit the designated undertakings from engaging in conduct falling within one of seven categories listed in the provision (ranging from self-preferencing by vertically integrated firms to the demanding of disproportionate compensation from business customers) ('abuse decision'). Firms may provide objective justification.

The '19a tool' is therefore only activated for a particular undertaking after it has been the subject of two decisions (which can be combined[30]). The instrument thus differs not only from traditional competition law (which contains self-executing obligations) but also from the DMA, in which the embodied obligations automatically apply to designated CPSs.

Section 19a of the Competition Act is designed to deal with unilateral conduct by undertakings in a gatekeeper position. In essence, the provision is aimed at undertakings that provide key intermediation services and thus control an interface between markets, regardless of whether their position could be characterised as dominant in a defined market.[31] While the actual criteria used in the law do not limit the scope of the instrument to digital business models (however precisely defined), the '19a tool' is clearly aimed at the (large) digital gatekeepers.

This concept has been implemented through two main criteria:[32] the instrument can only apply to undertakings that are 'active to a significant extent in markets within the meaning of section 18(3a) [of the Competition Act]', which in turn refers to 'multi-sided markets and networks'. The latter terminology seems to be misleading, since multi-sidedness is a characteristic at the firm level but not (or not necessarily) at the market level. Therefore, the reference means that only firms that operate a two-sided platform, thus acting as intermediaries between different user groups and creating cross-group network effects, can be designated.

Second, the undertakings addressed must have achieved a position of 'paramount significance for competition across markets' or, in the words of the drafting parliamentary committee, 'be particularly well placed to extend their power beyond market boundaries or to secure their unassailable position by virtue of their financial,

[28] For a detailed overview of the structure, scope, covered conduct, procedural and judicial remedies, see Franck and Peitz (2021), pp. 513–528. See also Bauermeister (2022).

[29] Franck (2024a), pp. 25–26.

[30] Section 19a(2), 5th sentence of the Competition Act. Hence, the designation procedure and the abuse procedure can be carried out in parallel.

[31] For a detailed analysis of whether and in what form an 'ecosystem concept' underlies section 19a of the Competition Act and what role such a concept plays in the Bundeskartellamt's designation decisions, see Hornung (2023).

[32] Franck (2024a), pp. 26–27.

technical or data resources or as a cross-market digital ecosystem or platform'. The provision lists five (non-exhaustive) criteria to be taken into account in this assessment: dominance in one or more markets; financial strength and access to resources; vertical integration and activities in otherwise related markets; access to competitively sensitive data; and the importance of its activities for third parties' access to supply and sales markets. A designation decision is valid for five years.

So far, the Bundeskartellamt has designated Amazon,[33] Meta,[34] Alphabet,[35] Apple[36] and Microsoft[37] as '19a firms'. With Amazon's[38] and Apple's[39] appeals having been rejected by the German Federal Court of Justice, the designation of all five major US digital gatekeepers has become final. Although it is easy to imagine other platform operators in addition to these five major digital gatekeepers for which a 19a designation could be considered,[40] from the Bundeskartellamt's point of view this seems to be a question of efficient use of resources: can the synergies and facilitations in abuse proceedings outweigh the costs of a designation procedure?

Section 19a of the Competition Act lists seven practices, drafted in a rather broad terms, that reveal the specific anti-competitive potential of 19a companies,[41] in particular practices that allow an undertaking to transfer market power to other markets. Looking at the list, it is clear that the provision covers much of the conduct regulated by the DMA:

- self-preferencing by vertically integrated firms,
- impediment of other undertakings' procurement and sales activities (e.g. exclusive pre-installation of own offers),
- impediment of other undertakings' activities on markets where the 19a undertaking can rapidly expand its position (e.g. exclusivity agreements, tying and bundling practices),
- processing and collecting data to raise entry barriers,
- refusing interoperability or data portability,
- providing other undertakings with insufficient information about the service provided (information about consumer click patterns, ranking parameters etc.),
- demanding disproportionate 'benefits' (e.g. transfer of data, rights) from business customers for intermediation services.

[33] Bundeskartellamt, 5 July 2022, B2-55/21.

[34] Bundeskartellamt, 2 May 2022, B6-27/21.

[35] Bundeskartellamt, 30 December 2021, B7-61/21.

[36] Bundeskartellamt, 3 April 2023, B9-67/21.

[37] Bundeskartellamt, 27 September 2024, B6-26/33.

[38] BGH, 23 April 2024, KVB 56/22 – Amazon.

[39] BGH, 18 March 2025, KVB 61/23 – Apple.

[40] See Franck and Peitz (2021), pp. 517–519 (considering Booking.com and CTS Eventim as possible candidates for a 19a designation).

[41] Franck (2024a), pp. 28–29.

These (exhaustive) categories are equivalent to 'rebuttable presumptions': the 19a undertaking may provide evidence of objective justification. It must demonstrate factors, in particular efficiencies, on the basis of which the practice in question should be considered not to be anti-competitive. This allocation of the burden of proof is intended to take account of the systematic information advantages of digital gatekeepers. The absence of an objective justification, however, does not automatically entitle the authority to impose a prohibition of conduct captured by section 19(2) of the Competition Act: this is not to be understood as a 'tick-box exercise' on the part of the authority.[42] Rather, the Bundeskartellamt is entitled to exercise its discretion in this respect. It must assess the economic and legal context and is bound by the principle of proportionality. It does not seem clear what the resulting requirements for an abuse decision would be. It has been argued that the authority must be able to present a theory of harm in the sense that it can at least plausibly argue that, taking into account the market situation and other contexts, the conduct in question poses a threat to open markets and undistorted competition, and that this can be remedied by the intervention. However, as the intervention threshold under section 19a of the Competition Act is deliberately lower than in traditional abuse control, it is important not to set too high a standard for the evidence required by the authority.[43]

2.2.2 Overview of Abuse Proceedings Under Section 19a of the Competition Act

So far, the Bundeskartellamt has initiated seven abuse proceedings against designated 19a firms, the statuses of which are presented in Table 1.[44]

The overview shows that three cases have been fully or at least partially closed because of commitments or changes in behaviour by digital gatekeepers.[45]

In the Meta VR Glasses case, the Bundeskartellamt persuaded Meta not to make the use of Oculus VR glasses (later branded 'Meta Quest') dependent on registering with Facebook. Instead, from August 2022, Meta allowed the use of VR glasses by logging in with a Meta account. The tying of Meta's VR glasses with Facebook registration is not covered by the DMA: while Facebook is designated as a CPS, tying a CPS with VR services is not explicitly prohibited by Article 5(7) of the DMA, and Meta's VR glasses are not designated as a CPS, so Article 5(8) of the DMA does not apply.

---

[42] Franck (2024a), pp. 30–31.

[43] See more in detail on normative calibrations for the efficiency and welfare analyses required under section 19a of the Competition Act Franck (2024a), pp. 31–32.

[44] For an overview of ongoing cases see https://www.bundeskartellamt.de/SharedDocs/Publikation/DE/Downloads/Liste_Verfahren_Digitalkonzerne.pdf?__blob=publicationFile&v=8 (in German) and at https://www.bundeskartellamt.de/SharedDocs/Publikation/EN/Downloads/List_proceedings_digital_companies.pdf?__blob=publicationFile&v=17 (in English).

[45] For a more detailed account of each of these three cases, see Franck (2024a), pp. 34–44. The following overview is based on these findings.

Table 1 List of Abuse Proceedings under Section 19a of the Competition Act

Case	Status
Google News Showcase (V-43/20)	Proceedings closed on 21.12.2022 following various measures taken by Google to address the competition concerns (Case Report of 1.8.2023)
Google Data Processing (B7-70/21)	Commitment Decision of 5.10.2023
Google Maps Platform and Google Automotive Services	Pending proceeding; initiated on 14.2.2022 (Press Release) Statement of objections of 21.6.2023 (Press Release) Market test regarding commitments proposed by Google (Press Release of 20.12.2023)
Amazon Price Control	Pending proceeding; initiated on 15.5.2020, extended to sec 19a(2) in November 2022 (Press Release of 14.11.2022)
Amazon Brandgating	Pending proceeding; initiated on 3.9.2020, extended to sec 19a(2) in November 2022 (Press Release of 14.11.2022)
Apple App-Tracking-Transparency Framework (ATTF)	Pending proceeding; initiated on 14.6.2022 (Press Release)
Meta VR Glasses (B6-55/20)	Pending proceeding; initiated on 10.12.2020, extended to sec 19a(2) on 28.1.2021 (Press Release) Meta responds to competition concerns (Press Release and Case Summary of 23.11.2022)

In the case of Google News Showcase, the Bundeskartellamt investigated the integration of the service into other Google services and the conditions under which it was offered to publishers. The case was closed by informal notice in December 2022 after Google implemented and committed to several measures. Google abandoned plans to integrate News Showcase into Google Search and promised not to treat press publishers differently in its search algorithm depending on whether they cooperated with Google Showcase or not. In addition, Google has made certain changes to the contractual agreements underlying the service that would or could have limited the ability of participating publishers to enforce their ancillary copyrights against Google. The case has an overlap with the (subsequently applicable) DMA: as Google Search has been designated as a CPS, any preferential treatment of News Showcase in the display of search results is prohibited under Article 6(5) of the DMA. Moreover, Article 6(12) of the DMA, which guarantees fair, reasonable and non-discriminatory (FRAND) access to online search engines, would not allow any preferential treatment of publishers that cooperate with Google News Showcase. However, other aspects of the case are not covered by the DMA: Google News is not a search engine within the meaning of the DMA and therefore access to the service cannot be subject to Article 6(12) of the DMA. Furthermore, as Google News (including Showcase) does not meet the criteria for being an 'online intermediation service', it could not be designated as such in order to then be subject to DMA obligations such as the prohibition on self-preferencing in ranking under Article 6(5) of the DMA.[46]

[46] Franck (2024a), pp. 40–41.

In a commitment decision dated 5 October 2002, Google agreed to significantly extend users' choice regarding the processing of data.[47] In effect, the Bundeskartellamt used the 19a instrument to supplement the DMA by extending beyond its scope the obligations to which Google was already subject under Article 5(2) of the DMA. To avoid overlap between the commitments and the scope of the DMA, the commitments apply only to the sharing and combination of user data (including data obtained from third-party websites or applications) across Google services that are not designated as CPSs. Thus, the commitments do not apply to any data processing activities in which a CPS is involved, such that Article 5(2) of the DMA applies. Should the Commission designate additional Google services, the scope of the commitments will automatically be reduced (and vice versa should services lose their status as CPSs in the future).[48] The Bundeskartellamt emphasised that it had been in regular contact with the Commission throughout the proceedings.[49] It was said that the latter had indeed commented on the draft commitments.[50]

2.2.3 Integration of Abuse Procedures Under Section 19a of the Competition Act with the DMA Framework

The legal basis for the additional role played by 19a procedures in regulating digital gatekeepers in a pro-competitive manner is provided by Article 1(6)(b) of the DMA:

> [The DMA] is … without prejudice to the application of … national competition rules prohibiting other forms of unilateral conduct insofar as they are applied to undertakings other than gatekeepers or amount to the imposition of further obligations on gatekeepers.

This transfers a key idea of Article 3(2) of Regulation 1/2003 to the DMA: with regard to unilateral conduct, national competition law may impose stricter rules on designated gatekeepers than those imposed by the DMA. The application of this rule, which has the potential to fragment the internal market[51], presupposes that abuse proceedings under section 19a of the Competition Act are to be regarded as 'national competition law.' This has been questioned in academic literature in relation to section 19a of the Competition Act.[52] It is true that the 19a proceedings and the role of the Bundeskartellamt differ significantly from traditional abuse

[47] Bundeskartellamt, 5 October 2023, B7-70/21.

[48] Bundeskartellamt (n 48), paras 74–75.

[49] Bundeskartellamt (n 48), para. 27.

[50] Bundeskartellamt (n 48), paras 36 and 38.

[51] See Franck and Peitz (2021) pp. 526–527. The Draghi Report (2024), Part B, p. 304, n. 9, contains the following note on this matter: '[T]he provision in art. 1(6.b) [of the DMA] about how the DMA Regulation is without prejudice to the application of national competition rules that "amount to the imposition of further obligations on gatekeepers" introduces uncertainties that need prompt clarifications to limit the risk of the potential of fragmenting the regulatory landscape of EU digital markets.'

[52] See Deselaers (2024), p. 369.

proceedings.[53] Nevertheless, the essential characteristics of 'national competition law' according to recital 10 of the DMA are fulfilled. It states:

> [S]ince this Regulation aims to complement the enforcement of competition law, it should apply without prejudice ... to other national competition rules regarding unilateral conduct that are based on an individualised assessment of market positions and behaviour, including its actual or potential effects and the precise scope of the prohibited behaviour, and which provide for the possibility of undertakings to make efficiency and objective justification arguments for the behaviour in question.

Thus, the DMA uses essentially the same criteria that have been established in the literature for the definition of 'national competition law' within the meaning of Article 3(2) and (3) of Regulation 1/2003.[54] Not only is the designation of a 19a gatekeeper based on an individual, multi-faceted analysis, but so is the determination of whether any particular conduct is abusive: The gatekeeper may submit an objective justification (including, for example, efficiency gains) and even without such a submission the Bundeskartellamt must assess the individual economic and legal context in order to argue that conduct falling under the categories listed in section 19a(2) of the Competition Act poses a threat to open markets and undistorted competition. Therefore, using the '19a tool', the Bundeskartellamt may indeed impose 'further obligations' on DMA gatekeepers.[55]

It has also been argued that the fact that Article 1(6)(b) of the DMA allows for the prohibition of 'other forms' of unilateral conduct means that only matters not covered by the DMA obligations can be addressed by national competition law. With regard to the Bundeskartellamt's Google Data Processing case, it is therefore argued that, if Article 5(2) of the DMA only restricts the cross-use and combination of data if a CPS is involved in the processing, this cannot be extended to data processing between non-CPSs on the basis of national competition law because it is not a question of prohibiting 'other forms' of conduct.[56] However, this is a misinterpretation of the provision: the expression 'other forms of unilateral conduct' refers to the previous point (a), which already provides for the applicability of national competition law to unilateral conduct in the form of 'abuse of a dominant position'. Thus, Article 1(6)(b) of the DMA refers to national competition law provisions such as section 19a of the Competition Act that do not correspond (in their scope of application) to Article 102 of the DMA.[57]

The application of section 19a of the Competition Act to gatekeepers designated under the DMA remains subject to the limitation that only 'further obligations' may be imposed on them. This includes not only the imposition of other categories of obligations but also the tightening of obligations in a matter covered by the

---

[53] See above Sect. 2.2.1; Franck (2024a), pp. 25–32.

[54] See Franck and Stock (2020), pp. 324 and 345–356.

[55] See Franck and Peitz (2021), p. 526; Schweitzer (2024), paras 44 and 61–67; Blockx (2023), pp. 330–331; Käseberg and Gappa (2024), para. 28.

[56] Deselaers (2024), p. 369.

[57] Käseberg and Gappa (2024), para. 24.

DMA. The condition that only 'further obligations' are allowed seems to be intended to prevent Member States from replicating DMA obligations through a specific competition instrument. Otherwise, the rules for the enforcement of DMA obligations, in particular the role of the Commission as the sole (public) enforcer, could be undermined.

Against this background, various scenarios can be outlined in which the Bundeskartellamt may impose 'further obligations' on gatekeepers designated under the DMA via section 19a of the Competition Act. First, the Bundeskartellamt can impose additional obligations in connection with a CPS designated under the DMA. For example, the authority prevented Meta from tying the use of its VR glasses to Facebook registration, which is not prohibited under Article 5(7) or Article 5(8) of the DMA.

Second, the Bundeskartellamt can use the '19a tool' to impose obligations on platform services operated by an organisation that is DMA gatekeeper, but which is not designated as a CPS under the DMA. On the one hand, this may be the case because the service is not covered by the list of possible CPSs under Article 2(2) of the DMA. For example, Alphabet's services Google News and Google News Showcase are of a type that cannot be considered a CPS because they do not qualify as online intermediation services[58] or as online search engines.[59]

On the other hand, this may also arise because a service included in the list of potential CPSs does not meet the threshold of being 'an important gateway for business users to reach end users'.[60] For example, Alphabet's Google Flights service qualifies as an online intermediation service (Article 2(2)(a) of the DMA), Android Automotive OS qualifies as an operating system (Article 2(2)(f) of the DMA) and Google Assistant qualifies as a virtual assistant (Article 2(2)(h) of the DMA). These services are not designated as CPS under the DMA, but the Bundeskartellamt's Google Data Processing decision effectively puts them on the same footing as the DMA with regard to the cross-platform use and aggregation of data.

All in all, the '19a instrument' is more flexible than the DMA. First, once designated, it applies to all platforms of the digital gatekeeper (not just the designated CPS) and, second, the catalogue of abusive practices is vaguer and therefore much broader. This means that the tool could be deployed more quickly, for example, in response to new developments such as the emergence of generative AI tools, in particular large language models, and the potential for abuse that these may entail. The Bundeskartellamt, using the '19a tool', could thus play a pioneering role by providing a basis for testing and considering possible extensions to the scope of the DMA. One obstacle, however, is that it will not always be clear to the Bundeskartellamt how far the obligations of the DMAs extend. However, the authority has to form an opinion on this, as its competence is limited to imposing 'further obligations' on the DMA gatekeepers. Finally, section 19a of the Competition Act does not provide for

[58] Article 2(5) DMA.

[59] Article 2(6) DMA

[60] Articles 1(b) and 3(9) DMA.

the possibility of imposing stricter merger control on digital gatekeepers or even structural measures such as ownership unbundling.[61] In this respect, the German instrument cannot go beyond the DMA.

3 Digital Gatekeeper Acquisitions: 'Case Procurement' for the European Commission?

Where mergers have a significant cross-border dimension in the internal market, the European Commission should be the competent authority to decide whether to clear or block them, taking into account the effects throughout the internal market and allowing for a single decision (including remedies). However, regarding acquisitions by digital gatekeepers, the thresholds of Article 1 of the EU Merger Regulation (EUMR) are too high, as the target firms are often acquired at a stage in their business life cycle where they have (yet) generated no or only a little revenue. Nevertheless, these acquisitions can have a significant impact on competition, as illustrated by the sometimes very high transaction values. In particular, there are fears that digital gatekeepers will discontinue or delay the scaling of business models, digital technologies or other innovations of the acquired firms, or at least replace their own innovation projects with the acquired capabilities, thereby significantly reducing the overall ability of the market to innovate.[62]

Against this background, I will first briefly explain how Article 14 of the DMA is intended to help extend the reach of EU merger control in practice. I will then examine the supporting role that German merger control law and the Bundeskartellamt can play in this context.

3.1 Article 14 of the DMA as an Instrument Facilitating the 'Article 22 EUMR Route' to Brussels

Under Article 14 of the DMA, digital gatekeepers are required to inform the European Commission of intended acquisitions, irrespective of whether they are notifiable under the EUMR or under national merger control law. The provision does not apply with regard to any acquisition by a designated gatekeeper but (only)

[61] To be sure, if an addressee infringes a behavioural obligation imposed on it under section 19a of the Competition Act, the general remedies available to the Bundeskartellamt apply, including (in a subsidiary manner) structural measures. See section 32(2), 3rd sentence of the Competition Act.

[62] For a comprehensive overview of the economics, and the antitrust theories or harm of so-called 'killer acquisitions' see Tzanaki (2023), sub I. ('The economics of killer acquisitions: why merger control thresholds and the law matter'), pp. 7–23.

'where the merging entities or the target of concentration provide core platform services or any other services in the digital sector or enable the collection of data'.[63]

The rationale behind this provision is essentially threefold. First, the Commission may use this information to verify the status of a gatekeeper and to adjust the list of CPSs provided by a gatekeeper.[64] Second, the information will be used to monitor 'broader contestability trends in the digital sector' and feed into market investigations under Articles 16 to 19 of the DMA.[65] Third, while Article 14 of the DMA does not impose a notification duty and thus, as such, does not extend EU merger review, it is intended to indirectly strengthen merger control of gatekeeper acquisitions on the basis of the EUMR. As explicitly endorsed by Article 14(4) and (5) of the DMA, the Commission should transmit the information to the competent authorities of the Member States so that they can consider, in particular, whether to refer concentrations to the Commission on the basis of Article 22 of the EUMR.[66] In other words, Article 14 of the DMA is intended to implement the 'Article 22 EUMR route' for (de facto) extending the scope of EU merger control. The minimum information listed in Article 14(2) of the DMA, which the gatekeeper must provide to the Commission, allows the Commission and subsequently the Member States to consider a referral under Article 22 of the EUMR.

This 'Article 22 EUMR route' is unsatisfactory for several reasons. The Commission cannot (unlike in the case of below-threshold referrals under Article 4(5) of the EUMR) examine the effects of an acquisition in relation to the whole internal market but only in relation to the territory of the Member States that actually make a referral. Whether the general interest in a 'one-stop shop' review in Brussels, which often seems to prevail in the case of digital gatekeeper acquisitions, is taken into account depends thus on the political will of individual Member States. In addition, following the ECJ's Illumina judgment, it is clear now that referrals under Article 22 of the EUMR are only possible where an acquisition is subject to merger control under national law.[67] The practical effectiveness of this route therefore depends not only on the political will of Member States in individual cases but also more generally on the legal framework for merger control in a Member State. But, for now,[68] it remains the only way to fill a gap in the scope of EU merger control in a particular case.

[63] Article 14(1) DMA.

[64] Recital 71, 1st sentence, DMA.

[65] Recital 71, 2nd sentence, DMA.

[66] Recital 71, 3rd sentence, DMA.

[67] ECJ, 3 September 2024, Case C-611/22 P, *Illumina v Commission*, ECLI:EU:C:2024:677.

[68] A pragmatic way to extend the Commission's competence to review mergers by legislation would be to use the simplified legislative procedure under Article 1(5) of the EU Merger Regulation to 'revise the thresholds and criteria' of Article 1(3) of the EU Merger Regulation. See ECJ, 3 September 2024, Case C-611/22 P, *Illumina v Commission*, ECLI:EU:C:2023:205, paras 183–184 and 216. However, it is not clear whether this simplified procedure would also allow for the introduction of an additional threshold based on the value of the transaction. For an overview of other possible options to extend the Commission's merger powers, see Tzanaki (2024), p. 7. The Commission is sceptical about amending the EUMR because it was adopted based on (now) Article 103 and Article 352 TFEU (the latter requiring unanimity in the Council). However, the EU has indeed the power to adopt merger legislation on the basis of Article 114 TFEU. See Franck et al. (2021).

It is therefore clear that the Commission will have to continue to rely on the cooperation of the Member States in order to fill the identified gap in merger control via the 'Article 22 EUMR route': Member State authorities must first be able to take up and control the relevant acquisitions under national law and second there must be the political will to refer these cases to Brussels where appropriate. Based on the above, I will turn in the following section to consider the legal framework and practice of merger review in Germany.

3.2 German Merger Law and Practice and the 'Article 22 EUMR' Route to Brussels

Two acquisitions of digital gatekeepers come to mind that the Commission reviewed on the basis of referrals under Article 22 of the EUMR: Apple/Shazam[69] and Meta/Kustomer.[70] While seven EEA states referred the Apple/Shazam merger to the Commission[71] and ten EEA states referred the Meta/Kustomer merger to the Commission,[72] Germany was not among them in either procedure. Why was this the case?

First of all, unlike the European Commission, the Bundeskartellamt has—rightly, as it turned out, if one follows the ECJ judgment in *Illumina*—taken the view that it is not in a position to refer cases under Article 22 of the EUMR to the Commission if the thresholds under German merger control law are not met. As German merger law does not provide for a 'call-in' power to require notification of acquisitions below the legal thresholds and as it appeared that the notification thresholds were not met (Apple/Shazam) or at least this seemed uncertain (Meta/Kustomer), the Bundeskartellamt abstained from making a referral:

> Germany did not join the application for referral to the EU Commission because in the Bundeskartellamt's general practice a referral requires a merger to be subject to notification based on national competition law, which still has to be clarified in the present case.[73]

According to the turnover-based notification criteria under German law, all parties together must have a combined worldwide turnover of more than EUR 500 million,

---

[69] 6.9.2018, Case M.8788 (clearance without commitments).

[70] 21.2.2022, Case M.10262 (clearance with commitments).

[71] European Commission, Press release of 6.9.2018, 'Mergers: Commission clears Apple's acquisition of Shazam' (noting that the Commission had accepted a request from Austria, France, Iceland, Italy, Norway, Spain and Sweden to assess the acquisition).

[72] European Commission, Press release of 2.8.2021, 'Mergers: Commission opens in-depth investigation into proposed acquisition of Kustomer by Facebook' (noting that the Commission had accepted a request from Austria, which was joined by Belgium, Bulgaria, France, Iceland, Ireland, Italy, the Netherlands, Portugal and Romania).

[73] Bundeskartellamt, Press Release of 23.7.2021, Bundeskartellamt Examines whether Facebook / Kustomer Merger is Subject to Notification https://www.bundeskartellamt.de/SharedDocs/Meldung/EN/Pressemitteilungen/2021/23_07_2021_Facebook_Kustomer.html.

one of the parties must have a turnover of more than EUR 50 million in Germany and another party must have a turnover of more than EUR 17.5 million in Germany.[74] The latter requirement may not be met in typical acquisitions of digital gatekeepers, even though they may have a significant impact on the competitive conditions in Germany. In order to close this gap,[75] a threshold based on transaction value was introduced in 2017: If no second party with a turnover in Germany of more than EUR 17.5 million is involved, notification is still required if:

- the consideration for the acquisition exceeds EUR 400 million, and
- the target has substantial operations in Germany.[76]

Thus, as far as can be seen, the Apple/Shazam merger did not have to be notified because the transaction value threshold was not met. The reported purchase price was USD 400 million,[77] equivalent to around EUR 340 million at the time.

In the Facebook/Kustomer case, where the reported purchase price was USD 1 billion[78] (around EUR 850 million), the issue at stake was whether Kustomer was sufficiently active in Germany within the meaning of the provision. Kustomer is a provider of customer relationship management (CRM) services, which it offers based on a software-as-a-service (SaaS) business model. The company had barely any customers in Germany. However, Kustomer's customers had a significant number of end users in Germany. After some initial uncertainty, the Bundeskartellamt finally concluded that the processing of these end customers' data constituted sufficient domestic activity. The authority ordered Meta and Kustomer to notify the merger.[79]

This led to the unusual situation that the Bundeskartellamt was investigating the acquisition in parallel with the European Commission, which caused some irritation in Brussels, to say the least. After all, given the potential cross-border effects of the merger, the Commission considered itself to be in the best position to assess the merger. The Commission cleared the merger subject to extensive commitments regarding public access to APIs to avoid foreclosing the CRM market.[80] The

---

[74] Section 35(1) Competition Act.

[75] Section 32f(2) of the Competition Act also allows for the extension of merger control to cases below the threshold. Following a sector inquiry, the Bundeskartellamt can require companies to notify any acquisition. The focus of this instrument is to protect competition in regional markets. See Franck and Peitz (2024b), pp. 7–8.

[76] Section 35(1a) Competition Act. The current version of the provision is based on an amendment made in 2021, which removed inconsistencies from the original version. The focus of this instrument is the protection of competition in regional markets.

[77] See BBC News (10 December 2017) 'Apple "to buy Shazam for $400m"', https://www.bbc.com/news/business-42299207.

[78] See Forbes (30 November 2020) 'Facebook confirms to buy Kustomer for $1 billion', https://www.forbes.com/sites/ilkerkoksal/2020/11/30/facebook-confirms-to-buy-kustomer-for-1-billion/.

[79] Bundeskartellamt, Press Release of 9 December 2021, 'Bundeskartellamt considers Meta/Kustomer merger to be subject to notification', https://www.bundeskartellamt.de/SharedDocs/Meldung/EN/Pressemitteilungen/2021/09_12_2021_Meta_Kustomer.html?nn=3591568.

[80] 21.1.2022, Case M.10262.

Bundeskartellamt investigated the merger based on a concurrent theory of harm, suggesting that significantly increased access to end user data would allow Meta to expand its digital ecosystem and gain an advantage over competitors in relation to various services. In the end, the authority cleared the merger in phase 1.[81] The Bundeskartellamt found that the acquisition could have negative indirect effects on competition in markets where Meta already had a strong position. However, these anti-competitive effects could not be predicted with the degree of probability required for a prohibition. Therefore, in the words of its president, the authority cleared the acquisition 'with unease'.[82]

Subsequently, however, the Düsseldorf Higher Regional Court, in proceedings concerning the Bundeskartellamt's decision on costs, found that the merger did not have to be notified because Kustomer did not have significant activities in Germany.[83] The court considered the provision of CRM services to customers based in Germany to be the only relevant factor for measuring Kustomer's domestic activities. Thus, the processing of data from German end customers was considered to be part of the activity in relation to Kustomer's customers. The court also acknowledged that Kustomer's data processing could have an impact on the competitive situation in Germany. However, while this may have been sufficient in the eyes of the court to establish the German legislature's power to regulate the merger,[84] it was not sufficient to establish market-related domestic activity within the meaning of section 35(1a) of the Competition Act.[85] As the share of the turnover that Kustomer generated with customers based in Germany was very small, the domestic activity of Kustomer was considered to be negligible.[86] Moreover, the court argued that the fact that the company serviced German customers from the United States, did not offer German support and did not provide the software in German indicated that the German market was not of particular importance to the company.[87]

In addition, the Higher Regional Court seems to have considered as an (unwritten) additional criterion that the relevant domestic activities of the target must not be in a 'mature' market. Otherwise, the (low) turnover of the target could be regarded as a sufficiently meaningful parameter and the threshold based on the transaction value should not apply. Without taking a final position on the issue, the court said that it doubted whether Kustomer was operating in an immature market, given that CRM services had been offered in the form of SaaS since the 1990s.[88] The

[81] Bundeskartellamt 11.2.2022, B6-21/22.

[82] Bundeskartellamt, Press Release of 11 February 2022, 'Bundeskartellamt clears acquisition of Kustomer by Meta (formerly Facebook)', https://www.bundeskartellamt.de/SharedDocs/Meldung/EN/Pressemitteilungen/2022/11_02_2022_Meta_Kustomer.html.

[83] OLG Düsseldorf, 23 November 2022, Kart 11/21 (V).

[84] Section 185(2) of the Competition Act.

[85] OLG Düsseldorf, 23 November 2022, Kart 11/21 (V), Juris, paras 63–70.

[86] OLG Düsseldorf, 23 November 2022, Kart 11/21 (V), Juris, paras 75–76.

[87] OLG Düsseldorf, 23 November 2022, Kart 11/21 (V), Juris, para. 77.

[88] OLG Düsseldorf, 23 November 2022, Kart 11/21 (V), Juris, para. 72.

Bundeskartellamt has appealed against the decision and the case is pending before the Federal Court of Justice.[89]

These details of the application of the transaction value-based threshold, as they have been endorsed by the Düsseldorf Higher Regional Court, make it clear that this interpretation, if it prevails,[90] is too restrictive to capture all potentially anti-competitive digital gatekeeper transactions. After all, the Bundeskartellamt pursued a plausible 'digital ecosystem-based' theory of harm in this case. Even if the merger is ultimately cleared, it is important that such acquisitions can be scrutinised because only then will the authorities have a chance to develop and test new theories of harm in the field of acquisitions of digital gatekeepers. Thus, if the Federal Court of Justice does not correct this restrictive view, a reform of the transaction value threshold should be considered.

Subsequently, the Bundeskartellamt, without applying a particularly strict standard in interpreting the criterion of 'substantial operations in Germany', concluded that this requirement was not met in the *Microsoft/OpenAI*[91] and *Microsoft/Inflection*[92] cases and that these merger cases could thus not be taken up by the authority. Therefore, even leaving the *Facebook/Kustomer* litigation aside, a legislative softening[93] and possibly even the abolition of the criterion that the target company must have significant domestic activities should be seriously considered.[94]

What seems rather unlikely, however, is the enactment of 'call-in' powers for the Bundeskartellamt, a reform along the lines much appreciated by the European Commission[95] in the wake of the ECJ's *Illumina* ruling:

> Another direction is to rely on Member States to expand their own jurisdictions, thus allowing for more referrals under the 'traditional approach' to Article 22 [EUMR]. This is already

---

[89] Subsequently, the Federal Court of Justice overturned the Düsseldorf Higher Regional Court's ruling and dismissed the appeal against the Bundeskartellamt, thereby affirming a broad interpretation of the criterion of 'substantial operations in Germany.' Bundesgerichtshof, 17 June 2025, KVR 77/22, Juris. For further details, see the addendum at the end of this chapter.

[90] For a critical account, see Göbel (2024), pp. 46–49.

[91] Bundeskartellamt 25.9.2023, B6-34/23. Crucially, the authority considered that the legal definition of a concentration would be met in 2019 and 2021. At that time, however, OpenAI had no significant domestic activities. Although the latter has been the case since January 2023, there has been no deepening of the cooperation since then that could be considered a notifiable concentration. However, if Microsoft were to increase its influence on OpenAI in the future, a notification obligation could arise. See Case summary of 15 November 2023, pp. 2–3.

[92] Bundeskartellamt, Press Release of 29.11.2024, 'Taking over employees may be subject to merger control in Germany – Bundeskartellamt not competent to review Microsoft/Inflection transaction as Inflection has no substantial operations in Germany.'

[93] According to an internal draft of the Federal Ministry of Economic Affairs and Climate Protection dated May 2024, it was planned to amend section 35(1a) of the Competition Act so that it would be sufficient if the target company was expected to carry out substantial activities in Germany within a projected period of three to five years. See Käseberg (2025), p. 1.

[94] See Göbel (2024), pp. 50–51.

[95] See Tzanaki (2024), pp. 7–8.

happening. Eight Member States [Denmark, Hungary, Ireland, Italy, Latvia, Lithuania, Slovenia and Sweden] have introduced such powers in their toolbox.[96]

In addition to political concerns that this would make Germany less attractive as a location for venture capital investments, the guarantee of legal certainty for companies has always been a high priority in the political debate,[97] and this was also emphasised by the Bundeskartellamt in the debate on Article 22 EU merger referrals prior to *Illumina*. A 'call-in' power would be in tension with this.

3.3 Conclusion

Germany has not yet proved to be a reliable 'case procurer' under Article 22 of the EUMR—in the sense desired by the European Commission—to fill the merger control gap at EU level for acquisitions of low-turnover targets by digital gatekeepers. Whether this will change in the future will depend, inter alia, on the pending decision of the Federal Court of Justice in the Facebook/Kustomer case and, possibly as a reaction to this decision and the then prevailing interpretation of section 35(1a) of the Competition Act, but also more generally, on the willingness of the German legislature to make the transaction value threshold less restrictive. However, the enactment of a 'call-in' competence for the Bundeskartellamt, which would allow it to refer all cases that the Commission would like to see in Brussels, seems at any rate rather unlikely from today's perspective.

On the other hand, it would be wrong to suggest that the Bundeskartellamt is unwilling to refer merger cases to the Commission. In particular, the authority does not appear to have advocated that Germany should refuse a referral in any of the numerous requests concerning acquisitions by digital gatekeepers under Article 4(5) of the Merger Regulation.[98] However, from the Bundeskartellamt's point of view, there seems to be an inappropriate post-*Illumina* debate in Brussels, according to which the thresholds under national law are only of practical relevance for these

---

[96] Speech by EVP M. Vestager at the 28th Annual Competition Conference of the International Bar Association (6 September 2024), https://ec.europa.eu/commission/presscorner/detail/en/speech_24_4582.

[97] Käseberg (2025), p. 2; see also Göbel (2024), pp. 74–76.

[98] The Bundeskartellamt's activity report ('Tätigkeitsbericht') for the years 2021 and 2022 mentions that the Bundeskartellamt has referred one merger case to the European Commission pursuant to Article 22 of the EUMR which was notifiable because the transaction value threshold pursuant to Section 35 (1a) of the Competition Act was met. Deutscher Bundestag, Bericht des Bundeskartellamtes über seine Tätigkeit in den Jahren 2021/2022 sowie über die Lage und Entwicklung auf seinem Aufgabengebiet. Drucksache 20/7300, 26.7.2023, p. 32. However, the case is not specified. It seems possible that the Bundeskartellamt has referred the *Booking/eTraveli* merger under Article 22 of the EUMR, but that this referral was ultimately irrelevant because the parties requested the case be referred to the Commission under Article 4(5) of the EUMR based on the fact that the transaction could have been reviewed under the national merger control laws of (at least) three Member States (Austria, Cyprus, Germany). 25.9.2023, Case M.10615 – *Booking Holdings / eTraveli Group*, paras. 6–8.

cases to be referred to the Commission. The authority is obviously confident enough to take up these cases itself if appropriate.

4 Administrative Enforcement of the DSA: The Bundesnetzagentur as the Principal Enforcer and Home of the Digital Services Coordinator

In Germany, the Digitale-Dienste-Gesetz (DDG),[99] the German Digital Services Act, came into force on 14 May 2024. The Act establishes a framework for the effective implementation and enforcement of the EU DSA. It confers powers to enforce the EU Digital Services Act and designates the competent authorities.

4.1 Competent Authorities and Coordination

The Bundesnetzagentur (the Federal Network Agency) plays the central role in the enforcement of the DSA. It acts as the default enforcer[100] and the Digital Services Coordinator[101]—referred to in the German legislative texts as the 'Koordinierungsstelle für digitale Dienste' (Digital Services Coordination Unit)—has been established as part of the Bundesnetzagentur.[102] Further, the German legislature has assigned certain specific tasks or sectors to other competent authorities:[103]

- For the protection of minors,[104] both a specialised authority at federal level (Bundeszentrale für Kinder- und Jugendmedienschutz) and various authorities at state level are designated as competent enforcement authorities.[105] This split in competences results from the differentiated distribution of regulatory powers for the protection of minors from harmful media between the federal level and the Länder.[106]
- Enforcement of the DSA in data protection[107] is the responsibility of the federal authority specialised in this area, the Federal Commissioner for Data Protection

[99] See https://www.gesetze-im-internet.de/ddg/.
[100] Section 12(1) German DSA.
[101] See Articles 49 to 51 DSA.
[102] Section 14(1) DSA. See https://www.dsc.bund.de/DSC/DE/_Home/start.html?r=1.
[103] See Article 49(2) DSA.
[104] Articles 14(3) and 28(1) DSA.
[105] Section 12(2) of the German DSA.
[106] See Jungbluth and Engel (2024), pp. 402–403.
[107] Articles 26(3) and 28(1) and (3) DSA.

and Freedom of Information (Bundesbeauftragter für den Datenschutz und die Informationsfreiheit).[108]

For a complainant, this fragmentation of responsibility in the enforcement of the DSA should not be detrimental. For this reason, section 20(1) of the German DSA designates the Digital Services Coordination Unit as the 'central contact point for complaints' (*zentrale Beschwerdestelle*) thus implementing a 'one-stop-shop principle'.[109] As a result, even if the Digital Services Coordination Unit transfers a complaint to another competent authority, it remains, by default, the contact point for the complainant.

Section 18(1) of the German DSA requires the DSA enforcement authorities to work together 'in a spirit of cooperation and trust'. In particular, they shall 'share with each other observations and findings that may be relevant to the performance of their respective duties'. Details may be set out in an administrative agreement between the authorities.[110] The authorities are authorised to exchange and use data, including personal data.[111]

The cooperation of the DSA enforcement authorities with other authorities, for example the Bundeskartellamt, is specifically dealt with in Section 19 of the German DSA. With regard to data protection law, for example, it is stipulated that, where the task of the Digital Services Coordination Unit includes the verification of compliance with the GDPR[112] or other data protection rules, decisions must be taken in consultation with the relevant data protection supervisory authority.[113]

The Federal Criminal Police Office (Bundeskriminalamt) has been designated as the central body (*Zentralstelle*)[114] for receiving reports of 'suspicions of criminal offences' under Article 18 of the DSA. German law requires the federal government to submit an annual report to the Bundestag on the type and number of offences reported to the Federal Criminal Police Office under this provision.[115] The information obtained in this way should contribute to the preparation of a proposal for a more precise definition of the offences to be reported under Article 18 of the DSA.[116]

---

[108] Section 12(3) German DSA.

[109] Kraul (2024), p. 520, para. 17.

[110] Section 18(2) German DSA.

[111] Section 18(3) German DSA.

[112] Regulation (EU) 2016/679 of the European Parliament and of the Council of 27 April 2016 on the protection of natural persons with regard to the processing of personal data and on the free movement of such data, and repealing Directive 95/46/EC (General Data Protection Regulation). OJ L 119, 4.5.2016, pp. 1–88.

[113] Section 19(1) German DSA. The competent data protection authorities are the data protection authorities of the respective German federal states or the Federal Commissioner for Data Protection and Freedom of Information.

[114] Section 13, 1st sentence, German DSA.

[115] Section 13, 2nd sentence, German DSA.

[116] Jungbluth and Engel (2024), p. 403.

4.2 *The Digital Services Coordination Unit and Its Head as a Key Figure in DSA Enforcement*

The institutional requirements for the Digital Services Coordinator set out in Article 50 of the DSA—resources, budget autonomy and independence—are implemented by sections 14(2) and (3) and 15 of the German DSA.

According to information provided by the federal government in August 2024, a total of 15 positions for the Digital Services Coordinator at the Bundesnetzagentur were earmarked in the 2024 federal budget, of which 12.5 positions were already filled. In addition, 33 positions were created by transferring tasks from another agency, although the final financing of these positions beyond 2025 had not been clarified at that time. It is said that the Bundesnetzagentur wanted to fill all the available positions by the end of 2024.[117] In spite of all the caution that must be exercised in making external assessments, it can be said that the staffing levels do not appear to be generous, at least so far.

In Germany, the independence of an authority, as provided for by law for the Digital Services Coordinator, is still the exception, although it can now be found in a few instances due to the influence of EU law in the area of economic regulation. It is noteworthy, for example, that the independence of the Bundeskartellamt from instructions from the Federal Ministry of Economic Affairs, although accepted in practice, is not explicitly laid down in the German Competition Act,[118] despite the fact that this is required by Article 4(2)(a) of the ECN+ Directive.[119] Traditionally, in Germany any break with the classic hierarchical administration has been seen as problematic because it weakens the legitimacy and accountability to parliament required by the principle of democracy. However, the ECJ did not consider these concerns to be legally compelling because:

> The existence and conditions of operation of such authorities [outside the classic hierarchical administration] are, in the Member States, regulated by the law or even, in certain States, by the Constitution and those authorities are required to comply with the law subject to the review of the competent courts. Such independent administrative authorities, as exist moreover in the German judicial system, often have regulatory functions or carry out tasks which must be free from political influence, whilst still being required to comply with the law subject to the review of the competent courts.[120]

The head of the Digital Services Coordination Unit has a crucial role to play, as they have to make all the decisions provided for by the DSA.[121] In particular, the head

---

[117] Bundesregierung (2024), p. 2.

[118] See Franck (2024b), pp. 640 and 644.

[119] Directive (EU) 2019/1 of the European Parliament and of the Council of 11 December 2018 to empower the competition authorities of the Member States to be more effective enforcers and to ensure the proper functioning of the internal market. OJ L 11, 14.1.2019, pp. 3–33.

[120] Case C-518/07, *Commission v Germany*, ECLI:EU:2010:125, para. 42.

[121] Article 16(1) German DSA.

represents Germany in the European Board for Digital Services[122] and exercises voting rights there.[123]

The head of the Digital Services Coordination Unit is a civil servant exercising a five-year term of office, though a one-off extension of five years is permitted.[124] This extension option is not ideal for ensuring independent management of the unit, as it may create incentives to meet political expectations. The eligibility requirements and the selection and appointment process are designed to ensure the democratic legitimacy and accountability of the head's actions, while avoiding undue politicisation of the process. Only those with the necessary qualifications, experience and expertise, in particular in business models for digital services and knowledge of the legal framework for digital services, are eligible to head the Digital Services Coordination Unit.[125] In any case, the principle of best selection applies to access to public office pursuant to Article 33(2) of the Grundgesetz (Basic Law), the German Constitution. Following a public call for tenders, the president of the Bundesnetzagentur proposes an individual to the Federal Ministry for Economic Affairs for the position of head of the Digital Services Coordination Unit. The federal president then appoints the head.[126] In order to ensure the independence of the unit, the head cannot own or be a member of the board of directors or the supervisory board of any company in the digital economy. The head must also not be a member of the government or a parliament.[127]

The position of head of the Digital Services Coordination Unit was publicly advertised on 12 December 2024. In the meantime, the president of the Bundesnetzagentur is managing the unit.[128]

4.3 *Investigatory Powers and Sanctions*

Under Article 51(1) to (3) of the DSA, the Digital Services Coordinator is granted certain investigatory powers and enforcement powers. Measures taken in the exercise of these powers:

> shall be effective, dissuasive and proportionate, having regard, in particular, to the nature, gravity, recurrence and duration of the infringement or suspected infringement to which those measures relate, as well as the economic, technical and operational capacity of the provider of the provider of the intermediary services concerned where relevant.[129]

---

[122] Articles 61 to 63 DSA.

[123] Section 16(2) German DSA.

[124] Section 16(3) German DSA.

[125] Section 16(4) German DSA.

[126] Section 16(5) German DSA.

[127] Section 16(6) German DSA.

[128] Section 16(5), 4th sentence, German DSA.

[129] Article 51(5) DSA.

Therefore, it is on the Member States to:

> lay down specific rules and procedures for the exercise of the [investigatory and enforcement] powers pursuant to [Article 51] paragraphs 1, 2 and 3 and shall ensure that any exercise of those powers is subject to adequate safeguards laid down in the applicable national law in compliance with the Charter and with the general principles of Union law.[130]

Against this background, sections 24 to 27 of the German Digital Services Act provide for complementary investigatory and enforcement powers: the power to conduct investigations and gather the necessary evidence; to request information, to conduct searches and to seize objects; and to enforce the resulting obligations and, in particular, to impose penalties in the event of non-compliance. Section 28 of the German Digital Services Act empowers the Digital Services Coordinator and other authorities responsible for enforcing the DSA to inform the public about their activities and the 'situation and developments in their area of responsibility'. To this end, they may disseminate any information that may be relevant from the perspective of consumers and other market participants, in particular through their websites. The measures permitted under Article 51(3) of the DSA are specified in section 29 of the German Digital Services Act.

The sanctioning of DSA infringements via fines—as provided for in Article 52 of the DSA—is specified in section 33(4) to (8) of the German Digital Services Act.

4.4 A Peculiar German Feature: The Advisory Board at the Digital Services Coordination Unit

A specific feature of the German implementation of the DSA is the Advisory Board, which is set up at the Digital Services Coordination Unit in accordance with section 21 of the German Digital Services Act. The Advisory Board is composed of members from academia (four members), civil society including consumer protection organisations (eight members) and business associations (four members). Representatives may be appointed if they have specific legal, economic, sociopolitical or technological experience or proven scientific knowledge of the activities of digital services. The members of the Advisory Board are nominated by the German Bundestag and appointed by the Federal Ministry of Economics in consultation with the Federal Ministry of Digital Affairs and Transport. On 18 September 2024, the Advisory Board held its first meeting.[131]

The role of the Advisory Board is, first, to advise the Digital Services Coordinator and the other enforcement authorities on fundamental issues relating to the application and enforcement of the DSA; second, to make general recommendations for the effective and consistent implementation of the DSA; and, third, to bring scientific

---

[130] Article 51(6), 1st sentence DSA.

[131] See https://www.bundesnetzagentur.de/1028472. The website lists the current members of the Advisory Board.

issues to the attention of the competent authorities, in particular with regard to data handling.

4.5 First Practical Steps Taken by the Bundesnetzagentur

The Digital Services Coordinator has launched a complaints portal where online users from Germany and institutions, organisations or associations tasked with safeguarding rights under the DSA can complain about violations of the DSA.[132] According to the authority, 222 complaints had been received through the portal by 12 August 2024, although not all of these were complaints under Article 53 of the DSA.[133]

As far as is publicly known, the Digital Services Coordinator has so far only carried out preliminary investigations;[134] it has not yet initiated any formal proceedings. However, it has already supported formal proceedings of the EU Commission under Article 66(1) of the DSA, e.g. in the case of the digital platforms TikTok and X.[135]

On 12 August 2024, the Digital Services Coordinator announced that it had certified the first (and so far only[136]) national out-of-court dispute settlement body under Article 21(3) of the DSA, namely User Rights GmbH, Berlin.[137]

The status of 'trusted flagger' was granted to an organisation for the first time on 1 October 2024, namely the 'Meldestelle Respect!' Foundation for the Promotion of Youth in Baden-Württemberg, based in Sersheim.[138] The original press release from the Digital Services Coordinator on this issue sparked a controversial debate about the role of the 'trusted flagger'. This was partly owing to an inaccurate wording in the press release, which implied that 'trusted flaggers' would have a privileged role in reporting not only illegal content (as is indeed foreseen under Article 22(1) in conjunction with Article 16 of the DSA), but also 'hate and fake news'.[139] However, even recognising the limited role of trusted flaggers as whistleblowers on illegal content, they are partly seen as a threat to freedom of expression, especially as the line between legal and illegal behaviour (as defined in Article 3(h) of the DSA) is

[132] See https://www.dsc.bund.de/DSC/DE/3Verbraucher/3VB/start.html. The total cost of developing the complaints portal was EUR 157,452.71, according to the authority. Bundesregierung (2024), p. 7.

[133] Bundesregierung (2024), p. 4.

[134] Bundesregierung (2024), p. 3.

[135] Bundesregierung (2024), p. 3.

[136] See https://www.dsc.bund.de/DSC/DE/5Streitb/start.html.

[137] See https://www.bundesnetzagentur.de/1019662.

[138] See https://www.bundesnetzagentur.de/1029736.

[139] See Ruschemeier (2024), sub 'Illegale Inhalte vs. "legal but harmful content"'.

often difficult to draw.[140] On 2 June 2025, the Bundesnetzagentur announced that it had certified three additional organisations as 'Trusted Flaggers.'[141]

It is too early to say how effective supervision will be in Germany. On the one hand, it is important to put in place the necessary human resources and technical infrastructure. On the other hand, as is always the case with bureaucratic enforcement, it will depend on good, motivating leadership with a realistic and appropriate prioritisation of tasks that makes the best use of limited resources.

5 Implementing the DSA: Amendments to Substantive Law

As a regulation,[142] the DSA is directly applicable in its entirety throughout the EU and is part of national legal systems without the need for an implementing measure. Indeed, the transposition into national law of the standards and rules laid down in a regulation may obscure their nature as EU law and may therefore be considered contrary to Article 288(2) of the TFEU.[143] This will require adaptations to national law, in particular the repeal of provisions relating to matters within the scope of the DSA. In addition, new rules may be enacted, or the scope of existing rules may be adjusted to deal with matters not covered by the DSA.

5.1 Ensuring Full Harmonisation by the DSA: Repeal of the Network Enforcement Act

The DSA sets out (fully) harmonised rules for 'the provision of intermediary services in the internal market'[144] with the aim of creating a 'safe, predictable and trusted online environment'.[145] In Germany, the Network Enforcement Act (Netzwerkdurchsetzungsgesetz) had been the functional equivalent of the DSA since 2017, as it imposed reporting obligations and the maintenance of an effective complaint management system for dealing with defined illegal, indeed criminal content on large social media platforms. The Act applied to platforms with more than 2 million registered users in Germany. In particular, social network operators

[140] See Lindner (2024).

[141] See https://www.bundesnetzagentur.de/SharedDocs/Pressemitteilungen/EN/2025/20250602_TrustedFlagger.html. Accessed 28 September 2025.

[142] Article 288(2) TFEU.

[143] Case C-34/73, *Fratelli Variola Spa v Amministrazione delle finanze dello Stato*, ECLI:EU:C:1973:101, paras 10–11.

[144] Article 1(2) DSA.

[145] Article 1(1) DSA.

had to remove or block access to 'manifestly illegal content' (as defined in the law) within 24 hours of receiving the complaint.[146]

As the provisions of the Network Enforcement Act are largely superseded by the DSA and therefore no longer applicable, they have been repealed by the German legislature. The current version of the Act[147] essentially only contains an obligation for social network providers from non-EU countries to appoint an authorised representative for service of process in Germany[148] and provisions allowing the continuation and termination of administrative fine proceedings for past offences.[149]

5.2 *Supplementing the DSA to Maintain the German Status Quo Ante: Liability of Intermediary Services Providers*

Articles 4 to 10 DSA provide for a (conditional) exemption from liability for intermediary service providers and thus replace[150] Articles 12 to 15 of the Electronic Commerce Directive.[151] Consequently, the provisions in German law[152] that had previously implemented the liability rules of the Electronic Commerce Directive have been repealed. However, the German legislature provided for the continued application of some provisions by incorporating them into the German Digital Services Act. It did so on the assumption that the DSA does not provide for an exhaustive regulation of the subject matter and thus leaves some room for national supplementary measures.

First, since Article 4(1) of the DSA does not specify what is covered by the liability from which exemption is granted, section 7(3) of the German Digital Services Act makes it clear that the exemption from liability under the DSA (also) excludes claims for injunctive relief and damages. Second, section 7(1) and (4) of the German Digital Services Act states that the conditional exemptions from liability, as provided for in the DSA and specified in the German Digital Services Act, also apply to public and free WLAN networks. Third, section 7(3) of the German Digital Services Act also ensures that claims for injunctive relief against access providers are excluded. This was not the case under Article 12(1) of the Electronic Commerce

[146] Section 3(2) no. 2 Network Enforcement Act.

[147] See https://www.gesetze-im-internet.de/netzdg/.

[148] Section 5 Network Enforcement Act.

[149] Section 6 no. 2 Network Enforcement Act.

[150] See Article 89 DSA.

[151] Directive 2000/31/EC of the European Parliament and of the Council of 8 June 2000 on certain legal aspects of information society services, in particular electronic commerce, in the Internal Market ('Directive on electronic commerce'). OJ L 178, 17.7.2000, pp. 1–16.

[152] Ex-sections 7 and 8 of the German Telemedia Act ('Telemediengesetz').

Directive, as interpreted by the ECJ,[153] which is why liability had been explicitly excluded under German law.[154]

As compensation for this exclusion of liability on the part of the access provider, German law grants a (subsidiary[155]) right to demand that access providers block information that infringes intellectual property rights. This right is now set out in section 8 of the German Digital Services Act. There is room for such a national rule,[156] since the DSA provides for limitations and procedural requirements with regard to the liability of access providers, but not 'when a provider can be held liable, which is for the appliable rules of Union or national law to determine'.[157] At the same time, Article 8, 3rd sentence of the Enforcement Directive[158] requires Member States to ensure that 'rightholders are in a position to apply for an injunction against intermediaries whose services are used by a third party to infringe an intellectual property right'.[159]

6 Concluding Remarks

Germany was and is one of the Member States that does not solely rely on the EU when it comes to regulating digital gatekeepers but has itself taken a hands-on approach with some results to show for it. Examples of legislative initiatives specifically targeting digital gatekeepers include the Network Enforcement Act of 2017, and the introduction of the '19a tool' in the Competition Act in 2021.

Against this background, it is not surprising that, on the one hand, Germany has not been reluctant to adopt legislative measures to implement the DSA and the DMA and to create the conditions for effective enforcement. In particular, Germany is one of the jurisdictions that has given its competition authority the power to investigate infringements of the DMA. On the other hand, it was necessary to react to the (partly) exhaustive nature of the EU regulation. The legislature had to repeal measures such as the Network Enforcement Act or to limit them to certain complementary functions to the DSA. The latter also applies to the '19a tool', as the Bundeskartellamt will have to take the requirements of the DMA into account when

[153] Case C-484/14, McFadden, ECLI:EU:C:2016:689, para. 79.

[154] Ex-section 8(1), 2nd sentence of the German Telemedia Act ('Telemediengesetz').

[155] See recital 27, 2nd sentence of the DSA.

[156] See Hofmann (2024), p. 82.

[157] Recital 17, 2nd sentence of the DSA. See also Article 4(3) DSA.

[158] Directive 2004/48/EC of the European Parliament and of the Council of 29 April 2004 on the enforcement of intellectual property rights OJ L 157, 30.4.2004, pp. 45–86.

[159] See also Case C-314/12, UPC Telekabel Wien, ECLI:EU:C:2014:192, para. 64 (relates to Article 8(3) of Directive 2001/29/EC of the European Parliament and of the Council of 22 May 2001 on the harmonisation of certain aspects of copyright and related rights in the information society. OJ L 167, 22.6.2001, pp. 10–19).

applying it. It is too early to assess the effectiveness of national enforcement instruments.

Of particular practical importance will be how the Bundesnetzagentur will fulfil its role as Digital Services Coordinator. For the time being, only institutional arrangements can be observed, such as the start of work of the Advisory Board, the certification of the first out-of-court dispute settlement body and the first recognition of an organisation as a 'trusted flagger'.

Finally, it will depend on the forthcoming decision of the Federal Court of Justice (and possible reactions by the legislator) how tightly the network is meshed with which digital gatekeeper (gap) mergers can be captured by the transaction value-based threshold. Whatever the outcome, only time will tell how actively the Bundeskartellamt will pursue the 'Article 22 EUMR' route to Brussels, as envisaged in Article 14 DMA for such acquisitions.

Addendum to Section 3.2

In a judgment of 17 June 2025 concerning the Facebook/Kustomer merger (KVR 77/22), the German Federal Court of Justice upheld the Bundeskartellamt's decision to review the transaction under the transaction value-based threshold of German merger control law. The Court held that a target undertaking may be deemed to have sufficient domestic operations if data concerning German end customers are processed on behalf of the target's German business clients.[160] This broad interpretation of the concept of 'domestic operations' reflects the Court's view that the transaction-value threshold is designed to capture the competitive potential of an acquisition. Given the objective of safeguarding competition in dynamic markets,[161] the assessment of substantial domestic activity in digital business models must also consider data processing activities conducted abroad, insofar as they relate to German customers. The Court left open[162] the question of whether the processing of German end-customer data would suffice even where the target's business clients are located exclusively outside Germany. However, since access to data is crucial for competitive advantage, it could be argued that such a scenario also meets the threshold for substantial domestic activity. The Court's expansive interpretation of the domestic nexus criterion may help ease pressure in the ongoing policy debate over whether to reform the German merger notification thresholds for acquisitions by digital gatekeepers.

---

160 Bundesgerichtshof, 17 June 2025, KVR 77/22, Juris, paras 29–59.

161 Bundesgerichtshof, 17 June 2025, KVR 77/22, Juris, para. 34.

162 Bundesgerichtshof, 17 June 2025, KVR 77/22, Juris, para. 45.

References

Bauermeister T (2022) Section 19a GWB as the German 'Lex GAFA' – lighthouse project or superfluous national solo run? Yearb Antitrust Regul Stud 15(26):75–102

Blockx J (2023) The expected impact of the DMA on the antitrust enforcement of unilateral practices. J Eur Compet Law Pract 14:325–333

Bundesregierung (2024) Antwort auf die Kleine Anfrage der Fraktion der CDU/CSU – Drucksache 20/12286 – Aktueller Stand der Umsetzung des Digitale-Dienste-Gesetzes und zur Einsetzung der Koordinierungsstelle für digitale Dienste in Deutschland. BT-Drs. 20/12584, 12.08.2024. https://dserver.bundestag.de/btd/20/125/2012584.pdf

Crémer J et al (2023) Enforcing the Digital Markets Act: institutional choices, compliance, and antitrust. J Antitrust Enforce 11:315–349

Deselaers W (2024) Die ersten Verfahren des Bundeskartellamtes nach § 19a GWB – gelöste und ungelöste Fragen. Neue Zeitschrift für Kartellrecht 12:366–369

Draghi M (2024) The future of European competitiveness. Part B. In-depth analysis and recommendations ('The Draghi report')

Federal Ministry for Economic Affairs and Energy, Ministère de l'Économie, des Finances et de la Relance, and [Dutch] Ministry of Economic Affairs and Climate Policy (2021) Strengthening the Digital Markets Act and its enforcement. https://www.bmwk.de/Redaktion/DE/Downloads/XYZ/zweites-gemeinsames-positionspapier-der-friends-of-an-effective-digital-markets-act.pdf?__blob=publicationFile&v=4

Franck JU (2024a) Abuse proceedings against digital gatekeepers under section 19a of the German Competition Act: taking stock of early results. In: Ruiz Peris JI, Estevan de Quesada C (eds) New European competition trends in digital markets. Atelier, pp 23–51

Franck JU (2024b) Das Bundeskartellamt zwischen Condor, Kranich und 'Mutterhaus': Von der Freiheit vor politischer Einflussnahme. Wirtschaft und Wettbewerb 639–646

Franck JU, Peitz M (2021) Digital platforms and the new 19a tool in the German Competition Act. J Eur Compet Law Pract 12:513–528

Franck JU, Peitz M (2024a) The Digital Markets Act and the whack-a-mole challenge. Common Market Law Rev 61:299–344

Franck JU, Peitz M (2024b) Germany's new competition tool: sector inquiry with remedies. J Eur Compet Law Pract 15:515–525

Franck JU, Stock N (2020) What is 'competition law'? – Measuring EU Member States' leeway to regulate platform-to-business agreements. Yearb Eur Law 39:320–386

Franck JU, Monti G, de Streel A (2021) Options to strengthen the control of acquisitions by digital gatekeepers in EU Law. TILEC Discussion Paper No. DP2021-16

Gappa S, Käseberg T (2024) Article 38 [DMA]. Cooperation and coordination with national competent authorities enforcing competition rules. In: Podszun R (ed) Digital Markets Act. Nomos, pp 454–462

Göbel M (2024) "Gotta catch 'em all?" – Instrumente zum Aufgreifen von "Gap cases" in der formellen Fusionskontrolle. Zeitschrift für Wettbewerbsrecht 37–77

Hofmann F (2024) Auf leisen Sohlen angeschlichen: Internetangebotssperren im Digitale-Dienste-Gesetz (DDG). Gewerblicher Rechtsschutz und Urheberrecht 81–82

Hornung P (2023) The ecosystem concept, the DMA, and section 19a GWB. J Antitrust Enforce 12:396–437

Hungarian Competition Authority (GVH) (2023) Changes in Competition Law: expanding GVH toolbox and less administrative burden for undertakings. Press Release of 1 January 2023. https://www.gvh.hu/en/press_room/press_releases/press-releases-2023/changes-in-competition-law-expanding-gvh-toolbox-and-less-administrative-burden-for-undertakings

Jungbluth A, Engel C (2024) Das Digitale-Dienste-Gesetz: Zentrale Punkte, regulatorische Herausforderungen und Lösungen. Computer und Recht 401–406

Käseberg T (2025) Ein 'Inflection'-Punkt für die Fusionskontrolle? Neue Zeitschrift für Kartellrecht (KartR) 1–2

Käseberg T, Gappa S (2024) Article 1 [DMA]. Subject matter and scope. In: Podszun R (ed) Digital Markets Act. Nomos, pp 17–27

Kraul T (2024) Die Durchsetzung des Digital Service Act nach dem neuen deutschen Digitale-Dienste-Gesetz: Behörden- und Aufsichtsstruktur. Gewerblicher Rechtsschutz und Urheberrecht in der Praxis (GRUR Prax) 16:529–531

Kumkar LK (2024) § 32g GWB. Untersuchung von möglichen Verstößen gegen die Verordnung (EU) Nr. 2022/1925 (Digital Markets Act). In: Jaeger W et al (eds) Frankfurter Kommentar zum Kartellrecht. Otto Schmidt, 107. Lieferung, 1/2024

Lindner JF (2024) Trusted Flagger als Gefahr für die Meinungsfreiheit: eine Replik auf Hannah Ruschemeier. VerfBlog, 2024/11/08. https://verfassungsblog.de/trusted-flagger-als-gefahr/

Monti G (2022) Procedures and institutions in the DMA. Centre on Regulation in Europe (CERRE), Issue Paper December 2022

MPI Innovation and Competition (2023) Drexl J et al. Position Statement of the Max Planck Institute for Innovation and Competition of 2 May 2023 on the Implementation of the Digital Markets Act (DMA). GRUR Int 72:864–875

Ruschemeier H (2024) Flagging Trusted Flaggers: Zur Rolle vertrauenswürdiger Hinweisgeber unter dem Digital Services Act. VerfBlog, 2024/11/04. https://verfassungsblog.de/flagging-trusted-flaggers/

Schweitzer H (2024) § 19a GWB. Missbräuchliches Verhalten von Unternehmen mit überragender marktübergreifender Bedeutung für den Wettbewerb. In: Körber T, Schweitzer H, Zimmer D (eds) Immenga/Mestmäcker, Wettbewerbsrecht, Band 2, GWB. CH Beck, pp 750–831

Tzanaki A (2023) Dynamism and politics in EU merger control: the perils and promise of a killer acquisitions solution through a law and economics lens. Working Paper. https://papers.ssrn.com/sol3/papers.cfm?abstract_id=4574948

Tzanaki A (2024) *Illumina*'s light on Article 22 EUMR: the suspended step and uncertain future of EU merger control over below-threshold 'killer' mergers. CPI Antitrust Chronicle December 2024

Wirtz M (2024) § 32g GWB. Untersuchung von möglichen Verstößen gegen die Verordnung (EU) Nr. 2022/1925 (Digital Markets Act). In: Körber T, Schweitzer H, Zimmer D (eds) Immenga/Mestmäcker, Wettbewerbsrecht, Band 2, GWB. CH Beck, pp 1379–1382

Jens-Uwe Franck is a Professor of Law at the University of Mannheim and a Co-Director of the Mannheim Centre for Competition and Innovation (MaCCI). His main area of research is competition law and policy with a focus on digital platforms.

Implementing DMA and DSA in France: Analysis of the Institutional Architecture and Regulatory Dynamics

Frédéric Marty

Contents

Abstract The law of 21 May 2024 aimed at securing and regulating the digital space implemented in French legal order the European regulations on digital markets and digital services. It has allocated the new responsibilities associated with the enforcement of these texts between regulatory authorities with horizontal jurisdiction (such as the Autorité de la concurrence) and regulatory authorities with vertical

F. Marty (✉)
CNRS, GREDEG, Université Côte d'Azur, Nice, France
e-mail: frederic.marty@univ-cotedazur.fr

F. Decarolis et al. (eds.), *The EU Digital Regulation and its Impact on Member States*, European Union and its Neighbours in a Globalized World 27,
https://doi.org/10.1007/978-3-032-06490-5_10

jurisdiction (such as Arcom and the CNIL). The purpose of this chapter is to analyse this new institutional framework and to shed light on the dynamics that may result from it in terms of guaranteeing competitive order and economic public order in response to the challenges posed by the major digital ecosystems and the manipulations they may entail.

1 Introduction

The SREN law of 21 May 2024 (law no. 2024–449 aimed at securing and regulating the digital space) establishes the institutional framework within which the DMA[1] and DSA[2] will apply but also leads to the introduction of provisions relating to the Data Act,[3] the Data Governance Act[4] and even the RGPD.[5] It amends several texts relating to market regulation, the protection of personal data and the regulation of the digital sector, in particular Law No. 2004-5757 of 21 June 2004 on confidence in the digital economy. Similarly, certain provisions are specific to French law. Overall, the new provisions introduced by the SREN Act should be seen in the context of broader issues relating to the regulation and management of the digital sector, which go well beyond simply adapting French law to DMA and DSA.

A distinction should be made between the ways in which the two texts are applied. The DMA, which came fully into force on 6 March 2024, is enforced by the Commission, which may enlist the help of national authorities in investigating possible infringements.[6] Under the DSA, which has been fully applicable since 17 February 2024, the Commission directly supervises only 25 very large online platforms and search engines. The Regulation is applied to the other platforms and search engines by the national regulatory authorities, which form part of a European Digital Services Committee.

Furthermore, the regulations forming the European digital package will be applied in parallel to existing legislation. The best example of this is the competition rules, in particular Article 102 of the Treaty on the Functioning of the European Union, which still applies to punish abuses of dominant positions. In some respects,

[1] Regulation (EU) 2022/1925 of 14 September 2022 on contestable and fair markets in the digital sector.

[2] Regulation (EU) 2022/2065 of 19 October 2022 on a single market for digital services.

[3] Regulation (EU) 2023/2854 of 13 December 2023 on harmonised rules on fair access to and use of data.

[4] Regulation (EU) 2022/868 of 30 May 2022 on European data governance.

[5] Regulation (EU) 2016/679 of 27 April 2016 on the protection of natural persons with regard to the processing of personal data and on the free movement of such data.

[6] National competition authorities can also exercise the powers they already hold within their competition-related competencies to address potential violations of the DMA and subsequently submit their findings to the Commission.

it targets practices that the DMA seeks to prevent. However, the very conditions under which it is implemented mean that the provisions of the DMA cannot replace it. The competition rules are applied ex post and have an efficiency objective. The rules resulting from the DMA apply ex ante and have the objectives of preserving the contestability of market positions and guaranteeing the fairness of the competition within the market.

This chapter presents the institutional framework set up in France, discusses the balance between the various regulatory authorities involved and places this framework in the context of the challenges of overseeing the digital sector.

As such, the chapter addresses several economic issues, particularly in the competition field. It examines the ability of the authorities responsible for enforcing these laws to regulate the market power of platforms, to control their private regulatory power, and to ensure that it is consistent with public regulation. It focuses on the ability to deter, prevent and remedy practices that could harm consumers, business partners and society as a whole and that were not, or poorly, countered before. It analyses the ways in which the objectives and scope of intervention of the various regulatory authorities and other government bodies responsible for preserving economic order can be made more complementary. It presents the coordination mechanisms between authorities with different mandates. Finally, it looks at the management of inter-regulatory situations.

To this end, the chapter is divided into five sections. The first two are devoted to the DSA and the DMA respectively. The third deals with initiatives taken to coordinate the regulatory bodies involved. The fourth section looks at current initiatives to adapt the French regulatory framework to the digital economy, focusing on the specific case of merger control insofar as it is emblematic of the supervision of market structures. A fifth section concludes by illustrating the complexities but also the potential benefits associated with this overall adaptation of the regulatory framework.

2 The DSA: The Pivotal Role of the Broadcasting Regulator for Operators not Supervised by the Commission

This first section looks at the application of the DSA in the French case by presenting the coordinating role assigned to Arcom, the regulator of audiovisual activities (A) and by looking at the coordination with two other regulatory bodies, the CNIL and the DGCCRF, which have been assigned some of the tasks defined by the DSA (B).

2.1 The Powers of Arcom in Applying the DSA

The implementation of the DSA requires each Member State to appoint a digital services coordinator.[7] In France, this task is carried out by Arcom, the French regulatory authority for audiovisual and digital communication. Arcom is the independent administrative authority responsible for regulating communication activities in the audiovisual and digital sectors. The convergence of these two sectors led to its creation in January 2022 to take over from two separate authorities, the Conseil Supérieur de l'Audiovisuel (CSA) created in 1989 and the Haute Autorité pour la Diffusion des Œuvres et la Protection des Droits sur l'Internet (Hadopi) created in 2009.

The responsibilities of Arcom cover both economic regulatory tasks (to preserve its economic equilibrium) and tasks relating to the defence of pluralism in the media and platforms and the promotion of creativity. In terms of regulation, Arcom's role includes the attribution of digital terrestrial television and radio frequencies, the protection of content on online platforms and the struggle against the manipulation of information, online hate and the protection of pluralism in both political and societal terms. Its responsibilities cover the supervision of online platforms and social networks, particularly as part of the application of Law no. 2018–1202 of 22 December 2018 on the fight against the manipulation of information, a law adopted in particular with regard to the prevention of foreign interference in public debate and electoral polls.

As part of the application of the DSA, the twenty-seven coordinators must ensure compliance with the obligations in their respective Member States. They can receive and investigate complaints against online intermediaries. In France, the SREN law has clarified the remit of the various public authorities as part of the implementation in France of the provisions relating to the entry into force of the Digital Services Regulation. Arcom has been appointed national coordinator and will implement the new provisions alongside the CNIL and the DGCCRF.

In this respect, Arcom is required to cooperate with the Commission's investigations into the very large online platforms, which remain under its exclusive jurisdiction (Article 51–1 of the DSA). This vertical cooperation between the European Commission and the national bodies responsible for applying the DSA also applies to the CNIL and the DGCCRF (article 64–4 of the DSA). The DSA is applicable to major online platforms and search engines with more than 45 million users in the EU. While the Commission is directly responsible for supervising the largest of these[8] (the VLOPSEs, i.e. very large online platforms (VLOPs) and very large online search engines (VLOSEs)), authorities selected by the Member States are responsible for supervising intermediary service providers.[9]

[7] SREN law, art. 51.

[8] The list is established by the EU Commission: https://digital-strategy.ec.europa.eu/fr/policies/list-designated-vlops-and-vloses

[9] Small operators are exempt from the obligations under the DSA.

These services can be grouped into four categories. The first are transport and cache services. These are network infrastructures and access services to these infrastructures. These activities include those of Internet access providers, domain name registry operators and domain registrars. The second services to be monitored include hosting services, whether for websites or data (cloud infrastructures). The third services targeted are those provided directly by the platforms. These include all services that enable information to be stored and shared online, i.e. social networks, video-sharing platforms, dating applications and marketplaces. The fourth and final services covered are those provided by marketplaces.

Within this framework, the responsibilities entrusted to Arcom can be divided into five groups.

Arcom's first role is to ensure that the practices of the operators concerned comply with the obligations arising from DSA. The second role is to ensure that operators complete the European database of statements of reasons sent to users when a moderation decision is made on their content. Arcom's third role is to designate trusted flaggers, i.e. entities whose reports of illegal content must be dealt with as a priority by the platforms under article 22 of the DSA.[10] Arcom's fourth responsibility is to certify the dispute resolution bodies proposed by the platforms for their disputes with users.[11] Finally, the fifth responsibility entrusted to the regulator is the centralisation of injunctions issued by the judicial and administrative authorities based on the DSA. These may include injunctions to act against illegal content and injunctions to provide information about a user or users.

Within the scope of its attributions, Arcom has new powers of investigation, injunctions (to cease a given market practice), fines and periodic penalty payments, and the ability to temporarily ban access to a platform.

Arcom sits on the European Digital Services Committee (article 61–1 of the DSA). Within this committee, Arcom, the twenty-six other coordinators and the Commission can coordinate their analyses, issue joint recommendations and conduct joint investigations. The authority may also support the Commission in its investigations of very large platforms and large search services in national matters.

2.2 *Coordination with DGCCRF and the CNIL in DSA Provisions Enforcement*

Two other institutions are involved in the application of the DSA in France: the CNIL and the DGCCRF.

[10] The first trusted flagger has been accredited by Arcom: the e-enfance association. The designation procedures are based on requirements concerning expertise and independence from online platform providers (see Arcom 2024).

[11] It is worth recalling that the sectoral inquiry conducted by the European Commission into online commerce in 2017 revealed that platforms often selected forums that were financially and geographically inaccessible to their complementors. See EU Commission (2017)

The Commission Nationale Informatique et Liberté (CNIL) is the French sector-specific regulator responsible for data protection. It was set up in 1978 and is responsible in France for implementing the RGPD. The DGCCRF (Direction Générale de la Concurrence, de la Consommation et de la Répression des Fraudes) is a directorate of the Ministry of the Economy. It is responsible for safeguarding economic public order, in other words, for the competitive regulation of markets and consumer protection.[12] Its consumer protection remit consists of punishing unfair commercial practices (fraud and deception), misleading information and product non-compliance with public health and safety standards. Its role in regulating competition in the markets is to support the Autorité de la Concurrence in punishing anti-competitive practices carried out by companies with a turnover of more than €1 billion.

However, the DGCCRF is not solely in charge of these micro-PACs ('micro' anti-competitive practices); in the French institutional architecture, it occupies a central position in the control of the balance and fairness of commercial practices. French law has long been concerned with the significant contractual imbalances that can result not only from abuse of exploitation within the meaning of competition law, but also from abusive exploitation of dissymmetrical bargaining power. This situation, which has long been particularly marked in the mass retail sector, is now characteristic of online intermediation platforms, particularly marketplaces. The DGCCRF is responsible for detecting, penalising and remedying such contractual imbalances and acts to ensure that vertical contracts are concluded under transparent and fair conditions. The link with the spirit of the European regulations in favour of equal opportunity on the market and guaranteeing fairness, initiated by the P2B Regulation of June 2019,[13] is obvious here.[14]

As part of the application of the DSA, these two bodies are each assigned responsibilities corresponding to their respective areas of expertise.

DGCCRF and CNIL may be called upon to take part in investigations launched by the Commission into major online platforms in areas that fall within their respective remits. They may also both be involved in the European Digital Services Committee under the same conditions.

The CNIL is responsible for ensuring that platforms comply with the obligations arising from the DSA in terms of advertising profiling. The DGCCRF is responsible for monitoring compliance by marketplace operators. The CNIL's responsibility covers the provisions of the DSA relating to transparency obligations or, conversely, the prohibition of advertising profiling targeted at minors or based on sensitive personal data (articles 26.1.d., 26.3 and 28.2 of the DSA and article 9 of the RGPD).

[12] The DGCCRF also carries out tasks related to the enforcement of regulations against money laundering and the financing of terrorist activities.

[13] Regulation (EU) 2019/1150 of 29 June 2019 on promoting fairness and transparency for business users of online intermediation services.

[14] See Bougette et al. (2019).

The DGCCRF is responsible for monitoring the behaviour of marketplaces.[15]

The obligations placed on marketplaces by the DGCCRF fall into three main categories. Firstly, there is an obligation to monitor product safety. This obligation may take the form of automated checks aimed at detecting illegal products and informing customers who have purchased non-compliant or dangerous products. Secondly, transparency obligations are imposed with regard to the identification of sellers and pre-contractual sales information. Lastly, it involves obligations of fairness vis-à-vis consumers relating to the prohibition of certain manipulative practices online, such as dark patterns, which we will consider below.

SREN law amends the Consumer Code in this respect and even introduces new obligations for the managers of e-commerce platforms. Failure to comply with these obligations could result in 2 years' imprisonment and a fine of 300,000 euros for individuals, but also (and more realistically) a fine of up to 6% of the turnover of the legal entities concerned. The powers of the DGCCRF also extend to the possibility of demanding that certain malevolent sites be blocked.

On 27 June 2024, the three regulatory authorities signed a cooperation agreement enabling them to coordinate their actions regarding the application of the DSA. This cooperation between the authorities is not unprecedented in that the law on confidence in the digital economy (law no. 2004–575, known as the LCEN law of 21 June 2004) initiated such a mechanism.

The agreement is based on rules for sharing information between the three entities, notably regarding the fulfilment of their respective responsibilities for supervising the application of the DSA (via the Agora information system set up by the European Commission (see DSA article 85–1)). Cooperation between the three entities also takes the form of joint participation in investigations and the sharing of information on the opening of proceedings to avoid parallel actions. In addition to these sharing rules, an institutional cooperation mechanism has been put in place with the appointment of contact points in each of the three entities and the organisation of technical follow-up meetings.

3 The DMA: The Competition Authority's Delegated Role in Relation to the Commission

This second section deals with the application of the DMA in the French case by presenting the coordinating role assigned to the Autorité de concurrence (A) and also considering the new responsibilities assigned to it by the SREN with regard to the supervision of cloud computing activities (B).

[15] These are Articles 25, 30, 31, and 32 of DSA. They led, through Article 52 of the SREN law, to an amendment of the Commercial Code to grant the DGCCRF these new sanctioning powers.

3.1 *The Attributions of the Autorité de la Concurrence in the DMA Enforcement*

While the sector regulator for audiovisual and digital communications plays a leading role in the application of the DSA, the role of national authority responsible for enforcing the rules of the DMA has been entrusted to the Autorité de la concurrence and the Ministère de l'économie.[16] The Autorité is also an independent administrative authority that was created in 2009 following the formation of the Conseil de la Concurrence in 1986. The Authority is responsible for sanctioning anti-competitive practices, ex ante merger control and certain regulatory tasks (in this case, controlling the creation of new offices for certain regulated legal professions). Its powers to enforce the DMA are complementary to those of the European Commission, insofar as its enforcement is centralised. The Authority may participate alongside the Commission and within the framework of the ECN (European Competition Network) in investigations into the compliance of gatekeepers' practices.[17]

The Autorité retains its powers to sanction anti-competitive practices and to run ex ante merger control. The DMA and the competition rules remain two complementary and non-substitutable tools.

3.2 *The Autorité de la Concurrence's New Responsibilities as Regard to the Cloud*

The SREN law also confers responsibilities on the Autorité de la concurrence, which do not exactly cover the supervision of dos and donts obligations under the DMA.[18] They relate specifically to the supervision of self-preferencing practices in the cloud. These powers are exercised in parallel with those assigned to ARCEP, the telecommunications regulator, which we shall present below. These powers relate to

---

[16] SREN law, art. 53.

[17] The gatekeepers' list is established by the EU Commission: https://digital-markets-act.ec.europa.eu/gatekeepers_en

[18] Cloud service providers (Article 2i) can be designated under the DMA as gatekeepers to essential platform services. As such, the obligations outlined in Articles 5 and 6 of the DMA may apply to them. The obligations and prohibitions imposed under the DMA are as follows: the requirement for real-time access to data when using the relevant essential platform service (Article 6(10)), ensuring free data portability (Article 6(9)), prohibiting the use of data from business users (Article 6(2)), banning the bundling of offers with essential services (Article 5(8)), and prohibiting the combination of personal data with other data without user consent (Article 5(2)).

However, the SREN law goes beyond the DMA by applying specific obligations to cloud service providers related to the Data Act. These requirements focus on ensuring data portability, the eventual ban on charging migration fees, and the implementation of technical measures to facilitate supplier switching. Partly, these two sets of prescriptions explain why some of the missions defined by the SREN law concerning cloud services are assigned to the Competition Authority, while others are assigned to ARCEP.

monitoring compliance with interoperability and data portability obligations. Assigning responsibility for controlling the risks associated with self-preference practices, i.e. discrimination between users of cloud services that unduly penalises users wishing to implement multi-homing strategies (multi-cloud strategies) or switch from one cloud to another. The theory of competitive damage would then be to foreclose user firms or create second-order discrimination.[19]

Article 26 of the SREN Act provides a definition of self-preferencing: 'where a cloud computing service provider, that also provides software, supplies a software to a customer via the services of a third-party cloud computing service provider under pricing and functional conditions that differ significantly from those under which the provider supplies the same software via its own cloud computing service, where such differences in pricing and functionalities are not justified[20]'.

The definition adopted differs from the one proposed by the Commission in its draft revised guidelines on the treatment of exclusionary abuses[21] in that it also covers pricing practices. It nevertheless follows the same logic. It is a form of discrimination that deprives companies that are not vertically integrated or not connected in some way to the company controlling the platform (via an exclusivity contract or otherwise) of equal opportunities in accessing the market. Article 156 of the Commission's draft guidelines, which is based on the Google Shopping judgment,[22] defines self-preference as 'the fact that a dominant undertaking actively accords preferential treatment to its own products over those of its competitors, mainly by means of non-price practices'.

The risks associated with self-preference are now well known in the field of competition.[23] In the cloud sector, they were analysed by the Autorité de la concurrence as part of its sector enquiry. Under SREN law, in addition to its powers to penalise anti-competitive practices, the Autorité has been given the task of ex-ante regulation. However, the strategies of anti-competitive foreclosure through the allocation of cloud credits[24] or exclusivity clauses, which it also identified in its sector

[19] The competition issue here concerns the specific position of a platform that holds a dual role as both a private regulator and an operator. This dual role can lead to conflicts of interest and may result in the platform distorting competition to its advantage. In this regard, the regulation of digital ecosystems can be seen as a (public) regulation of the exercise of (private) regulatory power.

See in particular Budzinski (2025).

[20] In French: Self-preferencing can be defined as the fact « pour un fournisseur de services d'informatique en nuage qui fournit également des logiciels, de fournir un logiciel à un client par le biais des services d'un fournisseur de services d'informatique en nuage tiers dans des conditions tarifaires et fonctionnelles qui diffèrent sensiblement de celles dans lesquelles le fournisseur fournit ce même logiciel par le biais de son propre service d'informatique en nuage, lorsque ces différences de tarifs et de fonctionnalités ne sont pas justifiées » (SREN law, art. 26)

[21] See EU Commission (2024).

[22] General Court, Judgement of November 10th 2021, Google and Alphabet v Commission (Google Shopping), Case T-612/17.

[23] See Bougette and Marty (2025).

[24] As noted by the French Competition Authority in its April 2023 opinion on the SREN draft law, credit clouds cannot be considered anticompetitive in themselves. They are legitimate when used

enquiry, and which may be required to sanction as part of its antitrust remit, are subject to regulation by Arcep, the incumbent telecommunications regulator, as we shall see below.

4 Coordination Between the Various Authorities Under SREN Law

This third section looks at the changes introduced into French law by the adaptation to the European texts by considering the coordination bodies between the various regulatory authorities within the framework of the DSA and DMA (A) and the new powers conferred on the regulatory authorities in the digital field beyond the DSA and DMA (B).

4.1 *The Coordination of the Authorities*

We consider in turn the questions of coordination at European level (a), the specific case of coordination between the Autorité de la concurrence and the CNIL (b) and that between the Autorité de la concurrence and the DGCCRF.

4.1.1 The National Coordination Network for the Regulation of Digital Services

As regards the DSA, a lead authority has been designated by law in application of Article 49 of the Regulation. As mentioned above, the designated coordinator is Arcom.[25] As such, it has a coordinating role with the other two authorities involved and must ensure the implementation of cooperation mechanisms involving exchanges of information and cross-consultations. One of the key points in facilitating these exchanges is the fact that they are exempt from constraints relating to business confidentiality, investigative secrecy and the protection of personal data. This first level of coordination is complemented by a second at European level. In

---

for testing the service. However, when implemented by a dominant firm, they may have exclusionary effects, as they can create barriers to entry or expansion for smaller competitors who are unable to replicate them. Nevertheless, the Competition Authority recommended in its opinion (§57) that the company concerned be allowed to justify its practice based on efficiency gains or an objective justification. This ex-post examination based on effects is one of the key advantages of antitrust enforcement compared to ex-ante regulation.

Autorité de la concurrence, avis n°23-A-05 du 20 avril 2023 concernant le projet de loi visant à sécuriser et réguler l'espace numérique).

[25] SREN law, art. 51.

the DSA field, Arcom sits on the European Digital Services Committee as national coordinator for digital services.[26]

A third level of coordination needs to be considered. This is at national level and involves all French stakeholders in the implementation of European regulations. This network brings together Arcom, CNIL, Arcep, the French Competition Authority, ANSSI (Agence Nationale de la Sécurité des Systèmes d'Information), the French Employment Platforms Social Relations Authority and the relevant government departments. The aim of this national coordination network for the regulation of digital services is to foster the exchange of information between its members, encourage coordination and promote a global policy for the regulation of digital services 'that integrates the issues of fairness, protection, innovation and competitiveness'. However, its action is circumscribed by the independence enjoyed by the various regulatory authorities.

4.1.2 Coordination Between the AdlC and the CNIL Regarding Data Law and the Data Economy

With the development of large digital ecosystems, the question of the relationship between the application of competition rules and those relating to the protection of personal data has become central and is even more acute with the development of artificial intelligence, particularly generative artificial intelligence. In 2016, the French Competition Authority and the Bundeskartellamt published a joint note on competition law and data.[27] The Court of Justice's Meta ruling, handed down on 4 July 2023,[28] confirms, if confirmation were still needed, the urgent need for the regulatory authorities with jurisdiction in each of the two fields to coordinate their actions.[29] Bruno Lasserre, former President of the French Competition Authority and current member of the CNIL's College, recently submitted a report to its President on the relationship between data protection and competition.[30]

While it is possible that under certain conditions initiatives taken to protect personal data may run counter to the opening up and maintenance of undistorted competition in the market (for example when a platform operator asymmetrically

[26] DSA, art. 61.

[27] See Autorité de la concurrence and Bundeskartellamt (2016).

[28] The Judgement allows a competition authority to incidentally identify a violation of the GDPR when establishing an abuse of a dominant position. Conversely, data protection authorities can consider competition-related data in their analyses, such as when assessing the characterization of freely and fully informed consent to the transfer of personal data (§39 of the judgement from July 4, 2023). The stance taken by the Court of Justice reaffirms the need for cooperation between the two competent authorities whenever competition issues involve access to personal data (§54 of the judgement).

[29] Court of Justice, Judgment of the 4 July 2023, Meta Platforms Inc., case C-252/51.

[30] See Lasserre (2024).

restricts the ability of third parties to collect information about users[31]), in most situations the protection of personal data, fair competition and the maximisation of consumer welfare are aligned.

These perspectives are likely to strengthen cooperation between the regulatory authorities.[32] Cooperation between the CNIL and the Autorité de la Concurrence is already well advanced, with the publication of a joint statement in December 2023.[33]

While data are central to the functioning of digital ecosystems and are the subject of close scrutiny by competition authorities to identify potential problems of self-preferencing in the area of predatory abuses, excessive extraction in the field of exploitative abuses,[34] and the assessment of competitive risks[35] and the effectiveness of remedies in mergers,[36] the fact remains that the issues of personal data protection and the preservation of a free and undistorted competitive process should not be confused.

Both the competition authorities and the personal data protection authorities face related but distinct challenges. It is more a question of encouraging exchanges and cross-understanding of the issues than of considering that the same positions should be taken by both types of authority. If the aim is to limit the risks of inconsistent decisions, the essential thing is for each to be able to grasp the other's issues and to construct decision-making mechanisms, particularly in terms of injunctions, that satisfy the various facets of the public interest.

In this regard, the Lasserre Report highlights several instances where competition law and data protection decisions may diverge. For example, identical data protection requirements can impose different relative compliance costs depending on a firm's size, thereby increasing the relative costs of smaller rivals or creating barriers to entry for potential competitors.

Similarly, rules restricting third parties' ability to track or collect user information within an ecosystem may strengthen the competitive position of a dual-role platform operator or enable it to increase its revenues by selling the collected data

[31] Autorité de la concurrence, décision n°21-D-07 du 17 mars 2021 relative à une demande de mesures conservatoires présentée par les associations Interactive Advertising Bureau France, Mobile Marketing Association France, Union Des Entreprises de Conseil et Achat Media, et Syndicat des Régies Internet dans le secteur de la publicité sur applications mobiles sur iOS.

[32] This cooperation is facilitated by Law No. 2017–55 of January 20, 2017, on the general status of independent administrative authorities and independent public authorities, which states in Article 15 that the concerned authorities can exchange information without being bound by professional secrecy.

[33] See Autorité de la concurrence and CNIL (2023).

[34] The disproportionate and undue extraction of data through the exploitation of a dominant position can be considered, particularly in digital ecosystems where prices may be zero for certain areas of activity, as an abuse of exploitation.

Directive (EU) 2019/770 on certain aspects concerning contracts for the supply of digital content and digital services (art. 3.1(2)).

[35] EU Commission, Apple /Shazam, case M.8787, 6 September 2018.

EU Commission, Microsoft / LinkedIn, case M.8124, 6 December 2016.

[36] EU Commission, Google / Fit Bit, case M.9660, 17 December 2020.

to data brokers.[37] Finally, competition remedies requiring an incumbent operator to grant new entrants access to customer data may also raise concerns regarding personal data protection.[38]

The consideration of perspectives from other regulatory authorities and the indirect effects of decisions on broader public policy objectives is increasingly prevalent and occurs through an expanding range of channels. For instance, the Competition Authority increasingly consults CNIL for decisions involving aspects of personal data protection, and regular exchanges are organized between the two agencies.[39] At the same time, data regulators at the European level have established a Consumer and Competition (C&C) task force within the European Data Protection Board in March 2023, aimed at assessing the impact of their policies on consumer protection and competition.[40]

4.1.3 Autorité de la Concurrence, DGCCRF, and the CNIL: Fairness Related Dimensions

Other practices implemented by digital platforms may raise issues that can be jointly addressed by different regulatory authorities or, at the very least, serve as grounds for sharing information and expertise. This is notably the case with deceptive and manipulative online choice architectures, which are among the topics covered by the agreement between Arcom, the CNIL, and DGCCRF. Dark patterns involve the exploitation of personal data (as well as users' cognitive biases) and consumer protection concerns,[41] but they may also raise competition issues. For instance, in the context of self-preferencing strategies, making vertically integrated offerings more accessible than competing ones can be facilitated using such practices.[42]

---

[37] The issue here is not whether the data held by a dominant operator could be considered essential facilities to which a third-party operator should have access on fair, reasonable, and non-discriminatory terms to operate in the market (or in a related vertically connected market). Rather, it is to consider that an operator in a pivotal position within an ecosystem can leverage a data-related advantage to potentially surpass, under certain conditions, its competitors.

[38] Autorité de la concurrence, décision n°14-MC-02 du 9 septembre 2014 relative à une demande de mesures conservatoires présentée par la société Direct Energie dans les secteurs du gaz et de l'électricité et arrêt de la chambre commerciale de la cour d'appel de Paris du 31 octobre 2014, n°157, 2014/19335.

[39] See Denis (2022).

[40] Bruno Lasserre specifically cites the example of initiatives launched a few years ago by Meta (such as "consent or pay") to illustrate one of the areas where European data protection authorities collaborate to develop a common doctrine. This is an area where both competition and consumer protection dimensions are central.

See Lasserre (2024), p 41.

[41] Dark patterns implementation scope is not limited to consent related issues. See Nataliia Bielova et al. (2024).

[42] See Ezrachi and Stucke (2022)

A dark pattern exploits consumer biases and, in an ideal-typical form, can be personalized and dynamic, meaning it may adjust in real time to each consumer's reactions. Broadly speaking, dark patterns can be categorized as forms of (bad) sludges and (bad) nudges. The former hinder consumers' ability to make decisions aligned with their interests by concealing options or making their selection unnecessarily cumbersome. The latter steer consumers toward suboptimal choices—through biased screen designs or stimuli—leading them to act against their own interests but in favor of the platform. Consequently, dark patterns represent a case where consumer data protection, protection against deceptive or unfair practices, and competition enforcement are closely aligned.

A firm's ability to leverage its dominant position to unduly extract data at the expense of its service users and ecosystem complementors places it in a position to gain an illegitimate advantage over competitors—one that may ultimately drive them out of the market. At the same time, such conduct enables the firm to engage in unfair strategies toward its own users, combining exclusionary self-preferencing practices with consumer surplus extraction through exploitative strategies.[43] The Lasserre Report, prepared for the CNIL, builds on this perspective to connect data protection, consumer protection, and competition law. This approach aligns with a longstanding position of the French Court of Cassation, which has held that an "undue competitive advantage [...] may constitute a fault of unfair competition.[44]"

One of the distinctive features of French competition law, in its broadest sense, is that the abuse of economic dependence exists both within the realm of the *Grand droit de la concurrence* (which governs abuses of dominant position) and the *petit droit de la concurrence* (which sanctions restrictive practices). In practice, sanctions for abuses of economic dependence are far more effective in the latter category, where it suffices to demonstrate harm to a commercial partner resulting from an imbalanced contractual relationship, rather than in the former, where proving consumer harm is required.

The issue of data provides a new illustration of how such abuses can manifest in both domains. As highlighted in the Lasserre Report: *"Abuse of economic dependence can also serve as an indicator of excessive data collection when it involves exchanges of personal data between companies. Indeed, this abuse is characterized by the excessive exploitation of a dependent relationship through abnormal, unbalanced, or excessive practices that directly or indirectly impose unfair transactional conditions.[45]"*

[43] Exploitative abuses are difficult to characterize in competition law and are the subject of controversies, particularly regarding the incentivizing effects of their sanction (see Werden 2021). However, they are observable in digital ecosystems where the pivot operator can exercise a private tax power due to its role as a gatekeeper and market organizer against its complementors. The Commission has sanctioned such practices, notably in the case of access to the App Store.

EU Commission, Apple – App Store Practices (music streaming), case AT.40437, 4 March 2024.

[44] Cass. Comm. 27 septembre 2023, n° 21–21.995.

[45] See Lasserre (2024), p. 22.

The implementation of the regulatory frameworks established by the European Digital Package—alongside earlier regulations such as the GDPR and the P2B Regulation—illustrates a potential convergence in the analytical approaches of various regulatory authorities (the Competition Authority, the DGCCRF, and the CNIL). This convergence arises from a shared focus on the fairness of competition, a central issue that underpins multiple regulatory objectives: safeguarding the competitive process, protecting consumer freedom of choice, ensuring balanced vertical relationships, and ultimately securing personal data against exploitative uses that could harm consumers—preventing what can be termed the weaponization of data.

These convergences can contribute to the competitiveness of firms by reducing the risk of inconsistent regulatory requirements across different authorities, as each integrates the objectives of the others. They may also help lower compliance costs and legal risks through the promotion of joint compliance programmes,[46] which become even more relevant as regulation increasingly incorporates voluntary corporate commitments, going beyond purely injunctive mechanisms.

4.2 *The Implications of the SREN Law Beyond the Integration of DMA and DSA Rules*

This subsection aims to briefly outline the additional responsibilities granted to French sectoral regulators under the SREN law. We will sequentially examine the new responsibilities of ARCEP (a), the CNIL (b), and Arcom (c).

4.2.1 The Missions Devoted to the ARCEP in the Cloud Sector Supervision

As noted above, Title II of the SREN law specifically addresses the cloud computing market. While the Competition Authority is responsible for enforcing the law in relation to self-preferencing practices, ARCEP, the Regulatory Authority for Electronic Communications, Postal Services, and Press Distribution (the successor of the Telecommunications Authority established in 1997), has been granted several responsibilities concerning the regulation of data intermediation providers and cloud services. Its actions are focused on preventing competitive lock-in situations for businesses using the aforementioned services.[47]

---

[46] See Lasserre (2024), p. 39.

[47] This point is present both in the opinion issued by the French Competition Authority following its sector inquiry into the cloud and in its opinion submitted to the government in April 2023 regarding the SREN bill (see French Competition Authority, opinion No. 23-A-05 of 20 April 2023 quoted above). The appeal of services provided by large vertically integrated digital operators (hyperscalers) means that users of cloud services have strong incentives to contract with them.

The goal is to enable the affected companies to switch from one provider to another without undue constraints and, if they wish, to adopt multi-hosting practices. The practices to be prevented involve anti-competitive lock-in phenomena, such as "credit clouds" and contractual clauses that force users into exclusive relationships. This is a well-known competition risk for complementors, which involves facilitating and subsidizing integration into an ecosystem to create a lock-in situation. From this point, these complementors would face sunk costs, making it impossible to exercise an exit option should the contractual terms deteriorate.[48]

In this regard, ARCEP must establish a regulatory framework designed to prevent undue obstacles to data portability and cloud system interoperability,[49] obstacles that can also be penalized by the Competition Authority under its mandate to sanction anti-competitive practices. Companies are required to implement technical procedures that ensure both of these objectives[50] and adopt cost-oriented pricing for services linked to them.[51] Finally, it should be noted that ARCEP can be called upon to resolve disputes related to cloud access contracts, can conduct investigations, and has sanctioning powers that could result in fines of up to 5% of the annual turnover of the companies involved in the case of repeated violations.[52]

Among the provisions introduced by the SREN law aimed at preventing lock-in phenomena are the limitation on the validity period of credit clouds, the prohibition of exclusivity clauses, and the conditioning of the sale of a specific service on the simultaneous conclusion of a cloud service contract, provided this conditioning constitutes an unfair commercial practice (Article 26 of the SREN law). The focus on unfair commercial practices clearly highlights that this is an issue of economic dependence i.e. practices potentially involving the abuse of economic dependence, for which the responsibilities are now shared between ARCEP, the Competition Authority, and the DGCCRF.

4.2.2 Additional Powers Devoted to the CNIL

CNIL has also seen its responsibilities expand within the framework of aligning European law with regulations related to the digital space, particularly through new tasks linked to the implementation of the Data Act and the Data Governance Act.

---

[48] See Marty and Warin (2023).

[49] See Vezzoso (2021).

[50] SREN law, art. 29.

[51] SREN law, art. 27.

Nevertheless, the focus on costs, particularly egress fees, is not self-evident in the digital world. As noted by the French Competition Authority in its April 2023 opinion (§79), the costs for providers associated with data transfers are essentially fixed costs related to the development, operation, and maintenance of bandwidth.

[52] SREN law, art. 30.

For instance, under the Data Governance Act (Article 26), CNIL is designated as the competent authority for managing the issue of data altruism.[53] Data altruism refers to the voluntary provision of data for public interest purposes. This provision must be based on the consent of the individuals concerned or on the authorization of data holders in the context of non-personal data.[54] The objective is to promote the flow of data and, in doing so, strengthen the competitiveness of the European economy while ensuring data protection. In this regard, the CNIL is granted new sanctioning powers in the event of non-compliance.

The SREN law also significantly extends the powers of the CNIL by modifying key parameters of the 1978 Data Protection Act (loi informatique et libertés, n° 78–17). This now includes the regulation of data processing carried out by entities located outside the European Union but targeting French users.

4.2.3 Additional Powers Attributed to Arcom

Arcom's responsibilities related to content have also been expanded through the provisions of SREN law.

On the one hand, its capacity to address problematic content has been strengthened. The areas under its jurisdiction include the regulation of pornographic content and content depicting acts of torture and barbarism (as defined under Article 221–1 of the Penal Code). For the former, the goal is to establish a general framework aimed at preventing minors from accessing such content and facilitating the rapid removal of such content. Non-compliance with the framework could result in access blocks[55] (without the need for a judicial decision[56]), removal of content by the affected online platforms,[57] and financial penalties in case of failure to respond to a formal notice.[58] For the latter, Arcom is granted experimental powers (for a 2-year

[53] SREN law, art. 57.

[54] In this regard, the CNIL manages the register of altruistic organizations in the field of data.

[55] SREN law, art. 2.

[56] A previous law from July 30, 2020, made a prior decision from the judiciary required.

[57] Article 3 of the SREN law allows Arcom to require app stores to make the loading of sanctioned apps impossible.

[58] Article 1 of the SREN law allows Arcom to require service providers and video-sharing platform providers to implement systems for verifying users' ages and protecting privacy. These verification mechanisms must undergo audits conducted by independent entities. Non-compliant behaviors with the regulator's requirements can lead to sanctions, which, in the case of repeated violations, may reach up to 4% of the concerned company's turnover. A key point regarding cooperation between regulatory authorities is that Arcom must seek the opinion of the CNIL before imposing any sanction. It is worth noting that cross-referencing by other authorities in the handling of cases is common in France. For instance, the French Competition Authority is consulted by the Energy Regulatory Commission regarding the setting of regulated electricity prices, Arcom was consulted by the Competition Authority for an opinion on Bouygues' proposed acquisition of the Métropole Télévision group (the TF1/M6 planned merger, eventually withdrawn), and the CNIL was consulted for an opinion in the Apple ATT procedure mentioned above.

period) to order the removal of such content from publishers and communication service providers.

On the other hand, its responsibilities related to combating disinformation and foreign interference aimed at manipulating information have been strengthened. Arcom now has the authority to instruct regulated firms to stop the dissemination of media subject to European sanctions within 72 h.[59]

5 Perspectives Related to Mergers Control

This fourth section focuses on the dynamics that could further adapt the competitive regulation of the digital sector, specifically considering the issue of merger control. We will sequentially examine the insufficiencies of ex-ante merger control in the digital sector (A) and the proposals by the Competition Authority to address the consequences of the restrictive interpretation of Article 22 of Regulation 139/2004, adopted by the Court of Justice in September 2024.

5.1 A Necessary Strengthening of Merger Control for Key Firms in Major Digital Ecosystems

One of the most debated aspects of strengthening potentially irreversible lock-in positions of dominance in the digital sector and extending them to related markets lies in the imperfect ex-ante merger control, both in the United States[60] and the EU.[61] The challenges faced by merger control stem from the difficulty in predicting the evolution of competitive dynamics in markets that are particularly complex and turbulent, as well as from the imperfect information framework within which competition authorities have to decide.[62] Specifically, these decisions and any corrective measures must be made within a 2- to 3-year evaluation period.

Competition authorities face several difficulties, including an information deficit ex-ante with respect to firms, the risk of moral hazard in the implementation of corrective measures, particularly behavioral remedies, and finally, the unpredictable evolution of markets.[63]

Ex-ante merger control therefore faces exacerbated difficulties in the digital sector, if it is even implemented. Indeed, ex-ante control is based on structural

---

[59] Failure to comply with this obligation would be sanctioned by a fine of up to 4% of the concerned company's turnover.

[60] See Kwoka (2014).

[61] See Valletti (2021).

[62] See Vezzoso and Kerber (2025)

[63] See Bougette et al. (2024).

thresholds. A transaction below these thresholds does not need to be notified. The existence of these thresholds is easily justified: they prevent overwhelming the authorities' processing capacities with transactions of little significance. However, in certain sectors, particularly digital, potential competitors that have not yet entered the market, or emerging competitors, can be acquired by dominant operators. These acquisitions are facilitated by the financial capabilities of these operators and the advantages they have in terms of advanced identification of opportunities and competitive threats, which are largely linked to the integration of these complementors into their ecosystems. The issue of the lack of control over acquisitions below these thresholds has been central to debates surrounding killer acquisitions, reverse-killer acquisitions, and consolidating acquisitions.[64]

The imperfections in control carry major competitive risks in terms of market foreclosure and the extension of dominant positions through leverage effects. The insufficiencies of ex-ante control thus harm the preservation of market contestability and the fairness of competition within ecosystems, as the incentives post-acquisition can be distorted for both the platform operator and the competitors of the acquired firm.

Despite these issues, the DMA does not provide any specific provisions regarding merger control, except for an obligation for firms designated as gatekeepers to inform the Commission about their acquisition plans.[65] This insufficiency has been addressed through an attempt to remediate by adopting a broad interpretation of Article 22 of Regulation 139/2004 concerning merger control, which allowed the Commission to intervene in transactions below the structural thresholds. The Article 22 route was opened by the Commission in September 2020. It enabled the transmission of transactions to the Commission that did not meet the ex-ante control thresholds in the concerned member states but raised competition concerns for the competition authorities.

5.2 *The Autorité de la Concurrence's Consultation Following the Court of Justice Judgement of September 2024*

The rejection of the broad interpretation of Article 22 by the Court of Justice in September 2024[66] prompted the French Competition Authority to consider the introduction of a merger control system targeting transactions that could harm competition

[64] See de Barsy and Gautier (2024).

[65] The DMA art. 14-1 states regarding the obligation to inform the Commission about concentrations: "A gatekeeper shall inform the Commission of any intended concentration within the meaning of Article 3 of Regulation (EC) No 139/2004, where the merging entities or the target of concentration provide core platform services or any other services in the digital sector or enable the collection of data, irrespective of whether it is notifiable to the Commission under that Regulation or to a competent national competition authority under national merger rules".

[66] Court of Justice, Judgment of 3 September 2024, Illumina Grail, cases C-611/22 et C-625/22P.

but do not meet the current notification thresholds. In this context, the Authority launched a public consultation in January 2025. The underlying rationale is to adapt national competition law to mitigate the consequences of the Court's ruling[67] by redefining the ex-ante review conditions for transactions falling below the existing thresholds[68] yet potentially having significant competitive effects.

The objective is therefore to adapt national competition law to address competition issues that are not covered by European regulations governing the digital sector, namely the DMA. In its consultation, the French Competition Authority sets out three options.

The first option is to establish a power of evocation, enabling the Authority to review a transaction even if it falls below the notification thresholds.[69] This evocation would be based on qualitative or quantitative criteria, such as the impact on competition or revenue thresholds. A mandatory notification mechanism would then be introduced.[70]

The second option would involve establishing specific thresholds for companies holding a particular market status, as determined in a previous decision by the European Commission or the French Competition Authority.[71] In other words, the conditions for merger control could be tailored to certain firms. The Authority distinguishes three scenarios:

1. A company that has previously faced a prohibition on a proposed external growth operation or received conditional approval.
2. A company that has been sanctioned for anticompetitive practices or has been subject to a decision imposing binding commitments.
3. A company designated as a gatekeeper under the DMA.

The third option proposed by the French Competition Authority involves implementing ex-post control based on the sanctioning of anticompetitive practices, following the logic of the *Towercast* ruling by the Court of Justice[72] and its decision of

---

[67] The French Competition Authority has already had the opportunity to dismiss, in previous public consultations (conducted in 2017 and 2018), solutions related to controls based on the transaction value (such as the Austrian and German models) or the reintroduction of threshold controls linked to market shares.

[68] These are defined in Article L.430–2 of the French Commerce code.

[69] Several member states have implemented mechanisms allowing them to consider public interest dimensions beyond competition concerns. In the French case, the Minister of the Economy can depart from a prior decision of the French Competition Authority by using their power of referral as defined in Article L.430–7-1 of the French Commercial Code. For a general analysis of the integration of public interest objectives in merger control, see: Budzinski and Stöhr (2021).

[70] Equivalent mechanisms already exist in Italy and other Member States.

[71] An equivalent mechanism also exists in Switzerland.

[72] EU Court of Justice, Case C-449/21, 16 March 2023, Towercast.

May 2, 2024, concerning practices in the rendering sector.[73] Unlike the other two options, this approach could be introduced without requiring legislative changes.[74]

The case of merger control highlights the need for national authorities to supplement the regulatory framework established at the European level. This issue is particularly relevant as it aims to address a gap in the DMA and the consequences of the Court of Justice's restrictive case-law approach.[75]

Among the proposed solutions, ex-post control is undoubtedly the most economically costly due to transaction costs and potential efficiency losses. The second option appears to be the most effective and entails less legal uncertainty than the first. It also complements the DMA well by shifting from a mere obligation to inform to a formal notification requirement. However, it raises concerns regarding the status of certain economic operators, given that French competition law lacks an equivalent to Germany's Article 19(a). This provision enables authorities to address systemic market power alongside absolute market power (individual dominance), collective market power (tacit collusion), and relative market power (asymmetric bargaining power).[76]

Such systemic market power can emerge within digital ecosystems due to the pivotal position of platform operators. Endowed with private regulatory power, these operators can shape the strategic choices of other market participants to their advantage—whether through self-preferencing, market foreclosure, or other exclusionary practices.

This example also illustrates the risks of internal market fragmentation, as different Member States pursue divergent regulatory initiatives.

6 Conclusion

The issues related to supplementing the DMA framework, as discussed in the previous section, illustrate the risks of internal market fragmentation as digital regulatory texts are implemented and further developed by national authorities. A second key challenge arises from the increasing regulatory complexity, both within each Member State and in the interactions between the European Commission and various national sectoral authorities. A third challenge concerns the growing hybridization of national authorities involved in the enforcement of these regulations and the need for effective coordination among them.

[73] Autorité de la concurrence, décision 24-D-05 du 02 mai 2024 relative à des pratiques mises en œuvre dans le secteur de l'équarrissage.

[74] Ex post control, which can lead to asset disposals, is often seen as carrying significant economic costs, although this assessment is debated in the literature. See for instance Kwoka and Valletti (2021).

[75] See Lindeboom (2025).

[76] See Budzinski and Stöhr (2024).

Hybridization here refers to the integration of multiple objectives traditionally associated with other regulatory authorities.[77] For instance, the French Competition Authority's consideration of data protection issues and the CNIL's growing attention to competition concerns illustrate this trend. While such cross-disciplinary approaches represent significant progress, they also introduce new challenges.

Coordination, in turn, requires the development of sophisticated institutional mechanisms and mutual commitments from each authority. The allocation of responsibilities may also generate transaction costs and create uncertainties for firms. However, enhanced coordination between authorities and the establishment of common compliance frameworks could gradually mitigate these risks and help address the challenges posed by regulatory silos.

More broadly, one of the key contributions of integrating European regulatory frameworks into French law is the dissemination of a common compliance culture across various regulatory requirements. This culture can be reinforced through commitment procedures, which are well established in competition law. A relevant example is the content moderation obligations derived from Article 49 of the DSA. In this context, the CNIL may accept commitments proposed by online platform providers to ensure compliance with regulatory obligations (Article 59). The CNIL's president also has the authority to render these commitments legally binding, even for a duration exceeding the initial proposal.

This compliance culture, facilitated by the convergence of regulatory frameworks, can be further strengthened through the implementation of automated audit mechanisms. Such systems would enable companies to proactively monitor their compliance, detect problematic content, and address market practices that could undermine the integrity of the competition process.

In this context, despite the inherent complexity of regulatory interventions and the multiplicity of regulatory actors, an ex-ante approach may be beneficial for firms. However, the dynamic issue lies in the rigidity of ex-ante rules, especially in a field characterized by rapid technological turbulence. The inclusion of provisions related to generative artificial intelligence in the AI Act,[78] as well as the withdrawal of the directive proposal on extracontractual liability for damages related to AI-incorporating services, highlights the intrinsic difficulty of regulating sectors that are particularly fast-evolving and complex.[79]

---

[77] Given that each authority already pursues composite objectives, whether related to sustainable development, competitiveness, or other factors, the integration of these diverse goals into regulatory frameworks can further complicate decision-making and coordination. See for a general view on the consideration of industrial policy based concerns by French regulatory authorities: See Glaser et al. (2024).

[78] Regulation (EU) 2024/1689 of the European Parliament and of the Council of 13 June 2024 laying down harmonised rules on artificial intelligence.

[79] See EU Commission (2025). Annex 4 of the Commission work programme announces the withdrawal of the proposed directive regarding the adoption of extracontractual civil liability related to AI (AI liability).

References

Arcom (2024) Press release from November 6 2024. https://www.arcom.fr/presse/mise-en-oeuvre-du-reglement-europeen-sur-les-services-numeriques-rsndsa-premiere-designation-dun-signaleur-de-confiance-e-enfance

Autorité de la concurrence and Bundeskartellamt (2016) Competition law and data, 10th May

Autorité de la concurrence et CNIL (2023) Concurrence et données personnelles: une ambition commune, 12 décembre

Barsy L de, Gautier A (2024) Big tech acquisitions and innovation: an empirical assessment. Cesifo Working Paper 11025

Bielova N et al (2024) The effect of design patterns on (present and future) cookie consent decisions. 33rd Usenix Security Symposium. https://www.usenix.org/conference/usenixsecurity24/presentation/bielova

Bougette P, Marty F (2025) Self-preferencing: an economic literature-based assessment advocating a case-by-case approach and compliance requirements. Competition Policy International Antitrust Chronicle

Bougette P, Budzinski O, Marty F (2019) Exploitative abuse and abuse of economic dependence: what can we learn from an industrial organization approach. Rev Econ Polit 129(2):261–286

Bougette P, Budzinski O, Marty F (2024) In the light of dynamic competition: should we make merger remedies more flexible? Eur Compet J. https://doi.org/10.1080/17441056.2024.2440228

Budzinski O (2025) Regulatory competition and platform companies: the economic perspective. In: Denga M, Hornuf L (eds) Regulatory competition in the digital economy – artificial intelligence, data, and platforms. Springer, pp 175–188

Budzinski O, Stöhr A (2021) Public interest considerations in European merger control regimes. In: Gal M, Bosco D (eds) Challenges to assumptions in competition law. Edward Elgar, pp 184–205

Budzinski O, Stöhr A (2024) Dynamic competition exclusionary and exploitative abuses, and Article 102 TFEU: towards a concept of systemic market power? Concurrences

Denis M-L (2022) Protection des données et concurrence dans l'économie numérique. Intervention devant le collège de l'Autorité de la concurrence, CNIL, 21 novembre

EU Commission (2017) Final report on the E-commerce Sector Inquiry. COM(2017) 229 final, 10th May

EU Commission (2024) Draft antitrust guidelines on exclusionary abuses, 1st August

EU Commission (2025) Commission work programme 2025. https://commission.europa.eu/strategy-and-policy/strategy-documents/commission-work-programme/commission-work-programme-2025_en

Ezrachi A, Stucke M (2022) Behavioural study on unfair commercial practices in the digital environment: dark patterns and manipulative personalisation. EU Commission report

Glaser E et al (2024) Le rôle des régulations sectorielles dans la mise en œuvre d'une politique industrielle européenne. Les Cahiers de Droit de l'Entreprise, dossier Régulation et Politique Industrielle 6:25–35

Kwoka J (2014) Mergers, merger control, and remedies: a retrospective analysis of US policy. MIT Press

Kwoka J, Valletti T (2021) Unscrambling the eggs: breaking up consummated mergers and dominant firms. Ind Corp Chang 30(5):1286–1306

Lasserre B (2024) Conclusions de la mission de réflexion portant sur l'articulation entre protection des données et concurrence. CNIL, 28 novembre

Lindeboom J (2025) Illumina/grail: flawed originalism and the judicial hunch. J Antitrust Enforc 13:223

Marty F, Warin T (2023) Multi-sided platforms and innovation: A competition law perspective. Comp Change 27(1):184–204

Valletti T (2021) How to tame the tech giants: reverse the burden of proof in merger reviews. ProMarket, 28th June

Vezzoso S (2021) Data portability: initial reflections on an ex ante approach. In: Viscasilla MP et al (eds) The digital economy-regulatory, contractual and competition aspects. Tirant lo Blanch, pp 163–177

Vezzoso S, Kerber W (2025) Competition and innovation: incorporating a more dynamic perspective into enforcement. In: First H (ed) Liber Amicorum. (in press)

Werden GJ (2021) Exploitative abuse of a dominant position: a bad idea that now should be abandoned. Eur Comp J 17(3):682–713

Frédéric Marty is a CNRS research director. PhD in economics, his work focuses on competition law and economics. He is a member of the Group of Research on Law, Economics, and Management (GREDEG), a join research unit of the CNRS and of the Université Côte d'Azur.

The Spanish Approach to Digital Regulation: From GSM to DSA/DMA

Néstor Duch-Brown and Estela Fernández López

Contents

Abstract This chapter examines the development of regulatory frameworks for two key areas in Spain, spanning from the 1980s to the latest EU initiatives. Initially, we provide an overview of the regulatory landscape for telecommunications and

---

Joint Research Centre, European Commission. Errors and omissions are the sole responsibility of the authors. The views expressed here are purely those of the authors' and may not in any circumstances be regarded as stating an official position of the European Commission.

N. Duch-Brown (✉)
Joint Research Centre, European Commission, Brussels, Belgium
e-mail: nestor.duch-brown@ec.europa.eu

E. F. López
University Carlos III, Madrid, Spain
e-mail: estela.f.lopez@alumnos.uc3m.es

F. Decarolis et al. (eds.), *The EU Digital Regulation and its Impact on Member States*, European Union and its Neighbours in a Globalized World 27,
https://doi.org/10.1007/978-3-032-06490-5_11

contrast its primary features with those of the newly introduced Digital Markets Act (DMA). Next, we trace the evolution of regulatory measures targeting information society services, beginning with an analysis of the e-commerce directive (ECD) and its implementation in Spain, followed by an examination of the Digital Services Act (DSA) and its potential implications for Spanish regulation. As the current regulatory framework is still in its early stages, we investigate the potential influence of case law on shaping the trajectory of these new regulations, drawing on historical precedents that have significantly impacted the development of previous regulatory frameworks. Furthermore, we investigate the institutions established to oversee these regulations, outlining the evolution of the organizational structure and discussing unresolved issues related to their effectiveness. Finally, we compare the initial approaches to regulating telecommunications and information society services with the recent EU initiatives, highlighting a significant paradigm shift towards a more proactive and interventionist approach, characterized by a move away from minimal, ex-post intervention and towards a more comprehensive and forward-looking regulatory strategy. We contend that as the digital transformation increasingly defines the economic, social, and political contours of the European Union, the regulatory approach has assumed greater importance and breadth, extending beyond traditional digital ecosystem domains.

1 Introduction

The liberalization of telecommunications in Spain, which began in the late 1980s, not only coincides in time with the country's entry into the European integration process but was crucial for creating a competitive market environment. The liberalization of the Spanish telecommunications sector was influenced significantly by European Union policies aimed at creating a competitive and integrated telecommunications market across Europe. Despite initial resistance, Spain adapted its laws to align with EU directives, leading to significant changes in the market landscape. This process dismantled the state monopoly and allowed new entrants to offer services, leading to improved infrastructure, lower prices, and better services. Liberalization encouraged investments in mobile networks and internet connectivity, which were foundational for the development of online services.

During the early days, the Internet emerged as a separate system from traditional telecommunications networks. Initially, the Internet relied on leased telephone lines for data transmission. These lines were dedicated and, unlike the circuit-switched system of telecommunications, which established a dedicated path for each call, the Internet used packet-switching, a method of breaking data into smaller packets that would travel across various routes, making the Internet more efficient and flexible than traditional telephone systems designed primarily for voice communication.

The rapid development and proliferation of digital technologies and the Internet paved the way for the emergence of information society services. These technologies enabled the creation, storage, and transmission of digital information on a large scale. The widespread adoption of the Internet provided a global platform for communication and information exchange, which allowed for the delivery of a wide range of services online, from e-commerce and online banking to digital media and social networking. As people became more familiar with digital technologies, there was an increasing demand for convenient, accessible, and efficient services. This demand drove the growth of information society services, as businesses sought to meet consumers' needs in areas such as communication, entertainment, and shopping, among others.

These goods and services were delivered directly over the Internet, bypassing traditional distribution methods, and the companies behind providing them were called over-the-top (OTT) service providers. OTT providers operate by hosting their content on their own servers or cloud platforms, accessible to users via Internet-connected devices. They employ content delivery networks (CDNs) to optimize performance, ensuring fast and reliable access to content regardless of user location. The rise of OTT services delivering content and services over the Internet, independent of traditional telecom networks, challenged existing regulatory frameworks and business models.

The distinction between the telecommunications network and the Internet as two separate dimensions, despite the technological convergence allowing the exact same type of information to be transmitted by either of the two, has also had important consequences in the way regulation has approached these activities. Today, we have a two-layered regulatory approach. On the one hand, telecommunication law handles the regulation of the carrier, essentially the infrastructure that allows the signals to be transmitted across the nodes of the network. On the other, information society or electronic commerce laws regulate the content that circulates through the network.

In this chapter, we look at the evolution of the regulation of these two elements in Spain, starting from the 1980s until the initiatives recently adopted by the European Union. First, we offer a brief overview of telecommunications regulation, and we compare its main characteristics with the recently adopted Digital Markets Act (DMA).[1] Second, we look at the evolution of the regulatory measures that have focused on information society services. Here, we first describe the role of the e-commerce directive (ECD) and its transposition in Spain. We then describe the recently adopted Digital Services Act (DSA)[2] and we identify the possible impacts it may have on the Spanish regulation. Third, as the current regulatory framework is relatively new, we delve into the possible effects that case law may have on the determination of the direction of these new regulations. In order to support our arguments, we rely on past examples that have had a decisive role in the evolution of the old regulatory frameworks. Fourth, we look at the institutions that were created to handle these regulations, we describe the evolution of the organisational setting and

[1] European Union (2022a), pp. 1–66.

[2] European Union (2022b), pp. 1–102.

discuss open issues regarding its efficiency. Fifth, we compare the early approaches to telecommunications and information society services regulations with the recently introduced initiatives by the European Union. We signal an important shift in the way these regulations are framed: they move from minimal ex-post intervention with a strong promotional effort, towards a positive, proactive, and more interventionist approach. We argue that as the digital transformation increasingly delineates the economic, social, and political dimensions of the European Union, the regulatory strategy has also gained greater significance and an enlarged scope. Hence, the new strategy goes beyond the traditional domains of the digital ecosystem.

2 From Telecommunication Regulation to the DMA

Although initially seemingly unrelated, there are relevant similarities between the more traditional telecommunications regulation and the recently enacted Digital Markets Act (DMA), as both instruments govern specific markets. The DMA is a significant piece of legislation enacted by the European Union (EU) to regulate digital markets, with a focus on large online platforms. It represents a broader effort within the EU to ensure fair competition and to address issues that traditional telecommunications regulations might not fully cover. On the other hand, traditional telecommunications regulation in Europe has primarily focused on regulating telecommunication markets, ensuring competition, consumer protection, and universal service within the telecommunications sector, including Internet service providers and mobile operators. The DMA extends these principles to the digital space, targeting large digital platforms, known as "gatekeepers," which control access to digital markets. The goal is to prevent anti-competitive practices and ensure a level playing field.

Telecommunications regulations historically dealt with physical infrastructure and service provision, ensuring that new entrants could compete with established operators (Fransman 2001). In contrast, the DMA addresses the digital ecosystem, where platforms like search engines, social media, and app stores can dominate. The act seeks to prevent these platforms from abusing their dominant positions, much like how telecom regulations prevent monopolistic practices. The enforcement mechanisms differ slightly due to the nature of the markets (Hernández López 2023). One important difference is that telecommunications regulations are typically enforced by national regulatory authorities, while the DMA provides the European Commission with direct enforcement powers over digital platforms. This centralization reflects the cross-border nature of digital services.

2.1 Telecom Regulation in Spain

Much has been written about the Spanish telecommunication sector and the evolution of its regulatory framework (see, for instance, Calzada et al. 2018; Martínez Soler 1998; Nadal 1995; Otero 2019; Rodríguez 2021). Hence, we will keep this section short and go over the most relevant aspects that connect it with the DMA as in Otero (2023).

Since the early 1990s, telecommunications services have been subject to extensive regulatory intervention. Initially, most countries were characterized by a market structure dominated by a single company, often with some degree of public ownership. This monopolistic setup was safeguarded and regulated directly by public administrations. In Spain, for example, Telefónica operated under a concession agreement with the State, exemplifying this model. In this context, economic literature emphasized the natural monopoly characteristics of telecommunications and explored ways to facilitate the entry of new competitors to enhance effective competition (Berg and Tschirhart 1988). A critical aspect of this discussion was the design of optimal tariffs to balance consumer interests and incentivize market participation (Hauge and Sappington 2010).

Three decades later, the liberalization of telecommunications is widely recognized as a successful process. Services are now provided on an arm's length basis, with retail activities largely free from price or other regulations. Regulatory intervention is now focused mainly on specific wholesale activities of the main operator, as many initial interventions have been phased out. Despite these advancements, the sector remains concentrated, presenting new regulatory challenges to ensure ongoing competition and innovation.

The liberalization model in telecommunications contrasts sharply with that of the other sectors—particularly energy—which have typically involved vertical disintegration and stringent regulation of transmission and distribution. In contrast, the telecommunications sector opted to facilitate non-discriminatory access to the incumbent's network, which remains vertically integrated. This approach was paired with regulatory incentives for new entrants to deploy network components and even establish parallel networks. This strategy has been particularly important as regulators address the need to deploy new high-capacity access networks.

Moreover, unlike homogeneous goods like electricity, telecommunications services encompass a variety of distinct options. These differentiated services are subject not only to significant economies of scale inherent in network sectors but also to economies of scope due to shared costs between services. Differentiation can be evident, such as between fixed and mobile telecommunications, or more nuanced, like variations in transmission content (voice, data) or quality, such as Internet speed. The distinct nature of telecommunications products has significant implications for competition and regulatory design, requiring tailored approaches to foster fair competition and innovation.

Telecommunications regulation in Spain is closely aligned with European regulatory frameworks. The General Telecommunications Law (LGT) of 2003[3] implemented the EU's regulatory framework, consolidating the liberalization process initiated in the late 1980s. The new LGT passed in 2014[4] further updated this framework with the directives adopted in 2009, further refined by the 2018 European Electronic Communications Code.[5] This code consolidated previous directives and was finally transposed to Spanish legislation in 2022.[6] This regulatory framework, alongside initiatives like the European Commission's Digital Agenda and Digital Single Market, has created a harmonized environment for telecommunications across the EU.

Moreover, the implementation of competition policy has significantly influenced the telecommunications sector, complementing sectoral regulations. This complementarity is evident in the interplay between ex ante regulatory measures and antitrust policies, particularly concerning anti-competitive practices and merger control. This relationship is expected to strengthen with the European Commission's new guidance for monitoring activities under the Digital Markets Act, further shaping the regulatory landscape to address the evolving challenges in digital markets.

The liberalisation of telecommunications activities required the creation of an independent sectoral regulator. In Spain, the national regulatory agency (NRA) was originally the *Comisión del Mercado de las Telecomunicaciones* (CMT) established in 1996. As will be explained later, the Spanish government decided to merge all regulatory agencies and the competition authority into the single institution in 2013, creating the *Comisión Nacional de los Mercados y la Competencia* (CNMC), which is the institution that oversees telecommunications regulation, among other activities. Alongside the CNMC, the *Ministry for Digital Transformation and Civil Service* (Ministerio para la Transformación Digital y de la Función Pública) plays a vital role in the regulatory framework. European legislation outlines a basic set of tasks for NRAs, leading to variations in their competences. A significant distinction in Spain is that spectrum management is handled by the Ministry rather than the CNMC, which in turn is tasked with developing obligations, resolving disputes between operators and other stakeholders, managing portability conditions and universal service, among others.

---

[3] Spain (2003), pp. 38890–38924.

[4] Spain (2014), pp. 35824–35938.

[5] European Union (2018)), pp. 36–214.

[6] Spain (2022a), pp. 91253–91411.

2.2 The Digital Markets Act

In recent years, a small group of OTTs gained significant size and dominance in some of the new digital markets that emerged with the Internet. Until recently, European countries and the European Commission dealt with various cases of abuse of dominance against these platforms through competition law. The difficulty and duration of these cases led to a collective reflection on the need for a more agile *ex-ante* regulatory tool to address the competition problems of these platforms (Vida Fernández 2021).

This is why in December 2020, the European Commission proposed the Digital Markets Act (DMA) which, following a complex debate, was adopted in November 2022. This initiative is one of the first *ex ante* regulations imposed on large digital platforms. The main objective of the DMA is to regulate the behaviour of large companies to ensure a level playing field in European digital markets.

The DMA is reminiscent of ex-ante regulation of telecommunications markets, where core services correspond to relevant markets, gatekeepers to operators with significant market power, and the obligations imposed are, in some ways, equivalent.

The DMA defines eight services where there are digital platforms that have a dominant position. The eight services, called core platform services (CPS) are: (i) online search engines; (ii) online intermediation services; (iii) social media; (iv) video-sharing platforms; (v) communication platforms; (vi) advertising services; (vii) operating systems; and (viii) cloud services. For each of these CPS, different digital platforms have been designated as gatekeepers.[7] These are defined as companies that have a strong economic position, a significant impact on the internal market and activities in many EU countries.[8] However, even if the above thresholds are met, the designation as a gatekeeper is not automatic, since an operator could reasonably oppose its designation and the European Commission will have to make a decision following a market investigation. Similarly, the European Commission can initiate an ex officio market investigation and designate gatekeepers that do not meet the above thresholds.

[7] On 6 September 2023 the European Commission designated six gatekeepers: Alphabet, Amazon, Apple, ByteDance, Meta, and Microsoft. On 29 April 2024, the Commission designated Apple with respect to its iPadOS, its operating system for tablets, as a gatekeeper under the DMA. On 13 May 2024, the Commission also designated Booking. In total, 24 core platform services provided by those gatekeepers have been designated until February 2025. More information at: https://digital-markets-act.ec.europa.eu/gatekeepers_en

[8] The thresholds established for designations require that they have an EU annual turnover of at least EUR 7500 billion (at group level) in each of the last 3 years (or average market capitalisation above EUR 75,000 billion in the last year), and that they offer the same CPS in at least three EU Member States. In addition, they should have a strong position as an intermediary platform, allowing it to connect a wide user base with a large number of companies, including at least 45 million monthly active end users and at least 10,000 business users active annually in the EU in the last year. Finally, gatekeepers should have an entrenched and durable position on the market, i.e., the thresholds laid down in the two previous criteria were exceeded in the last 3 years.

Once a CPS provider is designated as a gatekeeper, it has 6 months to fulfil the obligations included in Articles 5, 6 and 7 of the DMA. While in principle they should implement all the obligations, some must be directly implemented (Article 5), whereas the rest can be further specified in a dialogue between the Commission and the gatekeeper (Articles 6 and 7). Some obligations apply horizontally to all CPS, while others are clearly designed for specific types of CPS (e.g. online intermediation services, online advertising services, etc.).[9] Furthermore, emerging gatekeepers, which do not yet enjoy an entrenched and durable position but will reach it in the near future, are only subject to a subset of obligations specifically designed to prevent them from reaching a market tipping position.

Unlike telecommunications regulation, the European Commission will be responsible for implementing and enforcing the DMA.[10] The Commission has extensive powers, including requesting information—covering access to company data and algorithms—, conducting interviews and hearing natural or legal persons, carrying out on-site inspections—including access to IT systems, algorithms and business and data processing behaviour—ordering, "in case of urgency due to the risk of serious and irreparable damage" for users, interim measures against a gatekeeper on the basis of a "prima facie finding of an infringement of Articles 5, 6, and 7", and making the commitments offered by the gatekeeper in question binding by means of a decision.

The Commission must 'endeavour' to adopt its non-compliance decision within 12 months of the opening of the procedure. Before adopting a decision, the Commission must communicate to the gatekeeper its preliminary findings, together with an explanation of the measures that would be necessary to address them. At the same time, gatekeepers have the right to be heard on these preliminary findings. The Commission's non-compliance decision will force the gatekeeper to bring the infringement to an end and explain the measures it intends to take to comply with the decision.

The European Commission's decision may impose fines of up to 10% of the gatekeeper's overall annual turnover. However, if the latter commits the same or a similar infringement concerning the same CPS within 8 years, a higher maximum threshold of 20% of the overall annual turnover applies. Lower fines, up to 1% of the overall annual turnover, are also stipulated for less serious infringements, such as failing to notify the Commission when quantitative thresholds are reached.

The Commission shall determine the amount of the fine taking into account the 'gravity, duration and recurrence' of the infringement. In some cases, the Commission may also impose periodic penalty payments of up to 5% of the overall

---

[9] Most of these practices often stem from relevant competition cases in recent years. It could therefore be argued that the DMA uses 'ex post' cases to create new 'ex ante' rules and seeks to tackle identified problems related to anti-competitive practices at the root.

[10] According to the official documentation: "The European Commission is the sole enforcer of the DMA. A joint team in the Directorates-General for Competition (DG COMP) and Communications Networks, Content and Technology (DG CONNECT) is responsible for the implementation and enforcement of the DMA." See https://digital-markets-act.ec.europa.eu/index_en

average daily turnover. This could be done, for example, to force the gatekeeper to comply with the provisional measures ordered by the Commission.

While the Commission will be the institution responsible for enforcing the DMA, it will be assisted by different authorities and bodies: the Digital Markets Advisory Committee (DMAC), composed of representatives of EU Member States; national competition authorities (NCAs); and the DMA High Level Group, composed of 30 representatives from the following regulatory bodies: Body of European Regulators for Electronic Communications (BEREC), European Data Protection Supervisor (EDPS), European Data Protection Board (EDPB), European Competition Network (ECN), Consumer Protection Cooperation Network (CPCN), and European Regulatory Group of Audiovisual Media Regulators (ERGA). Both the Spain's Ministry of Economic Affairs and Digital Transformation and the Spanish Competition Authority participate in the DMAC.

The DMA complements and applies without prejudice to competition rules. However, the application of national or EU competition rules by national competition authorities cannot 'go against' a Commission decision adopted under the DMA. Therefore, the DMA includes provisions on cooperation and coordination between the Commission and NCAs through the European Competition Network (ECN), which is a cooperation mechanism between the European Commission and the national competition authorities in all EU Member States.

The DMA is conceptually simple: large digital platforms will be subject to a number of obligations and prohibitions for pre-determined digital services. However, implementation will be intricate. The obligations to be implemented are, in many cases, highly technically complex and the well-known asymmetry of information between the regulated entity and the regulator is particularly relevant in the case of large digital platforms.

In summary, there is no doubt that the DMA represents a major regulatory milestone at a global level, which will pose all kinds of challenges in its implementation. For the first time, an ex-ante regulatory regime is put in place to apply to large digital platforms. However, it should be recalled that the regulation of the telecommunications sector required the creation of independent national regulatory authorities with highly specialised staff, which became more effective as experience was gained. The regulation was refined over time, so it seems reasonable to expect similar developments in the practical implementation of the DMA, which is in its very early stages of deployment. In this case, in addition, the European Commission will be responsible for implementing the DMA,[11] which is a relevant development in relation to the decentralised model of regulation of the Telco sector.

[11] Without prejudice, as explained above, to the advisory functions of the different support groups composed of Member States, competition authorities and national regulators.

3 From the E-Commerce Directive to the DSA

The development and deployment of the Internet opened new ways to communicate and exchange information. In addition, it created new markets and economic activities that would eventually disrupt traditional industries. In the early phases of the adoption of these new technologies, the public sector's efforts were directed toward promoting the so-called "information society" (Feijóo et al. 2007). The extraordinary expansion of electronic communications networks, and in particular the Internet, and its incorporation into economic life and commercial activity, made it necessary to establish an appropriate legal framework that would give all the actors involved the confidence and legal certainty needed to use this new medium.

E-commerce emerged as a key driver of the Internet, offering numerous benefits such as speed, cost-efficiency, and global reach. In the 1990s, as the concept was new, there was a high demand for secure communication, safe payment services, and authentication, robust logistics, customer relationship software, and effective online advertising, among others. While some American companies thrived internationally, European businesses struggled and often had a more national focus. The European Commission proposed the e-Commerce Directive in 2000[12] to promote e-commerce across Europe, introducing the 'country of origin' principle and addressing liability issues related to illegal digital content through a 'notice and takedown' provision. The Directive allowed EU-based websites to sell across the region without additional formalities, but its liability provisions for illegal content were contentious.

Before that, there was no regulation or public management in this area in Spain, beyond what Telefónica itself, as an undertaking, could develop. The first telecommunications regulation in Spain was enacted in 1987, after the creation of the Directorate-General for Telecommunications that took place in 1985.[13] Since then, the public intervention in the area of telecommunications and information society has grown slowly and timidly, especially in the early years, progressively defining its own objectives (Nadal 1995; Soto et al. 2003). Telefónica, on the contrary, articulated its own development strategy also including considerations of public interest (Martínez Soler 1998; Jordana 1999). In any case, many of the activities that have since been carried out by the public sector were the result of some new developments and programmes promoted by the European Commission.[14]

---

[12] European Union (2000), pp. 1–16.

[13] The *Dirección General de Telecomunicaciones* was created in 1985 under the *Ministry of Public Works, Transport and Environment* (Ministerio de Obras Públicas, Transportes y Medio Ambiente). After a sequence of modifications due to changing governments, it has been renamed to *Secretary of State for Telecommunications and Digital Infrastructures* (Secretaría de Estado de Telecomunicaciones e Infraestructuras Digitales) under the *Ministry for Digital Transformation and Civil Service* (Ministerio para la Transformación Digital y de la Función Pública).

[14] An important exception to the situation described was the information society promotion activities initiated by the GSC, including the PISTA programme (Promotion and Identification of

3.1 The LSSI

In Spain, Law 34/2002 of 11 July on Information Society Services and Electronic Commerce (LSSI)[15] established the legal framework to ensure that commercial activities via the Internet are treated in the same way as similar activities carried out in the physical environment. It applies to Internet activities that are part of an economic activity, while excluding those that can be considered non-profit.[16]

The LSSI transposes into Spanish law Directive 2000/31/EC of the European Parliament and of the Council, which regulates certain legal aspects of Information Society Services,[17] in particular those relating to electronic commerce. The LSSI, in this regard, provides intermediary service providers, businesses offering their products or services online, and citizens holding a website with the necessary rules to ensure that the use and enjoyment of this network, as well as the potential economic activity generated around the purchase and sale of all types of products and services, are a positive, safe and trusted experience.

The LSSI is not the only rule governing commercial activities on the Internet. Depending on the specific nature of the online activities, other legal instruments would also be involved, such as Organic Law 3/2018 on the Protection of Personal Data and the Guarantee of Digital Rights,[18] which adapts the EU's General Data Protection Regulation (GDPR)[19] to Spanish law. Similarly, Royal Legislative Decree 1/2007 of 16 November 2015 on Consumer Protection and other complementary laws (TRLGDCU),[20] Directive (EU) 2015/2366 of the European Parliament and of the Council on payment services in the internal market;[21] Royal Decree-Law 19/2018 of 23 November 2015 on payment services and other urgent financial measures;[22] Law 7/1998, of 13 April, on general contract conditions[23]; Law 7/1996, of 15 January, regulating Retail Trade;[24] and finally, Royal Decree 3423/2000, of 15

Emerging Advanced Telecommunication Services) launched in 1996, with various lines of action defined in different areas of intervention (Nistal 1999).

[15] This is the abbreviated version of the full acronym LSSI-CE that comes from its name in Spanish, *Ley de Servicios de la Sociedad de la Información y de Comercio Electrónico*. https://www.boe.es/buscar/act.php?id=BOE-A-2002-13758

[16] For interesting early analysis of the law, see Boix Palop (2003), Campillos González (2001) and Jimena Quesada (2003).

[17] European Union (2000).

[18] Spain (2018a).

[19] European Union (2016), pp. 1–88.

[20] Spain (2007).

[21] European Union (2015a), pp. 35–127.

[22] Spain (2018b), pp. 114474–114568.

[23] Spain (1998).

[24] Spain (1996).

December, regulating the price labelling of products offered to consumers and users,[25] are also applicable.

The LSSI grants the Ministry for Digital Transformation and Civil Service (Ministerio para la Transformación Digital y de la Función Pública) the supervisory and control functions of the Information Society. In this control function, the Ministry may carry out the necessary inspection activities. Similarly, the power to impose penalties lies within the same Ministry through the Secretary of State for Digitalisation and Artificial Intelligence, except in the case it is related to commercial electronic communications (Articles 21 and 22), for which the Spanish Data Protection Agency has the power to impose penalties; and Article 38.2 (b)—for example, the Intellectual Property Commission.[26]

The power to impose penalties shall be exercised in accordance with the provisions of Law 39/2015 of 1 October 2015 on the Common Administrative Procedure of Public Administrations and its implementing rules. However, unlike the general scheme, the maximum duration of the simplified procedure for minor infringements shall be 3 months.

The enforcement of the LSSI in Spain involves multiple authorities, each responsible for different aspects of the law. First, the Agencia Española de Protección de Datos (AEPD) is responsible for enforcing data protection aspects of the LSSI, particularly concerning the use of personal data in electronic communications and privacy compliance. The State Secretariat for Digitalization and Artificial Intelligence (Secretaría de Estado de Digitalización e Inteligencia Artificial), part of the Ministry for Digital Transformation and Civil Service (Ministerio para la Transformación Digital y de la Función Pública), oversees the general application of the LSSI, including issues related to e-commerce and information society services. In addition, regional and national consumer protection agencies may also be involved in enforcing provisions related to consumer rights and unfair commercial practices as outlined in the LSSI. The CNMC can play a role in cases where LSSI intersects with market regulation and competition laws, particularly in the audiovisual sector. Depending on the nature of the service or specific issues arising under the LSSI, other sector-specific regulatory bodies might be involved, particularly where specific industries are affected. These authorities work together to ensure compliance with the LSSI, each focusing on their areas of expertise and jurisdiction. They may conduct investigations, impose sanctions, and provide guidance on compliance with the law.

[25] Spain (2000).

[26] The Intellectual Property Commission (CPI) is a collegiate body at the national level, attached to the Ministry of Culture and Sport, which is created to exercise the functions of mediation, arbitration, determination of rates, control of rates and safeguarding of intellectual property rights. It will also exercise advisory functions on any matters within its competence that are consulted by the Ministry of Culture and Sport. https://www.cultura.gob.es/cultura/propiedadintelectual/informacion-general/gestion-en-el-ministerio/comision-propiedad-intelectual.html

3.2 *The LSSI and the E-Commerce Directive*

The E-commerce Directive (ECD)[27] was established by the European Union to create a legal framework for electronic commerce within the internal market. It aims to ensure the free movement of information society services between EU Member States.

The ECD provides a broad framework by defining "information society services" as any service normally provided for remuneration at a distance, by electronic means, and at the individual request of a recipient. The LSSI incorporates this definition but uses specific Spanish legal terminology and includes additional clarifications to ensure that the definition is fully integrated with national legal concepts. This explicitly includes listing services considered part of the information society, such as online sales, advertising, and professional services offered electronically.

The ECD requires service providers to provide clear, comprehensive, and easily accessible information about their identity and terms of service. The LSSI aligns with this requirement but imposes additional obligations, such as mandatory registration or notification to national authorities for certain types of services. It specifies that information must be available before the conclusion of a contract, reflecting Spain's consumer protection standards.

In terms of commercial communications, the ECD sets out rules for unsolicited communications, requiring that they be clearly identifiable as such and providing opt-out mechanisms. However, the LSSI goes further by requiring explicit prior consent (opt-in) for sending promotional communications, which reflects a stricter stance on consumer consent compared to the directive's opt-out approach. This aligns with Spain's relatively robust data protection and privacy regime.

Both frameworks address the liability of intermediaries like Internet Service Providers (ISPs), caching services, and hosting providers. On the one hand, the ECD establishes conditions under which intermediaries (like ISPs, caching services, and hosting providers) are exempt from liability, provided they do not have knowledge of illegal content. On the other hand, while the LSSI closely follows these provisions, it adapts them to fit into the Spanish legal context, addressing issues such as the process for notification and takedown of illegal content and clarifying the responsibilities and duties of intermediaries in more detail.

The directive encourages the development of codes of conduct for certain areas of e-commerce to help implement the directive's principles effectively. The LSSI supports this provision, promoting the creation of codes of conduct specifically adapted to Spanish industry sectors. It may also require adherence to existing national codes, ensuring alignment with broader Spanish regulatory practices.

The ECD provides for cooperation between Member States and sets basic principles for legal remedies. The LSSI details mechanisms for legal redress, such as court action or administrative complaints, and specifies the roles of national authorities in enforcing the law. The LSSI often includes more comprehensive procedures for cooperation with other EU countries, reflecting Spain's administrative structure.

---

[27] European Union (2000).

Spain's transposition places a strong emphasis on consumer protection, sometimes going beyond the broad guidelines of the directive by adding more specific protections. The ECD focuses on ensuring transparency and fairness in e-commerce but leaves specific consumer protection measures to Member States. The Spanish approach has been to adopt stricter consumer protection measures, such as detailed requirements for contract formation, information disclosure, and consumer rights related to withdrawal and refunds.

The ECD introduces the country of origin principle, meaning that service providers are subject to the law of the Member State in which they are established. The LSSI integrates this principle providing additional detail on its application within Spain, ensuring clarity on jurisdictional issues, as well as how Spanish courts interpret and apply this principle in cross-border disputes.

3.3 Updating the Rules: The Expected Effects of the DSA

The Digital Services Act (DSA), part of the EU's broader digital strategy, aims to modernize the legal framework for digital services across the EU. It seeks to address challenges related to online platforms, especially large ones, focusing on transparency, accountability, and consumer protection. As an EU regulation, it is directly applicable in all Member States, including Spain, and national laws like the LSSI will require adjustments to ensure consistency and compliance with the new EU standards (Rodríguez de las Heras, 2021).

Although the DSA updates only some aspects of the E-commerce Directive, several elements of the LSSI will need to be revised. First, the DSA introduces new rules on the liability of online intermediaries, including clearer obligations for platforms to act against illegal content. Spain will have to adjust some LSSI provisions to align with these new liability frameworks, particularly regarding notification and action processes.

The DSA also demands greater transparency from online platforms, especially concerning algorithms and advertising. The LSSI might be updated to incorporate these requirements, ensuring that Spanish law reflects the EU's emphasis on platform accountability and transparency. The DSA strengthens consumer protection in digital environments. Spain may need to update its consumer protection provisions in the LSSI to ensure they meet the new standards, particularly regarding user rights and redress mechanisms.

The DSA imposes specific obligations on very large online platforms, such as risk assessments and the implementation of systemic risk mitigation measures. The LSSI might incorporate or reference these obligations to ensure comprehensive coverage of VLOPs operating in Spain. However, no VLOP or VLOSE has its European headquarters in Spain. The DSA introduces crisis protocols for platforms during extraordinary circumstances (e.g., pandemics or other crises). Spain might need to consider how these protocols integrate with national emergency frameworks and reflect this in the LSSI.

The DSA emphasizes cooperation among EU Member States and the European Commission for enforcement. Spain will likely need to enhance its mechanisms for collaboration, potentially requiring procedural updates in the LSSI. In this respect, the DSA proposes establishing national Digital Services Coordinators (DSC). The Spanish government has designated the CNMC as the DSC. This responsibility includes ensuring coordination, supervision, and consistent compliance with the DSA in Spain. The DSA grants the DSC broad powers of supervision, investigation, and sanction over service providers established in Spain. This includes the ability to request access to data and algorithmic systems for content moderation and advertising recommendations, as well as the authority to conduct inspections and impose fines on intermediaries in case of regulation violations. In addition, the CNMC will also be responsible for certifying "trusted flaggers" (preferred entities for reporting illegal content) and extrajudicial bodies for dispute resolution. However, on 16 December 2024, the European Commission decided to open infringement procedures by sending letters of formal notice to six Member States, including Spain, as they have designated their Digital Services Coordinators but have yet to empower them with the necessary powers and competences to carry out their tasks, including the imposition of sanctions in cases of non-compliance.

The implementation of the DSA will require careful coordination to ensure that national laws, like the LSSI and other relevant legislation, are aligned with EU regulations while respecting Spain's legal and administrative context. This process will involve legislative updates, stakeholder consultations, and possibly the development of new legal instruments or amendments to existing ones.

4 The Role of Case Law in Shaping Digital Market Regulation: From National Enforcement to the DMA/DSA Era

The enforcement of competition law in Spain's telecommunications and digital markets sector has played a vital role in ensuring fair market conditions, with the CNMC at the forefront of regulatory oversight. A key case exemplifying the authority's approach to addressing anti-competitive behavior on digital platforms is the Amazon/Apple Brandgating decision.[28] In 2023, the CNMC imposed fines totaling €194.15 million on Apple and Amazon for engaging in practices that distorted competition on Amazon Spain (amazon.es). The case centered on contractual agreements signed between the two companies in October 2018, which set restrictive terms governing how Amazon could sell Apple products. These agreements had significant consequences for competition in the online electronics market. Specifically, they drastically limited the number of independent resellers permitted to offer Apple products on Amazon Spain, restricted advertising space available to

[28] Comisión Nacional de los Mercados y la Competencia (CNMC) (2023).

competing brands, and constrained Amazon's ability to market alternative products to Apple customers.

As a result, over 90% of previously active independent Apple resellers were blocked from selling on Amazon Spain. This led to reduced competition in Apple product sales and left consumers with fewer choices, contributing to higher prices. The CNMC determined that these contractual restrictions breached Article 1 of Spain's Competition Law and Article 101 of the Treaty on the Functioning of the European Union (TFEU). Consequently, both companies faced financial penalties and were ordered to discontinue the restrictive practices.

However, the regulatory landscape has since shifted significantly. Both Apple and Amazon have now been designated as gatekeepers under the DMA, meaning that a similar case today would no longer be handled by the CNMC but rather fall under the exclusive competence of the European Commission. This marks a fundamental change in enforcement, centralizing oversight of the largest digital platforms at the EU level. Yet, the implementation of these regulations varies across Member States. In countries like Ireland or Luxembourg, where many major platforms have established their European headquarters, the impact of the DMA is expected to be far greater than in countries like Spain or Italy, where digital platforms do not have their main European offices. This structural difference means that while enforcement mechanisms have changed, the practical impact of the new digital regulations will likely be felt unevenly across the EU.

This case, among others, demonstrates how national competition authorities have historically been responsible for detecting and addressing anticompetitive practices in digital markets. However, with the entry into force of the DMA, the European Commission has taken over as the primary enforcer of competition rules for large digital platforms, or "gatekeepers." Under this new framework, the Commission will directly investigate and sanction non-compliance with the DMA's obligations, significantly reducing the role of national authorities like the CNMC in these matters. Yet, while enforcement is now centralized, case law remains an essential driver in shaping the application and interpretation of the DMA. This is already evident in the first ruling by the General Court of the European Union concerning the DMA, issued on July 17, 2024, in the ByteDance (TikTok) case.[29] In this case, ByteDance challenged its designation as a gatekeeper under the DMA, following a decision by the European Commission on September 5, 2023.[30] ByteDance argued that the Commission had misapplied the DMA's criteria, violated its rights of defense, and engaged in unequal treatment compared to other companies. However, the General Court dismissed all of ByteDance's claims, affirming that the Commission had correctly designated it as a gatekeeper based on its market influence, user base, and monetization potential.

[29] European Union (2024).

[30] European Commission (2023) Case DMA.100040 ByteDance – Online social networking services. Decision under the Digital Markets Act, Regulation (EU) 2022/1925, Article 3. September 5, 2023. https://ec.europa.eu/competition/digital_markets_act/cases/202344/DMA_100040_141.pdf

This ruling is just the first of many that will shape the future of the DMA's enforcement. Several other cases involving major tech companies, such as Meta and Apple, are currently pending before the General Court, and their outcomes will further clarify the DMA's scope and implementation. The transition from national-level enforcement to a centralized EU framework does not eliminate the role of case law; instead, it reinforces the judiciary's importance in interpreting and refining the regulatory landscape. As such, jurisprudence will continue to play a pivotal role in defining how digital markets operate under the new regime, ensuring that the DMA's ambitious goals of fair competition and market contestability are effectively upheld.

The enforcement of digital platform regulation in Spain has long relied on national authorities and judicial decisions to balance fundamental rights such as data protection, freedom of expression, and platform accountability. A key case illustrating this approach was the 2016 ruling by the Spanish Supreme Court against Google Spain,[31] which held the company liable for failing to remove outdated personal information from its search engine. The case involved an individual who, despite receiving a pardon in 1999, continued to have information about the pardon indexed by Google in 2010, long after the news had lost its public relevance. The Supreme Court ruled that the continued accessibility of these details was unlawful and disproportionate, as it infringed the individual's right to data protection, tipping the balance against the initial public interest in disclosure. Google Spain was ordered to pay €8000 in damages, and the court explicitly rejected Google's attempt to disclaim responsibility by arguing that it was merely an intermediary and that the affected person should instead litigate against Google Inc. in the United States. This ruling reinforced the principle that platforms bear legal responsibility for the impact of their content moderation decisions, setting a precedent for the "right to be forgotten" and shaping future litigation concerning online content removal.

However, much like competition law enforcement has transitioned from national authorities like the CNMC to the European Commission under the DMA, the introduction of the DSA has similarly centralized the oversight of large online platforms (VLOPs) at the EU level. Before the DSA, Member States had begun introducing increasingly strict digital regulations, which went beyond the scope of the EU's existing E-Commerce Directive, leading to significant legal fragmentation across the bloc. This patchwork of national laws created uncertainty for both platforms and users, prompting the European Commission to push for a harmonized legal framework. Spain, for instance, had taken an early step in addressing online content regulation with the Sinde-Wert Law, which entered into force on March 1, 2012, aiming to combat illegal online content.[32] However, as national measures diverged further,

---

[31] Spain, Supreme Court (2016) STS 210/2016, April 5, 2016. Sala de lo Civil, Pleno. https://vlex.es/vid/632311849

[32] The Sinde-Wert Law, part of the Telecommunications Package approved by the European Parliament in 2009, was a Spanish legislative initiative aimed at combating digital piracy. Unlike France's Hadopi Law, which penalized end users, this regulation focused on intermediaries that profited from unauthorized copyrighted content. It granted the Intellectual Property Commission the authority to order the removal of illegal material or even shut down websites that violated

the need for a single, directly applicable regulation became evident, culminating in the adoption of the DSA, which grants direct enforcement powers to the European Commission, preventing further legal fragmentation.

This transition is already being tested in the courts. The Amazon Services v. European Commission case,[33] ruled on in April 2024 by the Vice-President of the Court of Justice of the European Union (ECJ), became a defining early case in the implementation of the DSA. Amazon contested its designation as a Very Large Online Platform (VLOP), arguing that its marketplace should not fall under the same content governance obligations as social media platforms. Specifically, Amazon sought a suspension of the DSA's transparency obligations, which require platforms to explain how their algorithms influence user experiences. However, the ECJ rejected Amazon's request, affirming that the public interest in platform transparency outweighed Amazon's claims. The ruling served as a strong confirmation of the DSA's enforcement powers, ensuring that even non-traditional content platforms must comply with heightened transparency and accountability standards.

As with the DMA, this case highlights the pivotal role of case law in shaping the future enforcement of the DSA. Amazon's challenge is only the first of many legal battles expected in the coming months, as other platforms question the scope and application of their obligations. While the scope of enforcement covered by both the DMA and DSA has shifted from national to EU-level oversight, courts remain crucial arbiters in defining how these landmark regulations are applied in practice. The judiciary's role in interpreting and refining these new digital rules ensures that they remain effective, adaptable, and capable of achieving their broader objectives—whether in promoting fair competition under the DMA or safeguarding online accountability under the DSA.

5 Institutional Design and Efficiency

The development of independent regulatory agencies in the 1980s was driven by privatization, liberalization, and deregulation efforts initiated by conservative governments in the UK and the US. These changes, particularly in fields like telecommunications, were facilitated by technological advancements that challenged the traditional view of these sectors as natural monopolies (Segura 2018). In Spain,

copyright, following a swift procedure without prior judicial intervention. However, the law faced criticism for its limited legal safeguards for affected parties and its ineffectiveness against peer-to-peer (P2P) networks.

[33] European Union (2024) Order of the Vice-President of the Court of 27 March 2024. European Commission v Amazon Services Europe Sàrl. Appeal – Interim relief – Approximation of laws – Regulation (EU) 2022/2065 – Single market for digital services – Additional online advertising transparency – Decision to designate a very large online platform – Action for annulment. Case C-639/23 P(R). https://eur-lex.europa.eu/legal-content/EN/TXT/?uri=celex:62023CO0639%2801%29

independent organizations have a relatively short history due to political factors and a lack of tradition in bureaucratic administration. Despite this, key developments occurred in the 1980s and 1990s, including the creation of the telecommunications independent regulator in 1997. The formal recognition of independent administrations was consolidated with the enactment of a specific law[34] in that same year.

The *Comisión del Mercado de las Telecomunicaciones* (CMT) was pivotal in liberalizing Spain's telecommunications sector. Established in 1997, it transitioned the industry from a state-controlled monopoly to a competitive market. As an independent regulatory authority, the CMT regulated the telecommunications market to ensure fair competition, managing both incumbent operators (like Telefónica) and new market entrants. Its primary roles included preventing anti-competitive practices and ensuring a level playing field. The CMT's responsibilities also encompassed monitoring market behavior, addressing complaints, and implementing competition-promoting measures. One of the CMT's key functions was setting interconnection rules, allowing new operators to access the existing telecommunications network.

This was crucial for enabling competition, as it let multiple service providers offer services over shared infrastructure. Additionally, the CMT had the authority to regulate tariffs, particularly those of incumbent operators, to prevent market dominance abuse and protect consumers from excessive pricing. The CMT also issued licenses and authorizations to new market entrants, ensuring they met technical and financial standards and adhered to regulations. It protected consumer interests by ensuring pricing transparency and service quality, addressing telecommunications-related consumer complaints. The CMT encouraged investment in new technologies and infrastructure, aiding the rollout of broadband, mobile networks, and advanced telecommunications services. It provided advice to the government on telecommunications policy, shaping the legal and regulatory framework (Delgado and Otero 2015).

As part of its mandate, the CMT aligned Spain's telecommunications regulations with EU directives, facilitating integration into the broader European market. Overall, the CMT was instrumental in guiding Spain's telecommunications liberalization, fostering a competitive environment that benefited consumers and promoted innovation. Its work laid the foundation for today's dynamic telecommunications market in Spain.

In 2012, the Spanish government decided to merge several regulatory bodies to form the Comisión Nacional de los Mercados y la Competencia (CNMC).[35] The CNMC was created in 2013 by merging the former competition authority with the existing regulatory agencies for energy, telecommunications, railways, audiovisual, postal services and airports. This consolidation aimed to streamline regulatory oversight and improve efficiency across various economic sectors. The merger intended

---

[34] Spain (1997).

[35] National Commission for Markets and Competition, absorbing both the role of independent regulator and competition authority.

to reduce administrative costs and improve efficiency by combining several regulatory agencies into a single entity. The unified CNMC was expected to simplify the regulatory landscape, easing business compliance, as well as to adopt a consistent regulatory approach across the sectors under its mandate, enhancing policy coherence. By integrating the competition authority with sector-specific regulators, the CNMC sought to strengthen market competition oversight and prevent anti-competitive practices (Navarro Rodríguez 2013).

The CNMC's creation aligned with trends in other European countries, where integrated regulatory bodies oversee multiple sectors, ensuring alignment with EU directives and fostering European-level cooperation. The CNMC's broader regulatory capacity allowed it to address cross-sectoral issues more effectively. Since then, the CNMC has played a crucial role in regulating competition and markets in Spain, ensuring fair competition, consumer protection, and efficient economic sector functioning.

However, not all of the reform's expected benefits fully materialized in the short term. In the early stages of its functioning, the CNMC was unable to ensure improved decision-making or coordination, because its structure lacked explicit coordination mechanisms and sectoral silos persisted. In addition, its independence was questioned due to the senior staff appointment process as well as concerns about government influence. It faced concerns regarding accountability and decision-making capacity due to limited resources and extensive responsibilities. Hence, improving decision-making processes, enhancing financial and functional independence, and increasing transparency were elements that the newly created institution needed to develop over the years, as well as focusing on independent regulatory functions and simplifying its structure to create synergies.

Overall, while the CNMC's creation aimed to generate synergies and cost savings, its design did not fully achieve these goals in the short term. Institutional culture is crucial for promoting collaboration, and further improvements in the CNMC's design and operation were needed to realize the reform's benefits. For instance, conflicts between the CMT and the CNMC's predecessor, the Comisión Nacional de la Competencia (CNC), arose during and after integration. The merger aimed to eliminate contradictory decisions between sectoral regulators and the antitrust authority. Prior conflicts involved the CNC criticizing the CMT's handling of wholesale pricing, arguing that it discouraged alternative operators from investing in new networks, potentially harming consumers.

Overlapping responsibilities led to conflicts in regulatory approaches. For example, the CNC fined telecom operators for market dominance abuse in areas under the CMT's purview, which created an unstable regulatory environment. After forming the CNMC, internal conflicts persisted due to unresolved differences in regulatory philosophy. The lack of explicit coordination mechanisms hindered potential synergies, leading to less transparent decision-making and hindering the development of a cohesive regulatory strategy. In summary, conflicts between the CMT and the CNMC (via the CNC) resulted in contradictory decisions, overlapping responsibilities, and unresolved internal conflicts post-integration. These challenges highlighted the difficulties of merging sectoral regulation with competition law enforcement within a single regulatory body (Delgado and Otero 2015).

As explained before, both the DMA and the DSA foresee an organizational solution in which the European Commission takes the role of main regulator, assisted by the corresponding bodies of the different Member States. However, the previous approach to digital regulation relied heavily on transposing the proposed rules into the different national legal frameworks. There is some discretion as to how each Member State will adapt its existing government structures to support both the DSA and the DMA. In Spain, the mission to implement the DSA and to act as the Spanish Digital Services Coordinator (DSC) has been entrusted to the National Commission for Markets and Competition (CNMC). This institution is simultaneously the competition authority and the regulatory agency for relevant markets such as telecommunications and audiovisual services. It has responsibilities in supporting the DMA and participates in both the Digital Markets Advisory Committee (DMAC) and the European Competition Network (ECN).

6 A New Approach to Digital Regulation

Over the past decade, the European Union has significantly shifted its approach to digital regulation. In the past, the focus was only on minimal and occasional measures, primarily implemented to encourage innovation while promoting the adoption of digital technologies. This strategy relied on ex-post and purely corrective actions, which effectively served as external constraints on the sector's development. In the past decade, there has been a significant shift in approach due to the rising importance of digital transformation for economic growth and social development, along with the necessity of a trustworthy and secure environment to support it. As a result, the European Union is moving away from a traditional laissez-faire position and minimal last-resort measures. Instead, it is adopting a positive strategy with proactive and preventive actions, first evident in the proposal for a General Data Protection Regulation[36] in 2016.[37]

The European Union's evolving stance on the digital sector is evident in the progression of its digital strategies over the past two decades, which have positioned digital policy as central to EU initiatives. These strategies consistently emphasize enhancing digital infrastructure, the digital economy, and the digital skills of citizens, businesses, and administrations. However, their focus has shifted. They now extend beyond technical and economic advancements to ensure that the digital sector grows in line with the rights and values upheld by the EU's societal model. As digital policy increasingly defines the economic, social, and political framework of the European Union, its digital strategies have gained greater significance and

[36] European Union (2016), p. 1.

[37] For a more detailed exposition of this change of approach, see Vida Fernández (2022).

expanded their scope. These strategies now extend beyond the traditional domains of the digital ecosystem, such as telecommunications, audiovisual media, and information society services. They also address new concerns that surpass the mere protection of personal data.

The European Union's recent digital strategies have progressively introduced a growing number of initiatives, resulting in a broad and complex regulatory framework for the digital sector. This complexity makes it challenging to keep track of regulatory developments, as the increasing number of rules becomes more sophisticated and difficult to interpret, even for specialists. This is evident in the most recent digital strategy aimed at creating 'A Europe fit for the digital age,' one of the six priorities established by the Commission for the period up to 2023.[38] The current digital strategy was outlined in the 2020 Communication on Shaping Europe's Digital Future[39] and has been further supported by the Digital Compass Communication,[40] which presents the European approach for the Digital Decade, along with its program outlined in the proposed Decision Pathway to the Digital Decade 2030.[41]

These components of the European Union's digital strategy up to 2030 propose numerous measures impacting all areas of the sector reflecting a new and more interventionist approach. They represent the foundation of the digital sector's regulatory framework, which, when systematically organized, interconnect and provide a comprehensive view of the state of European digital policy.

An important component, dealing with information society services—now referred to as digital services—which have been growing exponentially, required urgent intervention. It was originally called the Digital Services Package, and it included the two recently approved regulations that have been explained in the previous pages: the Digital Services Act[42] and the Digital Markets Act,[43] both of which came into effect in 2023.

A second component is the set of electronic communications measures that apply to infrastructures and services to ensure the connectivity required for the development of digital activities. This includes the 2018 European Electronic Communications Code,[44] which continues the regulation of the telecommunications sector while introducing some new developments. After a significant delay, Spain

---

[38] European Commission (2019).

[39] European Commission (2020).

[40] Communication from the Commission to the European Parliament, the Council, the European Economic And Social Committee and the Committee of the Regions 2030 Digital Compass: the European way for the Digital Decade, COM/2021/118 final. https://eur-lex.europa.eu/legal-content/EN/TXT/?uri=celex:52021DC0118

[41] Proposal for a Decision of the European Parliament and of the Council establishing the 2030 Policy Programme 'Path to the Digital Decade' COM (2021) 574 final. https://eur-lex.europa.eu/legal-content/EN/TXT/?uri=celex%3A52021PC0574

[42] European Union (2022a), p. 1.

[43] European Union (2022b), p. 1.

[44] European Union (2018), p. 36.

has transposed this directive by adopting the General Telecommunications Law 11/2022 of 28 June,[45] which also incorporates the content of other European legislation such as Directive 2014/61/EU to reduce the cost of network deployment (BBCost Directive)[46] and Regulation (EU) 2015/2120 on net neutrality and roaming,[47] among others.

A third element addresses the audiovisual industry, which has been significantly transformed by new methods of transmitting and consuming audiovisual content. This transformation led to the adoption of the Audiovisual Media Services Directive,[48] implemented in Spain through the General Law on Audiovisual Communication 13/2022 of July 7.[49] More recently, efforts to enhance the media pluralism led to the proposal of the European Media Freedom Act[50] in September 2022, which entered into force on 7 May 2024. The new rules will take full effect on 8 August 2025.

Central to these sub-sectors is the data policy outlined in the 2020 European Data Strategy. This strategy extends beyond the protection of personal data, aiming to enhance data re-use and sharing to establish a single market for data, which is vital for the digital sector's development. In line with this, the Data Governance Act (Regulation (EU) 2022/868)[51] was adopted, and a proposal for a Data Act (Regulation (EU) 2023/2854)[52] introduced in 2022 finally entered into force on 11 January 2024. Additionally, the ePrivacy Regulation, which replaces Directive 2002/58/EC and seeks to regulate privacy and personal data protection in electronic communications, was proposed in 2017. However, it remains stalled due to a lack of agreement among institutions.[53]

Recent developments in digital policy include initiatives targeting disruptive technologies, such as artificial intelligence, which pose significant challenges. A proposal for an AI Regulation (AI Act) was introduced in 2021, followed by a proposal for an AI Liability Directive in 2022. The AI Act (Regulation (EU) 2024/1689)[54] finally entered into force on 1 August 2024 and will be fully applicable 2 years later, on 2 August 2026.[55] Partial regulation of blockchain and other distributed ledger

---

45 Spain (2003).

46 European Union (2014), pp. 1–14.

47 European Union (2015b), pp. 1–18.

48 European Parliament and Council (2018).

49 Spain (2022b).

50 European Parliament and Council (2024a).

51 European Parliament and Council (2022a).

52 European Parliament and Council (2023).

53 On February 11, 2025, the European Commission disclosed in its Work Programme for 2025 that it will withdraw the proposal for a new ePrivacy Regulation (replacing the current ePrivacy Directive). Hence, the current ePrivacy Directive of 2002 and its national transposition laws will remain in force.

54 European Parliament and Council (2024b).

55 With some exceptions: (i) prohibitions and AI literacy obligations entered into application from 2 February 2025; (ii) the governance rules and the obligations for general-purpose AI models

technologies (DLT) is also addressed in the European Digital Identity eIDAS2 (Regulation (EU) 2024/1183)[56] which took effect on 20 May 2024.

Other cross-cutting measures pertain to cybersecurity, which has gained increasing importance with the growing reliance on digital systems, as highlighted in the 2020 European Cybersecurity Strategy. In this context, two initiatives are relevant. First, the Cybersecurity Directive (NIS2, Directive (EU) 2022/2555)[57] had to be fully transposed by 17 October 2024. However, on 28 November 2024, the Commission decided to open infringement procedures, sending a letter of formal notice to 23 Member States, including Spain, for failing to fully transpose it. In addition, the Cyber Resilience Act (Regulation (EU) 2024/2847)[58] entered into force in 2024, and economic operators and Member States will have 36 months to adapt to the new requirements.

The final piece of the digital regulation puzzle, and perhaps the clearest sign of this shift, is the recognition of specific digital rights. The proposal for a European Declaration on Digital Rights and Principles for the Digital Decade, presented in January 2022, will play a central role in shaping all digital sector regulations. It embodies the principles of the digital society model to which European Union aspires and should be reflected in the development of all the rules and legislative proposals mentioned.

7 Conclusions

The evolution of digital regulation, particularly within the European Union (EU), has seen significant shifts from telecommunications regulation to the enactment of the Digital Markets Act (DMA) and the Digital Services Act (DSA). These changes reflect broader efforts to ensure fair competition and address challenges in digital markets that traditional telecommunications regulations did not fully cover. Traditional telecommunications regulation primarily focused on physical infrastructure and service provision, ensuring competition and consumer protection within the sector. The DMA, however, extends these principles to digital markets, targeting large platforms known as "gatekeepers" to prevent anti-competitive practices. It centralizes enforcement powers with the European Commission, reflecting the cross-border nature of digital services, which marks a departure from the nationally enforced regulations typical of telecommunications.

In Spain, the telecommunications sector underwent significant liberalization from the 1990s onwards, transitioning from a monopolistic market structure to a

become applicable on 2 August 2025; and (iii) the rules for high-risk AI systems—embedded into regulated products—have an extended transition period until 2 August 2027.

[56] European Parliament and Council (2024c).

[57] European Parliament and Council (2022b), pp. 80–152.

[58] European Parliament and Council (2024d).

more competitive environment. This was achieved through regulatory interventions that facilitated new market entrants and encouraged investment in network infrastructure. Despite these advancements, the sector remains concentrated, posing ongoing regulatory challenges. Spain's regulatory framework is closely aligned with European standards, as evidenced by the General Telecommunications Law and subsequent updates. The DMA marks a significant regulatory milestone for large digital platforms. It imposes ex-ante obligations on gatekeepers across eight core platform services. The European Commission is the primary enforcer, with powers including market investigations and the ability to impose fines for non-compliance. The DMA is conceptually similar to telecommunications regulation, where core services are akin to relevant markets. However, its implementation is complex, requiring careful coordination and ongoing regulatory refinement to address the dynamic digital landscape.

The e-Commerce Directive, established in 2000, laid the groundwork for electronic commerce within the EU by introducing the 'country of origin' principle and addressing liability issues. In Spain, the Law on Information Society Services and Electronic Commerce (LSSI) transposed this directive, providing a legal framework for internet activities. The DSA, part of the EU's broader digital strategy, aims to modernize digital service regulations, focusing on transparency, accountability, and consumer protection. It mandates greater platform transparency and imposes specific obligations on very large online platforms (VLOPs). Spain's LSSI will require adjustments to align with these new standards.

Case law has been pivotal in shaping digital market regulation, as seen in the CNMC's enforcement actions against anti-competitive practices. However, with the DMA and DSA centralizing oversight at the EU level, the role of national authorities like the CNMC has been diminished. At the same time, the judiciary remains crucial in interpreting these regulations, ensuring they effectively promote fair competition and online accountability.

The creation of independent regulatory agencies in the 1980s was driven by efforts towards privatization and liberalization. In Spain, the CNMC emerged from the merger of several regulatory bodies, including the competition authority and sector-specific regulators. While this consolidation aimed to streamline oversight, challenges related to coordination and independence persisted, highlighting the need for further institutional improvements.

The EU's approach to digital regulation has shifted significantly over the past decade, moving from minimal intervention to proactive strategies. This new approach is embodied in comprehensive digital strategies that not only address technical and economic advancements but also align with EU rights and values. The DSA and the DMA are central to this strategy, complemented by measures targeting electronic communications, audiovisual services, data policy, and emerging technologies like artificial intelligence.

In summary, the EU's evolving regulatory landscape reflects a more interventionist approach to digital markets, aiming to ensure fair competition, protect consumer rights, and foster innovation. The DMA and DSA represent a new era of digital regulation, centralizing enforcement at the EU level while addressing the unique challenges posed by large digital platforms.

We have argued that regulation of telecommunications—in a broad sense—is characterized by two main layers: the regulation of the physical network and the content. The first layer deals with the physical infrastructure, traditionally regulated by telecommunications law, while the second layer involves media and electronic commerce laws. The convergence of services on a single network, primarily the Internet, has rendered the traditional regulatory division obsolete, calling for more flexible and modern legislative approaches (Savin 2018). Furthermore, the complex interplay between national, European, and international regulations creates a challenging environment for telecommunications—or electronic communications—governance, necessitating political compromises and coordination across multiple jurisdictions. As telecommunications continue to evolve, the regulatory frameworks must adapt to reflect the realities of converged services and the global nature of the industry.

References

Berg SV, Tschirhart J (1988) Natural monopoly regulation. Cambridge University Press, Cambridge

Boix Palop A (2003) La LSSI y las diversas concepciones sobre la extraterritorialidad de las limitaciones a la libre expresión derivadas de la cláusula de orden público. Revista de Derecho 2:7

Calzada J, García-Mariñoso B, Ribé J, Rubio-Campillo R, Suarez D (2018) Fiber deployment in Spain. J Regul Econ 53(3):256–274

Campillos González GM (2001) La ley de Servicios de la Sociedad de la Información, marco jurídico de las actividades económicas a través de internet. Econ Ind Democr 338:51

CNMC (2023) Case S/0013/21 - Amazon/Apple Brandgating. Comisión Nacional de los Mercados y la Competencia, Spain. https://www.cnmc.es/sites/default/files/4889034.pdf

Comisión Nacional de los Mercados y la Competencia (CNMC) (2023) Expediente S/0013/21 – Amazon / Apple Brandgating. Case file resolution, 12 Jul 2023. https://www.cnmc.es/expedientes/s001321

Court of Justice of the European Union (2024) Order of the Vice-President of the Court, Case C-639/23 P(R), European Commission v Amazon Services Europe Sàrl. ECLI:EU:C:2024:277

Delgado J, Otero H (2015) La CNMC: La Historia de una Reforma Inacabada. Papeles Econ Española 145:18

European Commission (2019) Political guidelines for the next European Commission 2019–2024, Opening statement in the European Parliament plenary session, July 16, 2019; Speech in the European Parliament plenary session, November 27, 2019. Publications Office of the European Union. https://op.europa.eu/en/publication-detail/-/publication/62e534f4-62c1-11ea-b735-01aa75ed71a1

European Commission (2020) Communication from the Commission to the European Parliament, the Council, the European Economic and Social Committee and the Committee of the Regions – Shaping Europe's Digital Future. COM(2020) 67 final, 19 February 2020. https://eur-lex.europa.eu/legal-content/EN/TXT/?uri=celex:52020DC0067

European Commission (2023) Case DMA.100040 ByteDance – Online social networking services. Regulation (EU) 2022/1925, Article 3, 5 September 2023

European Parliament and Council (2018) Directive (EU) 2018/1808 of the European Parliament and of the Council of 14 November 2018 amending Directive 2010/13/EU on the coordination of certain provisions laid down by law, regulation or administrative action in Member

States concerning the provision of audiovisual media services (Audiovisual Media Services Directive) in view of changing market realities. Off J Law 303:69. 28 Nov 2018. https://eur-lex.europa.eu/eli/dir/2018/1808/oj/eng
European Parliament and Council (2022a) Regulation (EU) 2022/868 of the European Parliament and of the Council of 30 May 2022 on European data governance and amending Regulation (EU) 2018/1724 (Data Governance Act). OJ L 152/1, 03/06/2022. https://eur-lex.europa.eu/eli/reg/2022/868/oj/eng
European Parliament and Council (2022b) Directive (EU) 2022/2555 of the European Parliament and of the Council of 14 December 2022 on measures for a high common level of cybersecurity across the Union, amending Regulation (EU) No 910/2014 and Directive (EU) 2018/1972, and repealing Directive (EU) 2016/1148 (NIS 2 Directive). Off J Law 333:80–152. 27 Dec 2022. https://eur-lex.europa.eu/eli/dir/2022/2555/oj/eng
European Parliament and Council (2023) Regulation (EU) 2023/2854 of the European Parliament and of the Council of 13 December 2023 on harmonised rules on fair access to and use of data and amending Regulation (EU) 2017/2394 and Directive (EU) 2020/1828 (Data Act). Off J Law. 22 Dec 2023. https://eur-lex.europa.eu/eli/reg/2023/2854/oj/eng
European Parliament and Council (2024a) Regulation (EU) 2024/1083 of the European Parliament and of the Council of 11 April 2024 establishing a common framework for media services in the internal market and amending Directive 2010/13/EU (European Media Freedom Act). Off J Law 2024/1083, 17/04/2024. https://eur-lex.europa.eu/legal-content/EN/TXT/?uri=CELEX%3A32024R1083
European Parliament and Council (2024b) Regulation (EU) 2024/1689 of the European Parliament and of the Council of 13 June 2024 laying down harmonised rules on artificial intelligence and amending Regulations (EC) No 300/2008, (EU) No 167/2013, (EU) No 168/2013, (EU) 2018/858, (EU) 2018/1139 and (EU) 2019/2144 and Directives 2014/90/EU, (EU) 2016/797 and (EU) 2020/1828 (Artificial Intelligence Act). Off J Law, 12/07/2024. https://eur-lex.europa.eu/eli/reg/2024/1689/oj/eng
European Parliament and Council (2024c) Regulation (EU) 2024/1183 of the European Parliament and of the Council of 11 April 2024 amending Regulation (EU) No 910/2014 as regards establishing the European Digital Identity Framework. Off J Law, 30/04/2024. https://eur-lex.europa.eu/eli/reg/2024/1183/oj/eng
European Parliament and Council (2024d) Regulation (EU) 2024/2847 of the European Parliament and of the Council of 23 October 2024 on horizontal cybersecurity requirements for products with digital elements and amending Regulations (EU) No 168/2013 and (EU) 2019/1020 and Directive (EU) 2020/1828 (Cyber Resilience Act). Off J Law 20.11.2024. https://eur-lex.europa.eu/eli/reg/2024/2847/oj/eng
European Union (2000) Directive 2000/31/EC of the European Parliament and of the Council of 8 June 2000 on certain legal aspects of information society services, in particular electronic commerce, in the the Internal Market ('Directive on electronic commerce'). Off J Eur Union Law 178:1–16. https://eur-lex.europa.eu/eli/dir/2000/31/oj/eng
European Union (2014) Directive 2014/61/EU of the European Parliament and of the Council of 15 May 2014 on measures to reduce the cost of deploying high-speed electronic communications networks. Off J Eur Union Law 155:1–14. https://eur-lex.europa.eu/eli/dir/2014/61/oj/eng
European Union (2015a) Directive (EU) 2015/2366 of the European Parliament and of the Council of 25 November 2015 on payment services in the internal market, amending Directives 2002/65/EC, 2009/110/EC and 2013/36/EU and Regulation (EU) No 1093/2010, and repealing Directive 2007/64/EC (Text with EEA relevance). Off J Eur Union Law 337:35–127. https://eur-lex.europa.eu/eli/dir/2015/2366/oj/eng
European Union (2015b) Regulation (EU) 2015/2120 of the European Parliament and of the Council of 25 November 2015 laying down measures concerning open internet access and amending Directive 2002/22/EC on universal service and users' rights relating to electronic communications networks and services and Regulation (EU) No 531/2012 on roaming on pub-

lic mobile communications networks within the Union. Off J Eur Union Law 310:1–18. https://eur-lex.europa.eu/eli/reg/2015/2120/oj/eng

European Union (2016) Regulation (EU) 2016/679 of the European Parliament and of the Council of 27 April 2016 on the protection of natural persons with regard to the processing of personal data and on the free movement of such data, and repealing Directive 95/46/EC (General Data Protection Regulation). Off J Eur Union Law 119:1–88. https://eur-lex.europa.eu/eli/reg/2016/679/oj/eng

European Union (2018) Directive (EU) 2018/1972 of the European Parliament and of the Council of 11 December 2018 establishing the European Electronic Communications Code (Recast). Off J Eur Union Law 321:36–214. Accessible at: https://eur-lex.europa.eu/eli/dir/2018/1972/oj/eng

European Union (2022a) Regulation (EU) 2022/1925 of the European Parliament and of the Council of 14 September 2022 on contestable and fair markets in the digital sector and amending Directives (EU) 2019/1937 and (EU) 2020/1828 (Digital Markets Act). Off J Eur Union Law 265:1–66. https://eur-lex.europa.eu/legal-content/EN/TXT/?uri=uriserv%3AOJ.L_.2022.265.01.0001.01.ENG&toc=OJ%3AL%3A2022%3A265%3ATOC

European Union (2022b) Regulation (EU) 2022/2065 of the European Parliament and of the Council of 19 October 2022 on a Single Market for Digital Services and amending Directive 2000/31/EC (Digital Services Act). Off J Eur Union Law 277:1–102. https://eur-lex.europa.eu/eli/reg/2022/2065/oj/eng

European Union (2024) Case T-1077/23: Judgment of the General Court of 17 July 2024 – Bytedance v Commission (Digital services – Regulation (EU) 2022/1925 – Designation of gatekeepers – Online social networking service – Article 3(1), (2) and (5) of Regulation 2022/1925 – Requirements – Presumptions – Rebuttal of the presumptions – Rights of the defence – Equal treatment). Off J Eur Union C 5325. 9 Sep 2024. https://eur-lex.europa.eu/eli/C/2024/5325/oj/eng

Feijóo C, Gómez-Barroso JL, Karnitis A (2007) More than twenty years of European policy for the development of the information society. http://netcom.revues.org/2389

Fransman M (2001) Evolution of the telecommunications industry into the internet age. Commun Strateg 43:57–113

Hauge JA, Sappington D (2010) Pricing in network industries. In: Baldwin R, Cave M, Lodge M (eds) The Oxford handbook of regulation. Oxford University Press, Oxford

Hernández López C (2023) La regulación europea de los mercados digitales: justificación, técnicas y límites. Rev Adm Pública 221

Jimena Quesada L (2003) La técnica legislativa y otros aspectos constitucionales relativos a la Ley de servicios de la sociedad de la información y de comercio electrónico. Revista de Derecho 2

Jordana J (1999) El camino hacia la sociedad de la información. In: Jordana J, Sancho D (eds) Políticas públicas de telecomunicaciones en España. Tecnos, Madrid

Martínez Soler JA (1998) Telecomunicaciones: un sector en ebullición. Economistas 16(77):79

Nadal J (1995) La fusión de las telecomunicaciones y el multimedia. Perspectiva española. Estud Transp Comun 66:37

Navarro Rodríguez P (2013) La nueva Comisión Nacional de los Mercados y la Competencia: naturaleza, régimen jurídico e independencia. Rev Gen Derecho Adm 34

Nistal G (1999) El proyecto Ventanilla Única. Construyendo la Sociedad de la Comunicación. Presented at III Jornadas de Organización y Nuevas Tecnologías en la Administración Local, Blanes, 6–8 October 1999

Otero JD (2019) Competencia y regulación en los mercados de comunicaciones electrónicas: banda ancha y despliegues de nueva generación. Boletín Econ Inf Comercial Española 3111:19–30

Otero JD (2023) Regulación del sector de las comunicaciones electrónicas y de los mercados digitales: pasado, presente y futuro. FEDEA Estud Econ Española 2023/16

Rodríguez D (2021) Trece cuestiones sobre regulación en telecomunicaciones. FEDEA Estud Econ Española 2021/05

Rodríguez de las Heras Ballell T (2021) The background of the Digital Services Act: looking towards a platform economy. ERA Forum 22(1):75–86
Savin A (2018) EU telecommunications law. Edward Elgar, Cheltenham
Segura J (ed) (2018) Reguladores y supervisores económicos independientes: el caso español. Fundación Ramon Areces, Madrid
Soto J, Perez J, Feijoo C (2003) Veinticinco años la de sociedad de la información en España. Evolución tecnológica, globalización y políticas públicas. Econ Ind 349–350:63
Spain (1996) Ley 7/1996, de 15 de enero, de Ordenación del Comercio Minorista. BOE núm 15. 17 Jan 1996. https://www.boe.es/buscar/act.php?id=BOE-A-1996-1072
Spain (1997) Ley 6/1997, de 14 de abril, de Organización y Funcionamiento de la Administración General del Estado (LOFAGE). BOE núm 90. 15 de abril de 1997. https://www.boe.es/buscar/act.php?id=BOE-A-1997-7878
Spain (1998) Ley 7/1998, de 13 de abril, sobre condiciones generales de la contratación. BOE núm 89. 14 Apr 1998. https://www.boe.es/buscar/act.php?id=BOE-A-1998-8789
Spain (2000) Real Decreto 3423/2000, de 15 de diciembre, por el que se regula la indicación de los precios de los productos ofrecidos a los consumidores y usuarios. BOE núm 311. 28 Dec 2000. https://www.boe.es/buscar/act.php?id=BOE-A-2000-24118
Spain (2003) Ley 32/2003, de 3 de noviembre, General de Telecomunicaciones. BOE núm 264:38890–38924. 4 Nov 2003. https://www.boe.es/buscar/doc.php?id=BOE-A-2003-20253
Spain (2007) Real Decreto Legislativo 1/2007, de 16 de noviembre, por el que se aprueba el texto refundido de la Ley General para la Defensa de los Consumidores y Usuarios y otras leyes complementarias. BOE núm 287. 30 Nov 2007. https://www.boe.es/buscar/act.php?id=BOE-A-2007-20555
Spain (2014) Ley 9/2014, de 9 de mayo, General de Telecomunicaciones. BOE núm 114:35824–35938. 10 May 2014. https://www.boe.es/buscar/doc.php?id=BOE-A-2014-4950
Spain (2018a) Ley Orgánica 3/2018, de 5 de diciembre, de Protección de Datos Personales y garantía de los derechos digitales, known as LOPDGDD. BOE núm 294. 6 Dec 2018. https://www.boe.es/buscar/act.php?id=BOE-A-2018-16673
Spain (2018b) Real Decreto-ley 19/2018, de 23 de noviembre, de servicios de pago y otras medidas urgentes en materia financiera. BOE núm 284:114474–114568. 24 Nov 2018. https://www.boe.es/buscar/doc.php?id=BOE-A-2018-16036
Spain (2022a) Ley 11/2022, de 28 de junio, General de Telecomunicaciones. BOE núm 155:91253–91411. 29 Jun 2022. https://www.boe.es/buscar/doc.php?id=BOE-A-2022-10757
Spain (2022b) Ley 13/2022, de 7 de julio, General de Comunicación Audiovisual. BOE núm 163:08/07/2022. https://www.boe.es/buscar/act.php?id=BOE-A-2022-11311
Tribunal Supremo (2016) Sentencia STS 1280/2016, Recurso 3269/2014. ECLI:ES:TS:2016:1280, 5 April 2016
Vida Fernández J (2021) La articulación jurídica del entorno digital. Insuficiencias y soluciones en la delimitación de los sectores de referencia ante el desafío de los servicios over the top (OTT). Rev Derecho Adm 20
Vida Fernández J (2022) Una panorámica del puzzle de la regulación digital en la Unión Europea: Telecomunicaciones, Audiovisual, Mercados y Servicios Digitales, Datos, Inteligencia Artificial, Ciberseguridad y Derechos Digitales. Rev Gen Derecho Sect Regulados 10:9

Néstor Duch-Brown is a scientific officer and team leader at the Digital Economy Unit of the Joint Research Centre (European Commission). Before joining the JRC in 2012, he was an associate professor at the University of Barcelona and researcher at the Barcelona Institute of Economics. He holds a PhD in Economics from the University of Barcelona. His current research focuses on empirical digital economics, with a particular emphasis on online platforms, the economics of digital data, and the economic impact of European digital regulations.

Estela Fernández López is Legal Intern – IT/ES Legal Consumer Team at Amazon in Madrid. She graduated in Law and Business at Universidad Carlos III de Madrid. She has studied abroad at the University of Southern California and Università Bocconi. Her research interests include digital platform regulation, particularly its implications for user privacy and market competition.

Navigating the Intersection of National and European Digital Regulations: Estonia's Implementation of the DSA and DMA

David Ramiro Troitiño and Viktoria Mazur

Contents

Abstract This research provides an in-depth analysis of the implementation of the Digital Services Act (DSA) and the Digital Markets Act (DMA) in Estonia, examining how these European regulations interact with national laws and authorities responsible. Given Estonia's advanced digital infrastructure and its proactive approach on technology governance, the country faces unique challenges and opportunities lining up domestic regulations with European frameworks.

The Estonian Consumer Protection and Technical Regulatory Authority (TTJA) has been designated as the national Digital Services Coordinator (DSC) responsible for implementing the DSA. Therefore, it is fundamental to understand TTJA's role,

D. R. Troitiño (✉)
Department of Law, European Network on Digitalization and E-governance, Tallinn University of Technology, Tallinn, Estonia
e-mail: david.troitino@taltech.ee

V. Mazur
Department of Law, Tallinn University of Technology, Tallinn, Estonia
e-mail: viktoria.mazur@taltech.ee

F. Decarolis et al. (eds.), *The EU Digital Regulation and its Impact on Member States*, European Union and its Neighbours in a Globalized World 27,
https://doi.org/10.1007/978-3-032-06490-5_12

its collaboration with the Estonian Data Protection Inspectorate (AKI), and how these agencies coordinate to avoid overlapping related to data privacy, online content moderation, and platform accountability.

The relationship between Estonia's competition law and the DMA is another focal point. The Estonian Competition Authority (ECA) plays a critical role in overseeing market fairness, particularly concerning the DMA's focus on gatekeeper platforms. Additionally, the research explores the interactions between Estonia's DSC, the forthcoming AI Act supervisory authority, and the ECA. Through this analysis, the research offers insights into how Estonia navigates the complex interplay between national and European digital market regulations, highlighting the country's efforts to maintain its leadership in digital governance while complying with EU standards.

1 Introduction

The digital transformation of economies and societies has become a pivotal aspect of global development, particularly in Europe. The European Union (EU) has long advocated the idea of a Single Digital Market to foster innovation, economic growth, and regulatory integration across member states. Estonia, a small but digitally advanced country, has emerged as a relevant partner in this transformation. The Digital Single Market (DSM), an initiative launched in 2015 aimed at removing regulatory barriers and enabling seamless digital operations across member states. The DSM has three primary pillars: ensuring better access to digital goods and services, creating an environment where digital networks can thrive, and maximizing the growth potential of the digital economy.[1] Consequently, several EU directives and regulations have been enacted to support this vision, including the General Data Protection Regulation (GDPR), the Digital Services Act (DSA), and the Digital Markets Act (DMA). The GDPR set global standards for data protection and privacy, while the DSA and DMA aim to regulate digital platforms, improve user rights, and foster competition. Together, these policies represent the EU's efforts to strike a balance between promoting innovation and safeguarding the rights of citizens in the digital age.[2]

Estonia stands out within the EU as a pioneer in digital transformation, with a series of landmark initiatives that have redefined the relationship between citizens and the state. In the late 1990s, Estonia launched its "e-Estonia" project, a vision to create a digital society where citizens could interact with government services efficiently and securely. The cornerstone of this transformation was the development of

[1] See Heller (2017).

[2] See Björklund (2016).

e-government services and the digital ID system, both of which serve as models for digital governance worldwide.

- e-Government: Estonia's system allows citizens to perform nearly every bureaucratic function online, including filing taxes, registering businesses, voting in elections, and accessing healthcare services.
- Digital ID: Estonia's digital ID system, introduced in 2002, is another transformative innovation. The ID enables citizens to access a wide range of public and private services online using a secure electronic signature. The digital ID also underpins Estonia's X-Road system, a decentralized data exchange platform that facilitates the secure transfer of information between different government institutions.[3]

Estonia's digital advancements have enhanced civic participation and trust in government, setting a benchmark for other EU member states to follow. Nevertheless, as digital transformation accelerates, the need for comprehensive regulatory frameworks becomes critical to ensure that technological advancements align with societal values and legal norms.[4] Therefore, the importance of developing digital regulations that address key issues such as privacy, security, competition, and the accountability of digital platforms are a priority for both, Estonia, and the European Union:

- National Regulations in Estonia: Estonia's digital regulatory framework has been proactive and forward-thinking. It was among the first countries to implement strong cybersecurity measures through its Cybersecurity Act, which emphasizes the protection of essential services and critical infrastructure, due the threat of Russian cyberattacks. Additionally, Estonia has robust data protection laws that work in tandem with the GDPR to safeguard citizens' privacy rights.
- EU Digital Regulations: The European Union has taken the lead in setting global digital regulatory standards increasing the scope of its normative power. The GDPR, implemented in 2018, established the EU as a global pioneer in data protection, with its strict rules on data handling, storage, and processing. The DSA and DMA, introduced in 2020, mark the next phase of EU digital regulation, focusing on the responsibilities of online platforms and ensuring a competitive digital market. These regulations aim to restrain the monopolistic tendencies of large tech companies and protect users from illegal content, misinformation, and unfair business practices.

For Estonia, complying with these EU-wide regulations is crucial. As a highly digitalized society, the country is both a beneficiary and a key contributor to the EU's digital regulatory landscape. The European dimension provides Estonia with the power to halt the negative monopolistic tendencies of large technological corporations that could easily override the control in such a small digital landscape

[3] See Margetts and Naumann (2017).

[4] See Espinosa and Pino (2024).

and market, as Estonia, but cannot overrun a significant area such as the European Union.[5]

2 Digital Services Act (DSA) and Digital Markets Act (DMA) an Estonian Role in the Digital Universe

As digital platforms play an increasingly central role in our social, economic, and political lives, effective regulation has become a priority for governments and policymakers. The European Union (EU) has taken significant steps to address the challenges and opportunities presented by digital markets through two landmark regulations: the Digital Services Act (DSA) and the Digital Markets Act (DMA). Together, these regulations aim to create a safer, more transparent, and competitive digital ecosystem across the EU. The Digital Services Act (DSA), proposed in 2020 and adopted by the European Parliament in 2022, represents one of the most ambitious regulatory frameworks designed to govern the operation of digital platforms and services in the EU. The DSA applies to a wide range of online platforms, including social media networks, e-commerce platforms, and content-sharing websites. Its primary goal is to create a safer digital environment by ensuring that platforms are accountable for the content and activities they facilitate.

The DSA and DMA mark a transformative moment for digital governance in the EU, addressing a wide array of challenges posed by the dominance of online platforms and the evolving nature of the digital ecosystem. The significance of these regulations can be understood in terms of their impact on content moderation, market competition, and user empowerment by enhancing content moderation and accountability, creating a fair and competitive digital economy, protecting user rights and enhancing consumer choice and establishing global standards for digital regulation.[6]

Estonia, a small Baltic nation with a population of just over 1.3 million, has difficulties to protect its digital citizens from big corporations, limited digital market with a limited number of consumers and a crucial problem collecting data in an efficient way because of the reduce number of digital individuals. Therefore, its integration in the digital landscape of the European Union is a must. Nevertheless, the country emerged as a global leader in digital innovation and e-governance. Often referred to as the "world's most digital country," Estonia has pioneered several groundbreaking initiatives, such as e-government services and digital ID systems, which have transformed public administration and citizen engagement.[7] Estonia's digital achievements have not only solidified its reputation as a digital pioneer in Europe but have also positioned it as a key influencer of European digital

[5] See Robbins (2018).

[6] See Lamadrid de Pablo and Bayón Fernández (2021).

[7] See Troitiño (2022).

policies. Estonia's digital journey began in the early 1990s, following its independence from the Soviet Union. As a newly established sovereign state, Estonia faced the challenge of modernizing its public administration and infrastructure. Rather than following traditional models, the country chose to invest heavily in digital technology to jump ahead development and enhance efficiency. The necessity to change model, as Soviet system was obsolete and useless in a modern capitalist society, the willing of the population to accept changes and the relatively limited population, helped to implement novelties that would have been opposed by the citizens of most of Western states. Nevertheless, this decision made Estonia a global model for digital governance.

One of Estonia's most significant achievements has been its implementation of e-government services. Citizens can access nearly all public services online, from voting in elections to paying taxes and registering businesses. This system is underpinned by the country's X-Road platform, a secure data exchange infrastructure that enables seamless communication between government agencies. The efficiency of Estonia's e-government system is reflected in the fact that over 99% of government services are available online, and citizens can complete bureaucratic processes without visiting a government office, at least in theory. Estonia's digital ID system, introduced in 2002, is another groundbreaking innovation. Every citizen and resident receive a digital identity card that enables secure access to online services, digital signatures, and encrypted communication. In 2014, Estonia expanded this concept by launching its e-Residency program, which allows non-residents to obtain a digital identity and access Estonia's online services, such as registering a business or opening a bank account. This initiative has attracted thousands of entrepreneurs and freelancers worldwide, helping Estonia expand its digital influence far beyond its borders, but with doubtful effects, as it attracted, as well, people just interested to access the future EU Digital Market, people trying to avoid taxes or laundry money, and other illegal activities. These movements have been under the scrutiny of the Estonian state, reducing significantly the number of digital companies with non-European funds registered in the digital environment of Estonia.

On the other hand, Estonia's digital innovation extends to the realm of cybersecurity. After experiencing a large-scale cyberattack in 2007, the country developed robust cybersecurity measures to protect its digital infrastructure. In April 2007, Estonia experienced a coordinated series of cyberattacks that disrupted its digital infrastructure. These attacks, widely attributed to Russian actors, targeted government websites, financial institutions, media outlets, and other critical online services. While cyberattacks were not new, the scale, sophistication, and political implications marked a milestone, thrusting cybersecurity into the international spotlight. The attacks were precipitated by a contentious political dispute involving the relocation of the "Bronze Soldier," a Soviet-era monument, from central Tallinn to a military cemetery. The decision sparked protests among Estonia's ethnic Russian minority and drew sharp criticism from Moscow. Soviet army was seen as an occupation force by Estonians, and as a liberation force against the Nazis by the Russian minority. Therefore, there was a highly controversial divergence on the vision on the statute. Amid escalating tensions, the cyberattacks began, coinciding with physical protests and unrest. Mainly in Tallinn, the capital of the country. The 2007 cyberattack unfolded in three distinct phases:

- Initial Probes and Website Defacements: Attackers first targeted government websites, replacing official content with propaganda messages and incendiary images. These defacements were aimed at undermining public trust and demonstrating vulnerability.
- Distributed Denial-of-Service (DDoS) Attacks: The primary phase involved overwhelming servers with massive amounts of traffic, rendering websites and online services inaccessible. This method effectively paralyzed Estonia's digital infrastructure, affecting everything from banking to emergency services.
- Sustained Disruption: Over a 3-week period, attackers continued to target various sectors, adapting their methods and maintaining pressure on Estonia's cyber defences.

The immediate impact of the attacks was profound. Government communications were disrupted, financial transactions were stalled, and public confidence in digital systems was shaken. Estonia responded by implementing emergency cybersecurity measures, isolating critical systems, and seeking international assistance. Notably, NATO's Cooperative Cyber Defence Centre of Excellence (CCDCOE) was later established in Tallinn, underscoring the event's influence on global cybersecurity policy.

The incident highlighted several critical vulnerabilities such as:

- Reliance on Digital Infrastructure: Estonia's dependence on interconnected systems amplified the attack's impact.
- Lack of International Norms: At the time, there were no comprehensive frameworks for responding to cross-border cyberattacks.
- Challenges of Attribution: Identifying perpetrators in cyberspace proved complex, complicating legal and diplomatic responses.

These actions and initiatives gave a digital pioneer role to Estonia, providing a considerable influence in shaping European digital policies. Although it is one of the smaller member states, Estonia has strategically leveraged its expertise in digital governance to play a leading role in the development of EU-wide regulations and initiatives. Estonia's leadership in cybersecurity has positioned it as a key player in shaping the EU's cybersecurity agenda. The country has been instrumental in the development of the EU Cybersecurity Strategy and has supported the creation of the EU Agency for Cybersecurity (ENISA), which aims to strengthen cybersecurity coordination among member states. Estonia's proactive stance on cybersecurity has helped set the standards for protecting critical digital infrastructure and responding to cyber threats across Europe.

In addition, Estonia's extensive experience in digital governance has also influenced the development of the Digital Services Act (DSA) and Digital Markets Act (DMA). Both regulations aim to create a safer and more competitive digital market across the EU. Estonia's approach to content moderation, transparency, and platform accountability has provided a blueprint for the DSA's regulatory framework.

Additionally, Estonia's focus on promoting competition and innovation aligns closely with the DMA's goals of curbing the dominance of large digital platforms and fostering a level playing field for smaller businesses. Therefore, the early implication of Estonia on both initiatives, paved the way for their implementation in the national digital frame.

Parallel, Estonia frequently acts as a champion of digital innovation in EU policy discussions. The country has actively supported initiatives that promote the use of artificial intelligence (AI), blockchain, and digital identity solutions across the EU. For instance, Estonia has been a strong advocate for the development of a European Digital Identity, which would allow EU citizens to access public services and perform online transactions securely across borders. Estonia's push for digital innovation helps ensure that the EU remains at the forefront of technological development. Estonia's influence on EU digital policies was particularly evident during its presidency of the Council of the European Union in 2017. During this period, Estonia prioritized digital transformation as one of the key themes of its presidency. It fronted discussions on the DSM, data-driven innovation, and cybersecurity, emphasizing the importance of building a digitally connected Europe. Estonia's presidency left a lasting impact on EU digital policy by accelerating the adoption of several key initiatives, including the GDPR and the EU Cybersecurity Act. As the EU continues to expand its digital regulatory framework, Estonia's contributions still remain essential to shaping the future of Digital Europe. The country's experience with e-government, digital identity, and cybersecurity serves as a model for the broader EU, while its proactive stance on digital innovation positions it as a leader in emerging technologies. Estonia's role in influencing digital policies will likely grow in importance as the EU moves toward greater integration of digital markets and services.

Therefore, Estonia's expertise in creating seamless cross-border digital services will be crucial as the EU works to fully implement the Digital Single Market. Estonia's advocacy for interoperability and secure data exchange across borders could provide the foundation for future EU-wide digital services, such as cross-border e-health records and digital tax filing systems.[8] Estonia's experience with AI and blockchain technology positions it, as well, a valuable contributor to the EU's efforts to lead in emerging technologies. Estonia's focus on ethical AI and its transparent approach to blockchain governance could help shape future EU regulations on AI and other disruptive technologies, ensuring that innovation is pursued in a responsible and secure manner. Consequently, all these factors facilitated the Estonia's implementation of the DSA and DMA, but not without minor obstacles.

[8] See Troitiño and Mazur (2024).

3 National Digital Regulation in Estonia

Estonia's national digital policy framework is grounded, from the state perspective, on its commitment to innovation, protecting user rights, and ensuring the secure and ethical use of digital technologies. The country has implemented a series of laws and regulations designed to govern digital services, platforms, and data usage aiming to promote transparency, security, and competitiveness. The digital regulatory framework is built upon several foundational laws and initiatives that govern digital services and platforms. These laws reflect Estonia's status as a pioneer in digital governance and its commitment to maintaining a progressive and transparent digital environment, such as:

- Public Information Act (2000): This law requires government bodies to make public information freely available online, facilitating open access to government data. It was one of the first steps toward the digitization of public services and transparency in governance.
- Digital Identity and Electronic Signatures: Estonia's Digital Identity Act provides the legal foundation for the country's digital identity system, allowing citizens to use their digital ID cards to access services, sign documents, and authenticate their identity online. The Electronic Signatures Act further solidifies the legal standing of digital signatures, making them equivalent to handwritten signatures in legal contexts.
- Data Protection and Privacy: Estonia aligns closely with the EU's General Data Protection Regulation (GDPR), which sets stringent rules on data privacy and protection. Estonia has also implemented its own national privacy laws, such as the Personal Data Protection Act, which strengthens individual rights over personal data and outlines the responsibilities of data controllers.
- Cybersecurity Legislation: Estonia's Cybersecurity Act, introduced in 2018, sets the legal framework for safeguarding critical digital infrastructure and responding to cyber threats. It emphasizes the importance of cross-sectoral cooperation and the role of the public and private sectors in ensuring cybersecurity.
- e-Governance and e-Commerce Laws: Estonia has passed several laws related to e-governance and e-commerce, including the e-Government Act and the e-Commerce Act, which regulate online business activities and ensure the smooth functioning of digital transactions within the country.

These laws form the bedrock of Estonia's digital regulatory environment and are overseen by a network of government bodies, agencies, and independent institutions responsible for various aspects of digital governance. These stakeholders play a critical role in implementing, enforcing, and updating Estonia's digital policies. The Ministry of Economic Affairs and Communications (MEAC) is the central governmental body responsible for Estonia's digital strategy and policymaking. It oversees the development and implementation of digital laws and works to promote digital innovation and integration across the public and private sectors. The Estonian Information System Authority (RIA) is a key institution tasked with maintaining and securing Estonia's digital infrastructure. It manages the X-Road data exchange platform, ensures the security of digital services, and coordinates national cybersecurity efforts. The Data Protection Inspectorate is an independent authority and responsible for monitoring compliance with data protection laws, including the GDPR and Estonia's Personal Data Protection Act. It investigates breaches and ensures that both public and private entities uphold data privacy standards.[9] The Cyber Security Council comprise representatives from various ministries, security agencies, and private-sector actors, the Cyber Security Council plays an advisory role in shaping Estonia's national cybersecurity policy. It ensures coordinated responses to cyber threats and oversees the implementation of the Cybersecurity Act. Finally, the Estonian e-Governance Academy (eGA) is a public-private partnership that supports digital transformation in Estonia and other countries. It provides expertise in e-governance and digital policy, helping to develop Estonia's digital framework and expanding internationally its influence.

4 Interaction Between Estonian National Laws and EU Regulations

As a member state of the European Union, Estonia must ensure that its national digital regulations are harmonized with EU directives and regulations when required. The interaction between Estonia's national laws and EU-level regulations is crucial to maintaining a cohesive digital framework in the whole European Union, generating a common space with benefits and new necessities that, probably, will be solved with deeper integration, as generating new EU legislation and ne EU institutions addressing the common problems.

Estonia has a strong track record of aligning its national digital policies with EU regulations, often acting as a champion for EU-level digital initiatives. The country's ability to harmonize its own laws with broader EU directives reflects its commitment to ensuring that its digital services are interoperable across Europe and compliant with EU legal standards. Regarding GDPR Implementation, Estonia's adoption demonstrates its commitment to harmonizing national data protection laws with EU-wide standards. Estonia not only enforced the GDPR but has also strengthened its own privacy laws through the Personal Data Protection Act to ensure robust compliance. Additionally, Estonia has closely aligned its national cybersecurity policies with EU frameworks, such as the Network and Information Systems (NIS) Directive. This ensured that Estonia's digital infrastructure is integrated into the broader EU cybersecurity strategy, enabling coordinated responses to cross-border cyber threats.[10]

---

[9] See Metcalf (2019).

[10] See Troitiño and Mazur (2024).

4.1 Estonia's Legal Landscape Prior to the DSA and DMA

Before the introduction of the Digital Services Act (DSA) and Digital Markets Act (DMA), Estonia's legal landscape for digital services and markets was already relatively advanced. Nevertheless, like many EU member states, Estonia faced challenges in regulating the activities of large, cross-border digital platforms, particularly in areas such as content moderation, platform accountability, and market competition. Prior to the DSA, Estonia's regulatory framework for platform accountability was primarily focused on general cybersecurity and data protection measures. The lack of specific rules governing how platforms moderate content or handle illegal activities led to some gaps in regulation, particularly as digital platforms grew in scale and influence. On other relevant aspects, Estonia's laws on market competition, while robust, were primarily national in scope, limiting their ability to address the dominance of large, international digital platforms. It reflected the idea of independence based on integration, as just a strong union could have the means to control the large world digital platforms, therefore, protecting the independence of Estonia and other EU member states. The DMA, with its focus on regulating gatekeeper platforms and preventing anti-competitive practices, filled a critical gap that Estonia's national laws could not fully address.[11] On content moderation and transparency, Estonia's approach to content moderation prior to the DSA was largely reactive, relying on general legal frameworks related to illegal content. The DSA introduced a more proactive regulatory model, requiring platforms to take greater responsibility for their role in curating and disseminating content. This shift toward greater platform accountability aligned well with Estonia's commitment to transparency and user protection.[12] Estonia's legal landscape prior to the DSA and DMA was strong, but the introduction of these EU-wide regulations represented a significant step toward addressing the challenges posed by large digital platforms and ensuring a more transparent and competitive digital ecosystem across Europe.

5 Estonia's Implementation of the DSA

As part of the European Union's efforts to regulate digital services, the Digital Services Act (DSA) was introduced to enhance the transparency, accountability, and safety of online platforms. Estonia, a state deeply involved on digital governance, made significant adjustments to align its national laws with the DSA's requirements. To align with the DSA, Estonia undertook several legislative amendments aimed at harmonizing its national laws with the new EU standards. Key amendments included:

[11] See Colangelo (2023).

[12] See Buri and Hoboken (2021).

- Content Moderation and Transparency: Estonia revised its existing Electronic Commerce Act to incorporate new DSA rules on platform accountability, especially in the moderation of illegal content. Platforms were required to adopt transparent content moderation policies and provide users with clear information on how decisions are made.
- User Rights and Platform Accountability: Amendments were made to guarantee that users' rights were protected under the new digital regulations, particularly in terms of appeals and redress mechanisms when platforms remove content. Platforms must allow users to challenge content decisions through accessible and fair processes.
- Digital Advertising Transparency: The DSA's emphasis on transparency in digital advertising led Estonia to introduce provisions requiring platforms to disclose the use of algorithms in targeting users, as well as the criteria for personalized advertising.[13]

Nevertheless, Estonia encountered several challenges while adapting its laws to the DSA framework:

- Compliance Costs for Small Platforms: While large platforms were more equipped to meet DSA requirements, small digital platforms in Estonia faced significant compliance costs. Ensuring transparency and accountability measures can be resource-intensive for smaller players in the market.
- Alignment with Pre-Existing Regulations: Estonia's existing digital laws, such as those related to cybersecurity and e-commerce, had to be carefully re-aligned with DSA rules without creating overlapping regulations. This required a comprehensive review of pre-existing laws to avoid regulatory confusion.
- Public Awareness and Platform Readiness: Educating platform operators about new DSA obligations and ensuring that public and private stakeholders were prepared for the changes proved to be another challenge.

The Institutions Responsible for Enforcing the DSA in Estonia were the Ministry of Economic Affairs and Communications, responsible for overall digital policy in Estonia, MEAC coordinated with other agencies to ensure that platforms adhere to DSA requirements.[14] On the other side, Consumer Protection and Technical Regulatory Authority (CPTRA) was assigned the primary role in enforcing compliance with the DSA, particularly in cases related to content moderation, platform accountability, and digital advertising.

In terms of monitoring and compliance mechanisms Estonia set up several mechanisms to monitor compliance with the DSA, such as regular audits and reporting, as platforms must submit reports to the CPTRA outlining their content moderation practices, algorithm transparency, and measures for protecting users' rights. These reports are used to audit compliance and identify any regulatory breaches. Estonia also established an accessible system where users could file complaints regarding

---

[13] See Cevik (2023).

[14] See Pakutinskas and Šepetys (2023).

content moderation decisions. This allows for swift resolution of disputes in line with DSA provisions.

The implementation of DSA in Estonia has been a priority for the national government, including several practical examples, as moderation of hate speech. Platforms operating in Estonia have been required to introduce stricter measures for identifying and removing hate speech. For example, a major social media platform has adjusted its moderation policies and increased transparency around its decision-making processes for content removal. Implementation also included advertising transparency, as Digital advertisers in Estonia have started complying with DSA regulations by providing more detailed information about how user data is collected and utilized for targeted advertising. Therefore, the impact on Digital Service Providers, the compliance burden on smaller digital service providers has been noticeable, with several firms needing to invest in legal and technical infrastructure to meet new transparency and content moderation requirements.[15] Contrary, users are already benefiting from enhanced transparency on digital platforms. Greater clarity around content moderation processes has made it easier for users to understand how their content is handled and to challenge any unfair decisions.

6 Estonia's Implementation of the DMA

The Digital Markets Act (DMA) seeks to promote fair competition by regulating large online platforms, known as "gatekeepers." Estonia has had to adapt its legal and institutional structures to comply with the DMA, ensuring that both large and small digital players operate on a level playing field.[16] Estonia introduced several legal and institutional adjustments to comply with the DMA:

- Legal Adjustments: Estonia amended its Competition Act to include provisions specifically targeting large digital platforms that dominate the market, ensuring compliance with the DMA's rules on gatekeeping and anti-competitive behaviour.
- Institutional Adjustments: The Competition Authority of Estonia was strengthened, with expanded responsibilities for overseeing market dynamics in line with the DMA. This included hiring new experts in digital markets and creating a specialized unit to handle cases related to digital gatekeepers.

The introduction of the DMA has significantly impacted large platforms operating in Estonia increased Scrutiny. Large platforms, such as Google and Facebook, now face increased scrutiny from Estonian regulators, particularly regarding their data-sharing practices and market dominance. Additionally, it has foster fair market conditions. Smaller digital businesses have started experiencing more equitable market conditions, as the DMA prevents gatekeepers from engaging in unfair practices like

[15] See Denemark (2023).

[16] See Beems (2023).

self-preferencing or restricting access to essential services, but this benefit is still unclear from a practical vision.[17] The implementation of the DMA in Estonia meant also changes in its institutional frame, the Estonian Competition Authority (ECA) plays a key role in DMA enforcement. It oversees the implementation of fair competition rules and ensures that gatekeeper platforms do not exploit their dominant market positions. The ECA collaborates with other EU regulators to identify and address violations of DMA provisions.[18] Additionally, Estonia's Competition Authority coordinates closely with the European Commission to enforce the DMA. Joint investigations and data-sharing agreements have been established to ensure consistency in regulation and to prevent cross-border violations.

Contrary to the public position of the EU and Estonia, major digital platforms have expressed concerns about the increased regulatory burden but have generally adapted by complying with new rules regarding transparency and fair competition.[19] So far, the benefits they obtain from the market outline the new responsibilities and the general burden. On the other hand, smaller digital enterprises have largely welcomed the DMA, as it has created more competitive market conditions and reduced the dominance of large platforms.

7 Conclusions

One of the main challenges for Estonia is balancing national autonomy in its digital policies with EU-wide regulations like the DSA and DMA. This involves harmonizing national laws with European frameworks while ensuring that Estonia's digital priorities, such as innovation and cybersecurity, are not compromised. Certain areas, such as data localization and content regulation, have seen divergences between national and EU laws. Estonia has had to navigate these differences carefully to ensure compliance while protecting its national interests. Nevertheless, by being at the forefront of implementing the DSA and DMA, Estonia continues to strengthen its position as a digital leader in Europe. The country's ability to seamlessly integrate national and European regulations allows it to serve as a model for other EU member states.[20] Estonia's experience with the DSA and DMA opens up opportunities for further innovation, especially in areas such as AI governance, data ethics, and the regulation of emerging technologies.

Estonia's proactive approach to implementing the DSA and DMA provides valuable lessons for other EU member states. Key insights include the importance of early adaptation, stakeholder engagement, and robust enforcement mechanisms. As the digital landscape evolves, Estonia will face new regulatory challenges, particularly in the areas of AI regulation, cybersecurity, and the growing influence of global digital platforms.

---

[17] See Chiarella (2023).

[18] See Petit (2021).

[19] See De Streel et al. (2024).

[20] See Troitiño (2023).

References

Beems B (2023) The DMA in the broader regulatory landscape of the EU: an institutional perspective. Eur Comp J 19(1):1–29
Björklund F (2016) E-government and moral citizenship: the case of Estonia. Citizsh Stud 20(6–7):914–931
Buri I, Hoboken J (2021) The Digital Services Act (DSA) proposal: a critical overview. Digital Services Act (DSA) Observatory. https://dsa-observatory.eu/wp-content/uploads/2021/11/Buri-Van-Hoboken-DSA-discussion-paper-Version-28_10_21.pdf
Cevik I (2023) Analysis of digital services act of the European Union. YBHD, Ankara, p 387
Chiarella ML (2023) Digital Markets Act (DMA) and Digital Services Act (DSA): new rules for the EU digital environment. Athens J Law 14:33
Colangelo G (2023) DMA begins. J Antitrust Enforc 11(1):116–122
De Streel A, Bourreau M, Feasey R, Fletcher A, Kraemer MG (2024) Implementing the DMA: substantive and procedural principles. CERRE, Brussels
Denemark J (2023) Strengthening the European Union by regulating the digital single market. Acta Univ Carol Iur 69(2):107–123
Espinosa VI, Pino A (2024) E-government as a development strategy: the case of Estonia. Int J Public Adm 48(1):1–14
Heller N (2017) Estonia, the digital republic. The New Yorker 18:12
Lamadrid de Pablo A, Bayón Fernández N (2021) Why the proposed DMA might be illegal under article 114 TFEU, and how to fix it. J Eur Comp Law Pract 12(7):576–589
Margetts H, Naumann A (2017) Government as a platform: what can Estonia show the world. Research paper, University of Oxford
Metcalf KN (2019) How to build e-governance in a digital society: the case of Estonia. Rev Catalana Dret Pub 58:1
Pakutinskas P, Šepetys TL (2023) Algorithmic parody protection in the European Union: CDSM directive and DSA regulation perspective. Baltic J Law Polit 16(1):79–104
Petit N (2021) The proposed digital markets act (DMA): a legal and policy review. J Eur Comp Law Pract 12(7):529–541
Robbins M (2018) Myths, values and digital transformation: the exceptional case of Estonia
Troitiño DR (2022) The European Union facing the 21st century: the digital revolution. TalTech J Eur Stud 12(1):60–78
Troitiño DR (2023) Mapping e-governance in the EU. In: Digital development of the European Union: an interdisciplinary perspective. Springer, Cham, pp 303–317
Troitiño DR, Mazur V (2024) The strategy of the European Institutions on Digital Integration. In: E-governance in the European Union: strategies, tools, and implementation. Springer, Cham, pp 23–38

David Ramiro Troitiño is a professor at Tallinn University of Technology (TalTech). His research focuses on European integration, political history, and digital governance, with particular interest in EU institutions, civic participation, and the impact of digitalization on political processes.

Viktoria Mazur is a researcher and a project officer at Tallinn University of Technology. Her work focuses on EU interdisciplinary studies, innovation, digitalization & e-governance, and her publications examine the intersection of law, technology, and governance in the digital era.

MIX
Papier aus verantwortungsvollen Quellen
Paper from responsible sources
FSC® C105338

FSC
www.fsc.org

If you have any concerns about our products,
you can contact us on
ProductSafety@springernature.com

In case Publisher is established outside the EU,
the EU authorized representative is:
Springer Nature Customer Service Center GmbH
Europaplatz 3, 69115 Heidelberg, Germany

Printed by Libri Plureos GmbH
in Hamburg, Germany